Healthier Special Diets

HEALTHIER SPECIAL DIETS

Diet plans and recipes for allergies, deficiencies and healthy eating

RITA GREER

J. M. Dent & Sons Ltd
LONDON AND MELBOURNE

First published 1987

This book is set in 10/11½pt Plantin by
D. P. Media Ltd, Hitchin, Hertfordshire
Printed in Great Britain by
Cox and Wyman Ltd, Reading
for J. M. Dent & Sons Ltd
Aldine House, 33 Welbeck Street, London W1M 8LX

British Library Cataloguing in Publication Data

Greer, Rita
Healthier special diets: diet plans and over 500 recipes for allergies, deficiencies and healthy eating. — (Healthright).
1. Cookery for the sick
I. Title II. Series
641.5'63 RM219

ISBN 0-460-02421-3

CONTENTS

Acknowledgments vii
Introduction 1
Nutrition and Digestion Explained 9
General Diet for Healthier Eating 28

SPECIAL DIETS

Wheat-free Diet 35
Gluten-free Diet 40
Milk-free Diet 45
Egg-free Diet 50
Soya-free Diet 55
Citrus-free Diet 58
No Added Sugar Diet 61
Low Salt Diet 65
Corn-free Diet 69
Tapwater-free Diet 73
Slimming Diet 76
High Potassium Diet 78
Low Cholesterol Diet 80
Low Purine/Weight-reducing Diet 84
Mineral Booster Diet (1): High Calcium 86
Mineral Booster Diet (2): High Iron 89
The Hay Diet 92
Vegetarian Diet 98

RECIPES

Symbols and Special Ingredients 103
Breakfasts and Snacks 108
Soups and Starters 123
Pasta Dishes 153
Rice Dishes 181
Main Meals with Fish 191
Main Meals with Meat 209
Vegetarian Main Meals with Nuts, Cheese, Pulses, TVP and Grains 240
Cooked Vegetables 258

Salads and Salad Dressings 268
Puddings 299
Cakes, Biscuits, Cookies and Pastries 345
Breads, Scones, Crispbreads and Batters 366
Sauces, Gravies, Chutneys, Jams and Drinks 402
Further Reading 419
Index 420

ACKNOWLEDGMENTS

Figures and charts in this book are compiled from tables in McCance and Widdowson's *Composition of Foods*. With the exception of the Hay Diet, all diets have been designed by the author.

INTRODUCTION

In theory, humans can adapt to a wide variety of diets, enabling survival on foods which are available. However, it appears this is not so for everyone today. The development and progress of our civilization is to an extent affected by the way we cope with drastic changes in the structure of our diet. As an example, take the structuring of a new kind of diet for the people of Britain during the Second World War. The diet of the average person in Britain during this period was probably the healthiest it has ever been. With the exception of those few years, the diets we have adopted in the western world over the last hundred years may prove to be partly responsible for the increase in coronary heart disease, hypertension, some types of cancers and diabetes. Among surviving primitive tribes of hunter-gatherers, whose lifestyle closely resembles that of our ancient ancestors, these health problems are unknown.

Diet—Ancient and Modern

Looking at the history of our diet it is clear that it has undergone slow but drastic changes in the past. We probably began as mammals who ate insects, evolved as primates eating vegetables and fruit, and then developed into meat-eating man. Surprisingly, humans did not begin to eat fish and shellfish until a mere 20,000 years ago. About 10,000 years ago there was a swing to eating very little meat in favour of more vegetable foods (up to 90 per cent). This was due to the development of agriculture and, as a result, man became shorter in stature than his high-protein-eating ancestors. It was not until the Industrial Revolution that we began to eat more meat again and also began to produce taller people. Even so, today we are still not as tall as our primitive ancestors who hunted wild animals and foraged for wild vegetable foods. It has been calculated that the weekly diet of the ancient hunter-gatherers would probably have comprised about 12 lb (5 kg) wild meat (game) and 26 lb (13 kg) foraged, uncultivated vegetable foods.

The difference between wild meat and modern farmed meat is surprising. The average amount of fat found on wild meat is a mere 4 per cent. Domesticated (farm) animals yield up to 25–30 per cent fat. Even the type of fat differs, as the fat from wild animals can contain as much as five times more polyunsaturated fat than our modern farm animals. Domesticated plants usually contain a higher proportion of starch than their wild forms. The vegetable foods eaten by ancient hunter-gatherers were extremely varied compared with the range of such foods in the modern diet. Unlike our own diet, grains were of minor importance. A variety of roots, nuts, beans, tubers and fruits as well as flowers and gums were eaten. With wild meat this makes for a highly nutritious diet compared with our modern average diet and one with an entirely different balance of nutrients. For instance, the amount of meat protein consumed was enormous. Twice as much polyunsaturated fat was eaten as saturated. About sixteen times as much potassium as sodium was eaten, over 1½ oz (45 g) fibre per day, and much more in the way of vitamins and minerals (excepting perhaps iodine), than we eat today. The daily calcium intake was three times as much as the current UK RDA (Recommended Daily Allowance) and the Vitamin C, at almost 400 mg, works out at around nine times the current UK RDA.

As a result of their diet, the hunter-gatherers were able to build massive bones. They were tall and undoubtedly had to be strong and athletic to hunt game and probably walk many miles in a day on foraging expeditions. The greatest drawback to their diet would have been the extreme toughness of the meat, which would have worn down their teeth. However, there are some lessons to be learned here, particularly when the present-day agricultural populations of the underdeveloped countries of the world have widespread nutritional deficiencies.

By contrast, the current average diet in the western world is constructed from a different range of foods – milk, fats, oils, cheese, eggs, fish, farmed meat, farmed grains and cereals, processed sugars, farmed fruit and vegetables. These offer more in the way of saturated fat, a good deal less fibre (about 50 per cent less), fewer vitamins and minerals, far more starch and pure carbohydrate in the form of sugars. We eat about half the weight of food the hunter-gatherers ate and a good deal of it is not fresh or processed.

Our Diet a Century Ago

Country dwellers' diet

Going back to our diet of a hundred years ago, a very detailed first-hand account of what food was like for the country working-class people of that time is given in Flora Thompson's description of life in an English hamlet in her book *Lark Rise to Candleford*. It was a time when getting enough food to eat was a problem for poor families with too many children. Each dwelling in the main hamlet had its own patch of land or allotment for vegetable (and sometimes grain) cultivation and a sty in which to keep a pig. The pig meat was salted, cured and eked out as something to flavour the vegetable stews which were cooked in a large iron pot over an open fire.

The main meal of the day was eaten in the evening and was known as 'tea'. As a first course it featured a roly-poly pudding with fruit, currants or jam. (This was served to take the edge off the appetite.) A variety of boiled vegetables flavoured with meat from the pig or other meat followed. All the vegetables were fresh and home grown. Traditionally, they ate plenty of salad vegetables – lettuce, radishes and young onions – and bread spread with lard. The flour for the first course and the occasional plain cake could be had for nothing if the family went out gleaning after the harvesters. This grain was threshed at home and then sent to the local mill to be stone ground. To supplement the peas, beans, cabbage, kale, cauliflower and root vegetables, wild foods such as mushrooms, berries, nettles and nuts could be gathered free from the surrounding countryside. The actual amount of meat eaten was small. Bread was bought from the baker's cart unless the house had a suitable oven for baking bread. Some households never bought milk. Those who did obtained hand-skimmed from the nearest farm. Cheese was eaten in small amounts and eggs were eaten when cheap and plentiful or where fowls were kept.

Two of the three daily meals usually comprised bread spread with lard, mustard or jam and, very occasionally, butter. Margarine was available (then called 'butterine'), but home-made lard from the pig flavoured with rosemary from the garden was preferred by the adults. Children were given bread and black treacle or brown sugar. Tea without milk was the household drink and both the men and women drank beer, either home brewed or from the local inn. Flora Thompson's description of children brought up on this simple diet is a delight: 'They were stout limbed, rosy cheeked and full of life and mischief.' Most people worked very hard and long hours, often with a walk of several miles to and from work. After a day's work the men tended their gardens and allotments, which were sizeable. Both adults and children seem to have been fit and energetic as well as healthy.

City dwellers' diet

By stark contrast a book written in the 1890s about a slum family in the East End of London paints a very depressing picture. *A Child of the Jago* was written by Arthur Morrison, a civil servant who had first-hand experience of an area of extreme poverty. Honest toil was replaced by stealing to provide an income. For the tenants of the Jago there were no patches of land on which to grow vegetables and, for most of them, no cooking facilities. Food had to bought ready cooked. Apart from alcohol (mainly gin), which was cheap, the main beverage was coffee. A heavy kind of cake, cooked offal, tripe, saveloys and baked potatoes, fried fish, bloaters and bacon, bread, jam and pickles, and any food such as fruit which could be stolen or begged formed the basis of a very inadequate diet. There was much hardship and frightening violence as these slum-dwellers lived out their lives of squalor. They were the hunter-gatherers of a civilized society and it is interesting to note how much worse off they were nutritionally than our paleolithic ancestors.

Twentieth-century Food

The variety and scope of food eaten by the middle classes in Britain between the two World Wars is somewhat startling. Here are a few typical menus from the 1923 edition of a Mrs Beeton cookery book. First, two menus for an average sort of breakfast, followed by a more economical one:

Breakfast (average)

Grilled kidneys, baked halibut steaks, cold ham, stewed figs, marmalade, jam, butter, dry toast, toasted scones, bread, coffee, tea, hot and cold milk.

Breakfast (average)

Fried whiting, stewed kidneys, veal cake, marmalade, jam, butter, dry toast, rolls, bread, coffee, tea, hot and cold milk.

Breakfast (economical)

Grilled fresh herrings, boiled eggs, marmalade, butter, toast, bread, coffee, tea, cold and hot milk.

Here are a couple of dinners, each with four courses:

Dinner

Fillets of whiting with poulette sauce, haricot mutton, Jerusalem artichokes dressed in butter, potato croquettes, roast chicken, lettuce salad, pears and rice, cheese straws, cheese and dessert.

Dinner

Oxtail soup, crepinettes of chicken, beef braised and garnished with vegetables, celery stewed in gravy, potatoes Parisienne, cabinet pudding, cheese, dessert.

Suggested family suppers were substantial, as these two show:

Family supper

Beef steak and kidney pie, chaudfroid of chicken, cold ham, baked apples, swiss roll, custard, cheese, butter, biscuits, bread.

Family supper

Fish pie, cold beef, mashed potatoes, apple dumplings, cheese, butter, biscuits, bread.

Unwittingly all these menus, picked at random from many, put the emphasis on high-protein foods for all meals, particularly breakfast, a meal which has now largely died out. With large houses and an army of servants it was possible to produce this wide variety of dishes at each meal. After the First World War the number of servants dwindled and later after the Second World War they were to become something of a rarity.

Both World Wars brought austerity to the British diet, with rationing and far less variety of foods, especially in the way of imported items. The giant menus disappeared with the servants. When freezers were introduced a few years after the Second World War they paved the way for processed and precooked foods, readily acceptable by a society in which the majority of women were expected to go out to work as well as bring up a family. The average modern woman does not want to spend hours in the kitchen, without domestic help, preparing large meals. Buying in food which is already cooked and only needs serving or at the most warming up is obviously a far easier proposition. Eating out has gone the same way now that labour is expensive. Here are two 'eating out' menus from the London Freemasons' Shakespear No. 99 Lodge, with almost seventy years between them. The menu in 1907 comprised:

Clear Pontoise Soup

—

John Dorys aux fines herbes

—

Petits poulets à la Portugaise

—

Fore quarters of lamb
New potatoes
Peas

—

York ham
French salad

——

Asparagus

——

Iced macedoine of fruit

——

Cheese soufflés

——

By 1985 this kind of menu has shrunk from eight courses to four:

Prawn cocktail

——

Game pie
Parisienne potatoes
Brussels sprouts

——

Cheesecake

——

Cheddar cheese and biscuits

——

Coffee
After-dinner mints

——

The 1907 menu is more than substantial. It comprises soup, two fish courses, poultry, lamb, pork, a salad, three vegetables, fruit and a cheese dish. By contrast the 1985 menu offers prawns with lettuce and tomato, meat, two vegetables, two cheese dishes and chocolates. It is difficult to say which of the two menus is the worse as regards nutritional values! But it does show that, when it comes to healthy eating, catering is no wiser after seventy years. However, one point is worth mentioning. In 1907 everything would have been freshly cooked. In 1985 everything but the lettuce and tomato would have been precooked, processed (frozen or canned) and then warmed up or served defrosted as required.

A hundred years after Flora Thompson's experience of working-class family food, the British diet had become quite different, both in the types of food eaten, meal patterns and quality of food.

Average diet for 1981

The following information is based on figures from the National Food Survey for Britain, which monitors the amounts of food taken into the home for consumption. Here are approximate figures of the amounts of food for one person for one week in 1981:

Milk – 2 pints (1 litre)
Eggs – 3½
Fats/oils/cheese/cream – 14½ oz (400 g)
Meat – 2½ lb (1¼ kg)
Fish – 5 oz (150 g)

Sugar/preserves – 12½ oz (350 g)
Vegetables – 5 lb (2½ kg)
Fruit – 1 lb 11 oz (800 g)
Bread/grains/cereals – 3½ lb (1¾ kg)
Other foods (miscellaneous) – 2 lb (1 kg)

Added to these amounts should be any other foods bought and consumed outside the home such as restaurant or café meals, pub food, etc. and confectionery and snacks which are not taken into account in the National Food Survey as they are outside its limitations.

Comment

The majority of foods will have been processed – up to 75 per cent – so only a small amount of fresh fruit and vegetables will have been enjoyed. By now snacks had taken a real hold as an eating habit, especially among children, and breakfast as a meal had almost vanished. The eating pattern of three meals a day had also gone, too, for most households.

From a nutritional standpoint the 1981 diet has several faults, because of its structure. It is too high in fat, sugar and salt, but too low in fibre and fresh foods. Convenience foods, freezers and microwave ovens have undoubtedly helped to deskill the housewife and basic cooking skills that used to be handed down from one generation to the next are fast disappearing. Knowledge about nutrition, how to feed a family well and the whole purpose of food seem to pass by most people in modern Britain. There are several factors to blame. One is the disintegration of the family as a social unit. Where the family kitchen was once an ideal place for children to learn cooking skills, children are now more likely to be sent to the takeaway to buy ready-cooked food than to help the mother to prepare it. Nutrition has been largely ignored on a practical level in schools, both for school dinners and in teaching. The medical profession as a whole has little regard for its importance and nutrition does not feature as vital in the education of doctors. Advertising has kept up a steady pressure over several decades to promote the idea that food is a form of entertainment. Cookery writers and the media have also helped to further this idea, usually with a total disregard for the nutritional value of the food they produce.

The idea that food has some connection with health is a very old one among lay people. It is this idea that has led to self-treatment when medical treatment has failed or is not forthcoming. In the 1970s and 1980s there is evidence of bizarre diets being followed by people who believe, rightly or wrongly, that they have allergies. This is a fairly common phenomenon of modern eating patterns and often parents will impose a diet on children considered to be hyperactive or to have behavioural or learning problems.

In spite of this curious turn in the public attitude to diet, there is still a good deal of resistance to changing to healthier eating habits among the older generation. However, a genuine movement towards better eating among the more health conscious has put pressure on manufacturers to produce healthier food and more informative and honest labelling. This was brought about largely by the NACNE Report in 1983. First suppressed by the manufacturers, it caused something of a stir when it was released, and the COMA Report, which followed hard on its heels, reinforced matters. Manufacturers began to realize that the effects of these reports on public attitudes to health were not going to be a five-minute wonder and that they should take some action. Some manufacturers have responded by improving their products and labelling. Others have tended to sit out the crisis, trying to counteract all the good work done by the reports with clever advertising which claims the opposite. In the resulting turmoil the public has become confused.

It is against such a background that this book must stand. In the case of special 'medical' diets, the old idea that any food could be eaten provided it did not contravene the patient's list of banned foods is discarded. All diets, of no matter what type, should be structured in such a way that they promote health. Over-use of branded junk foods is not recommended as part of the diets and, within the limitations of each diet, whole fresh foods are used in preference to processed foods. This is not to be viewed as a fashionable quirk but as a sensible measure to make the diets as healthy as possible. Basically the maxims will be less salt, sugar and processed food and more fibre and fresh foods than the average British diet.

This book is written at a time when there is immense energy on the part of the public itself to improve the nation's health through diet (and exercise). Hopefully this will prevail against the endeavours and finance of the vested interests, who were quite happy with the way things were, and the intransigence of governments shy of telling voters what they should be eating. Hopefully, too, the following pages will provide a useful reference book with a broad spectrum of healthy diets and recipes to help with the radical changes that are required to bring about improvements in health, in relation to modern health problems.

NUTRITION AND DIGESTION EXPLAINED

Nutrition

To function, the human body needs food. A variety of food can supply the many nutrients needed to produce energy, movement and growth, to repair damaged or worn-out cells, to keep the body in a healthy state and, at some stages, to enable reproduction. While some foods are simple and can pass through the body virtually unchanged, most of the food taken in needs to be processed and treated chemically by the body for it to be of use. Digestion occurs to cope with this situation.

The basic nutrients and non-nutrients contained in food are carbohydrates, fats, proteins, vitamins, minerals and trace elements (nutrients), and water and fibre (non-nutrients).

Water

Water is essential for life. The amount of water that can be stored in the body tissues is small and soon used up in a crisis when water is not available. The body needs a regular supply of water as two-thirds of our body weight comprises water. Some water is taken into the body in the form of liquid and the remainder will be contained in various foods, especially fruit and vegetables. Water has an important link with fibre as it assists the passage of food through the body during the process of digestion.

Fibre

Fibre contains very few nutrients. Its main function is to provide non-digestible bulk in the diet, for it can remove and dispose of toxins in food by absorbing them and then passing them out of the body along with other waste debris from the digestion process. When the diet is low in fibre a very slow passage of food through the body results. On the other hand, a too speedy transit can result in food being wasted because the body is not given enough time to process out the nutrients (especially minerals) it needs before the food is excreted.

Carbohydrates and Fats

Carbohydrates and fats are mainly energy providers. Energy produces heat and enables the body to move and work. A constant body temperature of 37°C is ideal for body function and high energy foods help maintain this. To keep up a constant supply of energy fortunately does not require constant eating. Instead, the body can store surplus energy-producing foods in the form of body fat. This means we can eat meals at intervals. When required, the body fat can be converted to energy and used up. Both carbohydrates and fats can be converted to this kind of stored energy. When too much food is stored in this way the fat stores will become too large and this leads to a state of obesity. The body becomes too heavy for its framework (skeleton) and muscles, with resulting health problems.

Proteins, Vitamins and Minerals

Proteins are mainly needed for repair and growth. Excess protein taken in can be turned into energy and heat, just like carbohydrate and fat. This means the body has to be able to adapt the digestive process according to the variety and amount of food that is eaten. Vitamins and minerals as well as trace elements have a part to play in the efficient working of the body. There are many different kinds of these and individual foods contain a variety of them, with each food offering its own selection.

Results of Lack of Food

If the body takes in too little in the way of food the result can be deficiencies in vitamins, minerals and trace elements, loss of body weight due to using up the stored fat and body tissues, and eventual wasting away of the muscles. Movement becomes impossible as the body becomes unable to produce the required energy, incapable of repair or making new cells. This starvation of nutrients would eventually cause a very painful death.

Nutrients

With rare exceptions, individual foods contain a variety of nutrients and not just one. For instance, mushrooms contain fibre, calcium, iron, thiamin, riboflavin, nicotinic acid and Vitamin C, but no fat or Vitamin A and D. Almonds contain fibre, protein, fat, carbohydrate, calcium, iron, thiamin, riboflavin, nicotinic acid, but no Vitamin A, C or D. Sardines, canned in oil, contain protein, fat, calcium, iron, thiamin, riboflavin, nicotinic acid and Vitamins A and D but not C.

The amount of individual nutrients varies enormously from one food to another. Wheat germ contains 26.5 per cent protein, wheat bran 14.1 per cent, oats 12.4 per cent and lettuce merely 1 per cent. However, there are groups of foods which bear a certain similarity as regards their nutritional profiles. For instance, fruit and vegetables are more likely to contain Vitamin C than, say, grains. Meat will have high concentrations of protein whereas vegetables have very little. It is possible, therefore, to group foods as being high protein, high carbohydrate, high fat, high vitamin, high mineral, high fibre, etc. Here are a few examples:

High protein foods

Wheat germ, low fat soya flour, starch-reduced wheat crispbread, dried milk (skimmed), Cheddar-type cheese, Parmesan, grilled back bacon, stewed steak, roast leg of lamb or pork and corned beef all have over 25 per cent protein.

High carbohydrate foods

Pearl barley, cornflour, wheat flour, boiled rice, muesli, rye crispbread, digestive biscuits, raisins, sultanas and jams are all high carbohydrate foods with over 60 per cent carbohydrate.

High fat foods.

Butter, margarine, lard and cooking oil all contain over 80 per cent fat. Walnuts, almonds, brazil nuts and coconut contain over 50 per cent fat.

High vitamin foods

Vitamin A – liver, cod liver oil, broccoli tops, carrots, spinach, spring greens, dried apricots, Cantaloupe melon.

Vitamin B1/thiamin – bread with wheat germ, lean pork and ham, brazil nuts, fresh peanuts.

Vitamin B2/riboflavin – fortified breakfast cereals, kidney, liver, almonds.

Vitamin B3/niacin – eggs, whole grains, meat, milk, organ meats, nuts, seafood, poultry, liver, yeast.

Vitamin B5/pantothenic acid – dates, cereals, brewer's yeast, eggs, mushrooms, liver, legumes, green vegetables, peanuts, milk, bran, molasses.

Vitamin B6 – yeast, liver, cereals, meat, green vegetables, nuts, fresh and dried fruits.

Vitamin B12 – liver, meat, eggs, fish.

Folic acid – eggs, liver, leafy green vegetables, milk, grains.

Vitamin C – citrus fruits, green peppers, fruit and vegetables generally, new potatoes.

Vitamin D – fish oils, egg yolks, organ meats, bone meal and milk; Vitamin D can also be made in the body from exposure to sunlight.
Vitamin E – soya beans, wheat germ, sprouting seeds, dark green vegetables, eggs, nuts, vegetable oils.
Vitamin F/essential fatty acids – sunflower oil, safflower oil, wheat germ oil, corn oil, fish oils.
Biotin – brewer's yeast, egg yolks, whole grains, organ meats.
(Some vitamins are water soluble and others are oil soluble.)

High mineral foods

Calcium – milk, cheese, cereals, fish, bones, dried apricots.
Copper – oysters, shellfish, liver, legumes, nuts, raisins.
Iodine – seafood.
Iron – meat, poultry, cereals, seafood, molasses, liver.
Magnesium – green vegetables, cereals, honey.
Manganese – cereals, green leafy vegetables, nuts, legumes, celery.
Potassium – green vegetables, fresh fruit, dried fruit, nuts, seafood, sunflower seeds, legumes.
Sodium – salt, milk, cheese.
Zinc – nuts, grains, legumes, oysters, seafoods, liver, meat.

High fibre foods

Wheat bran, wholewheat flour, oats, low fat soya flour, wholewheat bread, beans, root vegetables, peas, sweet corn, dried raw apricots, passion fruit, raspberries, dried raw figs.

Digestion and Absorption of Food

Food can be in solid or liquid form. To qualify as a food it must be able to produce heat, movement or other kinds of energy, or be suitable for growth, repair and sometimes reproduction, or contain substances needed to control growth and repair or the production of energy. The inclusion of fibre in this definition is inappropriate, but it is nevertheless very important in the diet, and so is water.

No matter what its form, food must be processed by the body in such a way that the nutrients from the food can pass into the bloodstream and into the cells of the body. Food comes in great variety, so different processes are required for different foods. Apart from a few foods, such as salt, glucose and alcohol which can pass straight into the bloodstream, almost all the other foods we eat need to be broken down by enzymes, of which there are many kinds, each with a special job to do.

Hunger and Appetite

We can experience the sensation of hunger when the stomach is empty, when there has been a reduction in our fat (energy) stores, or when the appetite is stimulated by the smell, appearance or even just the thought of food. The salivary glands are stimulated to produce saliva, and other gastric juices in the body will begin to flow and prepare for the digestion and absorption of food yet to be consumed. The actual taste of food in the mouth will continue the work of stimulation.

The Digestive Tract

Digestion and absorption take place in the digestive tract of the body. This is basically a series of tubes all joined together, with ducts that lead into it from the parts of the body that produce the various digestive juices. The tract is about five metres long; it starts with the mouth as its entrance and ends with the anus as its exit.

The Mouth

Food is taken into the body via the mouth. It can be taken in in large chunks, but it must be chewed into smaller pieces there before it can be swallowed. As some food will be dry, lubrication with saliva occurs during the chewing process. Glands at the back of the mouth and under the tongue can produce a steady flow of saliva, encouraged by the smell, taste and thought of food as well as the action of chewing. The teeth at the front of the mouth are shaped for cutting through the food. Those at the sides of the mouth are of a different shape and their function is to grind the food to make a kind of coarse paste that can be swallowed. The chemical process of digestion begins even in the mouth, for the saliva contains an enzyme (ptyalin) that begins to convert some (not all) the starch in the food to maltose. The action of swallowing pushes the food down the first part of the tract, the oesophagus. Three seconds later it passes into the stomach.

Mouth problems

Good teeth are important in maintaining health. A diet high in unrefined carbohydrates, especially sugar, can lead to dental caries. Poor performance by the teeth because of the decay of tooth enamel or gum disease, poorly fitting dentures or lack of dental care can cause digestive problems. If food is not chewed and lubricated properly (or if it is bolted due to lack of time devoted to a meal, or stress), then the pieces of food that are passed down into the stomach will be too large for the remainder of the digestive system to cope with easily. Chewing difficulties can even deter some people from eating, especially the elderly.

The Stomach

After the oesophagus the tube widens to become the stomach. Food can be contained here for several hours because the stomach is so large, rather like a bag. Without a stomach we would need to be eating constantly, to maintain a supply of food for the remainder of the tract.

As some bacteria will inevitably be present in the food taken into the body, the stomach contains a strong antiseptic in the form of hydrochloric acid. This can destroy bacteria as well as working closely with an enzyme to break up protein. In normal situations the amount of bacteria the acid can destroy relates well to what is taken into the body. However, sometimes there are too many bacteria and not enough acid. The result can be infection or illness.

To break down the food particles the stomach produces up to three litres of gastric juice per day. This contains the acid mentioned above, the enzyme pepsin which starts to digest protein (with the help of the acid), and the 'intrinsic factor' needed for the eventual absorption of Vitamin B12. The food in the stomach is usually a mixture of several foods, so the length of time it remains there varies according to the mixture. Carbohydrates are the quickest to pass through, while fats take the longest. Food will stay in the stomach for between two and four hours in normal circumstances. The walls of the stomach are capable of contractions to help break down the foods until they are semi-liquid and ready to pass into the next part of the tract, the duodenum. A few foods such as alcohol, sugars, some water-soluble vitamins and minerals, and water can pass straight through the stomach walls and into the bloodstream.

To protect itself from the effects of hydrochloric acid the stomach secretes mucous, which is used as a barrier.

Stomach problems

The stomach of a baby is equipped to digest milk. It takes some time for the digestive system to develop so that adult food (solids) can be digested. Weaning babies too soon leads to problems if their digestive systems are not ready to cope. (The main difficulty is with starch.)

When the stomach loses its ability to withstand the effects of hydrochloric acid a peptic ulcer can develop. Aspirin and similar drugs can also affect the stomach by producing ulcers. Caffeine causes extra acid to be secreted, as does alcohol, although the latter stimulates the secretion of mucous as well. Acid from the stomach which enters the oesophagus can cause the burning sensation of heartburn.

The Small Intestine

The duodenum is the first part of the small intestine, and this is where most of the nutrients in food are absorbed. Bile enters the duodenum to help with this process. Bile is produced in the liver, which is connected to the duodenum by the gall bladder (where bile is stored). Muscular contractions in the duodenum cause the bile to start flowing into it, and this also helps to start the flow of gastric juices and saliva further up the tract, in the mouth and stomach. (The walls of the small intestine also produce gastric juices.) Bile contains bile salts which help to break down fats ready for absorption, by making them into minute droplets, aiding the digestion of protein and carbohydrate, as well as the absorption of the fat-soluble Vitamins A, D and K. The pancreas also has a duct into the duodenum and this too releases enzymes to help digest food in the small intestine.

As the food passes through the small intestine and is processed (broken down), nutrients are absorbed into the bloodstream via the large surface area of the digestive tract. Villi (hair-like structures) line the tract and on the villi are even smaller 'hairs' (the brush border). They all enable the absorption of some water, alcohol, sugars, minerals, water-soluble vitamins, amino acids (broken-down proteins), fatty acids, fat-soluble vitamins and broken-down starches. The villi and the brush border make a surface area of up to forty square metres to carry out the absorption process.

The first part of the small intestine, the duodenum, connects with the second part, the jejunum, and this in turn leads to the ileum, the third part. By the time the food has passed down to the ileum most of the available nutrients have been absorbed, leaving a soft, wet mixture to be passed into the large intestine.

Small intestine problems

Peptic ulcers can occur in the small intestine as well as in the stomach, causing similar problems.

Lactose intolerance: one of the enzymes found in the small intestine is called lactase. Its job is to change milk sugar (lactose) into glucose (a sugar) and galactose which can then be absorbed. Not everyone can produce the necessary enzyme for this and consequently their digestive system cannot cope with milk (which contains lactose). Our western style of diet makes good use of milk products. People from cultures who do not have a tradition of dairy farming like us are often unable to tolerate milk and milk products. Those most frequently affected are Chinese, Latin American, African, Indian and Middle Eastern peoples.

Coeliac disease: this disease is most prevalent in areas of the world where wheat is a staple food. In coeliac disease the small intestine becomes damaged by a reaction to the gluten in wheat, rye, barley and (possibly) oats. Instead of being hair-like, the villi become shorter and flattened and so cannot absorb nutrients as they should. Although the patient seems to be eating well, a state of malnourishment is the result.

When solids are introduced to the diet of a coeliac baby it will fail to thrive because this is when gluten-containing foods are first eaten. If gluten is excluded from the diet the small intestine can return to normal and resume its job of digesting and absorbing nutrients. Usually, coeliacs need to be on a gluten-free diet for life. Occasional dietary lapses can damage the villi again and cause problems.

Diabetes: the gastric juices produced by the pancreas and fed into the duodenum are alkaline, to neutralize the very acid mixture from the stomach as it passes down the tract. If there is a deficiency of insulin in the pancreatic juices, or if the insulin is not as effective as it should be, there will occur a concentration of glucose in the blood, leading to the condition known as diabetes. The excess glucose is passed out of the body via the kidneys. Extra insulin is required to control the disease or, in older people, it can be controlled by a diet with restricted carbohydrate intake.

The Large Intestine

The digestive tract becomes larger in diameter to form the last part, the large intestine. Any remaining nutrients are absorbed from this, and most of the water, leaving comparatively dry waste and debris. If the large intestine provides the right conditions, helpful bacteria will grow in it and try to process any remaining food as well as manufacturing B group vitamins. After all possible food processing and nutrient absorption has taken place, the waste material is accumulated and then passed out of the body via the anus.

Digestive tract problems

Indigestion: food which cannot be absorbed passes down the whole length of the digestive tract and into the large intestine. Here it will be fermented by the bacteria, often producing gas and diarrhoea. The term 'indigestion' usually refers to the discomfort or even pain in the digestive tract caused by indigestible foods or emotional upsets.

Poor absorption: if laxatives are taken they usually speed up the passage of food through the tract. Dietary fibre in excess of requirements can have the same effect. The result may be poor absorption of nutrients as the food passes too quickly through the tract, not allowing enough time for it to be broken down thoroughly or absorbed.

The time that food takes to pass through the body is called the 'transit time'. This may vary from a few hours to several days. High or low fibre diets can be used to manipulate the speed of food through the tract.

Useful Nutritional Information

Fibre

Best Sources of Fibre in Foods*

food	*approx % of fibre*	*food*	*approx % of fibre*
wheat bran	44	haricot beans, boiled	7
wholewheat flour	10	beansprouts, cooked	3
oats, raw	7	beetroot, raw or cooked	3
low fat soya flour	14	broccoli tops, cooked	4
wholewheat bread	9	carrots, raw	3
Puffed Wheat	15	leeks, boiled	4
Shredded Wheat	12	mushrooms, cooked	4
rye crispbread	12	fresh peas, boiled	5
French beans, cooked	3	dried peas, boiled	5
runner beans, cooked	3		
broad beans, cooked	4		
butter beans, boiled	5		

*Although some of these figures for fibre may not seem to be very high, the foods can be eaten in quite large quantities, e.g. potatoes. All Bran (the breakfast cereal) has added bran to make it 27 per cent bran, but it also has added sugar and salt.

food	*approx % of fibre*	*food*	*approx % of fibre*
new potatoes, boiled	2	bananas	3
jacket potatoes, including skins	2	blackberries, stewed	6
spring greens, cooked	4	black currants, stewed	7
sweet corn, canned	6	passion fruit	16
apricots, dried raw	24	raspberries	7
apricots, stewed dried	9	strawberries	2
		figs, dried raw	19

Other Sources of Fibre in Foods

food	*approx % of fibre*	*food*	*approx % of fibre*
pearl barley, cooked	2	Brussels sprouts, cooked	3
white flour	3	carrots, boiled	3
brown flour	8	cauliflower, raw or cooked	2
brown bread	5	celery, raw	2
brown bread with wheat germ	5	lentils, cooked	4
white bread	3	lettuce	2
muesli	7	mushrooms, raw	3
made with white flour:		spring onions	3
Christmas cake	3	parsley	10
Madeira cake	1	parsnips	3
sponge	1	green peppers, raw	1
mince pies	3	crisps (high fat/salt)	10
flaky pastry	2	radishes	1
shortcrust pastry	2	spinach, boiled	6
fruit pie	3	swede, boiled	3
baked beans (high salt/sugar)	5	tomatoes, fresh	2
		tomatoes, canned	1
		turnips, boiled	2

food	approx % of fibre	food	approx % of fibre
watercress	3	oranges	2
apple, eating	2	peaches, dried raw	14
apricots, fresh stewed	2	pears	2
avocado pears	2	pineapple	1
cherries	2	plums	2
gooseberries, stewed	3	currants	7
lemons	5	dates	9
		prunes, stewed	8
		sultanas	7

Carbohydrates

Good Sources of Carbohydrate in Foods (Healthy)

food	approx % of carbohydrate	food	approx % of carbohydrate
wholewheat flour	68	butter beans, boiled	17
pasta, boiled	25	haricot beans, boiled	17
rice, boiled	87	split peas, boiled	22
wholewheat bread	42	old potatoes, baked	25
muesli	66	raisins	64
Shredded Wheat	68	sultanas	64
rye crispbread	71		
muesli	66		

Other Sources of Carbohydrate in Foods

food	*approx % of carbohydrate*	*food*	*approx % of carbohydrate*
wheat germ	44	carrots, old	5
wheat bran	29	cauliflower, boiled	1
cornflour	92	cucumber	2
white flour	75	leeks, boiled	5
oat porridge	8	lettuce	1
rye flour	76	mushrooms	0
soya flour	24	onion, raw	5
brown bread	45	peas, boiled	8
white bread	50	green pepper, raw	2
All Bran	43	chips	37
cornflakes	85	spinach	1
plain digestive biscuits	66	sweet corn, boiled	22
		tomatoes	3
rich fruit cake	58	watercress	1
shortcrust pastry	56	apples	12
fruit pie	57	apricots	7
milk pudding	24	bananas	19
cow's milk	5	blackberries	6
most cheeses	trace	cherries	12
natural yoghurt	6	figs, stewed dried	34
fruit yoghurt	18	dates	64
eggs	trace	grapes	16
oils/fats	0 or trace	grapefruit	5
meat/poultry	0 or trace	melon	5
liver	1–2	oranges	9
sausages, grilled	15	pears	11
fish/molluscs	0	pineapple	12
French beans	1	raspberries	6
broad beans	7	strawberries	6
baked beans	10	almonds	4
beetroot, cooked	10	brazil nuts	4
broccoli tops, boiled	2	coconut	4
		peanuts	9
Brussels sprouts	2	peanut butter	13
red cabbage, raw	4	walnuts	5

food	*approx % of carbohydrate*	*food*	*approx % of carbohydrate*
glucose	85	mincemeat	62
sugars	100	boiled sweets	87
black treacle	67	chocolate bars	58–67
honey	75	toffees	71
jam/marmalade	69	wines and spirits	very low
marzipan	49		

Fats and Oils

We have grown used to referring to fats and oils by what they feature most in their composition. Margarines are described as being 'polyunsaturated', although they do not comprise *all* polyunsaturated fat. Popular myths are that all animal fats are bound to be saturated and all vegetable oils are polyunsaturated. This is a wrong assumption as all fats and oils are a mixture of several types of fat – saturated, unsaturated (polyunsaturated), mono-unsaturated and other more obscure fats and oils. Two of the most highly saturated oils are vegetable in origin – coconut oil and palm oil.

Saturated fats are known to be reasonably stable. Butter will keep for a long time if the water is removed from it, even in a hot climate such as that of India. Ghee, which is clarified butter, is frequently used in Indian cooking and exploits this factor. Unsaturated fats are inclined to turn rancid more quickly.

Another popular myth is that if fats and oils set into a soft consistency when cold (even when taken from the fridge), they are unsaturated. Many cookery writers use this as a rule of thumb, not realizing that it is wrong. Manufacturers can process saturated fats and oils to remain soft when cool. The following chart shows the levels of saturated and unsaturated (polyunsaturated) fat in fats and oils.

Approximate Levels of Saturated and Unsaturated (Polyunsaturated) Fats in Fats and Oils

animal fat	*% saturated fat*	*% unsaturated fat*
cream	61	3
butter	61	3
suet	58	1
lard	44	10
egg yolk	38	11

vegetable oils/fats	*% saturated fat*	*% unsaturated fat*
vegetable oil, hard block	38	16
olive oil	15	12
coconut oil	80	2
palm oil	49	9
peanut oil (groundnut)	21	30
soya bean oil	15	60
safflower seed oil	11	76
sunflower seed oil	15	52
corn oil (maize)	17	52
polyunsaturated margarine	25	55

mixtures of animals fats/ vegetable oils	*% saturated fat*	*% unsaturated fat*
hard margarine	38	16
ice cream	67	33

Some foods are easily recognized as containing fat — cheese, cream, butter, cooking oil, margarine, etc. In other foods it is harder to spot – avocado pears, chocolate, pastry, cakes, milk, yoghurt, nuts, sesame and sunflower seeds. Some fat is visible in meat, either as strips of fat or as 'marbling' within the meat fibres.

Foods Containing Animal Fats

food	*% of fat*	*food*	*% of fat*
lard, dripping	99	corned beef	12
margarine (some)	85	ham	5
butter	82	single cream	21
bacon	27–49	double cream	48
pork	7–26	Cheddar cheese	36
lamb	8–29	Stilton	40
beef	4–29	Edam	23
calves' liver	7	eggs	11
chicken	5	milk, whole	4
turkey	1–7	milk, dried skimmed	1
veal	3		
sausages, fried	18		

Food Containing Vegetable Oils*

food	*% of oil*	*food*	*% of oil*
cooking oil	100	olives	9
low fat spreads	41	coconut, desiccated	62
oats	9	brazil nuts	62
wholewheat bread	3	almonds	54
white bread	2	walnuts	52
white flour	1	peanuts	49
wholewheat flour	2	margarines (some)	85
pasta	1		
rice	1		
avocado pears	11–39, depending on season		

*Vegetables and fruit contain only a trace of fat, except for avocado pears.

Fat Content of Meat (Approximate)

Under 10% – low fat

meat	*% of fat*	*meat*	*% of fat*
beef sirloin, lean only	9	chicken, light meat	4
beef topside, roast, lean only	4½	chicken, dark meat	7
lamb, roast leg, lean only	8	turkey, light meat	1
		veal cutlet, fried	8
		pigs' liver, stewed	8

Over 10% fat

beef		pork, roast leg	11½
brisket	24	*poultry*	
rumpsteak, fried	16	chicken, roast meat and skin	14½
sirloin, including fat	29	duck, roast meat and skin	29
silverside	14	*veal*	
topside, roast, including fat	12	roast	11½
lamb		*offal*	
breast	37	calves' liver, fried	13½
loin chops	35	lambs' liver, fried	14
cutlets	36	chicken liver, fried	11
leg, roast, including fat	18	ox tail, stewed	13
scrag and neck	21	ox tongue	24
shoulder, roast	26	lambs' sweetbreads	15
ham/bacon/pork		*meat products*	
collar ham	27	salami	45
gammon ham	19	beef sausages	18
bacon, fried back rasher	40½	pork sausages	25
(lean only)	(19)	liver sausage	27
bacon, grilled streaky rasher	36	beefburger, fried	17–50
pork, belly rasher	35	cornish pasties	20½
loin pork chops, grilled	24	pork pie	27
		sausage roll	36

Oil Content of Fish

fatty fish	*% of oil*	*fatty fish*	*% of oil*
herring	15	salmon, canned	8
kipper	11	sardines, canned	14
mackerel	8		

non-fatty fish	*% of oil*	*non-fatty fish*	*% of oil*
plaice	2	cod	1
sole	1	haddock	1

The popularity of high fat foods such as sausages and hamburgers is not surprising: they remain in the stomach longer than food lower in fat, so they tend to be very satisfying.

Fat Problems

Our bodies can store any excess food taken in by converting it to body fat for later use. A diet which provides too much in the way of food, therefore, can lead to over-large fat stores being made in the body. The result is overweight or obesity. This can overload the framework of bones and muscles, not only making the body an ugly shape but also making life harder for the heart, lungs, limb movements, etc. There are also psychological problems arising from the anti-social nature of obesity, for fat people often see themselves as unattractive in appearance and performance.

Deficiencies

As some vitamins are fat soluble, e.g. Vitamins A, D, E, F and K, too little fat in the diet can lead to deficiencies in these very important micronutrients. Fats and oils also contain essential fatty acids and these too will be deficient in a diet that contains too little in the way of fats and oils.

Cholesterol

Cholesterol is not a kind of fat but a fat-like substance – a lipid. It is only found in animal fats. The body can produce its own cholesterol and does not seem to need a supply from outside. There is much controversy about the dangers of too much cholesterol in the blood, and cholesterol has been linked with heart disease for many years, despite a lack of true scientific evidence to support such a link. However, most lay people seem to take a common-sense attitude to cholesterol and feel too much should be avoided. Doubtless the scientific arguments will continue for years, as the data on mortality and heart disease are investigated. By coincidence, vegans are usually found to have very much lower levels of cholesterol than people who eat an ordinary diet. (See pp. 80–3).

Margarines

Margarine was originally invented as a substitute for butter, which was often in short supply before the days of refrigeration and large-scale dairy farming. The technique of solidifying liquid oils to a solid form made margarine possible. A variety of oils is used today to produce several different kinds of margarine. Vegetable sources are soya beans, sunflower seeds, palm fruits and kernels, rapeseed, coconuts, safflower seeds and corn cobs. Animal sources are beef fat and fish oils. To make the final product other ingredients are added – colour, flavouring, whey from milk, salt, Vitamins A and D (UK) and emulsifiers extracted from fats and oils.

Protein Content of Some Foods

food	*approx % of protein*	*food*	*approx % of protein*
Cereals/grains (and products)			
wheat germ	26.5	Shredded Wheat	10.6
wheat bran	14.1	starch reduced wheat crispbread	45.3
wholewheat flour	13.2	rye crispbread	9.4
raw oats	12.4	bread and butter pudding	6.1
porridge	1.4	egg custard	5.8
boiled pasta	4.3	fruit pie with pastry top	2.0
boiled rice	2.2	pancakes	6.1
low fat soya flour	45.3	Yorkshire pudding	6.8
wholewheat bread	8.8		
white bread	7.8		
muesli	12.9		

food	approx % of protein	food	approx % of protein
Milk and milk products			
fresh whole milk	3.3	Cheddar type cheese	26.0
dried skimmed milk	36.4	Parmesan	35.1
made up	3.4	cottage cheese	13.6
butter	0.4	natural yoghurt	5.0
Eggs			
boiled egg (1 average)	6.2	egg white	9.0
Meat			
grilled back bacon, lean and fat	25.3	roast leg of pork, lean only	30.7
cooked, lean minced beef	23.1	roast chicken, lean only	24.8
stewed steak, lean and fat	30.9	roast turkey, light meat	29.8
loin lamb chops, grilled, lean only	27.8	fried lamb's liver	22.9
		corned beef	26.9
roast leg of lamb, lean only	29.4	ham	18.4
		beef stew	9.6
Fish			
baked cod	21.4	tuna	22.8
fried haddock	21.4	prawns	8.6
plaice fried in batter	15.8	scampi	12.2
canned salmon	20.3	fish cakes	10.5
sardines	23.7		
Vegetables containing over 4 per cent protein*			
broad beans	4.1	raw parsley	5.2
boiled butter beans	7.1	boiled peas	5.0
baked beans in tomato sauce	5.1	boiled dried split peas	8.3
cooked lentils	7.6	boiled spinach	5.1

*Fruits are very low in protein, being around 1 per cent or less. Dried fruits such as apricots, figs and prunes have slightly higher concentrations of protein, but none is as high as 4 per cent.

GENERAL DIET FOR HEALTHIER EATING

There have been disturbing trends in the average British diet since the Second World War. The average person in the UK is eating far too much fat, particularly saturated fat, far too much sugar and salt, but too little fibre. Other trends are the consumption of too little fresh food, especially vegetables and fruit, and a great deal of convenience food. Over 70 per cent of food is taken in the form of snacks such as crisps, bakery items and fast foods, and advertising exerts much pressure on the individual to continue the habit, while general lack of knowledge about nutrition compounds the problem. Teaching in schools, either by lessons or by example (i.e. school meals) and the examination syllabuses have not helped matters. There is also strong evidence of a second generation of mothers who do not know how to cook or care nutritionally for their offspring. (Unfortunately the tendency for children to carry through into adulthood the same eating habits as their parents is common.)

As we saw in the Introduction, although the NACNE and COMA Reports, both published in the early 1980s, drew attention, through the media, in a rather sensational way, to the mounting problems of wrong nutrition, failure on a practical level to put matters right has left the average British citizen confused and lacking in direction. Cookery writers and broadcasters, presented with doubts about the suitability of their work for the new thinking on nutrition, have tended mainly to continue with their old, bad advice and habits, merely paying lip-service to the new thinking by labelling their work 'healthy'.

If anything, advertising has tried even harder to promote unhealthy products since the public has become interested in healthier food. As advertising revenues are vital in commercial life – most magazines and independent TV stations would be unable to continue without them – a gulf has opened between the editorial content and the actual adverts which appear in magazines and newspapers. Editorial extols the virtues of healthier eating but its credence may be lowered by the extremely unhealthy adverts that follow, which say exactly the opposite. Or some TV and radio presenters praise the new interest in better nutrition and then proceed with the same old unhealthy cookery demonstrations and recipes, but passing them off as 'healthy'. There is no doubt that the unhealthiest food is the most attractive and likely to be the most popular. Viewing and listening ratings are of great importance, so the situation is unlikely to change. What alarms most people anxious for a change for the better is that the media, who could bring about the changes, seems to pay only lip-service to the subject and in fact is doing more harm than good by pretending to have changed its ideas. New blood could probably work wonders but there are very few openings if any for the would-be TV cook who specializes in healthy cooking, as the stalwarts of the old unhealthy cooking brigade cling to their jobs like limpets.

Manufacturers, at first believing the new interest in the health value of their food products to be a 'flash in the pan', have tended to use the word 'healthy' as a gimmick. Although some efforts have been made to improve the nutritional quality of a number of products, even more energy seems to have been directed at disguising bad quality products, particularly with health conscious symbols and labelling. Lack of effort by the government to come to terms with the situation and fear of upsetting manufacturers in a time of unemployment has produced a frustrating inertia. The British public has become confused but happily has not given up. Polls in 1985 still showed a willingness to accept the idea that a better style of diet could improve health and should be followed.

A national feeling that people do not want to be told what to eat, and indeed should not be told, any more than they should not be told not to smoke or take excessive amounts of alcohol, is a difficult obstacle. Nevertheless, there are people who welcome advice and will act upon it. Here then is a chart which gives specific amounts of food for one person per week. It is based on a good deal of research and leans heavily on the NACNE Report of 1983 for its underlying nutritional goals.

Basic Diet for Health
Suggested amounts of food for one adult for one week

High Vitamin/Mineral Foods

Vegetables	3 lb (1.5 kg) potatoes (fresh) 2½ lb (1.25 kg) fresh green and other vegetables

Vegetables cont.	(allow at least one portion of leafy greens per day)
	3 oz (75 g) frozen vegetables
Fruit	over 2 lb (1 kg) fresh fruit
	3 oz (75 g) dried fruit and nuts
	2 oz (50 g) canned fruit without sugar

High Sugar Foods

Sugar	not more than 5 oz (150 g)
Jam/sweet spreads	4 oz (110 g)
Biscuits	4 oz (110 g), or 1 per day
Cakes/buns/pastries	under 3 oz (75 g), or about 2 items per week

High Carbohydrate Foods

Pulses	1½ oz (40 g) dried beans, split peas, lentils, etc.
Rice/wholewheat pasta/noodles	1 lb (450 g), or 2 portions of rice and 3 portions of pasta
Flour	about 6 oz (175 g) of wholewheat
Bread	1¼ lb (550 g) wholewheat/granary/high fibre
	12 oz (350 g) white
	4 oz (110 g) of other breads
Breakfast cereals	8 oz (225 g), or about 5 portions

High Protein Foods

Meat – lean only from about 2 lb (1 kg) weight; bone, gristle and fat to be discarded	4½ oz (125 g) beef/veal
	2½ oz (65 g) pork
	1½ oz (40 g) liver
	1½ sausages (low fat)
	2½ oz (65 g) lamb
	4 oz (110 g) bacon/ham
	10 oz (280 g) poultry
	about 4½ oz (125 g) of other meat products
Fish	about 10 oz (280 g) mixed fresh and canned fish, shellfish
Milk	about 2 pints (1 litre) skimmed milk
Eggs	3½

High Fat/Oil Foods

	under 3 oz (75 g) polyunsaturated margarine
	under 2 oz (50 g) butter (saturated fat)
	9 fluid oz (250 ml) oil high in polyunsaturates such as sunflower, safflower, corn, soya
	4 oz (110 g) cheese, preferably low fat
Beverages	about 2½ oz (65 g) tea, coffee, cocoa, etc.
Other foods	9 oz (250 g)

Cookery Advice

Wherever possible, meat should be trimmed of excess fat before cooking. Grill rather than fry, and avoid deep fat frying as a method of cooking.

Make your own sausages at home (see recipe on p. 113).

Preference should be given to fresh fruit and vegetables rather than canned, frozen or processed varieties.

Cook jacket potatoes and eat the skin as well as the flesh. Boil new potatoes in their skins.

Avoid salt in cooking and at table if possible.

Make your own pasta at home with wholewheat flour (see recipes on p. 154).

Use brown rice in preference to white.

Use the stir/cook method for vegetables at least three times per week.

Eat a raw salad at least five times a week.

Eat one good portion of a leafy green vegetable every day.

Eat bread three times a day to use up the bread allowance.

SPECIAL DIETS

WHEAT-FREE DIET

Wheat is probably the most common allergen in Britain today. It features largely in most diets as it is a staple food, and is cheap, nutritious, can be stored easily for long periods and has a wide variety of uses. Wheat's main characteristic is that when liquid is added to wheat flour it reacts with the gluten it contains and will make a strong elastic dough, enabling large bakery items such as bread to be made without crumbling or collapsing during baking. Wheat is also used widely in food manufacture, being a useful and cheap thickener and binder. Wheat bran is considered to be the most effective of all the available brans and is used extensively for high fibre slimming foods. Although other flours are available – rye, rice, soya and barley – they are more expensive and do not perform in baking as well as wheat.

Processing of wheat flour to make refined white flour results in the loss of micronutrients. Some of these are put back in before the flour is used but the fibre (bran) lost is not. Gluten can be extracted for use in slimming foods such as crispbreads as it provides cheap protein. The waste product from this process is wheat starch and this is used extensively for gluten-free bakery products, even though its nutritional profile is nothing short of a disaster. (Wheat starch is also used for animal feed, for making paper white in the paper industry and for starching clothes to make them stiff, e.g. stiff collars.)

In the factories and mills where wheat is ground and processed wheat is everywhere in the air, on the workers' clothes, on machinery, etc. As other flours may be milled in the same conditions, contamination of those other flours with wheat is inevitable. Unless milled in a mill where wheat is not processed, rye and barley flours may be contaminated with wheat flour. Soya and corn flours are obtainable from mills which deal only with those flours and so contamination in these is rare.

The Nutritional Value of Wheat in the Diet

Although wheat is a high carbohydrate food (66 per cent), it also contains protein (13 per cent). It has a low fat content (2 per cent) but contains iron, zinc, thiamin, riboflavin, nicotinic acid and Vitamin E.

Wheat bran contains 27 per cent carbohydrate, 14 per cent protein and 6 per cent fat. It has a high level of phosphorus, iron and zinc, and useful levels of Vitamin B6, folic acid, pantothenic acid and biotin. Because of its grain structure wheat can easily be separated into bran, germ and starch. The germ (wheat germ) is high in protein (26·5 per cent) but much lower in carbohydrate than the wholeground flour, containing only 45 per cent. Wheat germ is valued for its iron content of 10 mg per 100 g of Vitamin E, as well as good levels of thiamin, riboflavin and nicotinic acid. (All these figures relate to wholewheat flour.)

The greatest alteration to a normal diet by exluding wheat is the loss of wheat bread, which is a very important part of most diets. It is known as 'the staff of life' for good reason, and people who are suddenly told they cannot eat it any longer can feel very deprived. As bread is a very bulky food this often results in a much reduced intake of food until they learn to cope. Weight loss is usual during the first weeks of adjustment, because of the reduction in the amount of food consumed. As wheat is so widely used in the manufacture of processed foods, a wide variety of ready-made foods also has to be excluded, meaning more home cooking and less intake of 'junk foods'. People who have been very dependent in the past on processed foods fare the worst during the initial period of adjustment.

Substitutes

Other flours can be used to imitate wheat flour, but most will need a binder added to replace the elastic gluten. The protein can be supplied by using soya flour, but as this has a rather musty taste it is best mixed with other, blander-tasting flours such as rice flour, cornflour, ground rice or barley flour. Rye flour can also be blended with other wheat-free flours. This too has a very strong taste and is normally used in a blend with wheat flour for that very reason. Useful binders are dried pectin (expensive), fresh grated apple (for its pectin), methylcellulose (synthetic version of pectin, made from wood pulp), and egg.

Supplements

It may be necessary to take B complex vitamins on a wheat-free diet, and these too should be wheat free.

Basic wheat foods

wheat flour, brown, granary, white and wholewheat
wheat bran
wheat germ
wheat wholegrains
cracked wheat

Foods normally made with wheat

- bread
- breadcrumbs
- biscuits
- cakes, sponges
- buns
- pastries
- mixes for cakes, biscuits, sponges, pastry, crumble toppings, batters, pancakes
- blancmange powders (some)
- baking powders (some) (see recipe on p. 105)
- wheat-based breakfast cereals
- breakfast cereals with bran, e.g. oats with bran
- chocolate and confectionery (some brands)
- chutneys (some)
- cocoa and drinking chocolate
- cheap instant coffees
- cornflours (some)
- crispbreads (some)
- curry powders (some)
- custard powder, packet mixes or ready made canned custard
- gravy powders and stock cubes
- soy sauces (some)
- ice creams (some)
- pastas – macaroni, noodles, lasagne, tagliatelli, vermicelli, etc.
- mustard (made)
- mustard powder
- pickles (some)
- pie fillings
- salad dressings
- savoury and sweet spreads and pastes
- sausages and pâtés
- sauces, sweet and savoury
- food in sauces, e.g. fish in white sauce, baked beans
- canned and packet soups
- TVP (some)
- sauce mixes
- imitation, thickened or extended creams
- instant puddings and desserts
- fruit-flavoured yoghurts
- alcoholic drinks (some) e.g. rye whisky
- baby foods (some)
- white pepper (in restaurants and cafés – often extended with wheat flour)

Reading Labels

As wheat flour is used for both thickening and binding, it is found in many processed foods. Manufacturers do not always state clearly on their labels exactly which type of starch has been used in their product. Often the starch used is the cheapest available at the time of manufacture, and so it can change from one batch of food to the next.

Any of the following terms on a label could mean that wheat has been used: wholegrain; wheat meal; flour; starch; modified starch; rusk; wheat protein; cereal protein; cornflour; edible starch; food starch; cornstarch; vegetable protein; thickening; thickener.

Basic Wheat-free Diet Suggested amounts of food for one person for one week

Milk	3 pints (1.5 litres) skimmed milk
Eggs	4
Fats/oils	about 4 oz (110 g) polyunsaturated margarine and under 2 oz (50 g) butter
	4 oz (110 g) cheeses, preferably low fat
	9 fluid oz (250 ml) sunflower, safflower, corn, soya or olive oil (varied)
Vegetables	4 lb (2 kg) potatoes (fresh)
	3 oz (75 g) frozen peas
	2½ lb (1.25 kg) fresh green and other vegetables
Meat (lean only from)	4½ oz (125 g) beef or veal
	2 oz (50 g) liver
	2½ oz (65 g) lamb
	10 oz (280 g) poultry
	4 oz (110 g) bacon/ham without breadcrumbs
	2½ oz (65 g) pork
	2 home-made sausages (see recipe on p. 113) made with special wheat-free breadcrumbs
Fish	about 12 oz (350 g) oily and white fish, fresh and canned in oil or water
Sugar	5 oz (150 g)
Jam/honey	4 oz (110 g)
Wheat-free flours	4 oz (110 g)
*Rice/buckwheat**/ wheat-free pasta*	1 lb (450 g)
Fruit	over 2 lb (1 kg) fresh fruit
	2 oz (50 g) low sugar canned fruit
	8 oz (225 g) dried fruit including apricots and nuts
Biscuits	6, wheat free (see recipes)

*Not a member of the wheat family – Saracen corn.

Bread	2–3 small wheat-free loaves and crispbreads to total 1½ lb (750 g) (see recipes)
Cereals	8 oz (225 g) oats, rice-based cereals, barley, rye, and millet flakes
	2 oz (50 g) rice bran/soya bran
Cakes/buns/ pastries	about 3 oz (75 g), wheat free
Pulses	2 oz (50 g) dried weight
Beverages	2–3 oz (50–75 g), wheat free
Other foods	9 oz (250 g), wheat free

Note If wheat-free bread is a problem and cannot be organized or supplied, increase the amount of breakfast cereals, rice, buckwheat and wheat-free crispbreads by about 1 lb (450 g). If necessary, supplement with a wheat-free B complex tablet. If no bread at all is taken, supplement with brewer's yeast.

Cookery Advice

Avoid all wheat flours: white, granary, brown and wholewheat. Instead use maize, rice flour and ground rice, millet, buckwheat, barley, rye and soya flours. Oats and oatmeal can also be used.

For binders use grated apple, dried pectin or methylcellulose. Yellow split pea flour will also bind a little but should be used more for adding colour to otherwise unappetizing coloured flour blends. Use in small amounts or the taste will come through too strongly.

For thickening gravies, casseroles, etc. use maize flour. For coating fish, rissoles, etc. use millet, oatmeal or maize flour.

Instead of ordinary bread for breadcrumbs use special bread (see recipes on pp. 374, 378, or Trufree loaves using Nos 1, 3, 4 and 5 flours. Some recipes will be able to use cooked rice instead of breadcrumbs.

For stock, find a brand of thin wheat-free soy sauce which can be tolerated (check the label), or use yeast extract.

Find a brand of wheat-free pasta, e.g. buckwheat, that is acceptable, or substitute with buckwheat or rice.

GLUTEN-FREE DIET

As gluten is found in four grains – wheat, rye, barley and oats – these must all be excluded from the diet. Wheat is the staple grain of the four so the diet is not an easy one to follow at first. Rye and barley are rarely eaten in a normal diet, except in crispbreads, but oats are eaten as porridge, in baking and as a base for the now popular breakfast dish, muesli. For more information about wheat, see the wheat-free diet on pp. 38–9.

Because gluten is the natural binder in wheat, rye, barley and oats, and other flours such as rice, soya and cornflour do not contain such a substance, a binder usually has to be added to them.

The Nutritional Value of Gluten-containing Grains in the Diet

By excluding wheat, rye, barley and oats from the diet carbohydrate is lost as well as some cereal protein and micronutrients such as Vitamin B6, thiamin, riboflavin, biotin, pantothenic acid, nicotinic acid, Vitamin E, folic acid and the minerals iron, zinc and phosphorus. Cereal fibre is also an important loss as it is considered to be the most useful fibre there is in the normal diet. Wheat is widely used in the manufacture of foods as it is not only a good binder but thickens well. Being cheap and readily available it is found in a great variety of processed foods and is also used a good deal for home baking and cooking. In particular it is made into bread, and this will be seen as the greatest loss in a gluten-free diet. Weight loss is common during the first few weeks of adjustment to a gluten-free diet, because it excludes so many foods.

Substitutes

Ground rice, rice flour, sago flour, cornflour, millet, soya flour and buckwheat can be used in blends with a binder to mimic both the nutritional value and the performance of wheat flour. The traditional answer to the gluten-free dieter's flour problem has always been to use wheat starch. (For more details of this nutritional disappointment see p. 35). Although a good deal of processing is applied to remove the gluten, some inevitably remains in the wheat starch and it should not be regarded as 100 per cent gluten free unless it carries a declaration 'maximum gluten content nil'. There is a loophole in the law regarding the labelling of wheat starch which allows manufacturers to label it 'gluten free' even if does contain a little gluten. Even such a small amount can cause the acutely allergic to suffer distressing symptoms. Wheat starch should be avoided totally on a gluten-free diet for best results.

Binders that are useful are: methycellulose (made from wood pulp), pectin (dried), fresh grated apple and, of course, the versatile egg.

Supplements

It may be necessary to take B complex vitamins (gluten free) on a gluten-free diet.

Basic gluten-containing foods

wheat flour: brown, white, wholewheat and granary
wheat bran
wheat germ
wheat wholegrains
cracked wheat
wheat starch
pearl barley
pot barley
barley flakes
barley flour
oats
oatmeal and flour
rolled oats
porridge oats
rye flour
rye flakes
some cornflours (look for pure maize instead)

Foods normally made with gluten-containing grains

gravy powders and stock cubes
breakfast cereals made with wheat, rye, barley or oats
cocoa
baby foods
soups, canned, packet and cartoned
pâtés and pastes
pasta – noodles, spaghetti, macaroni, vermicelli, lasagne, tagliatelli, etc.
baking powders (see recipe on p. 105)
bedtime drinks
drinking chocolate
salad dressings, mayonnaise (commercially produced)
sandwich spreads, sweet or savoury
cakes, sponges
biscuits, pastries, cookies
crispbreads
porridge
muesli
breakfast cereals
malt
malt vinegar
malt flavouring (except for synthetic types)
malt whisky, rye whisky

Foods normally made with gluten-containing grains cont.

alcoholic drinks based on wheat, rye, barley or oats
made mustard, unless genuine French
mustard powder
sauces, including most soy sauces
sauce mixes
food in sauces, e.g. baked beans
chutneys, pickles
yoghurts with flavourings or fruit
pie fillings
imitation, thickened or extended cream
instant puddings and desserts
blancmanges, custards, ready made or powder
cheap brands of instant coffee
curry powders (some)
some spices, e.g. mixed spice
ice creams (some)
sausages
bread, yeasted buns
batter and batter mixes
pancakes
scones and dropscones
crumble topping mixes
cake, biscuit, sponge, bun mixes
cheap chocolate
confectionery (some)
cake decorations (some)
snack nibbles
white pepper (in restaurants and cafés)
TVP (some)

Reading Labels

As flours are useful for both thickening and binding or making foods 'go further', they are used widely in the manufacture of foods. Manufacturers do not always state clearly on the label which kind of flour they have used. Any of the following declarations on a label could mean the presence of gluten: wholegrain; wholemeal; wheat meal; flour; starch; cornstarch; modified starch; special gluten-free starch (usually wheat starch); rusk; wheat protein; cereal; cereal protein; edible starch; foodstarch; thickening; thickener; binder; vegetable protein.

Basic Gluten-free Diet Suggested amounts of food for one person for one week

Milk	3 pints (1.5 litres) skimmed milk
Eggs	4
Fats/oils	about 4 oz (110 g) polyunsaturated margarine and under 2 oz (50 g) butter

Fats/oils cont.	4 oz (110 g) cheese, preferably low fat
	9 fluid oz (250 ml) sunflower, safflower, corn, soya and olive oils, varied
Vegetables	4 lb (1.75 kg) fresh potatoes
	2½ lb (1.25 kg) fresh green and other vegetables
	3 oz (75 g) frozen peas
Meat (lean only from)	4½ oz (125 g) beef or veal
	2 oz (50 g) liver
	2½ oz (65 g) lamb
	10 oz (280 g) poultry
	4 oz (110 g) bacon/ham without breadcrumbs
	2½ oz (65 g) pork
	2 sausages, home made (see recipe on p. 113)
Fish	about 12 oz (350 g) oily and white fish, fresh and canned in oil or water
Sugar	5 oz (150 g)
Jam/honey	4 oz (110 g)
Gluten-free flours	total of 4 oz (110 g) rice flour or ground rice, buckwheat,* maize flour
Rice/buckwheat/ gluten-free pasta	total 1 lb (450 g)
Fruit	over 2 lb (1 kg) fresh fruit
	2 oz (50 g) low sugar canned fruit
	8 oz (225 g) dried fruit and nuts (plain)
Biscuits	4–6, gluten free (see recipes)
Bread	3 small loaves, gluten free (see recipes)
Cereals	8 oz (225 g) rice-based cereals, millet
	2 oz (50 g) rice bran, soya bran
Cakes/buns/ pastries	about 3 oz (75 g), gluten free
Pulses (if tolerated)	2 oz (50 g) dry weight
Beverages	2–3 oz (50–75 g), gluten free
Other foods	9 oz (250 g), all gluten free

Note If gluten-free bread is a problem and cannot be made or supplied, increase the amount of gluten-free breakfast cereals, rice,

*Buckwheat is not a member of the wheat family. It is naturally gluten free.

buckwheat and potatoes. It may be necessary to supplement with B complex vitamins. Some women may need an iron supplement daily. If no bread at all is eaten, supplement with brewer's yeast.

Cookery Advice

Avoid wheat, barley and rye flours, oats and oatmeal. Instead use pure maize, rice flour, ground rice, millet and buckwheat.

For binders use grated apple, egg, pectin (dried) or methylcellulose. Use yellow split pea flour in small amounts to bind and give a good colour to food.

For thickening gravies, casseroles, etc. use pure maize flour. For coating fish, rissoles, etc. use pure maize flour or millet.

Make breadcrumbs from any of the gluten-free bread recipes (pp. 374, 378) or from bread made with Trufree flours, Nos 1, 3, 4 and 5. Cooked rice can be used in some recipes instead of breadcrumbs.

For stock, find a brand of soy sauce or similar that is gluten free, or use yeast extract instead.

Make your own gluten-free pasta (see recipe on p. 154). Rice or buckwheat can be substituted for pasta in some recipes.

Make your own soups, sauces, etc. at home.

MILK-FREE DIET

Milk is used in liquid form as a food and can be made into other foods such as cheese, yoghurt, butter and cream. The manufacturing industry uses the components of milk as fillers for pharmaceutical products such as tablets and pills (lactose) and to make foods creamy (whey). Other useful milk components are milk solids, curds, lactic acid, albumin, casein and caseinates (zinc, iron, magnesium, sodium, potassium, calcium).

As dairy farming is an important industry in Britain it is no surprise that milk has become a staple in the diet and is used by most people every day. In particular it is used in tea and coffee, which is drunk throughout the day. Yoghurt was first introduced to use up surplus milk and is now a part of most peoples' diet.

The Nutritional Value of Milk in the Diet

Milk contributes a variety of nutrients to the diet: protein 3 per cent, 4 per cent fat for whole milk but less than 1 per cent for skimmed milk, 120 mg per 100 g calcium, 0.05 mg per 100 g iron, 1.5 mg per 100 g Vitamin C, over 30 mcg Vitamin A and other vitamins and minerals. As it appears in the diet in different forms, e.g. as cheese, yoghurt, butter and cream, a milk-free diet represents a considerable loss of important nutrients. Cheese contributes various levels of protein, with Cheddar-type cheese being 26 per cent protein. The positive aspect of a milk-free diet is that a good deal of saturated fat will also be lost by not eating cheese or butter.

As milk is almost a complete food the nutrients lost by excluding it from the diet need to be put back in a variety of foods, and even supplements for a healthy diet. You will find recipes in this book for making staple foods without milk. A milk-free diet means much more home cooking and the people who will find it most difficult to cope are those who cannot cook and are used to buying and eating a good deal of junk food. Weight loss is usual during the initial adjustment period.

Substitutes

Most people would understand 'milk' to mean milk from the cow, but goat's milk is also available and may be tolerated by some people who cannot take cow's milk. Goat's milk cheese can also be bought from specialist cheese shops and health stores, and in some supermarkets.

Soya milk is a very nutritious milk made from the soya bean. However, it has the characteristic musty taste of soya and many people find this distasteful. Tofu is a kind of white cheese made from soya bean protein. Its main drawback is that it has very little taste and needs to be flavoured in some way to make it palatable.

The majority of margarines are made with whey, a milk by-product. Tomor and Vitaquel are two margarines made without animal products and so are milk free. Tomor can be bought at most Jewish grocers and Vitaquel at health food stores. Look for the 'non-dairy' flash or some indication that the products are made without ingredients of animal origin.

Some people may be able to tolerate the 'Carnation' brand of evaporated milk because, having been heat treated, some of the large protein molecules are destroyed, making it easier to digest than whole milk.

Foods likely to contain milk

commercially made baking powders
bread from the bakers
enriched breads, buns, e.g. hot cross buns
rolls
butter
margarine, unless 'no dairy' or milk free
low fat spreads
sauces made with butter, milk, cheese
cakes, sponges, cookies, biscuits, doughnuts
crumpets, pikelets, muffins
cheese and cheese spreads
cream and creamed foods
mashed potato with cream or milk
cocoa and chocolate drinks
chocolate, confectionery, sweets
curd
custards
blancmanges
junket
desserts made with milk
scrambled egg made with butter and milk
ice cream
rarebit
malted milk, bedtime drinks
mixes for baking
milk – fresh, dried, whole, soured, curds, whey, milk solids, skimmed milk, buttermilk, semi-skimmed milk, powdered milk, milk granules, condensed milk, evaporated milk
Yorkshire pudding
batter pudding
fritters
toad in the hole
pastry

soufflés
quiches and savoury flans with milk or cream
creamed foods
milk puddings
salad dressings (commercial)
mayonnaise, commercial
crispbreads and water biscuits, crackers
some soups, especially 'cream of . . .'
pancakes
dropscones
scones made with milk, yoghurt, cream or cheese
cheese dishes, e.g. cauliflower cheese, pizza
cheesecake
cream liqueurs
instant whips
milky drinks

Reading Labels

The use of milk by-products in processed foods is widespread and makes identification difficult – for instance, it may be used in improvers for commercially made bread, which will not carry a label if bought unwrapped, so the customer will never know about it. The following E numbers indicate milk or milk by-products, so foods which display these on the label should be avoided: E270, E325, E326, E327 and E472(B).

Totally Milk-free Diet
Suggested amounts of food for one person for one week

Milk	none avoid yoghurt
Eggs	3½
Fats/oils	6 oz (175 g) milk-free margarine ¼ pint (150 ml) sunflower, safflower, corn or soya oil cheese: none butter: none
Vegetables	3½ lb (1.75 kg) potatoes 3 oz (75 g) plain frozen vegetables 10 oz (280 g) vegetables canned in water 2½ lb (1.25 kg) fresh leafy greens, carrots and other vegetables

Meat (lean only from)	4 oz (110 g) beef or veal
	3 oz (75 g) liver
	2½ oz (65 g) lamb
	4 oz (110 g) bacon/ham
	2 sausages, home made
	12 oz (350 g) poultry
	4 oz (110 g) other meats
Fish	12 oz (350 g) white and oily fish, fresh and canned in oil or water
Fruit	over 2 lb (1 kg) fresh fruit
	2 oz (50 g) canned fruit without sugar
	8 oz (225 g) dried fruit and plain shelled nuts
Bread (home made)	approx 1¼ lb (550 g) wholewheat
	12 oz (350 g) white
	12 oz (350 g) brown
Rice/pasta	4 oz (110 g) other breads without milk
	1 lb (450 g) brown rice or wholewheat pasta
Biscuits	4 oz (110 g) home made, with milk-free margarine
Flour	6 oz (175 g) wholewheat
Cereals	8 oz (225 g) milk-free oats, millet, rye and barley flakes
Cakes/buns/ pastries	under 3 oz (75 g), made without milk and using milk-free margarine
Pulses	1½ oz (40 g) dried beans, peas or lentils
Beverages	2½ oz (65 g) tea, coffee, served without milk
Sugar	5 oz (150 g)
Jam/marmalade	4 oz (110 g)
Other foods	about 9 oz (250 g), avoiding those with milk, butter, cheese, yoghurt and other milk by-products.
Supplements	low dose cod liver oil, low dose dolomite or bone meal (calcium).

Note If soya milk can be tolerated, cut down the meat by 4 oz (110 g) and use 1 pint (600 ml) per week.

Cookery Advice

Use fruit juice on cereals instead of milk. Make a variety of fresh fruit juices at home (see recipes).

Make savoury sauces for meat and fish with tomato and other fruits.

Make scrambled egg with water instead of milk.

Make your own baking powder at home (see recipe).

Make sorbets to serve instead of ice cream.

Serve weak, black tea with a slice of lemon instead of milk.

Recipes that use a little milk to bind can be bound with a little apple juice or orange juice instead, e.g. scones.

Use milk-free margarine for cooking. See recipe section for milk-free recipes.

Make oil/vinegar or oil/lemon dressings for salads.

EGG-FREE DIET

Eggs are used widely throughout the diet in both sweet and savoury dishes, and as a high protein food that makes a good and inexpensive substitute for meat or fish. However, it is often forgotten that they are also a source of saturated fat and have a high cholesterol level (in the yolk).

An egg comprises three parts – the shell, which is discarded, the white (albumen) and the central yolk. (After the shell is removed the yolk and white can easily be separated.) As regards cooking, the egg is an extremely versatile and useful ingredient. The white will bind ingredients together in cakes, rissoles, burgers, pancakes, batters, etc. and eggs can give foods a shiny glaze, e.g. bread and pastries. Eggs will emulsify to make sauces, mayonnaise and drinks. They can be used to enrich foods and give them a higher nutritional value. Dipping food in beaten egg before frying can given a crisp, attractive and tasty finish to fish cakes, rissoles, and some fish and meat dishes. Eggs will set to make a custard for quiches, while light cakes such as sponges can be made from quite heavy ingredients, with the addition of an egg. Whites can be whisked to incorporate air and become extra light, as in meringues, soufflés, sorbets and other desserts. Eggs can be cooked on their own – boiled, baked, scrambled, fried, poached or made into omelets – all things considered a very versatile food!

Although eggs contain only a trace of carbohydrate they have good levels of protein (12 per cent) and fat (11 per cent). They contribute the following micronutrients in significant amounts: Vitamin E and biotin (in the yolk), Vitamins B1 (thiamin), B2 (riboflavin), B6, B12 and D, folic acid and pantothenic acid. In free-range eggs the Vitamin B12 value can be almost double that of the battery produced egg (2.9 mcg for free range and 1.7 mcg for battery eggs per 100 g). This point is important for the vegetarian who cannot rely on meat as a source of this important vitamin.

Some people react to just the white of egg, others to just the yolk. Some people react to the whole egg. It is thought that as many as one in ten people may be allergic in some way to egg in the UK. In view of the many uses of eggs in the average diet it is not surprising that a great number of foods need to be excluded from an egg-free diet – not just egg dishes but a host of foods that contain egg in some way. Many drugs are cultured on egg white, another point to remember.

Substitutes

There is no satisfactory substitute for an egg. 'Egg replacers' can be obtained which are usually just a kind of powdered binder plus a filler of starch. Milk-based products are more successful, such as 'Bipro', but they are very expensive. It is quite easy to follow an egg-free diet providing home cooking is available. People who will find an egg-free diet difficult are those without any knowledge of cooking who eat out a good deal. The avoidance list is long and should be available for reference in a small notebook until well known to the dieter.

Foods made with egg white

sorbets
ice cream
fruit snow
macaroons
marshmallows
meringues
consommé (egg shells are used to 'clear' this soup)
frostings for cakes
Royal icing
confectionery made with egg white

Foods made with egg yolk

mayonnaise and salad cream
Hollandaise sauce
tartare sauce
all mayonnaise-based sauces
marzipan
margarines enriched with lecithin
mashed potato enriched with egg yolk
chocolate mousse and other mousses

Foods which contain egg

custard powder
batter mixes
cake, sponge and biscuit mixes
sauce mixes

Savoury foods made with whole egg

omelets
boiled eggs, soft or hard boiled
baked or coddled eggs
scrambled eggs
poached eggs
fried eggs
pickled eggs
Scotch eggs
food cooked in batter made with egg – fish cakes, fish, fritters, toad in the hole
food cooked in egg and breadcrumbs – fish fingers, fish, scampi, croquettes, rissoles
foods which use egg as a binder – burgers, fish cakes, rissoles, croquettes, meat balls, meat loaf, terrines, nut savouries
savoury pancakes
latkes
quiches
savoury tarts

Savoury foods made with whole egg cont.

gnocchi
sauces enriched with egg
mashed potato enriched with egg
soufflés (savoury)
egg pasta, noodles, macaroni, spaghetti, tagliatelli, fettucine, lasagne, etc.
piperade
Yorkshire pudding
savoury mousses
savoury pâtés made with egg
kedgeree

Sweet foods made with whole egg

home-made or commercially made cakes, sponges, biscuits
cookies, brownies
doughnuts
eclairs, profiteroles
choux buns, and other items made with choux pastry
pastries
custard tarts
egg custard, crème caramel
items made with egg-enriched pastry
desserts made with egg
dropscones made with egg
Welshcakes
scones made with egg
crumpets made with egg
muffins, pikelets
pancakes, waffles, crèpes
sweet sauces made with egg
sweet soufflés
sorbets
ice cream
bedtime drinks enriched with egg
'nogs' or creamy enriched alcoholic drinks
batter pudding
bread and butter pudding
egg-enriched buns, e.g. hot cross buns, currant buns, Bath buns, teacakes, fruit buns
bakery items glazed with egg
fruit breads, tea breads
enriched breads
croissants
mousses
cheesecakes

Reading Labels

Look on the labels of commercial foods for the following: albumen; lecithin (this is often from soya but may also be from egg); E322 (may be from egg). Foods which indicate that these substances are included in manufacture should be avoided, as well as the more obvious ones such as egg white, egg yolk or just egg.

Basic Egg-free diet
Suggested amounts of food for one person for one week

Milk	2½ pints (1¼ litres) skimmed milk
Eggs	none
Fats/oils	4 oz (110 g) butter
	4 oz (110 g) low fat cheeses
	9 fluid oz (250 ml) oil high in polyunsaturates
Vegetables	3 lb (1.5 kg) potatoes
	3 oz (75 g) plain frozen vegetables
	2½ lb (1.25 kg) fresh green and other vegetables
Meat (lean only from)	4 oz (110 g) beef or veal
	2 oz (50 g) liver
	3 oz (75 g) lamb
	12 oz (350 g) poultry
	2 sausages, home made
	4 oz (110 g) bacon/ham
	2½ oz (65 g) pork
	4½ oz (125 g) other meat products that do not contain egg
Fish	about 12 oz (350 g) fresh and canned in oil or water, a mixture of oily and white fish
Sugar	5 oz (150 g)
Jam/marmalade	2 oz (50 g)
Rice/pasta/noodles	1 lb (450 g) total. NB pasta should not be made with egg
Flour	about 6 oz (175 g) wholewheat
Fruit	over 2 lb (1 kg) assorted fresh fruit including citrus
	2 oz (50 g) canned, low sugar fruit
	4 oz (110 g) dried fruit
	3 oz (75 g) plain nuts, assorted, shelled
	1 oz (25 g) sunflower and sesame seeds
Bread	1¼ lb (550 g) wholewheat/granary
	12 oz (350 g) plain white (avoid enriched breads)

Cereals	8 oz (225 g), especially Shredded Wheat, Puffed Wheat, oats
Cakes/buns/pastries	under 3 oz (75 g), all made without egg
Pulses	1½ oz (40 g) dried beans, peas, lentils
Beverages	2½ oz (65 g) tea, coffee, cocoa. NB avoid egg-enriched bedtime drinks
Other foods	about 9 oz (250 g), all without egg

Cookery Advice

For binding rissoles, meatballs, meat loaf, nut savouries, sausages, etc., grated apple makes a good egg substitute.

To replace frying in egg and breadcrumbs, dip food in milk and then wholewheat flour, cornflour, rice flour or potato flour.

To replace egg batter use a batter made with flour and milk, or flour and water. Make pancakes, dropscones, biscuits without egg (see recipes). Make cakes without egg (see recipes)

Some pastas are available which are not made with egg. Check labels carefully.

It is possible to make salad creams and mayonnaise-type salad dressings without egg at home (see recipes).

It is in the nature of egg, especially beaten egg, to stick to things, in particular the prongs of forks and other cutlery. Extra care when washing up is required.

SOYA-FREE DIET

Soya beans can be used to make flour, milk, oil and TVP. Soya is a highly nutritious food with a high level of protein (37 per cent) (figures are for full fat soya flour). It is also high in fat (24 per cent), but this is largely polyunsaturated. As a cheap and easy-to-grow food it is now used widely in the manufacture of many kinds of processed foods. The oil is extracted for cooking oil and also used in margarines. The protein is used to extend animal protein and for TVP (Textured Vegetable Protein). The beans themselves take a good deal of cooking and soaking, and all soya products have a characteristic 'musty' taste. The flour produced is yellow and fine and is used in the bakery industry to boost protein levels of food.

Soya is a food that has been used more and more over the last two or three decades and has gradually become a minor staple in the diet. Soya by-products are found in many kinds of manufactured goods, not just in foods. Anyone on a soya-free diet would therefore be wise to avoid: celluloid, printing inks, enamels, paint, varnish, adhesives, textile dressings, cosmetic creams, soaps and candles.

As soya is spread through the average diet in small amounts, a diet excluding soya is not difficult except for the vegetarian who may have relied heavily on tofu and TVP for protein. However, other beans and nuts will put this protein back into the diet.

Substitutes

For soya oil substitute sunflower, safflower and corn oils. For soy sauce substitute either home-made stocks or yeast extract. Meat and fish will provide good protein to replace soya in the diet. Soya bran can be replaced with wheat bran or rice bran.

Foods likely to contain soya flour, oil or beans

margarines
low fat spreads
salad dressings (commercial)
soya oil
mixed vegetable oils
hard block vegetable fat
sausages
canned meats
corned beef
pasties, pies
pâtés, spreads
cereals (some)
breads (some)
soya bran
bread with bran
soya milks

Foods likely to contain soya flour, oil or beans cont.

sprouted soya beans
soya beans
tofu
soups
gravy mixes, stock cubes
miso
crumble toppings and mixes
TVP
soya lecithin
ice cream
desserts
pastas (some)
meat pie fillings
vegetarian savoury products (some)
sweets, toffees
cakes, biscuits, pastries
soy sauce
sauces
gravies, casseroles
ready prepared meals

Reading Labels

Avoid foods with vegetable protein listed on the label, as this could mean soya.

Soya-free diet
Suggested amounts of food for one person for one week

Milk	2 pints (1 litre) skimmed milk, but no soya milk
Eggs	4
Fats/oils	4 oz (110 g) butter
	6 oz (175 g) low fat cheeses
	9 fluid oz (250 ml) sunflower, safflower and corn oil; avoid soya oil
Vegetables	3½ lb (1.75 kg) potatoes
	4 oz (110 g) frozen peas
	2½ lb (1.25 g) fresh greens and other vegetables
	10 oz (280 g) canned vegetables, but not soya beans
Meat (lean only from)	4 oz (110 g) beef or veal
	2 oz (50 g) liver
	2½ oz (65 g) lamb
	4 oz (110 g) bacon/ham
	2 sausages, home made
	2½ oz (65 g) pork

Meat (lean only from)	10 oz (280 g) poultry 3 oz (75 g) other meat products, without soya oil or protein or soya bran
Fish	about 10 oz (280 g) white fish and oily fish, canned or fresh
Fruit	over 2 lb (1 kg) fresh fruit 2 oz (50 g) canned fruit without sugar 8 oz (225 g) dried fruit and nuts
Bread	all bread to be made without soya flour or oil 1¼ lb (550 g) wholewheat 12 oz (350 g) white 12 oz (350 g) brown 4 oz (110 g) other breads
Rice/pasta	1 lb (450 g) wholewheat pasta, brown rice
Biscuits	about 4 oz (110 g), made without margarine, soya oil, soya bran or flour
Flour	6 oz (175 g) wholewheat
Cereals	8 oz (225 g) breakfast cereals, oats, millet
Cakes/buns/ pastries	under 3 oz (75 g), made without soya oil, soya bran or flour, or margarine
Pulses	1½ oz (40 g) peas, beans, lentils
Beverages	2½ oz (65 g) tea, coffee, cocoa, etc.
Sugar	5 oz (150 g)
Jam/marmalade	4 oz (110 g)
Other foods	about 9 oz (250 g), without soya beans, soya flour, bran or oil, or margarine, or TVP

Cookery Advice

If you wish to avoid butter, find a brand of margarine that does not contain soya oil. See p. 26 for details of margarine manufacture.

CITRUS-FREE DIET

Nutritional Value of Citrus Fruit in the Diet

Oranges, lemons and grapefruit are available all year round, as are orange and grapefruit juice, both fresh, frozen, canned and cartoned. Seasonal citrus fruits are clementines, satsumas, mandarines, tangerines, limes and uglifruit. All these fruits are valued for their high level of Vitamin C, although oranges can also contribute folic acid and a little Vitamin A. Citrus fruits are low in protein (about 1 per cent) but contain about 9 per cent carbohydrate. Ripe fruit is usually sweet but poorer quality and unripe fruit can be extremely sour and provide an excuse for a good deal of sugar. This is particularly true of fruit juices which require several fruits to make a portion.

Usually the fruit peel is removed and just the segments eaten, but the peel can also be used fresh in cooking if grated, or chopped and candied. Citrus peel makes a good flavouring for both sweet and savoury foods, e.g. cakes and fish dishes. Lemon is a much used garnish for all kinds of food. Grapefruit is a popular starter and breakfast fruit.

Citrus is one of the most widely used flavourings in food manufacture, from squashes and desserts to sauces and confectionery, toothpaste and vitamin pills. Bioflavonoids are extracted from the skins of citrus fruit for use as food supplements.

Substitutes

Totally synthetic flavours can mimic the taste of citrus fruits to an extent, but they are never as good as the real thing. Bioflavonoids can be manufactured synthetically for use in supplements.

Foods to avoid on a citrus-free diet: citrus fruits

orange
lemon
grapefruit
lime
tangerine
satsuma
mandarin
clementine
uglifruit
angostura
hybrid fruits such as 'sweeties' which are obviously from the citrus family

Foods that contain the juice, peel, flavour or flesh of citrus fruit

citrus-flavoured sweets, confectionery and chocolates, usually coloured yellow, green and orange, or red
orange, lemon, lime, grapefruit ice cream/sorbets
candied peel
mixed dried fruit containing candied peel
orange flower water
marshmallows made with orange flower water
citrus fruit juice – orange, grapefruit, lime, etc. (fresh juice, canned or frozen)
fruit drinks containing citrus
fruit squashes containing citrus
lemonade, orangeade, limeade, lemon barley water
cakes with citrus – rind or juice
biscuits with citrus
cookies with citrus
sponges containing rind or juice of citrus fruit
lemon meringue pie
marzipan and some icings, e.g. Royal icing
citrus fruit jellies
citrus-flavoured cheesecake
yoghurts flavoured with citrus fruit
alcoholic drinks decorated with citrus fruits, e.g. gin and tonic with lemon
alcoholic drinks made with citrus fruits, e.g. vodka and orange curacao, drinks with angostura bitters
savoury sauces, especially for fish
sweet sauces for puddings, e.g. lemon or orange sauce
fish dishes cooked with orange, lemon, lime
chicken dishes cooked with lemon, orange, lime
pickles and chutneys made with citrus fruits
tea with lemon
oil and lemon salad dressing
cream-type salad dressings (some)
garnishes, e.g. slices or twists of lemon
angostura bitters and dishes made with it
citrus marinades for fish and meat, e.g. for kebabs
sweet and sour sauce made with orange juice
marmalades

vitamin supplements made with natural bioflavonoids or Vitamin C from citrus
citrus-flavoured toothpaste

Reading Labels

Foods with the following E numbers include citrus: E330; E331; E332; E334; E440(A); E450(B); E472(C).

Cookery Advice

Do not use any of the following in cooking and baking: the grated rinds of citrus fruits; citrus fruit juice; candied peel; dried mixed fruit with candied peel; angostura bitters; any kind of citrus in fruit salad; slices of citrus fruit for garnish; citrus for fruit juice; orange flower water.

Avoid the kind of cakes that specify citrus rind, juice or fruit. Make fruit cakes with a mixture of sultanas, currants, raisins and chopped dried apricots. Avoid using marzipan.

Avoid garnishing food with lemon slices. Garnish savoury foods with watercress or parsley, and sweet foods with grapes or slices of other kinds of fruit, e.g. strawberries, raspberries, slices of peach or nectarine.

NO ADDED SUGAR DIET

Many foods contain natural sugars, e.g. milk contains lactose, fruit contains fructose, so this diet should not be regarded as sugar free but instead free of added sugar.

One of the problems with this kind of diet is a craving for sweet things, which is seldom satisfied. An attempt should be made to lower the amount of sweetness that can be accepted in foods to the extent that fresh grapefruit can be eaten and enjoyed without sugar or any kind of sweetening. At this level of sweetness awareness, many foods considered to be savoury will taste sweet, e.g. peas, carrots, onions.

Addiction to sugar can start at an early age when children are given highly sweetened rusks for teething. Sweets and chocolate are still given to children as 'treats', making sugary foods desirable and associated with loving and caring adults. The use of jam or marmalade as a spread to make bread more palatable has a very strong hold on the western diet. Extra sugar is often taken in tea and coffee, although these two beverages are quite acceptable without any sweetening. Biscuits, cakes, pastries and other bakery items are eaten as snacks and these have a high sugar content. Over-sweet cakes are made for celebrations such as Christmas, birthdays, weddings and anniversaries. A good deal of sugar is consumed from habit rather than need, and because of this factor people can develop a 'sweet tooth'.

Substitutes

Artificial sweeteners (or intense sweeteners) are available from chemists and stores. They are much sweeter than sugar and so need only to be used in very small quantities. Their nutritional contribution to the diet is negligible. As none of the sweeteners has the bulk of sugar they are difficult to use in baking. However, they are welcome as flavourings and table-top sweeteners. Their main drawback is that for those with a sweet tooth the habitual craving for sweet foods is perpetuated when really it would be better to lessen it. Artificial sweeteners are probably most useful in beverages, for those who fail to give up sugar in tea and coffee.

Four main types of sweetener are available and they are as follows:

sweetener	*sweetness quality*	*known brand names*	*remarks*
saccharin	bitter aftertaste	Saxin Hermesetas Sweetex	synthetic, often bulked with lactose, over-use not recommended
Aspartame	good	Equal Nutrasweet Canderel	synthetic, 180–200 times as sweet as sugar
Acesulfame	slight aftertaste		synthetic
Thaumatin	delay in taste	Talin	natural

The following should be avoided as they are all kinds of sugars

granulated sugar
caster sugar
icing sugar
coffee sugar or crystals
soft brown sugar
soft moist sugar
muscovado sugar
barbados sugar
demerara sugar
black treacle
molasses
golden syrup or treacle
fructose (fruit sugar)
dextrose
sucrose
glucose
lactose
cane and beet sugar
honey, thick and thin
corn syrup
maple syrup
frostings
icings
low sugar sweeteners

No Added Sugar Diet
Suggested amounts of food for one person for one week

Milk	3 pints (1.5 litres) skimmed milk
Eggs	4
Fats/oils	under 3 oz (75 g) polyunsaturated margarine
	under 3 oz (75 g) butter
	9 fluid oz (250 ml) polyunsaturated oil, e.g. sunflower
Vegetables	3½ lb (1.75 kg) potatoes
	4 oz (110 g) frozen peas
	2½ lb (1.25 kg) fresh leafy greens and other vegetables
	10 oz (280 g) canned tomatoes
Meat (lean only from)	4½ oz (125 g) beef
	2 oz (50 g) liver
	2½ oz (65 g) lamb
	4 oz (110 g) bacon/ham
	2 sausages, home made
	2½ oz (65 g) pork
Fish	about 10 oz (280 g) both white and oily fish, fresh and canned
Fruit	over 2 lb (1 kg) fresh fruit, including 5 citrus fruits
	4 oz (110 g) fruit canned without sugar
	8 oz (225 g) dried fruit and plain shelled nuts
Rice/pasta	1 lb (450 g) wholewheat pasta and brown rice
Bread	approx 1¼ lb (550 g) wholewheat
	12 oz (350 g) white
	12 oz (350 g) brown
	avoid teabreads, malt bread and breads with sugar
Biscuits	4 oz (110 g): avoid unless made without sugar
Flour	6 oz (175 g) wholewheat
	1 oz (25 g) wheat bran

Cereals	8 oz (225 g) sugar-free oats
Cakes/buns/pastry	2 items per week: avoid unless made without sugar
Pulses	1½ oz (40 g) home-cooked dried beans, lentils, split peas
Beverages	2½ oz (65 g), sugar free
Sugar	none
Jam/marmalade	2 oz (50 g) sugar-free quick jams (see recipes)
Other foods	about 9 oz (250 g), sugar free

Note Artificial sweetener (sugar free) can be used in moderation, if desired, but avoid encouraging a sweet tooth by its use.

Coping

A diet with plenty of variety can break the habit of sweet snack eating. Fruit consumption should be increased to cope with a persistent sweet tooth. Replace sweets, chocolate and confectionery with dried fruit and plain shelled nuts. Sweet spreads such as jams can be made as required and sweetened with artificial sweetener, if necessary. Savoury spreads can be used instead of sweet ones. Some bakery items can be made using artificial sweeteners instead of sugars.

LOW SALT DIET

This diet avoids adding salt to foods, and also avoids those foods which have already had salt added to them as part of their manufacture.

We use salt to preserve and flavour food, as we have done for hundreds of generations. Most of us like the taste, which is very sharp and clean, but a good deal of the salt we take in is purely out of habit or addiction. All foods contain salt to some extent, as a natural part of their make-up. Salt is in our body cells and bones but mainly in the bloodstream. By eating food we are able to top up our salt level, making up for any lost through sweating. Unless we are involved in heavy manual work or exercise, which makes us sweat and lose extra salt, the amount of salt found naturally in food is usually enough to supply the needs of most people. By adding salt to food in cooking and at table we can take in more than we need.

To cope with this situation our kidneys are able to excrete a certain amount of excess salt. However, if we take in too much for the kidneys to cope with, two things happen. The first is that the salt will make us thirsty and that leads to taking extra liquid to quench the thirst. The body holds on to some of the extra fluid and begins to bloat. The second complication can be high blood pressure, which may lead to strokes and heart disease. There is much controversy about the role of too much salt in the diet and, as usual, one group of experts believes it to be nonsense and another group thinks there is cause for concern.

From a common-sense point of view there seems no point in taking in a nutrient that the body does not need and has difficulty in getting rid of, with other possible health hazards that can only (and not always) be rectified by drugs.

The average person trying to cut down on salt will feel pressurized by the food industry, which adds salt to food willy nilly, making use of its low price and its effectiveness as a flavouring and preservative.

Substitutes

The salt substitute market has always been dominated by the use of high potassium products. However, these do not have the same kind of taste as salt and most people find them unpleasant. People who smoke and have to a certain extent lost some of their sensation of taste seem to accept such substitutes more easily than non-smokers. Other ways round cooking without salt are flavouring food more with herbs and adding the sharp taste of lemon juice.

Foods that have salt added during manufacture

soups
breakfast cereals
muesli
pastas, noodles, spaghetti, macaroni, tagliatelle, lasagne, etc.
salted butter
margarine
cheeses
salted nuts
snack nibbles and crisps
baking soda
baking powder
self-raising flour
canned and frozen food in sauce
canned beans
canned vegetables
burgers, rissoles
sweet, savoury and plain biscuits
bread, baked commercially
buns, cakes, cookies, sponges, scones, pastry items, baked commercially
mixes for buns, cakes, cookies, sponges, scones, crumble toppings, pastry
chapatis
sauces, sweet and savoury, commercially made
fruit pies
cocoa
coleslaw
chutneys and pickles
salad creams, dressings and mayonnaises, commercially made
dessert and pudding mixes
ice cream
sweets, chocolate, confectionery
flavoured salts, e.g. celery salt, garlic salt and flavour enhancers
low salt substitutes with added salt
gravy mixes
stock cubes
soya sauce, tamari
haggis
faggots
kippers
smoked fish, e.g. smoked trout, smoked haddock, smoked salmon
caviar, lumpfish roe
fish pastes and spreads
salted fish (dried)
mustards
nut butters, e.g. peanut butter
pizza, commercially made
ready prepared meals
instant potato
sausages, sausage rolls
bacon/ham, salted meat
meat pies, pasties
quiches
pâtés, terrines
luncheon meats, corned beef
yeast extracts
yoghurt

Basic Low Salt Diet
Suggested amounts of food for one person for one week (avoids adding salt during cooking and at table, and also high salt foods)

Milk	2 pints (1 litre) skimmed milk
Eggs	4
Fats/oils	under 3 oz (75 g) salt-free margarine
	under 2 oz (50 g) unsalted butter
	9 fluid oz (250 ml) polyunsaturated oil, e.g. sunflower, corn, soya, safflower
Vegetables	3 lb (1.5 kg) potatoes (fresh)
	3 oz (75 g) plain frozen vegetables, without salt
	2½ lb (1.25 kg) fresh leafy green and other vegetables, including carrots
	10 oz (280 g) canned vegetables, without salt
Fresh meat (lean only from)	4 oz (110 g) beef or veal
	1½ oz (40 g) liver
	2½ oz (65 g) lamb
	10 oz (280 g) poultry
	4 oz (110 g) pork
Fish	12 oz (350 g) fresh fish, both white and oily
Sugar	5 oz (150 g)
Jam/honey	4 oz (110 g)
Rice, home-made pasta	1 lb (450 g)
Flour (plain)	about 6 oz (175 g)
Fruit	over 2 lb (1 kg) fresh
	2 oz (50 g) canned without sugar
	8 oz (225 g) dried fruit and plain shelled nuts without salt
Biscuits (home made)	4 oz (110 g)
Bread (home made)	1¼ lb (550 g) wholewheat
	12 oz (350 g) white
	4 oz (110 g) other breads
Cereals	8 oz (225 g) including oats, salt free

Cakes/buns/pastries (home made)	under 3 oz (75 g)
Pulses	1½ oz (40 g) dried weight, lentils, split peas
Beverages	2½ oz (65 g), salt free
Other foods	9 oz (250 g), salt free

Note Salt-free or low salt substitutes may be used, providing they do not contain more than 0.02 per cent sodium. Check labels carefully as there is a loophole in the law which allows manufacturers to label such products as 'low salt' even if they contain 50 per cent salt.

Some small bakers will bake bread without salt if you place a regular order and there are more than one of their customers who will buy it regularly. Do not expect it to keep as well as the salted kind.

Cookery Advice

You will need to buy a salt-free baking powder such as 'Salfree', made by the Cantassium company, or get your chemist to make up the following formula: 13.5 g tartaric acid, 50 g cornflour or potato or rice flour, 70 g potassium bicarbonate, 100 g cream of tartar. Use half the quantity specified in recipes for ordinary baking powder.

Make your own pasta without salt (see recipe).

Make your own bakery items at home, with oil or unsalted butter or margarine. Make your own chapatis.

Make your own salad dressings, cream, mayonnaise, chutney, etc., and home-made vegetable stock.

Use carob instead of cocoa.

Make good use of fresh and dried herbs and citrus juices in your cooking.

Find a brand of plain low fat yoghurt that does not have added salt.

CORN-FREE DIET

Although 'corn' can be taken to mean any grain as a kind of blanket term, in this instance it refers to corn made from maize (corn on the cob). It is available as maize meal, cornmeal (coarsely ground) or cornflour, a very finely ground whitish powder. This can be used for thickenings and coatings, and will blend well with wheat flour to make it lighter. Cornflour turns up in unexpected places, such as adhesives and gums. It is used on the back of postage stamps and to seal envelopes. Most toothpastes are thickened with it and it is also found in talcum powder. Avoiding the hazards of breathing in talcum powder, absorbing toothpaste in the mouth, and licking stamps and envelopes are just a few of the points to note in this diet, as well as a long list of foods which contain corn. Cardboard and paper cartons, plates, cups, etc. often have cornflour in the special coating that covers them. Some people are allergic enough to react to foods from this type of carton, even if the food itself does not contain corn.

Glucose for sweetening can be made from corn, and this is widely used in the manufacture of processed foods as well as cornflour for thickening them. Laundry-grade cornflour is used for starch in laundries to make clothes stiff or crisp. Corn can be fermented to make alcohol, especially ales, beers and some kinds of whisky (e.g. bourbon).

Poorer grades of sweet corn are used for animal feed. Some people may be unable to tolerate corn-fed meat, which is easily recognizable by its golden yellow colour; chickens in particular will appear bright yellow on the supermarket shelf.

Foods which are likely to contain corn (maize)

aspirin and other tablets
cough syrups
baking powders
foods made with baking powder – cakes, scones, biscuits, pastry, crumbles, cookies, doughnuts, pancakes, fritters, waffles
carbonated drinks
ales, beers, bourbon and other alcoholic drinks
confectionery, candies, chocolate
Chinese food
soy sauce
some instant coffees – look for brands marked 'pure coffee'
instant tea
cornflakes
cornbread
tortillas

Foods which are likely to contain corn (maize) cont.

tacos
corn syrup
glucose
corn oil, maize oil
frying fats
blended vegetable oils and margarines
hard block vegetable oils
custard powder and canned custard
peanut butter
sweet spreads
sandwich spreads, pastes
canned peas, beans and other vegetables
food canned in sauces, e.g. baked beans (some brands)
corn on the cob (sweet corn)
thickened puddings and desserts, quick whips
pâtés
sauce mixes
tomato sauce and ketchup
cheese sauce, commercially made
parsley sauce, commercially made
sherberts
frostings and icings
ice cream
syrups for ice cream and desserts, e.g. melba sauce
crisps and nibbles
popcorn
stuffings
sausages
thick soups, cream soups
some brands of soya milk
distilled vinegar
gravy mixes, stock cubes
trifle
pie fillings
lemon meringue pie and similar pies
pasties
meat pies
imitation cream
jams and jellies made with glucose
pastilles

Reading Labels

Avoid foods labelled E300, E301, E302, E474.

Substitutes

Other flours can be used instead of corn for thickening, such as wheat, potato or rice flour. Safflower, soya and sunflower oils are high in polyunsaturates, like corn oil. Use yeast extract instead of soy sauce. Make bakery items at home without cornflour, using home-made baking powder (see recipe). Use butter instead of margarine, unless you can find one made without corn oil.

Corn (maize)-free Diet
Suggested amounts of food for one person for one week

Milk	2 pints (1 litre) skimmed milk
Eggs	3½
Fats/oils	4 oz (110 g) low fat cheeses
	5 oz (150 g) butter
	¼ pint (150 ml) sunflower, safflower, soya, olive oil
Vegetables	3½ lb (1.75 kg) potatoes
	4 oz (110 g) frozen peas
	2½ lb (1.25 kg) fresh greens and other vegetables, but not sweet corn
	10 oz (280 g) canned vegetables, but not sweetcorn
Meat (lean only from)	4½ oz (125 g) beef or veal
	1½ oz (40 g) liver
	2½ oz (65 g) lamb
	4 oz (110 g) bacon/ham
	2 sausages, home made
	10 oz (280 g) poultry, not corn fed
Fish	about 10 oz (280 g) oily and white fish, fresh or canned in oil
Fruit	over 2 lb (1 kg) fresh fruit
	2 oz (50 g) canned fruit without sugar
	8 oz (225 g) dried fruit without glucose coating and plain fresh nuts
Bread	1¼ lb (550 g) wholewheat
	12 oz (350 g) white
	12 oz (350 g) brown
	4 oz (110 g) other breads without corn or glucose
Rice/pasta	1 lb (450 g) brown rice and wholewheat pasta
Biscuits	4 oz (110 g), made with corn-free oil or butter and without glucose
Flour	6 oz (175 g) wholewheat, plain
Cereals	8 oz (225 g) corn-free breakfast cereals, oats, oatmeal, millet

Cakes/buns/pastries	under 3 oz (75 g), made without cornflour, commercial baking powder or glucose
Pulses	1½ oz (40 g) home-cooked dried peas, beans, lentils
Beverages	2½ oz (65 g) fresh tea and coffee (pure)
Sugar	5 oz (150 g), but not glucose
Jam/marmalade	4 oz (110 g), glucose free
Other foods	about 9 oz (250 g) corn-free and glucose-free foods

TAPWATER-FREE DIET

Tapwater varies in different parts of the country and can contain chemicals and chlorine. In Britain, where water is cheap, tapwater features largely in the diet. It is used to make the popular beverages tea and coffee, for boiling vegetables, etc., and in food preparation. Dried foods such as milk are reconstituted with it, other foods are diluted with it. Ice cubes are made with it and it is also drunk as just plain water out of the tap. By cleaning the teeth with tapwater some will be taken into the mouth. Washing food, such as salad vegetables, before use will also be a source of tapwater in the diet. Foods are canned and frozen with tapwater and it is used in the preparation of processed foods.

A tapwater-free diet is expensive because all water, for washing and cooking vegetables, for making tea and coffee, for teeth cleaning, must not come out of the tap. Processed convenience foods cannot be used. Bottled water, which is available in both 'still' and carbonated ('fizzy') form, is not cheap and it is heavy to carry. Some people may be able to tolerate the use of boiled and cooled tapwater for the less important tasks, such as washing vegetables, but those acutely allergic to tapwater will have to use bottled water for all tasks.

Tapwater-free Diet
Suggested amounts of food for one person for one week

Milk	2 pints (1 litre) bottled water mixed with 4 oz (110 g) dried skimmed milk granules (low fat)
Eggs	3½
Fats/oils	3 oz (75 g) butter
	¾ pint (450 ml) polyunsaturated vegetable oil, e.g. sunflower, safflower, corn, soya
Vegetables	3½ lb (1.75 kg) potatoes
	3 lb (1.5 kg) fresh greens and other vegetables, including carrots

Meat (lean only from)	avoid canned and frozen meats; all meat should be fresh and washed in bottled water before use:
	3 oz (75 g) liver
	4 oz (110 g) beef or veal
	2½ oz (65 g) lamb
	4 oz (110 g) bacon/ham
	2 home-made sausages
	2½ oz (65 g) pork
	10 oz (280 g) poultry
Fish	10 oz (280 g) fresh fish and fish canned in oil
Fruit	over 2 lb (1 kg) fresh fruit
	8 oz (225 g) dried fruit and nuts – wash in bottled water before use
Bread	make at home with bottled water
	1¼ lb (550 g) wholewheat
	12 oz (350 g) each of white and brown
	4 oz (110 g) other breads
Rice/pasta	1 lb (450 g) brown rice and home-made wholewheat pasta, using bottled water for making and cooking
Biscuits	4 oz (110 g), home made
Flour	6 oz (175 g) wholewheat
Cereals	8 oz (225 g) oatmeal, millet for porridge/muesli (avoid breakfast cereals)
Cakes/buns/pastries	under 3 oz (75 g), home made, using bottled water
Beverages	2½ oz (65 g) tea, coffee, made with bottled water
Sugar	5 oz (150 g)
Jam/marmalade	4 oz (110 g), home made with bottled water
Other foods	9 oz (250 g), providing they are made without tapwater. Stocks must be home made (see recipes), using bottled water.

Note Use bottled water for washing, preparing and cooking vegetables and fruit. Supplement the diet with low dose cod liver oil.

Cookery Advice

Make your own fruit juices (see recipes) instead of using canned, frozen or cartoned ones. Make your own lemonade using bottled water, instead of buying squashes etc. Use bottled water to make ice cubes.

Make your own bread at home, using bottled water.

The least expensive way to cook vegetables is the stir/cook method (see recipe). Any water added should be bottled. Add home-made stock if you want to strengthen the gravy at the bottom, not soy sauce. Wash salad items in a very little spring water and pat dry with kitchen paper. Some vegetables only need peeling, e.g. potatoes, carrots, swede, parsnip, etc.

The least expensive way to cook fruit is to bake it.

Use bottled water for cleaning and rinsing teeth. Avoid tapwater near the mouth when washing.

SLIMMING DIET

This diet is for slow but steady weight loss without the bother of weighing foods for each meal and counting calories. Glucommanan may be taken with water between meals to satisfy hunger pangs, if necessary.

Suggested approximate amounts of food for one person for one week

Milk	2 pints (1 litre), skimmed milk
Eggs	3
Fats/oils	2 oz (50 g) polyunsaturated margarine
	1 oz (25 g) butter
	4 oz (110 g) cottage cheese
	¼ pint (150 ml) polyunsaturated oil – about 1 tablespoon per day
Vegetables	2 lb (1 kg) root vegetables, including carrots
	1½ lb (750 g) leafy green vegetables – 1 portion daily
	1½ lb (750 g) fresh potatoes – about 1 medium per day
	2 medium cans tomatoes
Meat (lean only, trim off fat, etc.)	3 oz (75 g) beef
	1½ oz (40 g) liver
	lean from 1 lamb chop
	2 oz (50 g) bacon/ham
	2 oz (50 g) pork
	6 oz (175 g) poultry
Fish	8 oz (225 g) fish canned in water or fresh fish
Fruit	2 lb (1 kg) fresh fruit
	2 oz (50 g) fruit canned without sugar
	4 oz (110 g) dried fruit and nuts, including apricots, but avoid peanuts
Rice/pasta	8 oz (225 g) brown rice or wholewheat pasta

Flour	2 oz (50 g) wholewheat
	1 oz (25 g) wheat bran
Cereals	4 oz (110 g), including oats
Bread	1½ lb (750 g) wholewheat
	4 oz (110 g) brown
	4 oz (110 g) white
Biscuits	2 oz (50 g), about 2 or 3 per week
Cakes/buns/pastries	1 per week
Pulses	1 oz (25 g) dry weight
Beverages	2 oz (50 g) tea and coffee
Other foods	about 9 oz (250 g), including 1 tablespoon of single cream
Supplements	a comprehensive multivitamin, e.g. Cantamega 1000 and brewer's yeast: follow dose on bottles or cartons.

Note One small portion of TVP or two heaped tablespoons of low fat dried milk granules, or one heaped tablespoon of plain shelled nuts can be exchanged for the meat portions.

Cookery Advice

With one meal per day serve a good selection of cooked vegetables: see the stir/cook recipe on p. 264. Serve a salad every day. Make your own salad dressings from the recipes in this book.

Avoid frying; grill instead. Avoid mashed potato.

For a quick meal serve a milkshake with fruit.

Use an artificial sweetener if you wish, in moderation.

Make soup at least twice a week.

General Advice

Take some exercise every day such as a brisk walk, a simple workout or dancing.

HIGH POTASSIUM DIET

Most people either do not take in enough potassium or waste this valuable mineral by poor cooking methods. A good deal of potassium is poured down the kitchen sink, for instance, after boiling vegetables. As potassium has to maintain a balance with sodium in the body the habit of taking too much salt in the diet is detrimental to the potassium level.

The easiest way to boost potassium in the diet naturally is to structure the diet so that, within the food groups, the high potassium/low sodium foods are used most. Raw vegetables and fruit are excellent sources of potassium as they are low in sodium and no potassium is lost in cooking. Stir/cook vegetables (see recipe) are better value than boiled as the juices are saved and served with the vegetables. Dried fruit has a concentration of potassium and, with the exception of figs, sultanas and raisins, is also low in sodium. Nuts have a good potassium level and low sodium content if they are eaten fresh and not salted. Butterbeans are exceptionally high in potassium and low in sodium (400 mg potassium and 16 mg sodium per 100 g). Home-made bread can be made without salt and boosted with bran and wheat germ, two good sources of potassium, making a high potassium loaf.

As much raw food as possible should be eaten for maximum potassium levels and, if possible, no salt should be added to cooking or at the table.

Foods high in potassium and low in sodium

wheat germ
wheat bran
soya flour (low fat) (an excellent source)
wholewheat flour
asparagus
avocado
white and red cabbage, raw
cauliflower, raw
mushrooms, raw
lettuce
tomatoes
jacket potatoes
new boiled potatoes
roast potatoes
Brussels sprouts
raw parsley
bananas
cherries
apricots
grapes
butterbeans (excellent)
currants
dates

raw dried peaches
prunes
raw dried apricots
almonds
brazils
chestnuts
walnuts
black treacle
sweet sherry

Cookery Advice

Use the Basic Diet for Health and increase the amount of vegetables and fruit. Omit the white bread and increase the wholewheat by the same amount. Make high potassium bread at home instead of buying baker's bread.

Use cold cooked butterbeans in salads or serve them hot as a vegetable.

Serve a salad of raw vegetables every day, especially those on the high potassium/low sodium list.

Snacks of dried fruit and nuts are an excellent source of potassium. Make fruit cakes with dried fruit, nuts and black treacle.

Make pastry with soya flour (see recipes).

Take a glass of sweet sherry each day as a tonic.

See pp. 29–31 for the Basic Diet for Health.

LOW CHOLESTEROL DIET

The foods which contain cholesterol are all of animal origin. Cholesterol is found in animal fats and is often confused with fat. (In fact cholesterol is not a fat but a fat-like substance or lipid.) It is found in the following basic foods and the chart shows which foods are high and which are low in cholesterol, within food groups.

Cholesterol in Foods in mg per 100 g

food	*mg*	*food*	*mg*
		whole fresh cow's milk	14
		longlife	14
dried whole milk	120	dried skimmed milk	18
salted butter	230		
single cream	66		
double cream	140		
whipping cream	100		
Camembert-type cheese	72		
Cheddar-type cheese	70		
Parmesan	90		
Stilton	120		
cream cheese	94	cottage cheese	13
		low fat natural yoghurt	7
egg yolks	1260	egg white	0
boiled eggs	450		
beef dripping	60		
lard	70		
suet	74	vegetable oils	0
fried bacon, lean and fat	80		
beef	82		
lamb	110		
pork	110		
roast chicken			
white meat	74	nuts	0
dark meat	120	TVP	0
roast duck	160	tofu	0

food	*mg*	*food*	*mg*
turkey			
light meat	49	beans	0
dark meat	100	vegetables	0
calves'/lambs' brains	2200	fruit	0
fried lambs' kidneys	610	grains	0
fried lambs' liver	400	sugar	0
fried calves' liver	330	honey	0
corned beef	85		
ham	33		
tongue	110		
liver sausage	120		
pork sausages	53		
pork pie	52		
suet pastry	125		
beef stew	30		
beefburgers	68		
baked cod	60		
steamed haddock	75		
steamed plaice	90		
grilled herring	80		
canned salmon	90		
canned sardines	100		
lobster	150		
prawns	200		
scampi	110		
mussels	100		
fried herring roe	500		

As cholesterol is found only in foods of animal origin, a vegan diet, which excludes all animal foods, is totally free of cholesterol. However, this does not mean vegans have no cholesterol in their bodies as humans are able to synthesize cholesterol in both the liver and the intestines.

Vegetarians, by not eating meat and fish, would seem to enjoy a diet lower in cholesterol than their meat- and fish-eating cousins. However, by increasing dairy produce and eggs to make up for the protein lost by not eating meat and fish, there is very little difference in the cholesterol intake of the average vegetarian, compared with those on an ordinary diet.

Many processed foods contain cholesterol and some have a high level of it. Cakes which contain butter, eggs and cream probably have the highest content. Food fried in lard or dripping, especially meat, and dishes made with meat, cheese and eggs have high levels of cholesterol.

Foods to avoid on a low cholesterol diet

dried whole milk
butter
cream
most cheeses
egg yolks and whole eggs
cakes made with egg
pastry made with egg
mayonnaise made with egg
egg dishes, omelets, scrambled, poached, fried, baked, boiled
soufflés
pancakes
fritters, batter-coated foods
quiches
Yorkshire pudding
egg-coated foods (egg/breadcrumbed)
mashed potato with egg yolk
pastas made with egg
cakes, sponges, doughnuts, biscuits, cookies, brownies made with egg
choux pastry, e.g. items such as eclairs, profiteroles
scones made with egg
crumpets, pikelets
ice creams (some)
bedtime drinks enriched with egg
nogs or cream-enriched alcoholic drinks
bread and butter pudding
egg-enriched bread, buns and teabreads
croissants
cheesecake
rissoles, burgers bound with egg
egg custard
meat and foods containing meat, e.g. pies, brawn, pâtés, pastes, soups, broths, burgers
fish and foods containing fish, e.g. fish pie, fish cakes, fish paste
food cooked in lard or dripping, e.g. chips
food containing suet, e.g. suet pastry, sweet mincemeat
pastry made with butter
butter on vegetables
full fat yoghurt
chocolate and confectionery with butter/egg

Low Cholesterol Diet Suggested amounts of food for one person for one week

Milk 3 pints (1.5 litres) skimmed milk (fresh)
Eggs none

Fats/oils	4 oz (110 g) low cholesterol polyunsaturated margarine
	½ pint (300 ml) sunflower, safflower, soya, corn or olive oil
	6 oz (175 g) cottage cheese (without added cream)
Vegetables	3½ lb (over 1.5 kg) fresh potatoes
	3 lb (1.5 kg) wide variety fresh vegetables, including 1 portion of leafy greens daily and 8 oz (225 g) carrots (per week)
	10 oz (280 g) plain, canned vegetables
	6 oz (175 g) frozen peas
Pulses	1 lb cooked weight (450 g) haricot or other beans
	4 oz (110 g) dry weight TVP
	2 oz (50 g) dry weight lentils/split peas
Meat and meat products	none
Fish and fish products	none (see cookery advice regarding fish cakes)
Fruit	over 2 lb (1 kg) fresh fruit, including 6 citrus fruit
	8 oz (225 g) dried fruit, including apricots
	8 oz (225 g) shelled nuts and seeds (no peanuts)
Bread	1¼ lb (550 g) wholewheat bread
	4 oz (110 g) plain white
	4 oz (110 g) granary or wheatgerm enriched
Flour	8 oz (225 g) wholewheat
Cakes/biscuits/cookies	3 oz (75 g), all without egg yolks and butter (see recipes)
Cereals	8 oz (225 g) wholegrain, e.g. Shredded Wheat, Puffed Wheat, oats
	2 oz (50 g) wheat germ
Rice	8 oz (225 g)
Pasta	8 oz (225 g), made without egg
Sugar/honey	not more than 5 oz (150 g)
Jam	not more than 2 oz (50 g), including marmalade

Beverages	2 oz (50 g) tea, coffee, cocoa, etc.
Other foods	9 oz (250 g), all cholesterol free
Diet supplements	175 mcg vitamin B12 (per week)

Cookery Advice

Do not use whole eggs for cooking. Some items can be made with just the egg white, e.g. nut cookies, langues de chat. Digestive biscuits, fruit cakes, dropscones, scones, etc. can be made without eggs (see recipes).

For binding nut/bean burgers etc. use grated apple instead of egg. Dip food in flour to coat before frying and avoid egg batters and egg and breadcrumbs.

Do not use butter for cooking, and do not serve vegetables with butter on them.

If low cholesterol fish is allowed, use the fish cake recipe in this book and use either cod or haddock.

LOW PURINE/WEIGHT-REDUCING DIET

A diet low in purines is often used for gout, together with a slow weight-reducing regime if the patient is obese.

High purine foods to be avoided

Fish	*Meat*
herring roe (soft)	sweetbreads
whitebait	heart
sprats	liver
sardines	kidney
herring	goose
mussels	venison
bloater	meat extracts
cods' roe	meat soups

Moderate purine foods to be avoided

Fish	*Meat*
trout	pheasant
whiting	veal
salmon	lamb
haddock	chicken
cod	bacon
crab	pork
	ham
	beef

Diet Low in Purines
Suggested amounts of food for one person for one week for a slow weight loss

Milk	3 pints (1.5 litres) skimmed milk
Eggs	4
Fats/oils	2 oz (50 g) polyunsaturated margarine
	2 oz (50 g) butter
	½ pint (300 ml) polyunsaturated oil
	8 oz (225 g) cheeses, preferably low or medium fat
Vegetables	3½ lb (over 1.75 kg) fresh potatoes
	3 lb (1.5 kg) wide variety of fresh vegetables
	10 oz (280 g) canned vegetables
	4 oz (110 g) frozen peas
Meat	none, or meat products
Fish	none, or fish products
Pulses	6 oz (175 g) (dry weight) beans, peas, lentils, TVP
Fruit	over 1½ lb (750 g) fresh fruit, including 4 citrus fruits
	2 oz (50 g) dried fruit
	4 oz (110 g) shelled nuts and seeds, excluding peanuts
Bread	1 lb (450 g) wholewheat
	2 oz (50 g) white
	8 oz (225 g) brown
Cakes/biscuits/buns	4 oz (110 g)
Cereals	4 oz (110 g) wholegrain, including oats
Rice/pasta	8 oz (225 g) wholewheat pasta, brown rice
Sugar/honey	2 oz (50 g)
Jam/marmalade	1 oz (25 g)
Beverages	2 oz (50 g) tea or coffee, or herb teas and spring water (plenty), especially last thing at night
Other foods	4 oz (110 g) low purine items
Alcohol	avoid if possible, or very moderate amounts
Diet supplement	175 mcg Vitamin B12, low dose B complex or brewer's yeast

MINERAL BOOSTER DIET (1): HIGH CALCIUM

Calcium is the most abundant mineral in the body, found in bones, teeth and nails. After middle age is reached, women lose calcium gradually from their bones. This causes the bones to become brittle and older women, in particular, are prone to fractures, especially of the hip bones.

Good sources of calcium in the diet

muesli
white bread and flour (fortified with calcium)
dried skimmed milk
Parmesan cheese
Cheddar cheese
yoghurt
haddock
pilchards
sardines
sprats
whitebait
shrimps
boiled spinach
watercress
almonds
black treacle
milk chocolate
figs (dried)

Note The high calcium value of the smaller fish is due to the fact that the bones can be eaten after cooking.

Diet High in Calcium Suggested amounts of food for one person for one week

Milk	2 pints (1 litre) skimmed milk 2 small cartons yoghurt 4 oz (110 g) dried skimmed milk granules (low fat)
Eggs	4
Fats/oils	under 3 oz (75 g) polyunsaturated margarine under 2 oz (50 g) butter 3 oz (75 g) cottage cheese 3 oz (75 g) Cheddar or Parmesan

Vegetables	3½ lb (1.75 kg) fresh potatoes
	3 oz (75 g) frozen vegetables
	10 oz (280 g) canned vegetables
	2 oz (50 g) watercress in season
	8 oz (225 g) spinach in season
	2 lb (1 kg) other leafy greens and root vegetables
Meat (lean only from)	4 oz (110 g) beef or lamb
	2 oz (50 g) liver
	3 oz (75 g) bacon/ham
	2 sausages, home made
	2 oz (50 g) pork
	10 oz (280 g) poultry
Fish	8 oz (225 g) white fish
	2 small cans sardines or pilchards
	2 oz (50 g) shrimps
	2 oz (50 g) whitebait or sprats, when available
Fruit	over 2 lb (1 kg) fresh fruit
	2 oz (50 g) fruit canned without sugar
	6 oz (175 g) dried fruit, including figs and apricots
	2 oz (50 g) almonds (shelled)
	2 oz (50 g) other nuts
Pasta/rice	1 lb (450 g) white pasta, brown rice
Bread	1 lb (450 g) wholewheat, made with added calcium (see note)
	1 lb (450 g) white
	12 oz (350 g) brown
	4 oz (110 g) other breads
Biscuits	4 oz (110 g)
Flour	6 oz (175 g) wholewheat, with added calcium (see note)
	2 oz (50 g) wheat bran
Cereals	8 oz (225 g) wholegrain e.g. Shredded Wheat, oats
Cakes/buns/pastries	3 oz (75 g)
Pulses	1½ oz (40 g) dried peas, beans, lentils
Beverages	2 oz (50 g) tea, coffee, cocoa, etc.
Sugar	4 oz (110 g)
Jam/marmalade	4 oz (110 g)

Other foods 9 oz (250 g), including black treacle and milk chocolate

Note Adding calcium to bread or flour: buy calcium carbonate at the chemists and add a half teaspoon to every 1 lb (450 g) flour. Mix well before using to make bread etc.

Cookery advice

Make your own wholewheat bread at home, with added calcium. Add bran to baking.

Use the dried milk to make milkshakes with fruit.

Use the dried fruit, nuts, bran and oats to make muesli.

MINERAL BOOSTER DIET (2): HIGH IRON

Iron is not a mineral that is well absorbed by the body, for as little as one-tenth may be taken in. Some people, therefore, need to take in extra to make sure of an adequate supply. Iron supplements are obtainable, but in some people can cause problems such as headaches and constipation, while iron salts can cause gastric irritation. Iron not only helps us to cope with stress but is necessary for the reproduction of haemoglobin, which is vital to the oxygen-carrying capacity of the blood. Brittle fingernails, breathlessness, pale skin and fatigue may be helped by a diet high in iron, if iron deficiency has been diagnosed.

Good sources of iron in the diet

wheat germ and bran
wholewheat bread
bread with bran and wheat germ (see recipes)
Special K and Weetabix (fortified breakfast cereals)
game meats, e.g. pheasant, venison
kidney and liver
black pudding (contains blood)
cockles
cooked haricot beans
almonds
curry powder
cocoa
black treacle
spring greens
leeks
low fat soya flour
raw oats (as in muesli)
dried fruit, especially apricots, peaches and figs
corned beef
lean leg of lamb
dark chicken meat
beefburgers
oatcakes
rye crispbread
raw parsley
yeast
mustard
pepper
ground ginger
curry powder
tomato purée

Diet High in Iron
Suggested amounts of food for one person for one week

Milk	2 pints (1 litre), skimmed milk
Eggs	3½
Fats/oils	under 3 oz (75 g) polyunsaturated margarine
	4 oz (110 g) low fat cheeses
	9 fluid oz (250 ml) polyunsaturated oils
Vegetables	3½ lb (1.75 kg) fresh potatoes
	3 oz (75 g) frozen vegetables
	2½ lb (1.25 kg) spring greens, leeks, parsley and other vegetables
	10 oz (280 g) canned vegetables
Meat (lean only from)	4 oz (110 g) beef, especially corned beef
	4 oz (110 g) liver
	3 oz (75 g) lambs' kidneys
	2 oz (50 g) bacon/ham
	10 oz (280 g) poultry, preferably dark meat
	4 oz (110 g) venison or other game bird
Fish	about 10 oz (280 g) white and oily fish, canned and fresh
Fruit	over 2 lb (1 kg) fresh fruit
	2 oz (50 g) canned fruit without sugar
	6 oz (175 g) dried fruit – figs, apricots, peaches
	2 oz (50 g) shelled almonds
Rice/pasta	1 lb (450 g) brown rice and wholewheat pasta
Bread	1¼ lb (550 g) wholewheat bread with bran and/or wheat germ
	8 oz (225 g) white bread or rye crispbreads
	12 oz (350 g) brown, with wheat germ
	4 oz (110 g) other breads, preferably fruit breads
Biscuits	about 4 oz (110 g) with dried fruit

Flour	about 6 oz (175 g) wholewheat 1 oz (25 g) wheat bran
Cereals	8 oz (225 g) Special K, Weetabix and oats
Cakes/buns/pastry	under 3 oz (75 g), with cocoa, ground ginger, almonds, dried fruit, or oatcakes
Pulses	1½ oz (40 g) dried lentils, peas, beans
Beverages	2 oz (50 g) cocoa, coffee, tea
Sugar	5 oz (150 g) 2 oz (50 g) black treacle
Other foods	about 9 oz (250 g), including curry powder, tomato purée, mustard, yeast extract

THE HAY DIET

This is not, as its title suggests, a diet which includes a great deal of dried grass but one which takes its name from the American doctor who formulated it! William Hay was born in 1866 in the USA. By his mid-twenties he had graduated in medicine from the University of New York. He evolved 'The Hay Diet' to cope with his own health problems – Bright's disease, obesity, high blood pressure and a dilated heart – all of which he managed to overcome. Thereafter he treated his patients by similarly improving their diets, advising against eating refined carbohydrates, too much meat and too much food generally. Hay stressed the importance of avoiding constipation and he recommended sunshine, fresh air, daily baths, exercise and rest. Harmony between the physical and spiritual states he felt was also important. In his own lifetime such ideas were thought to be outrageous and he was branded a quack. By coincidence, many of his ideas are now accepted, although not by a medical profession which seems to be more interested in heroic surgery and potent drugs than preventive medicine.

Dr Hay's diet is based on the theory that meals should not comprise starches and sugars mixed with proteins and acid fruits. By starches and sugars, Dr Hay referred to high carbohydrate foods – grains, bread, cakes, bakery items, cereals, potatoes and sugars. By protein foods he indicated animal proteins – meat, poultry, fish, eggs and cheese. He believed that the acid state of the stomach required for digesting proteins was interfered with by eating high starch and sugar foods (at the same time), which require an alkaline situation for digestion.

Acid-forming foods should be regarded as meat, poultry, eggs, cheese, fish and shellfish (all animal proteins); some nuts, rice, wheat, barley, rye, oats, breads, flours and all foods made from cereal starches; sugars (all carbohydrate foods), dried beans and peas, heat-treated milk and cream.

Alkali-forming foods should be regarded as all vegetables and salads, including potatoes in their skins, some nuts, milk and most fresh fruits.

The principle of the diet is to choose 'compatible foods' to produce the correct balance of alkali/acid in the body chemistry (ratio 4:1).

Note By 'acid' fruits most of us will think of citrus fruits, such as orange, lemon and grapefruit. However, you will see in the lists that follow that the picture is much broader, and there are many more fruits to be considered.

Do not confuse *acid* foods with *acid-forming* foods or *alkali* foods with *alkali-forming* foods.

The Hay Diet

Here are six important points to consider:

1. Proteins, fats and starches are not eaten in large quantities.
2. The basis of the diet is vegetables, fruits and salads.
3. Wholefoods should be eaten, and not refined or processed foods.
4. High starch/sugar foods should not be eaten at the same meal as animal proteins/acid fruits.
5. Allow at least four hours between meals as a general rule.
6. Balance the diet with 20 per cent acid-forming foods and 80 per cent alkali-forming foods (see lists).

Legumes present a problem as they are high in both protein and starch; however, by sprouting them they can be made compatible. On the whole this is a diet most suited to meat and fish eaters. The vegetarian approach, which will include sizeable amounts of legumes in order to obtain sufficient protein, is much more difficult to follow.

Probably most benefit from the diet will be for those people who experience constant indigestion, but it has been claimed that it has been used successfully for some people with stomach ulcers and other high acid-related disorders.

Once the principles of the diet have been learned and several days' food planned out, the diet should be easy enough to follow. Eating out is less problematical than with most diets. Benefits may include comfortable digestion, possible weight loss or gain as a stabilizing effect, and higher alkali and lower acid levels in the body. Stumbling blocks will be the 'cranky' or 'quack' label that still attaches itself to this kind of diet, non-acceptance or even derision by doctors, and resistance to eating such large amounts of vegetables and salads. The eating of meat or fish with potatoes as a national habit may be hard to break, as will the prohibition on drinking tea and coffee.

Milk Products

These should be used very sparingly by adults and regarded as a food. Milk should not be included at all in a meal which contains meat, and only very little should be used with grains and sugars (high carbohydrate foods).

Milk which is heat treated becomes more acid forming. Whole milk, skimmed milk, fresh cream, cream cheese and yoghurt are all classed as milk products.

Pure vegetable oils such as sunflower seed, safflower seed and olive oils (first pressing) are foods to be used with either acid- or alkali-forming foods. Butter, being a high fat food, to be used sparingly, is preferable to margarine which is a complicated mixture of oils/fats and additives. Butter can also be used with both acid-forming and alkali-forming foods.

Some foods are less acid/alkali forming than others. These are termed 'free' and can be used as part of either high protein or high starch meals.

The Hay Diet is probably easiest to arrange in the following way:

1. Plan for three meals per day and eat only when hungry.
2. Main meal of protein (see List A) plus compatible vegetables and fruit.
3. Light meal of starches (see List B) and compatible vegetables and fruit.
4. One small meal, suitable for breakfast, comprising mainly fruits.

The following lists give specific information on what foods should be combined.

'Free' Foods to Combine with either List A or List B

Nuts

all nuts

Fats/dairy foods

olive oil (first pressing)
sunflower oil, safflower oil
egg yolks
butter, cream, milk
yoghurt (small amounts)

Vegetables

All cooked vegetables except potatoes, e.g.

asparagus
green beans
broccoli
Brussels sprouts
cabbage
calabrese
spinach
carrots

swede
turnips
parsnips
beetroot
cauliflower
celery
courgettes
marrow
leeks
mushrooms
onions
peas
aubergines

All raw salad vegetables, e.g.

avocado
cucumber
peppers (red, green, yellow, black)
lettuce
mustard and cress
watercress
radishes
spring onions
tomatoes
celery
sprouted seeds/legumes
sunflower and sesame seeds

Flavourings

parsley
sage
thyme
mint
chives
garlic
grated rind of lemon, lime and orange

Alcohol

whisky
gin

List A: for High Protein Meals

All kinds of meat, poultry, game, fish, shellfish, eggs, cheese.

Combine with these less sweet fruits

apples/pears/grapes
pineapples/raspberries
strawberries/tayberries
loganberries/black currants
red currants/ white currants
gooseberries (ripe)
nectarines/peaches
kiwi fruit/mangoes
plums/prunes
oranges/lemons
limes/grapefruit
uglifruit/tangerines
satsumas/clementines

salad dressings of oil/lemon are suitable

avoid sugar

Alcohol

dry wines and cider

Combine with foods from the 'free' list.
Do not combine any of the foods on List A with those on List B at the same meal.

List B: for High Starch Meals

wheat, rye
barley, oats, oatmeal
corn (maize), millet
buckwheat
rice, all kinds of bread
potatoes, pasta

Combine with these extra sweet fruits

currants, raisins, sultanas
ripe pears, papaya, grapes
ripe bananas, dates
fresh and dried figs
raw cane sugar
honey (as little as possible)

to dress salads use yoghurt, olive oil-based dressings or sour cream

Alcohol

beer, ale

Combine with foods from the 'free' list.
Do not combine List B foods with foods from List A at the same meal.

Cookery Advice

Use wholefoods such as brown rice and wholewheat flour.

Melon is a fruit best eaten on its own and not as part of a meal.

Legumes are not included in the diet unless sprouted (dried beans, peas, peanuts (which are not classed as nuts as they are really legumes), chick peas, etc.).

Avoid using vinegars, pickles, chutneys and sauces as well as some condiments. Freshly ground black pepper may be used and French mustard.

Beverages

Avoid tea, coffee, soft drinks, fruit squashes, etc. Instead drink herb teas, spring water, or freshly made fruit juices.

Stock

Make your own vegetable stock at home or use a small amount of yeast extract. Avoid stock cubes or products which contain additives.

Thickenings/coatings

As so little is used potato flour is acceptable.

Typical Day's Food

Breakfast – dried apricots or fresh fruit with a little plain yoghurt.
High protein meal – cottage cheese, fish or grilled meat and mixed salads, fruit salad.
High starch meal – pasta with a sauce, sandwiches with wholewheat bread, or risotto, baked bananas and cream.
Drinks – spring water, herb tea, wine with high protein meal.

The Hay Diet should provide a regime which is low in fat, sugar and salt, high in vegetable but not cereal fibre, and with plenty of fresh vegetables and fruit. Protein may seem a little on the mean side by today's standards, also the milk intake.

Long-term adherence to this diet may mean that supplements for calcium, the B vitamins and extra fibre in the form of wheat bran should be taken at appropriate meals.

See p. 419 for Further Reading on the Hay Diet.

VEGETARIAN DIET

The average vegetarian diet in the UK is far too high in fat, because of heavy reliance on dairy foods. A greater variety of pulses is normally consumed to make up for the protein in meat and fish. Nuts are also used for the same reason. Sesame and sunflower seeds will increase the amount of polyunsaturates taken in the diet.

A Healthier Diet for Vegetarians Suggested amounts of food for one person for one week

Milk	3 pints (1.5 litres) skimmed milk
	½ pint (300 ml) yoghurt
Eggs	6
Fats/oils	2 oz (50 g) polyunsaturated margarine
	2 oz (50 g) butter
	9 fluid oz (250 ml) polyunsaturated oil
	6 oz (175 g) low fat cheeses (especially cottage)
Vegetables	3½ lb (over 1.5 kg) potatoes
	3 lb (1.5 kg) wide variety fresh vegetables, including fresh greens daily, sprouted seeds, carrots, etc.
	10 oz (280 g) canned vegetables
	3 oz (75 g) frozen vegetables
Pulses	6 oz (175 g) dry weight beans/peas/lentils, TVP
Meat and meat products	none
Fish and fish products	none
Fruit	over 2 lb (1 kg) fresh fruit including 6 citrus fruit
	4 oz (110 g) dried fruit
Nuts/ seeds	8 oz (225 g) shelled nuts and seeds, excluding peanuts
Bread	1¼ lb (550 g) wholewheat
	4 oz (110 g) white
	12 oz (350 g) brown
	4 oz (110 g) other breads

Cakes/biscuits/buns	7 oz (200 g)
Cereals	8 oz (225 g) wholegrain, including oats
Flour	8 oz (225 g) wholewheat
Rice/pasta	1 lb (450 g) brown/wholewheat
Sugar/honey	5 oz (150 g)
Jam	2 oz (50 g)
Beverages	2 oz (50 g)
Other foods	8 oz (225 g) vegetarian
Diet supplement	175 mcg Vitamin B12 (per week)*

*The amount of B12 suggested as a supplement is well above the RDA as it is poorly absorbed in this form.

RECIPES

SYMBOLS AND SPECIAL INGREDIENTS

The symbols used with the recipes will give you a quick guide as to whether they are suitable for a particular kind of cooking, or what can be done to make them suitable, if this is possible.

Wheat free Recipes marked with this symbol are free from wheat, white or brown flours made from wheat, wheat germ, wheat bran and wheat starch.

Gluten free Recipes marked with this symbol are free from wholewheat, wheat flours, wheat bran, wheat germ, rye flour, rye flakes, pot barley, barley flour, barley flakes, oats, oatmeal and rolled oats.

Milk free Recipes marked with this symbol are free from all kinds of milk, cream, cheeses, whey, curds and yoghurt. Most margarines contain whey, but milk-free brands are available from health stores and kosher grocers.

Egg free Recipes marked with this symbol are free from whole egg, egg yolk or egg white. Some pastas are available which are made just from flour, and not flour and egg.

Soya free Recipes marked with this symbol are free of soya beans, soya flour, soya bran, soy sauce, tofu and soya oil. If a soya-free margarine is unobtainable, then butter should be used as a substitute for margarine.

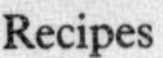

Citrus free Recipes marked with this symbol are free from both the rind and juice of orange, lemon, lime, grapefruit, satsuma, clementine and other citrus fruits.

Sugar free Recipes marked with this symbol are free of all added sugars such as fructose, honey, barbados sugar, icing sugar, treacle, molasses and any ingredient likely to contain sugar such as jam or sweetened fruit juice.

Salt free Recipes marked with this symbol are free from added salt, MSG or bicarbonate of soda, as well as any other ingredient which may contain salt – butter, margarine, tomato purée, ham, bacon, soy sauce, yeast extract, cheeses and baking powder. Unsalted butter can sometimes be substituted for margarine in the recipes.

Corn free Recipes marked with this symbol are free of cornflour, sweet corn, maize, maize flour, maize or corn oil, cornmeal, corn syrup, masa harina. Corn-free margarine should be used, or replaced by butter.

Vegetarian Recipes marked with this sign are free of meat or meat-derived products, gelatine, fish and fish-derived products. Where cheese is used in the recipes care should be taken to use that made without rennet. Health food stores and some supermarkets sell genuine vegetarian cheeses and these will be marked as such.

Wheat Free/Gluten Free

As wheat-free and gluten-free ingredients overlap to a certain extent, this can cause a good deal of confusion to those not used to preparing food of this type. Here are two lists to help you.

Wheat-free ingredients (flours, flakes, brans)

rye flour, rye flakes,
barley, pot barley, barley flakes, barley flour

oats, oatmeal, rolled oats
buckwheat, buckwheat flour†
millet flakes, millet flour
ground rice, rice flour, rice, rice bran
arrowroot
potato flour
soya flour, soya bran
split pea flour
maize flour
cornmeal, cornflour*

Gluten-free ingredients (flours, flakes, brans)

buckwheat, buckwheat flour
millet flakes, millet flour
ground rice, rice flour, rice, rice bran
arrowroot
potato flour
soya flour, soya bran
split pea flour
maize flour
cornflour, cornmeal*

Note *Cornflour (gluten/wheat free) must comprise pure maize starch and *not* a blend of unidentifiable flours. Look carefully at the label before buying.
†Buckwheat is not a grain, in spite of its name, and therefore is both gluten free and wheat free, although it does look rather like wheat in appearance.

The lists above are 100 per cent wheat-free and gluten-free ingredients, **providing they are not processed in mills where wheat, rye, barley and oats are ground**. Some manufacturers guarantee such purity on their packs, so look for these.

Gluten-free and Wheat-free Baking Powder

Most baking powders have a gluten/wheat base. However, baking powder can be made at home, with a gluten-free and wheat-free base using potassium bicarbonate, which can be bought at the chemists.

   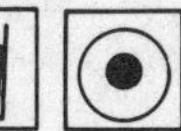      

¼ oz (7 g) potassium bicarbonate
4½ oz (125 g) potato flour or rice flour

Method
Mix the two ingredients together and store in an airtight jar. Use instead of ordinary baking powder.

SPECIAL INGREDIENTS

Health food stores are the most likely source for unusual ingredients. However, some manufacturers specialize in them and will supply by mail order. Some chemists and pharmacies, too, now have a special food section devoted to ingredients and foods for the allergic.

Trufree Flours
Larkhall Laboratories, 225 Putney Bridge Road, London SW15 2PY specialize in wheat-free and gluten-free ingredients and Trufree flours. Send a SAE for details of products and mail order service.

Trufree Nos 4 and 5 flours

Trufree No. 6 flour

Trufree No. 7 flour (self-raising)

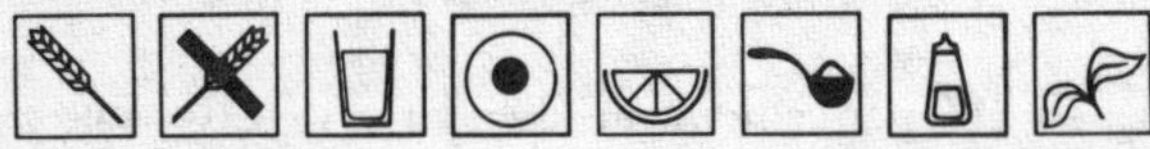

Soy Sauce
This is also known as soya sauce and is usually made from a fermentation of soya beans and wheat. Thickening of some kind is added to the end product. This is most often wheat, but some brands use corn instead of wheat. MSG is used in many brands and these should be avoided.

Soya-free diets. All kinds of soy sauce are unsuitable for soya-free dieters.

Wheat-free diets. Most wheat-free dieters will be able to tolerate soy sauce if thickened with corn.

Corn-free diets. Those following a corn-free diet should use a brand of soy sauce thickened with wheat and not corn.

Gluten-free diets. Most gluten-free dieters will be able to tolerate soy sauce if a corn-thickened brand is used. Wheat-thickened brands should be avoided.

One of the major ingredients in soy sauce is usually salt. However, low salt or salt-free brands are available in the USA and should appear in UK stores and shops over the next few years, if the interest in salt-free foods continues.

BREAKFASTS AND SNACKS

PORRIDGES

Simple versions of a very ancient kind of food, gruel, which was made by gathering wild cereal grains and seeds and making a kind of porridge with water. Nowadays we tend to limit the grain to just one at a time and use milk instead of water. Use for breakfast instead of toast.

Oat Porridge

Probably the most popular porridge as it is so quick and easy to make, using rolled oats which have already been cooked and dried. For a stiffer porridge, use less liquid.

Serves 1–2

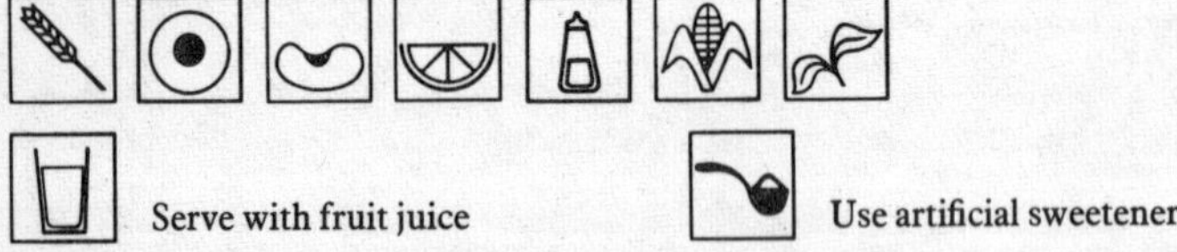

2 tablespoons (heaped) rolled oats
Just under ½ pint (300 ml) cold water or skimmed milk

Method

Put the oats and liquid into a saucepan and stir well. Bring to the boil and continue stirring over a moderate heat for another 3 or 4 minutes until creamy. Serve hot with skimmed milk and brown sugar.

Oatmeal Porridge

Serves 1–2

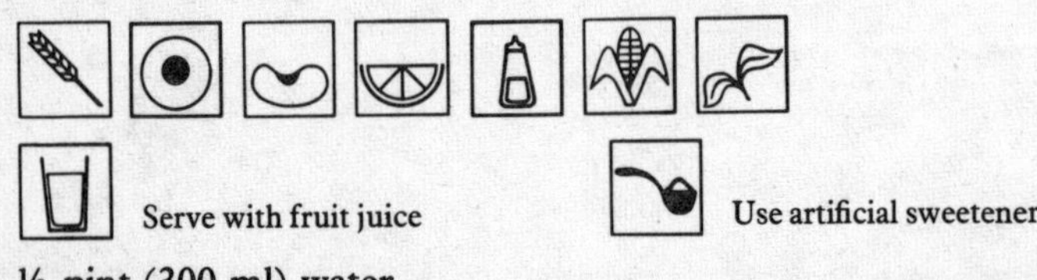

½ pint (300 ml) water
2 oz (50 g) medium oatmeal

Method

Put the water into a saucepan and bring to the boil. Sprinkle in the oatmeal and bring back to the boil while stirring. Continue to cook while you stir for about 4 minutes. Pour into a porridge bowl and leave to cool a little and thicken. Serve with skimmed milk and brown sugar, honey or fructose to taste.

Rice Porridge (gluten free)

Serves 1–2

2 generous tablespoons ground rice, preferably brown
½ pint (300 ml) skimmed milk or water
2 teaspoons sunflower oil
Sugar or honey to taste
1 tablespoon ground almonds (optional)
1 tablespoon sultanas or raisins (optional)

Method

Put the rice and liquid into a saucepan and stir until smooth. Mix in the oil and bring to the boil while stirring. Turn the heat down and, still stirring, simmer for 3 or 4 minutes. Take off the heat and stir in the sweetening to taste and the dried fruit and almonds if used. Serve hot with a little skimmed milk poured over.

Millet Porridge (gluten free)

A useful porridge for babies who cannot tolerate gluten.

Serves 1

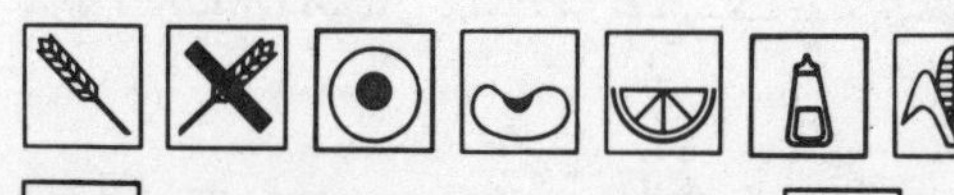

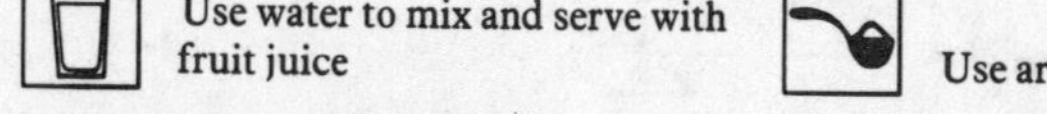

2 oz (50 g) millet flakes
Just over ¼ pint (150 ml) water or skimmed milk

Method

Put the millet flakes into a saucepan and cover with the water. Stir well and bring to the boil, still stirring. Turn down the heat and simmer while you stir for about 4 minutes. Serve hot with skimmed milk and sugar or honey to taste.

Roasted Buckwheat Porridge

Buckwheat can be bought at some health stores already roasted. It will most likely be labelled 'kasha'.

Serves 1

1½ oz (40 g) buckwheat
Just under ¼ pint (150 ml) skimmed milk or water

Method

To roast the buckwheat, put it into a heavy based frying pan and heat, tossing it to toast evenly for about 3 minutes. Put into a small saucepan with the milk and bring to the boil while stirring. Put the lid on the pan and simmer for about 10 minutes, or until the buckwheat is soft enough to eat. Serve with skimmed milk and a little honey or sugar to taste.

Granola

This is a kind of DIY breakfast cereal, very popular with children and one which can be eaten warm.

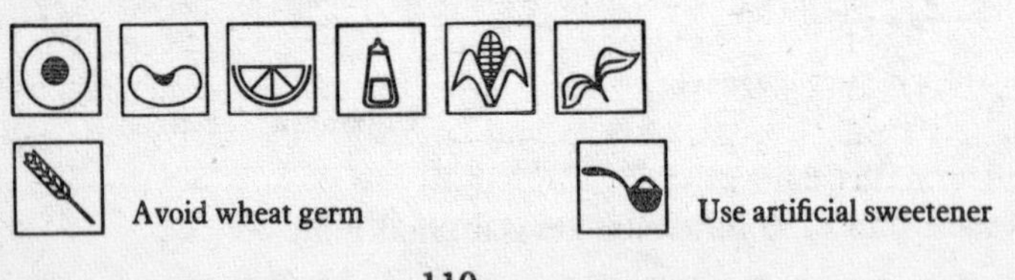

For each serving you will need:

1 scant tablespoon sunflower oil
2 heaped tablespoons rolled oats, or a mixture of oats and barley flakes
1 tablespoon chopped nuts – almonds, walnuts, cashews, hazelnuts
1 heaped teaspoon wheat germ
2 heaped teaspoons sunflower seeds
2 heaped teaspoons soft brown sugar or demerara, or 1 heaped teaspoon fructose, or a little honey, to taste
1 heaped tablespoon sultanas or raisins (seedless)

Method

Use a small saucepan with a heavy base. Put in the oil and the cereal flakes/oats. Heat gently while you stir and the cereal absorbs the oil. Sprinkle in all the other ingredients, except the dried fruit, and continue to heat and stir for about 10 minutes over a very low heat. Turn up the heat, to brown it while you stir, then serve mixed with the dried fruit and with a little warmed skimmed milk poured over.

MUESLI

Popular as a breakfast dish or snack, muesli can be made from a variety of ingredients. Some kind of cereal base is required, plus fresh fruit, dried fruit and nuts. Seeds and brans can also be used and the dish should be moistened with either some kind of milk or fruit juice. Although the dish should not be a sweet one, honey, brown sugar or fructose can be used to sweeten it, to taste.

The best place to buy ingredients for muesli is the health food store. Commercially made mueslis are never as good as the home-made kind and most of them have left the original idea of muesli far behind. (The first muesli was formulated by Dr Bircher-Benner many decades ago for use in his clinic. His 'raw fruit porridge' comprised 1 tablespoon medium oatmeal or rolled oats soaked overnight in a little water, 1 tablespoon fresh lemon juice, 3 tablespoons raw milk, 1 tablespoon of grated hazelnuts or almonds, and 2 eating apples, grated.)

Muesli Recipes

The following suggestions for muesli ingredients indicate amounts for 1 person.

 Avoid wheat bran and wheat germ

 Use millet flakes and avoid wheat bran, wheat germ, rye flakes, barley flakes and rolled oats

 Avoid milk and yoghurt

 Avoid soya milk and bran

 Avoid orange juice

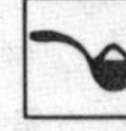 Avoid sugars and honey

Suggested bases for muesli

1 heaped tablespoon of any of the following (or a mixture) soaked overnight in 3 tablespoons of water: medium oatmeal; rolled oats; barley flakes; millet flakes; rye flakes.

Suggested fresh fruit for muesli

Fruit should be washed well and the skins left on, if digestible. Choose from: apple; pear; ripe peach (peel); ripe nectarine; ripe plums (2 or 3); sliced pineapple (trimmed and cored); banana (peeled); kiwi fruit (peeled); a handful of fresh raspberries, strawberries, tayberries or loganberries, or a mixture of these.

Suggested dried fruit for muesli

Wash the dried fruit well before using. About 1 slightly heaped tablespoon will be enough: sliced, stoned dates; chopped dried apricots; raisins (seedless); sultanas; chopped dried nectarines or peaches.

Suggested nuts for muesli

Wash the nuts before chopping. Use just one kind or a mixture; 1 slightly heaped tablespoon will be sufficient: walnuts; hazelnuts; almonds; cashews; brazils.

Suggested brans for muesli

1–3 heaped teaspoons of bran will be sufficient as an optional extra: coarse wheat bran; rice husk bran; soya bran, preferably toasted.

Suggested seeds etc. for muesli

Use 1–2 heaped teaspoons as an optional extra: sesame seeds; sunflower seeds; wheat germ (this will increase the protein content of the muesli).

Liquids for muesli

Skimmed milk; soya milk; plain, low fat yoghurt; unsweetened orange juice; unsweetened pineapple juice; unsweetened apple juice; a handful of raspberries or strawberries, liquidized with a little water.

Pork Sausages

Makes 4

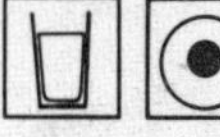

Use wheat-free bread and soy sauce, coat with potato flour

Use ½ teaspoon yeast extract and 1 tablespoon hot water instead of soy sauce

Use gluten-free bread and soy sauce, coat with potato flour

Avoid soy sauce, use ½ teaspoon yeast extract and 1 tablespoon hot water

1 pork fillet, trimmed of all fat and cut into pieces
1 slice bread, preferably wholewheat, broken into pieces
½ medium cooking apple, peeled, cored and cut into pieces
1–2 teaspoons thin soy sauce
Freshly ground black pepper, to taste
Pinch allspice
Pinch mixed herbs
Wholewheat flour for coating
Sunflower oil for frying

Method

Put the pork, bread, apple, soy sauce, seasoning, spices and herbs into a food processor. Mix to a coarse paste and divide into four. Roll into sausage shapes and coat in flour. Fry in a little hot sunflower oil, turning once, for about 5 minutes. Serve with grilled or canned tomatoes.

Creamed Mushrooms on Toast

Serves 1

 Use wheat-free bread

 Avoid lemon juice

 Use gluten-free bread

 Use potato flour

2 teaspoons sunflower oil
1 spring onion, finely chopped
2 oz (50 g) mushrooms, sliced
Few drops lemon juice
1 teaspoon cornflour
1 tablespoon single cream mixed with 2 tablespoons skimmed milk
Freshly ground black pepper, to taste
1 slice wholewheat toast

Method

Heat the oil in a small pan and fry the onion for a few seconds. Put in the mushrooms and lemon juice and cook while you stir for 2 minutes. Sprinkle in the cornflour and cook for another 2 minutes, while stirring. Add the cream and lower the heat. Heat through gently (do not let it boil) and season to taste. Put the hot toast on a plate and cover with the mushroom mixture. Serve immediately.

Potato Pancakes

Serves 4–5

1 lb (450 g) old potatoes, peeled and grated
1 medium onion, chopped finely
2 eggs, beaten
2 good pinches grated nutmeg
Freshly ground black pepper, to taste
Sunflower oil or similar for frying

Method

Put the grated potato into a basin of water while you are preparing them. Drain in a colander, pressing to drain well. Put into a basin with the onion, eggs, nutmeg and black pepper. Mix with a fork. Oil a griddle or heavy based frying pan with a little oil on a screw of kitchen paper. Heat until it begins to smoke and then drop spoonfuls of the mixture on to it. Spread them out with the back of a spoon. Cook for about 4 minutes on one side, then turn over with a spatula and cook on the other side until golden and crisp. Keep them hot in the oven and serve as soon as they are all made.

Fish cakes and pancakes are also good for breakfast: see the recipes on pp. 191–2 and 399.

EGGS

Soft Boiled Eggs

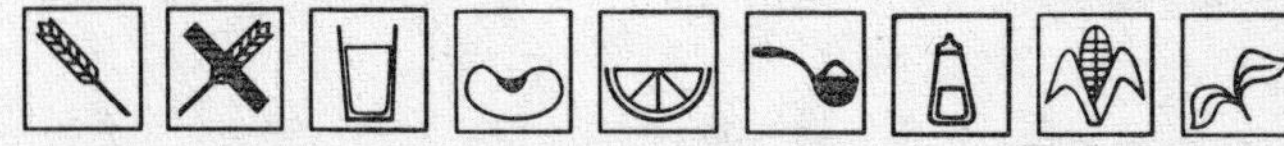

Allow 1 egg per person, preferably a free-range one

Method

Put enough water in a small saucepan to cover the egg and bring the water to the boil. Take off the heat and carefully lower the egg into the water on a spoon. Put back on the heat and bring to the boil again. Continue to boil for exactly 1 minute, then take off the heat. Leave to cook slowly in the saucepan for 5 minutes, or 6 minutes if the egg is fresh. Serve with fingers of wholewheat toast and suitable polyunsaturated margarine: this makes a good breakfast.

Hard Boiled Eggs

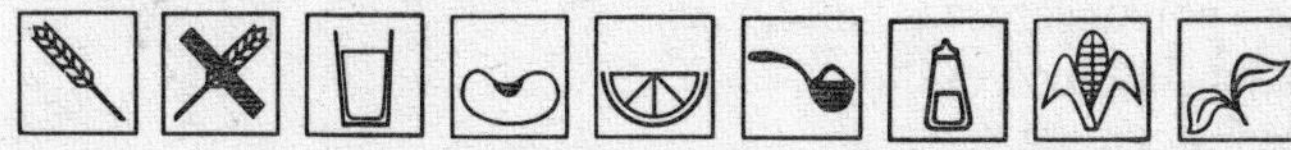

Allow 1 egg per person, preferably a free-range one

Method

Put enough water in a small saucepan to cover the egg. Bring the water to the boil and lower in the egg on a spoon. Bring back to the boil and cook steadily for 10 minutes. Plunge the egg into cold water and leave to cool. Break the shell and peel off the pieces. Rinse under the cold tap and leave to grow cold. Serve halved or chopped, but leave whole for curries.

Baked Egg

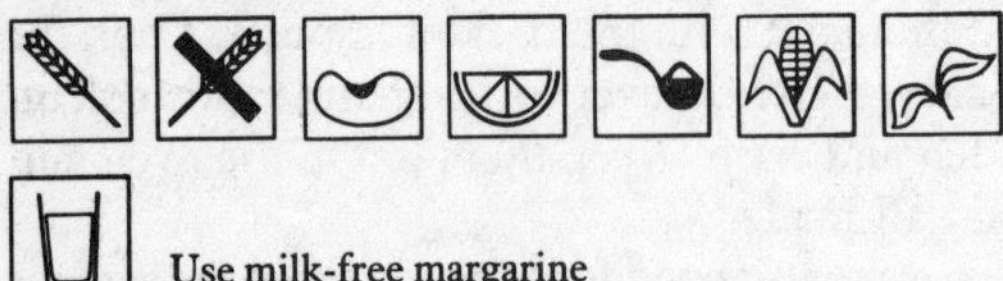

Use milk-free margarine

Allow 1 egg per person, preferably a free-range one

Method

Liberally grease a ramekin with polyunsaturated margarine. Break an egg into it and place in a roasting tin half filled with boiling water. Put on the top shelf of a preheated oven at Gas Mark 4, 180°C or 350°F. Bake for about 8 minutes or less, until the white has set but the yolk is still runny. Serve right away with toast.

Scrambled Eggs

A good breakfast dish.

Serves 1

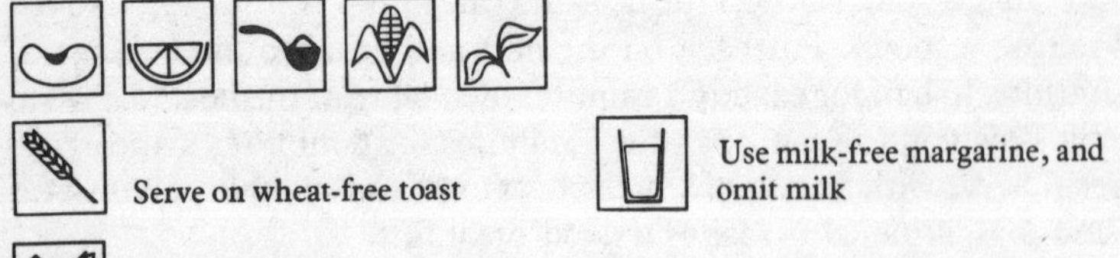

Serve on wheat-free toast

Use milk-free margarine, and omit milk

Serve on gluten-free toast

Small knob polyunsaturated margarine
1 tablespoon skimmed milk
1 fresh free-range egg

Method

Melt the margarine gently in a small frying pan or saucepan. Add the milk and break in the egg. As the egg begins to cook break it up with a fork. Serve when still shiny and a little runny, as it will continue to cook even after it is out of the pan. Serve on dry wholewheat toast.

Poached Eggs

This makes a good breakfast, or serve on spinach or potatoes for a main course.

     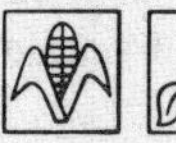 

 Serve on wheat-free toast

 Serve on gluten-free toast

Allow 1 egg per person, preferably a free-range one

Method

Heat about 1 pint (600 ml) of water in a frying pan. Break in an egg and continue with the heat until the white has set and the yolk looks pale. Lift out of the water with an egg slice and place on wholewheat toast.

Omelet

Serves 1

1 fresh free-range egg
2 teaspoons cold water
Sunflower oil for the frying pan (or preferably a real omelet pan)

Method

Whisk the egg and water lightly, in a cup. Grease the pan and heat. Pour in the egg mixture and allow the egg to set underneath. Make breaks in the omelet to let the runny egg through and underneath to set, tilting the pan as required. Loosen all round the edge and flip one half over the other. Turn out on to a plate and serve immediately.

Filled Omelet

   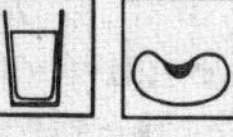   

 Avoid ham and salted fish

 Avoid meat and fish fillings

Prepare 2 heaped tablespoons of filling before you make an omelet and spoon over one half before flipping over the other half to enclose it. Chopped lean chicken or ham, watercress and spring onion, slices of tomato and flaked tuna, canned salmon, prawns and hot boiled potatoes with a sprinkle of parsley can all be used for fillings.

Herb Omelet

Make as for plain omelets, without a filling, but stir in 1 teaspoon fresh or ¼ teaspoon dried herbs to the egg mixture before cooking.

PACKED FOODS

 Use wheat-free bread and pastry

 Use gluten-free bread and pastry

 Use milk-free margarine, avoid butter, avoid milk shakes

 Use salt-free home-made bread and fillings, and unsalted butter

 Avoid meat and fish fillings

It is important for anyone on a special diet who is away from home for meals to be able to take packed food that can be enjoyed and will be sustaining. Reliance on takeaways and commercially packed foods is not possible, and such food is certainly not as nutritious as the home-made variety.

Food that can be eaten with the fingers, without the bother of a plate, cutlery, etc., is usually the most popular packed food. Sandwiches, quiches, pizza, salads to be eaten out of their container and both fresh and dried fruit are probably the easiest things both to prepare and to eat. Avoid too much carbohydrate and sugary food and try to make the packed meals resemble the nutritional balance of a meal eaten at home. In winter soups can be taken in a vacuum flask, but remember their greatest value will be in providing a warm drink. Milk shakes or other cooling drinks can also be put into vacuum flasks for summer. Sandwiches can be prepared, packed in plastic bags and kept overnight in the fridge for a quick getaway the following morning. Fruit just has to be taken from the fruit bowl and washed or peeled and makes a very easy sweet part to the meal. Dried fruit and nuts can be mixed in a small bag. Salad items will stay fresher if they are not cut up or grated: take loosely packed in plastic bags. Avoid crisps and chocolate bars.

SANDWICHES

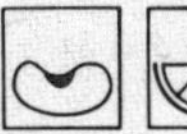   

 Use wheat-free bread

 Use gluten-free bread

 Avoid butter and cheese, and use milk-free margarine

 Avoid egg fillings

 Avoid cheese, meat and fish fillings with added salt, e.g. ham; use home-made salt-free breads, unsalted butter

 Avoid meat and fish fillings

As well as being a very useful food for snacks and packed lunches, sandwiches make good suppers or light meals. The problems with them include: not enough filling; the filling being too dry; and bread which is allowed to get too dry and stale. The traditional sandwich has a base and top of bread and a filling of meat, egg, fish, cheese, salad vegetables, nuts or fruit, so a good variety is possible. Open sandwiches have a base only and can be made very attractive with various garnishes while using the same ingredients as for the traditional sandwich.

Here are fillings or toppings to be used with slices of wholewheat or special bread (for gluten-free/wheat-free diets), lightly spread with polyunsaturated margarine to prevent the bread from taking moisture from the filling.

Sandwich Fillings or Toppings

Lean cold roast pork, trimmed of all fat, thin slices of eating apple and a spread of fresh chutney.

Lean cold roast beef, trimmed of all fat and spread with a little French mustard or fresh chutney, topped with watercress or lettuce leaves.

Cold chicken, skin removed and sliced thinly, spread with fresh chutney.
Canned salmon, mashed with chopped tomato, thin slices of cucumber and tomato.
Sardines, drained and mashed with a little tomato purée and a few drops of lemon juice, and a sprinkle of freshly chopped parsley.
Tuna fish, drained and flaked, mixed with chopped tomato and lettuce with a little chopped celery or celery leaves and freshly ground black pepper to taste.
Canned salmon, drained and mashed, covered with thin slices of cucumber and watercress sprigs.
Cottage cheese, spread generously and topped with chopped watercress.
Cottage cheese and a sprinkle of raisins, sultanas or chopped, stoned dates.
Mashed hard boiled egg and chopped cress.
Any of the pâtés in this book topped with tomatoes and lettuce.
Few defrosted prawns, spoon of home-made mayonnaise (see recipes on pp. 273–5), lettuce and tomato.
Low fat cream cheese and a sprinkle of freshly chopped parsley topped with tomato slices.
Hard boiled egg, mashed with a little skimmed milk and 2 or 3 pinches curry powder to taste, the same of ground coriander, plus tomato slices and lettuce.
Cottage cheese and chopped walnuts topped with watercress.

French Bread Sandwich

Use the end of a fresh French loaf (stick). Slice down one side but do not cut right through so that you are left with a 'hinge' of crust down one side. Spread inside with a scrape of polyunsaturated margarine. Trim a slice of ham of all fat and line the bread. Now add as much salad as it will hold – lettuce, tomato, watercress, cucumber, etc.

Quiche

Serves 4

 Avoid meat and fish fillings

4 oz (110 g) plain wholewheat flour
2 oz (50 g) polyunsaturated margarine
Cold water
4 heaped tablespoons low fat dried milk granules
½ pint (300 ml) cold water
2 eggs
Filling†

Method

Preheat the oven to Gas Mark 8, 230°C or 450°F. Put a baking sheet to heat on the top shelf. Make the pastry. Put the flour into a bowl and add the margarine. Rub in with the fingertips until the mixture resembles breadcrumbs. Add enough cold water to mix to a soft, sticky paste. Add more flour to make a workable but soft dough. Knead lightly in the bowl and then turn out on to a floured worktop. Roll out and line a 9 in. (23 cm) quiche dish. Trim off the edges neatly with a knife and very carefully pull the pastry slightly over the rim of the dish. (This is to stop it collapsing.) Prick the base all over with a fork. Bake on the top shelf, on the baking sheet, for about 12–15 minutes.

While the pastry is baking, make the filling. Sprinkle the milk granules into the ½ pint (300 ml) of water and whisk to combine, removing any lumps. Add the eggs and whisk again. When the pastry case is ready, take it out of the oven. Turn the oven down to Gas Mark 5, 190°C or 375°F. Cover the pastry with the filling of your choice and steadily pour in the milk/egg mixture. Carefully, as it is inclined to slop, put the quiche back into the oven on the centre shelf. Bake for about 25 minutes, until the egg has set and risen. Eat hot or cold. (NB As the quiche cools down, so the filling will sink.)

Fillings for quiches†

Choose one of these (* indicates vegetarian fillings):
*4 oz (110 g) cottage cheese mixed with chopped tomato.
2 slices lean ham, trimmed of fat and cut into little squares.
1 small can tuna fish, drained, with 2 chopped tomatoes.
*Watercress – use ½ bunch and chop coarsely after a thorough wash in cold water; shake dry before chopping.
*1 heaped teaspoon freshly chopped herbs (fresh thyme, parsley, sage, etc.).
*2 oz (50 g) mushrooms, chopped and fried in a little sunflower oil.
2 rashers unsmoked back bacon, all fat removed and the lean chopped into small pieces and fried in a little sunflower oil until crisp.

*1 medium onion, finely chopped and fried for 5 minutes in a little sunflower oil, mixed with 1 heaped teaspoon of freshly chopped parsley.
*½ red pepper, deseeded, chopped and fried in a little sunflower oil for 5 minutes.

Pizza

Although associated with Italian cooking this dish is made throughout the Mediterranean and was actually introduced to Britain by the Romans. Its ability to adapt to the takeaway trade and its inexpensive ingredients have made it a commercial success as a fast food. However, the home-made version is much lower in fat and higher in fibre and protein than its takeaway cousin.

 Use bread dough made with Trufree No. 4 or 5 flours

 Use ground almonds instead of cheese

 Use bread dough made with Trufree No. 4 or 5 flours

 Omit ham, increase cheese

For each person you will need:

About 2 oz (50 g) freshly made bread dough (see recipes on pp. 366, 374)
2 tomatoes, sliced
½ slice lean ham, trimmed of fat and cut into small squares
1 mushroom, chopped
1 heaped tablespoon finely grated Parmesan cheese
Sprinkle of freshly chopped parsley, or dried basil or oregano

Method

Preheat the oven to Gas Mark 7, 220°C or 425°F. Grease a baking sheet and put it to warm in the oven. On a floured worktop, roll out the dough until it looks like a thick pastry. Transfer to the baking sheet. Cover with the tomato slices and then with the ham and mushroom. Sprinkle with the cheese and herb, then leave to rise in a warm place for just 10 minutes. Put into the oven on the top shelf for about 12–15 minutes and serve hot.

SOUPS AND STARTERS

SOUPS

Beetroot Soup

Adding the vinegar to this soup during the final stages needs careful attention, as too much will spoil the taste. Exactly how much to add depends on the sweetness of the variety of beetroot used.

Serves 3

   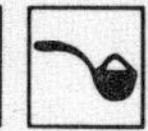 

 Use wheat-free soy sauce

 Use salt-free home-made stock

 Use gluten-free soy sauce

 Avoid soy sauce, use potato flour

 Avoid soy sauce

1 small onion, peeled and sliced thinly
2 teaspoons sunflower oil
1 stick celery, trimmed, scrubbed and chopped
About 8 oz (225 g) raw, peeled beetroot, cut into pieces
¾ pint (450 ml) water
2 teaspoons thin soy sauce, or 1 teaspoon yeast extract, or home-made stock to taste
Wine or cider vinegar, to taste (about 1 teaspoon +)
Freshly ground black pepper, to taste
2 tablespoons cold water mixed with 1 level teaspoon maize flour (cornflour)

Method

In a large saucepan fry the onion in the oil for 3 or 4 minutes. Put in the celery, beetroot and about half the water. Bring quickly to the boil and put a lid on. Turn down the heat and simmer for about 15–25 minutes, depending on the age of the beetroot. When tender, take off the heat and pour in the remainder of the water. Liquidize in a blender. Pour back into the pan through a fine mesh wire sieve and discard the residue. Add the stock of your choice and stir well. Taste and add the vinegar, a quarter teaspoon at a time, until the flavour is right. Add the pepper and the maize flour/water mixture and bring to the boil. Simmer while stirring for about 2 or 3 minutes to thicken the soup. Serve hot.

Split Pea Soup

This very substantial soup is an attractive golden colour. It makes a cheap but nourishing snack or, with sandwiches and fruit, it can provide a complete meal.

Serves 4–5

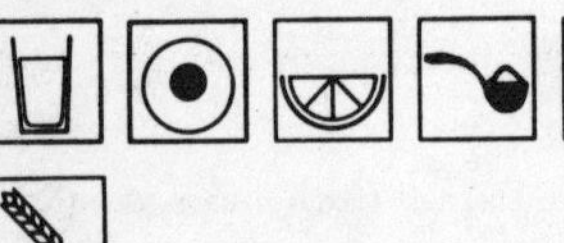

Use wheat-free soy sauce

Use salt-free home-made stock

Use gluten-free soy sauce

Avoid soy sauce

Avoid soy sauce

8 oz (225 g) split peas
1 large onion, peeled and sliced
1 tablespoon sunflower oil
1 pint (600 ml) water
1 tablespoon thin soy sauce, or 2 teaspoons yeast extract, or home-made stock to taste
2 medium carrots, scrubbed, trimmed and cut into slices
Freshly ground black pepper, to taste

Method

Put the split peas into a colander or wire mesh sieve. Rinse under the cold tap. Put into a large bowl and cover with at least 1½ pints (900 ml) cold water. Leave overnight to swell. The next day fry the onion in the oil for 3 or 4 minutes in a large saucepan. Pour in the 1 pint (600 ml) of water and the stock of your choice. Strain the split peas and add to the saucepan with the carrots. Bring to the boil and give a good stir. Simmer with the lid on for at least 1 hour, giving a stir from time to time. (If it starts to get too thick, add a little more water.) Allow to cool and liquidize for a smooth soup. Alternatively, leave just as it is. Season to taste with the pepper and serve hot.

Lentil Soup

A thick, substantial soup.

Serves 4

 Use wheat-free soy sauce

 Use salt-free home-made stock

 Use gluten-free soy sauce

 Avoid soy sauce

 Avoid soy sauce

5 oz (150 g) dried lentils
2 medium onions, peeled and sliced
1 tablespoon sunflower oil
1 medium potato, peeled and sliced thinly
1 tablespoon thin soy sauce, or 2 teaspoons yeast extract, or home-made stock to taste
About 1 pint (600 ml) water
Freshly ground black pepper, to taste

Method

Put the lentils into a wire sieve and wash them well under the cold tap. Leave them overnight to soak in a large bowl, with plenty of water. Use a large saucepan to fry the onion in the oil. Add the potato, the stock of your choice, the strained lentils and the pint of water. Bring to the boil and simmer with the lid on for about 40–45 minutes, or until the lentils are soft. (If the soup begins to get too thick while the lentils are cooking, add more water and stir.) Remove from the heat, allow to cool and then liquidize into a creamy apricot-coloured soup. Season to taste with the pepper – this may be omitted if the lentils are very peppery themselves. Reheat when required and serve hot.

Onion and Potato Soup

A very filling soup to serve on its own.

Serves 3

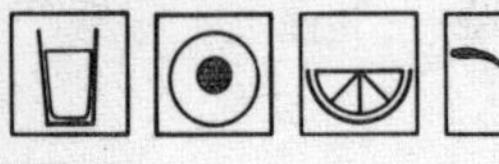

Use wheat-free soy sauce

Use home-made salt-free stock

Use gluten-free soy sauce

Avoid soy sauce

Avoid soy sauce

2 medium onions, peeled and sliced thinly
1 tablespoon sunflower oil
1 clove garlic, peeled
2 medium potatoes, sliced thinly
2 teaspoons thin soy sauce, or 1 teaspoon yeast extract, or home-made stock to taste
¾ pint (450 ml) cold water
Freshly ground black pepper, to taste
1 tablespoon freshly chopped parsley

Method

Fry the onion in the oil for 2 minutes while you stir. Crush in the garlic through a garlic press. Stir and put in the potato slices, stock and just over half the water. Bring to the boil and simmer with the lid on for about 10–15 minutes, until the potatoes are cooked. Take off the heat, add the remaining water and blend in a liquidizer. Pour back into the pan. Bring back to the boil and serve hot, seasoned with the black pepper and the parsley, stirred in at the last minute.

Fresh Pea Soup

A beautiful emerald green soup. Best made with fresh peas, but can also be made with defrosted frozen ones.

Serves 3–4

 Use wheat-free soy sauce

 Use home-made salt-free stock

 Use gluten-free soy sauce

 Avoid soy sauce

 Avoid soy sauce

1 medium onion, peeled and chopped finely
1 tablespoon sunflower oil
12 oz (350 g) shelled peas
¾ pint (450 ml) water
2 teaspoons thin soy sauce, or 1 teaspoon yeast extract, or home-made stock to taste
Freshly ground black pepper, to taste

Method

Fry the onion in the oil until transparent, but do not let it brown or it will spoil the colour of the soup. Add the peas, about half the water and the stock of your choice. Bring to the boil and put on a lid. Simmer for just 8 minutes, or a little longer if the peas are end-of-season. Add the remaining water and liquidize. Season with the black pepper to taste and serve hot.

Onion Soup (1)

Serves 4

  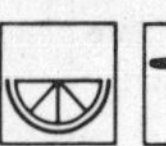  

 Use wheat-free soy sauce and potato flour

 Use salt-free home-made stock

 Use gluten-free soy sauce and potato flour

 Avoid soy sauce

 Avoid soy sauce

About 1 lb (450 g) onions, chopped finely
1 tablespoon sunflower oil
1 tablespoon wholewheat flour
1½ pints (900 ml) water
1 tablespoon thin soy sauce, or 2 teaspoons yeast extract, or
home-made stock to taste
½ teaspoon tomato purée
Freshly ground black pepper, to taste

Method

Use a large saucepan to fry the onions in the oil. Stir while you fry them gently and do not let them brown. Sprinkle in the flour and continue cooking while you stir for a minute. Pour the water into the pan gradually. Add the stock and tomato purée. Stir and bring to the boil. Turn down the heat and simmer with the lid on for about 25–30 minutes. Season to taste with the pepper and serve hot.

Variations

Serve with grated cheese sprinkled into the hot soup just before serving. Or serve plain, with a little freshly chopped parsley stirred in just before serving. Avoid the cheese variation for milk-free diets.

Onion Soup (2)

Serves 4–5

 Use wheat-free soy sauce

 Use gluten-free soy sauce

 Avoid soy sauce

Use salt-free home-made stock

 Avoid cornflour – use potato flour instead – and avoid soy sauce

4 medium onions, peeled and sliced
1 tablespoon sunflower oil
1 pint (600 ml) water
1 tablespoon thin soy sauce, or 2 teaspoons yeast extract, or
home-made stock to taste
Freshly ground black pepper, to taste

1 pint (600 ml) skimmed milk
Pinch or two mace
1 tablespoon cornflour mixed with 2 tablespoons water
Cheese for sprinkling

Method

Stir/fry the onions in the oil for about 4 or 5 minutes without letting them brown. Pour in the water and stock of your choice and season with black pepper. Bring to the boil and simmer with the lid on for about 30 minutes. Take off the heat. Put about half the milk into the blender goblet and spoon in the cooked onion. Blend and return to the pan. Add the remaining milk, the mace and the cornflour mixture. Bring to the boil again and stir while it simmers for 4 minutes. Serve hot with a sprinkling of cheese stirred in.

Clear Onion Soup (Broth)

A light but very tasty soup. Serve as a starter before a substantial main course such as pasta.

Serves 4

 Use wheat-free soy sauce

 Use artificial sweetener, if necessary

 Use gluten-free soy sauce

 Use home-made salt-free stock

 Avoid soy sauce

 Avoid soy sauce

1½ lb (750 g) onions, peeled and sliced thinly
1½ tablespoons sunflower oil
1 clove garlic, peeled
1½ pints (900 ml) water
1 tablespoon thin soy sauce, or 2 teaspoons yeast extract, or home-made stock to taste
Brown sugar, to taste (may not be necessary if the onions are sweet)
Freshly ground black pepper, to taste
1 heaped tablespoon freshly chopped parsley

Method

Fry the onions in the oil for about 5 or 6 minutes, stirring over a medium heat to brown them. Add the garlic through a garlic press. Stir and add the water. Bring to the boil and then simmer gently with the lid on for about 20–25 minutes. Strain through a fine mesh wire sieve into a basin. Press the residue with the back of a wooden spoon to release all the juices you can. Discard the mush. Pour the liquid back into the saucepan and add the stock of your choice. Taste and season with a pinch of sugar if required. Add black pepper to taste and sprinkle in the parsley. Serve hot.

Celery Soup

The best celery for this kind of soup is the green, unblanched type which always has more flavour. This soup is useful for using up the tough outer stalks that would otherwise be discarded. It is a soup which actually improves for standing, and is excellent with cheese straws, or cheese scones, or cottage cheese sandwiches.

Serves 4

1 medium onion, peeled and sliced
1 tablespoon sunflower oil
5–6 stalks of celery, including the leaves, scrubbed and chopped
½ pint (300 ml) water
2 teaspoons thin soy sauce, or 1 teaspoon yeast extract, or home-made stock to taste
Pinch celery seeds
Freshly ground black pepper, to taste

Method

Fry the onion in the oil for about 4 minutes, making sure it does not brown. Add the celery pieces and stir/fry for about 3 more minutes. Pour the water into the liquidizer goblet and spoon in the partially cooked vegetables. Blend and pour into the saucepan. Bring to the boil, then simmer for about 8 minutes. Strain through a fine mesh wire sieve. Press the residue with the back of a wooden spoon to free the juices. Add the stock of your choice, celery seeds and black pepper to taste. Leave to stand for a few hours and then reheat.

Mushroom Soup

Serves 4

 Use wheat-free soy sauce

 Avoid soy sauce

 Use gluten-free soy sauce

 Use salt-free home-made stock

 Avoid cream of mushroom soup variation

 Avoid soy sauce

1 medium onion, peeled and sliced
1 tablespoon sunflower oil
4 oz (110 g) fresh mushrooms, washed and chopped
2 teaspoons thin soy sauce, or 1 teaspoon yeast extract, or home-made stock to taste
¾ pint (450 ml) water
Freshly ground black pepper, to taste

Method

Fry the onion in the oil for about 4 minutes, while you stir. Put into the liquidizer goblet with the raw mushrooms and the stock of your choice. Add the water and blend. Bring to the boil and simmer for about 4 or 5 minutes while you stir. Season with the black pepper. Serve hot.

Cream of Mushroom Soup

Serves 4

Make as for Mushroom Soup but use skimmed milk instead of the water. This soup should not be allowed to boil or it will be spoiled.

Avocado Soup

This soup should be served immediately it is made as it will discolour. The avocados should be ripe but still firm.

Serves 4

 Use wheat-free soy sauce

 Use salt-free home-made stock

 Use gluten-free soy sauce

 Avoid soy sauce

 Avoid soy sauce

1 medium onion, peeled and sliced finely
1 tablespoon sunflower or safflower oil
2 avocado pears
1 pint (600 ml) cold water
1 tablespoon soy sauce, or 2 teaspoons yeast extract
Freshly ground black pepper, to taste

Method

Fry the onion in the oil for about 3 or 4 minutes, taking care not to let the onion brown or it will spoil the colour of the soup. Peel the avocados and remove the stones. Chop the flesh and put into the blender goblet with the cooked onion. Pour in the water and add the stock of your choice. Blend and pour into the saucepan. (If the soup looks too thick, add more water.) Heat and simmer for just 3 minutes. Season with the black pepper and serve immediately.

Cauliflower Soup

The cauliflower for this rather subtle soup should have creamy white curds and be firm and crisp. Be careful not to put in too much nutmeg: a mere pinch is all that is required just to round off the flavour. Serve immediately it is made; not suitable for a thermos flask.

Serves 2–3

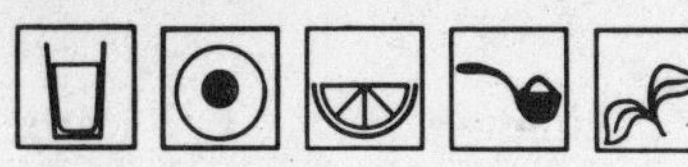

 Use wheat-free soy sauce

 Use salt-free home-made stock

 Use gluten-free soy sauce

 Use potato flour, instead of cornflour, and avoid soy sauce

 Avoid soy sauce

1 small onion, peeled and sliced finely
2 teaspoons sunflower oil
About 6 oz (175 g) cauliflower florets
½ pint (300 ml) water mixed with 1 heaped teaspoon cornflour
1 teaspoonful soy sauce, or ½ teaspoon yeast extract, or home-made stock to taste
Pinch freshly grated nutmeg
Freshly ground black pepper, to taste

Method

Use a large saucepan to fry the onion in the oil. Chop the florets and put into the pan with about half the water. Bring to the boil and simmer with the lid on for about 5–8 minutes, or until the cauliflower is tender but not mushy. Add the remaining water, liquidize and pour back into the saucepan. Add the stock of your choice and the nutmeg. Heat through and simmer for about 3 minutes while you stir. Taste, season and serve hot immediately.

Spinach Soup

Serves 4

  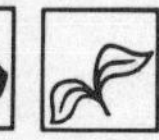

 Use wheat-free soy sauce

 Use salt-free home-made stock

 Use gluten-free soy sauce

 Avoid soy sauce

 Avoid soy sauce

1 small onion, peeled and chopped finely
Scant tablespoon sunflower oil
1 lb (450 g) fresh spinach, washed thoroughly
1½ pints (900 ml) water
Scant tablespoon thin soy sauce, or 2 teaspoons yeast extract, or home-made stock to taste
2 teaspoons fresh lemon juice
Freshly ground black pepper, to taste

Method

In a large saucepan fry the onion in the oil for about 3 minutes. Tear the green parts of the spinach leaves away from the coarser stems, and discard the stems. Put the spinach, torn into pieces, about two-thirds of the water and the stock of your choice into the saucepan and bring to the boil. Poke the spinach down with a wooden spoon as it heats. Simmer for about 15 minutes, or a little longer if the leaves are large. Put in the remaining water and liquidize. Return to the saucepan and reheat. Stir in the lemon juice and pepper to taste. Serve hot.

Thin Leek Soup

This is a very splashy soup to liquidize. Put a double thickness of kitchen paper over the goblet after putting on the lid.

Serves 4

 Use wheat-free soy sauce

 Use salt-free home-made stock

 Use gluten-free soy sauce

 Avoid soy sauce

 Avoid soy sauce

1 medium onion, peeled and sliced thinly
1 tablespoon sunflower oil
1 lb (450 g) leeks, trimmed, cut lengthways and washed thoroughly
1½ pints (900 ml) water
3 teaspoons soy sauce, or 1 generous teaspoon yeast extract, or home-made stock to taste
Freshly ground black pepper, to taste

Method

Fry the onion in the oil for 3 or 4 minutes. Add the leeks, cut into pieces and stir/fry for another 3 minutes, without letting them brown. Pour in about half the water and the stock of your choice. Bring the mixture to the boil and simmer for about 15 minutes with the lid on. (Very young leeks will only need about 10 minutes.) Take off the heat and add the remaining water. Spoon into the liquidizer goblet. Pour off about half the liquid into the pan. Blend what remains in the goblet and pour into the pan. Season with black pepper, bring to the boil, stir well and serve hot.

Turnip Soup

A very creamy soup. Only small, new season turnips are suitable for this recipe.

Serves 4

 Use wheat-free soy sauce and bread

 Use salt-free home-made stock

 Use gluten-free soy sauce and bread

 Avoid soy sauce

 Avoid soy sauce

2 medium onions, peeled and sliced thinly
1 tablespoon sunflower oil
1 lb (450 g) turnips, trimmed, peeled and sliced thinly
1½ pints (900 ml) reconstituted low-fat dried milk
1 tablespoon thin soy sauce, or 2 teaspoons yeast extract, or home-made stock to taste
Freshly ground black pepper, to taste
4 slices wholewheat bread

Method

Fry the onion in the oil for 4 or 5 minutes. Add the turnip slices, milk and stock of your choice. Bring to the boil carefully as the milk will be inclined to boil over. Simmer gently for about 25 minutes. Take off the heat and allow to cool a little. Liquidize and return to the pan. Gently reheat. Put a slice of bread into the base of each of four soup bowls. Pour the hot soup over the bread and serve immediately.

French Country Soup

One of the few soups that can be made without onion.

Serves 4–5

  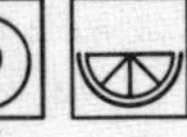  

 Use wheat-free soy sauce

 Use salt-free home-made stock

 Use gluten-free soy sauce

 Avoid soy sauce

 Avoid soy sauce

1 lb (450 g) leeks, trimmed, sliced, washed thoroughly and sliced
2 medium carrots, trimmed and sliced
1½ tablespoons sunflower oil
3 medium potatoes, peeled and cut into thin slices
Just over 1½ pints (900 ml) water
1 tablespoon thin soy sauce, or 2 teaspoons yeast extract, or home-made stock to taste
Freshly ground black pepper, to taste
1 heaped tablespoon finely chopped fresh parsley

Method

Put the leeks into a large saucepan with the carrots and oil. Stir/fry for about 4 minutes. Put in the potato slices with about two-thirds of the water and the stock of your choice. Bring to the boil and simmer for about 20–25 minutes, with the pan covered. Take off the heat, add the remaining water and blend in a liquidizer for a few seconds, but not long enough to make the soup too smooth. Return to the pan, reheat, season with black pepper and stir in the parsley. Serve hot.

Minestrone Soup

As nourishing as a main course meal if made at home with fresh vegetables. The beans, if cooked at home, should be soaked overnight, brought to the boil and boiled steadily in plenty of water for at least 10 minutes as well as simmering until tender, before using in the soup. Alternatively, use commercially prepared beans which will be already cooked; just strain these and add to the soup. *(See p. 265 for cooking details for haricot beans.)*

Serves 4–6

 Use gluten-free pasta and soy sauce

 Use ground almonds instead of cheese

 Use egg-free pasta

 Use wheat-free pasta and soy sauce

 Avoid soy sauce

 Use home-cooked salt-free beans and home-made salt-free stock

 Avoid soy sauce

3 oz (75 g) haricot beans, cooked
1 large onion, peeled and sliced
1½ tablespoons sunflower oil
2 cloves garlic, peeled
1½ pints (900 ml) water
1 medium carrot, trimmed and cut into small dice
1 stick celery, trimmed and sliced finely
½ medium green pepper, deseeded and cut into small dice
4 canned tomatoes, chopped
1 tablespoon thin soy sauce, or 2 teaspoons yeast extract, or home-made stock to taste
2 or 3 cabbage leaves, finely shredded
2 oz (50 g) wholewheat pasta – shells or spaghetti broken into short pieces
2 heaped tablespoons freshly chopped parsley
Freshly ground black pepper, to taste
Grated Parmesan cheese

Method

Fry the onion in the oil for 3 or 4 minutes, using a large saucepan. Crush in the garlic through a garlic press and add the water, carrot, celery, green pepper, tomatoes, stock of your choice, cabbage and pasta. Stir and bring to the boil. Turn down the heat so that the mixture will simmer and put on the lid. Simmer gently for about 30 minutes, adding the cooked beans after 20 minutes. Season with black pepper to taste and sprinkle in the parsley. Serve hot with a light sprinkling of Parmesan cheese.

Leek and Potato Soup

Serves 4

 Use wheat-free soy sauce

 Use salt-free home-made stock

 Use gluten-free soy sauce

 Avoid soy sauce

 Avoid soy sauce

1 medium onion, peeled and chopped
1 tablespoon sunflower oil
2 medium leeks, trimmed
2 medium potatoes
¾ pint (450 ml) water
2 teaspoons thin soy sauce, or 1 teaspoon yeast extract, or home-made stock to taste
Freshly ground black pepper, to taste

Method

Fry the onion in the oil but do not let it brown. Cut the leeks in half along the length and separate out the layers. Wash thoroughly to remove any grit. Chop coarsely and add to the saucepan with the potatoes and about half the water. Bring to the boil and then simmer for about 15 minutes (or less if the leeks are young), with the lid on. Add the remainder of the water and blend in a liquidizer. Return to the pan and reheat. Season with the pepper to taste and serve hot.

Bean and Pasta Soup

A very thick, nourishing soup, especially good for winter days. It makes a meal with a green salad and fruit to follow.

Serves 2–3

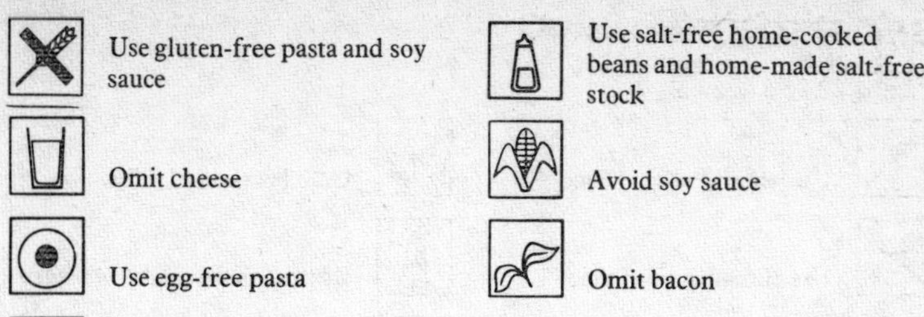

Use gluten-free pasta and soy sauce

Use salt-free home-cooked beans and home-made salt-free stock

Omit cheese

Avoid soy sauce

Use egg-free pasta

Omit bacon

Avoid soy sauce

1 medium onion, peeled and chopped finely
1 tablespoon sunflower oil
1 small clove garlic, peeled
1 heaped tablespoon each diced carrot and diced celery
1 sliced unsmoked back bacon, trimmed of all fat and cut into small pieces
1 heaped tablespoon finely chopped parsley
3 skinned tomatoes, chopped (fresh or canned)
1 heaped teaspoon tomato purée
About 1 pint (600 ml) water
3 teaspoons thin soy sauce, or 1 generous teaspoon yeast extract
3 oz (75 g) pasta – any small shapes will do, or spaghetti broken into short lengths
4 oz (110 g) haricot beans (red or white), cooked
Freshly ground black pepper to taste
Cheese for sprinkling

Method

Fry the onion in the oil for about 3 minutes, using a large pan. Crush in the garlic, add the carrot, celery and bacon, and stir. Fry while you stir for another 2 or 3 minutes and then add the parsley, tomatoes, tomato purée, water and stock of your choice. Sprinkle in the pasta and cooked beans and bring to the boil. Turn down the heat and simmer for about 15 minutes or until the pasta is tender. Season to taste with the pepper and serve hot, sprinkled with cheese.

Chicken Broth

The chicken can be old and tough – it doesn't matter – as it is only put in to flavour the broth. The residue should be discarded after straining.

Serves 4

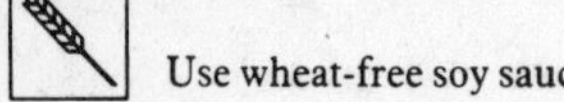

Use wheat-free soy sauce

Omit lemon rind

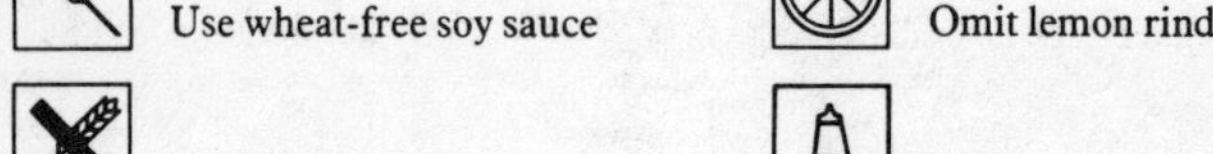

Use gluten-free soy sauce

Use salt-free home-made stock

Avoid soy sauce

Avoid soy sauce

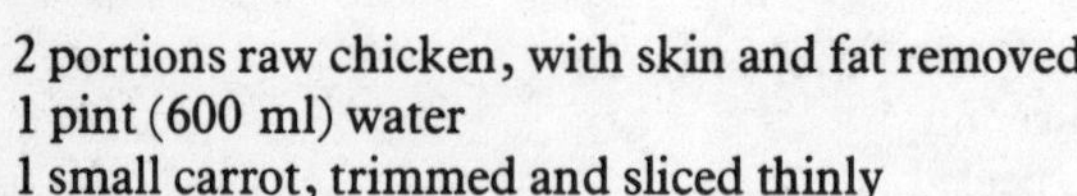

2 portions raw chicken, with skin and fat removed
1 pint (600 ml) water
1 small carrot, trimmed and sliced thinly
1 onion, peeled and sliced thinly
1 stick celery, scrubbed and chopped
1 tomato, cut into quarters
4 peppercorns
1 bay leaf
1 tablespoon thin soy sauce, or 2 teaspoons yeast extract, or home-made stock to taste
Finely grated rind of ¼ of a lemon
1 tablespoon freshly chopped parsley

Method

Put the chicken into a large saucepan and pour in the water. Bring to the boil and skim off any scum that forms. Put in all the other ingredients except the stock, lemon and parsley. Bring back to the boil and turn down the heat to let it simmer slowly for about 50–60 minutes. Strain through a fine mesh sieve into a bowl. Pour the liquid back into the pan and add the stock of your choice, lemon rind and parsley. Stir and serve hot.

Green Pepper and Tomato Soup

This thin, ginger-coloured soup can also be served chilled for summer.

Serves 4

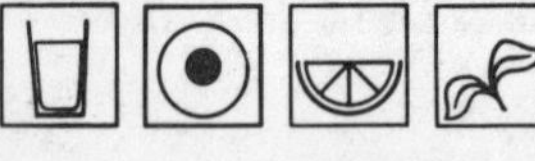

 Use wheat-free soy sauce

 Use artificial sweetener

 Use gluten-free soy sauce

 Use salt-free home-made stock

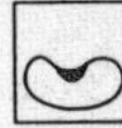 Avoid soy sauce

 Avoid soy sauce

1 medium onion, peeled and sliced thinly
1 tablespoon sunflower oil
1 clove garlic, peeled
3 small green peppers, stalks and seeds removed, flesh coarsely chopped
5 canned or 4 fresh, peeled, tomatoes, chopped
1 teaspoon brown sugar
1 tablespoon thin soy sauce, or 2 teaspoons yeast extract, or home-made stock to taste
1 pint (600 ml) water
1 tablespoon freshly chopped parsley
Freshly ground black pepper, to taste

Method

Put the onion and oil into a saucepan and stir/fry for about 3 or 4 minutes. Crush in the garlic through a garlic press. Add the peppers, tomatoes, sugar, stock of your choice and about half the water. Bring to the boil and then turn down the heat to simmer the soup for about 5 minutes. Add the remaining water and blend in a liquidizer. Pour back into the pan through a fine wire mesh sieve, discarding the residue. Sprinkle in the parsley, add black pepper to taste. Reheat and serve.

Courgette Soup

Serves 2–3

 Use wheat-free soy sauce

 Use home-made salt-free stock

 Use gluten-free soy sauce

 Avoid soy sauce

 Avoid soy sauce

½ medium onion, peeled and chopped finely
2 teaspoons sunflower oil
8 oz (225 g) small courgettes (baby marrows), trimmed and sliced thinly
1½ teaspoons thin soy sauce, or ½ teaspoon yeast extract
Just over ½ pint (300 ml) water
Freshly ground black pepper, to taste

Method

In a saucepan fry the onion in the oil until transparent. Add the courgettes, stock of your choice and most of the water. Bring to the boil and simmer for about 8 minutes or until the courgettes are tender, giving the soup a stir now and then. Add the remaining water and liquidize into a creamy light soup. Return to the pan, season to taste and serve hot. In summer, serve chilled from the fridge.

Tomato Soup

If you wish to serve this soup chilled then be a little more generous with the sugar. Adjust this when the soup has been chilled, as chilling will make it taste less sweet than the hot version.

Serves 4–5

 Use wheat-free soy sauce

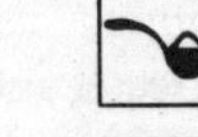 Use artificial sweetener if necessary

 Use gluten-free soy sauce

 Use home-made salt-free stock

 Avoid soy sauce

 Avoid soy sauce

1 medium onion, peeled and chopped
1 tablespoon sunflower oil
1 medium can tomatoes
Just under 1 pint (600 ml) water
3 teaspoons thin soy sauce, or ¾ teaspoon yeast extract, or home-made stock
Brown sugar, to taste
Freshly ground black pepper, to taste
1 heaped tablespoon freshly chopped parsley

Method

Fry the onion in the oil for 5 minutes while you stir. Add the tomatoes and their juice and a little of the water. Pour into the liquidizer goblet and blend. Return to the pan and add the remainder of the water and the stock of your choice. Stir well and taste. Add sugar, a pinch at a time, until the taste is right. (If the tomatoes are very sweet then there will be no need to add any sugar.) Season with black pepper to taste and sprinkle in the parsley. Serve hot.

Cold Cucumber Soup

Serves 3

½ average cucumber, peeled and chopped
1 small carton plain, low fat yoghurt (about 5 oz/150 g)
2–3 fresh mint leaves, chopped finely
Freshly ground black pepper, to taste
Chilled, skimmed milk

Method

Put the cucumber into the blender with the yoghurt. Blend and spoon into a bowl. Stir in the mint and season with the black pepper. Stir in a little chilled milk if you think it is too thick. Serve cold, from the fridge.

Clear Vegetable Broth

Serves 3–4

  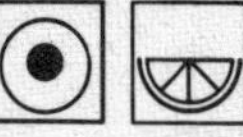  

 Use wheat-free soy sauce

 Use home-made salt-free stock

 Use gluten-free soy sauce

 Avoid soy sauce

 Avoid soy sauce

2 medium onions, peeled and sliced thinly
1 tablespoon sunflower oil
2 medium carrots, sliced
2 or 3 cabbage leaves, shredded
2 sticks celery, chopped
2 or 3 mushrooms, sliced
1 leek, thoroughly washed and sliced (optional)
1 heaped teaspoon tomato purée
1 pint + (600 ml +) water
3 teaspoons thin soy sauce, or 1 generous teaspoon yeast extract, or home-made stock to taste
Freshly ground black pepper, to taste
1 heaped tablespoon freshly chopped parsley

Method

Fry the onion in the oil for 1 minute while you stir. Add all the other ingredients except the parsley and bring to the boil. Simmer with the lid on for about 25–30 minutes, until all the vegetables are soft. Strain into a basin through a fine mesh wire sieve and discard the vegetables. Pour the liquid back into the pan. Reheat and sprinkle in the parsley. Serve hot.

Variation

Instead of cabbage, use spinach leaves, Brussels sprouts or broccoli.

Parsley Soup

Serves 3

 Use wheat-free soy sauce

 Use home-made salt-free stock

 Use gluten-free soy sauce

 Avoid soy sauce

 Avoid soy sauce

½ medium onion, peeled and chopped finely
2 teaspoons sunflower oil
2 oz (50 g) fresh parsley, washed and coarsely chopped
2 medium potatoes, peeled and sliced thinly

1 pint (600 ml) skimmed milk
3 teaspoons thin soy sauce, or 1 generous teaspoon yeast extract, or home-made stock to taste
Freshly ground black pepper, to taste

Method

Fry the onion in the oil for about 3 or 4 minutes, while you stir. Put in the parsley and potato. Stir/fry for a minute and then pour in the milk and add the stock of your choice. Bring just to the boil and then simmer with the lid on for 25–30 minutes. Remove from the heat and allow to cool a little before blending. Return to the pan, taste and season with the pepper. If it seems too thick, then add a little water. Serve either hot or chilled from the fridge.

Lettuce Soup

Serves 2–3

 Use wheat-free soy sauce

 Use gluten-free soy sauce

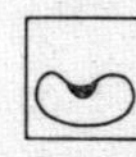 Avoid soy sauce

 Use salt-free home-made stock

 Use potato flour instead of cornflour and avoid soy sauce

¼ cucumber, chopped
½ lettuce, washed and shredded
2 spring onions, trimmed and chopped
3 teaspoons sunflower oil
Freshly ground black pepper, to taste
1 pint (600 ml) water
3 teaspoons thin soy sauce, or 1 generous teaspoon yeast extract
2 teaspoons cornflour mixed with 2 tablespoons skimmed milk
1 heaped tablespoon freshly chopped parsley

Method

Put all the ingredients except the cornflour mixture and the parsley into a saucepan and bring to the boil. Simmer with the lid on for about 30 minutes. Allow to cool a little, then blend in a liquidizer. Pour back into the pan and add the cornflour mixture. Bring to the boil again and stir while the soup simmers for 3 minutes. Put a little of the parsley into the bottom of each soup bowl and pour the soup over. Serve hot.

Quick Beef Broth

Serves 3

 Use wheat-free soy sauce

 Use salt-free home-made stock

 Use gluten-free soy sauce

 Avoid soy sauce

 Avoid soy sauce

1 medium onion, peeled and chopped finely
1 tablespoon sunflower oil
About 4 oz (110 g) cooked beef from a joint, or scraps
¾ pint (450 ml) water
3 teaspoons thin soy sauce, or 1 generous teaspoon yeast extract
1 tablespoon freshly chopped parsley
Freshly ground black pepper, to taste

Method

Fry the onion in the oil for 5 minutes, letting it brown evenly. (This will give the soup a good colour.) Trim and discard all visible fat, gristle, etc. from the meat, then cut it into small dice or mince coarsely. Add to the onions and pour in the water. Stir in the stock of your choice and bring to the boil. Turn down the heat and simmer for 10–15 minutes. Stir in the parsley and serve hot, seasoned with the black pepper.

STARTERS

In these days of overnutrition, very simple starters seem a better idea for a meal than those with a good deal of extra calories. The following starters are quickly prepared and very easy to make. Their simplicity should not devalue the purpose of starters as an appetizer to make the digestive juices flow.

Grapefruit

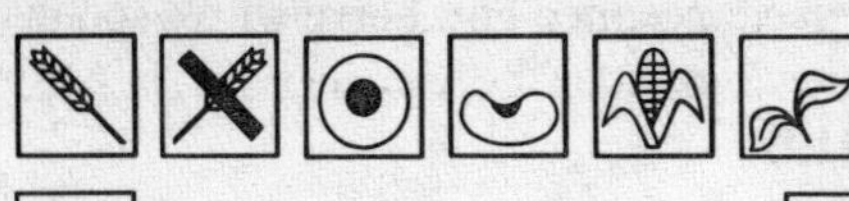

Use milk-free margarine

Use artificial sweetener

Allow ½ grapefruit per person

Method

This can be served hot or cold. Halve and put into bowls. Cut round the flesh and between the segments and serve with a little sugar or liquid honey. Eat with a teaspoon.

To serve hot, prepare in the same way but remove the centre pith/membrane. Sprinkle with a little sweetening and put a knob of polyunsaturated margarine in the middle. Grill for a few minutes and serve hot, with a teaspoon.

Tomato Appetizer

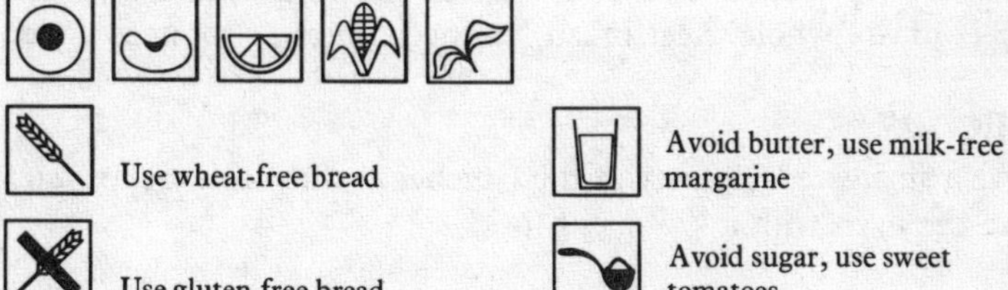

Use wheat-free bread

Avoid butter, use milk-free margarine

Use gluten-free bread

Avoid sugar, use sweet tomatoes

Allow 2 fresh, good quality tomatoes per person

Method

Slice the tomatoes, season to taste with black pepper and a pinch or two of sugar, and sprinkle with a little freshly chopped parsley and spring onion or chives. Serve with brown bread and butter or polyunsaturated margarine.

Melon

Wash the melon. Cut out wedges and remove the seeds. Cut away the peel and serve in long slices on a plate with a knife and fork. Small melons can be halved and the seeds scooped out. Serve with a spoon.

Orange and Grapefruit

  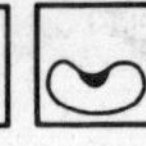   

 Use artificial sweetener

Serve a mixture of orange and grapefruit segments with a little sweetening to taste, in small glass dishes or bowls. Serve with a teaspoon.

Salads

See also the section on Salads in this book. Serve a half portion of any of the mixed ones.

Soups

See also Soups. Serve a small portion of any of the thin soups with fingers of dry wholewheat bread (or special bread), toasted.

Quiches

Serve a small wedge of any of the Quiches in this book. Serve warm from the oven with a knife and fork.

Pâtés

Serve any of Pâtés from this book with dry, toasted bread – wholewheat or special as appropriate.

Stuffed Mushrooms

Serves 2

 Use wheat-free bread

 Use milk-free margarine

 Use gluten-free bread

 Omit bacon garnish

4 large flat mushrooms
1 small onion, finely chopped
1 tablespoon polyunsaturated soft margarine
1 slice wholewheat bread without crusts, made into crumbs
2 tablespoons dry white wine or water
1 tablespoon freshly chopped parsley
1 small clove garlic, peeled and put through a garlic crusher
Freshly ground black pepper, to taste

Garnish

1 rasher unsmoked back bacon, trimmed of fat, chopped and fried in 1 teaspoon sunflower oil

Method

Preheat the oven to Gas Mark 4, 180°C or 350°F. Wash the mushrooms and take off the stalks. Chop the stalks finely and fry with the onion in the margarine for 4–5 minutes, while stirring. Put the breadcrumbs into a bowl and cover with the wine or water, stirring to make the crumbs soak up the liquid. (If it is too dry add a little water.) Stir in the mushroom stalks and onion mixture, the parsley and garlic, and add pepper to taste. Grease an ovenproof dish and arrange the mushroom caps, gills upwards, on the base. Fill with the breadcrumb mixture and bake for about 15 minutes. Sprinkle with the chopped bacon garnish and return to the oven for another 3 minutes. Serve hot.

Variation

Garnish Stuffed Mushrooms with 1 tablespoon of grated cheese instead of the bacon.

Hummus

Chickpeas are a vegetarian high protein food, which are sometimes called 'garbanzos'. They need to be soaked overnight and then boiled in plenty of water the following day. Depending how hard they are, they will require from 1–2 hours cooking. When they are soft, strain in a colander. They can be used instead of beans in casseroles, soups and stews, as well as forming the basis of hummus.

Serves 3–4 as a starter

 Serve with wheat-free bread or rye crispbreads

 Serve with gluten-free bread or crispbreads

8 oz (225 g) chickpeas, cooked
1 generous tablespoon tahini (sesame seed paste)
1 small clove garlic, peeled
Juice 1 small lemon
1 tablespoon sunflower oil
Freshly ground black pepper, to taste

Method

Blend the chickpeas to a paste, either in a liquidizer or a food processor, adding a little water as necessary. Put into a basin and add the tahini. Stir in well and then crush in the garlic through a garlic press. Add a little lemon juice and the oil and mix well. Taste and adjust with more lemon and black pepper, as required. Beat well, adding a little more water if the consistency is too thick. Serve in a bowl, with bread or crispbreads.

Walnut Pâté

Wholewheat flour or rice flour will make good substitutes for the split pea or bean flour.

Serves 1

 Avoid wholewheat flour

 Avoid tomato purée, use a finely chopped or puréed fresh tomato instead

 Avoid wholewheat flour

1 spring onion, finely chopped
3 teaspoons sunflower oil
1 teaspoon split pea or bean flour
4 tablespoons water
2 heaped tablespoons grated walnuts (use a coffee grinder)
¼ teaspoon freshly chopped thyme, or use 3 pinches dried thyme
1 level teaspoon tomato purée
Few drops fresh lemon juice
Freshly ground black pepper, to taste

Method

Stir/fry the onion in the oil, using a small frying pan, for 30 seconds. Add the flour and mix well to absorb the oil. Continue to stir/fry for about 1 minute over a gentle heat. Add the water and cook while you stir for another 3 minutes, until you have a stiff paste. Take off the heat and add the nuts, thyme, tomato purée and lemon juice. Mix well. If it seems too stiff, add a little more water. Season to taste and turn into a small dish to get cold. Cover and store in the fridge.

Nut Pâté

This pâté can be served hot with toast or cold in sandwiches.

Serves 2

1 tablespoon sunflower oil
1 spring onion, chopped finely
½ clove garlic, peeled
1 oz (25 g) yellow split pea flour (available from Asian stores or health food shops)
About 6 tablespoons water
2 oz (50 g) ground almonds or cashews
1 pinch nutmeg
Freshly ground black pepper, to taste

Method

Heat the oil in a small saucepan and fry the onion for 30 seconds while you stir. Crush in the garlic through a garlic press and continue to stir/fry for another 30 seconds. Put in the pea flour and stir until the oil has all been absorbed. Fry while you stir for another minute. Pour in the water and cook for 3 or 4 minutes, stirring with a wooden spoon to prevent lumps from forming. When the mixture has become a stiff paste, add the nuts, spice and pepper. Turn out into a small dish and flatten with a knife. Leave to get cold, then store in the fridge.

Liver Pâté

 Use wheat-free soy sauce

 Use 1 teaspoon yeast extract

 Use gluten-free soy sauce

 Use 1 teaspoon yeast extract instead of soy sauce

8 oz (225 g) chicken livers
1 small onion, chopped finely
1 tablespoon sunflower oil
½ clove garlic, peeled and put through a garlic press
1 pinch dried mixed herbs
Freshly ground black pepper, to taste
2 heaped teaspoons low fat dried milk mixed with 1 tablespoon cold water
1 teaspoon sherry
2 teaspoons soy sauce

Method

Wash the chicken livers and pick them over, discarding any stringy or yellow parts. Chop. Fry the onion in the oil for about 4 minutes, while you stir. Crush in the garlic, then add the liver, herbs and seasoning to taste. Stir/fry using a wooden spoon or fork to break up the livers as they cook. After about 4–5 minutes they should be crumbly and have changed colour. Allow them to cool a little then put into a blender with the remaining ingredients. Blend to a thick paste. (If it turns out too thin put back into the pan and heat to reduce.) Spoon into a small dish. Serve with toast.

Crudités

See Salad section on p. 298.

PASTA DISHES

Although home-made pasta can be excellent, very good commercial brands are also available and store well. The best grain for making pasta at home is durum wheat, which has a high gluten content; however, ordinary wholewheat flour can be used successfully. Some wholewheat flours have added durum wheat bran and are labelled 'high fibre' or 'high bran'. The healthiest kinds of pasta are the wholewheat varieties. Pasta made with white flour is not only less nutritious, it also has much less taste. Pasta with spinach (green pasta) leaves itself open commercially to be simply white pasta dyed green. For special diets pasta can be made at home with gluten-free and wheat-free flours. Commercially made buckwheat pasta is available in some areas, often in health stores.

Commercially made pasta falls into two categories – the fresh kind, with a short shelf life of two or three days, and the dried sort, which has a long shelf life. Fresh pasta takes only a few minutes to cook but the dried brands will need much longer. Many shapes are available which add visual interest to dishes – shells, spirals, tubes, shapes, flat noodles, round noodles, flat pieces for main meals and tiny shapes for soups.

The influence of Italian peasant cooking is, of course, obvious in pasta recipes. However, Chinese cooking also features wide use of this basic item. As a cheap and nourishing food it is now part of the western diet and looks as if it is here to stay.

There is a tendency in pasta recipes for far too much fat to be used, either in the sauce, or by using too much cheese on top, or by coating the cooked pasta with oil or butter before adding a sauce. The recipes that follow are restricted in their use of fat. By using wholewheat pasta instead of white the fibre content of the diet can also be improved. Pasta may be eaten hot with a sauce or cold with salads. As part of a healthy diet it can be eaten two or three times per week.

Amounts of Pasta

For an average serving of pasta for a main meal allow about 4 oz (110 g) of raw pasta. For a starter or snack allow just half, i.e. 2 oz (50 g) of raw pasta. In salads allow at the most 2 oz (50 g) cold, cooked pasta. (A generous raw handful is a good guide to the latter: cooking pasta in water makes it swell so it ends up heavier after boiling than its raw weight.)

Cooking Home-made Pasta

Put a large pan of water on to boil – about 5 pints (2¾ litres). Put in the pasta a little at a time and bring back to the boil. Boil steadily for 3–5 minutes, or until the pasta is tender but still a little firm. Tip into a colander and strain. Serve with a sauce and sprinkled with Parmesan cheese or ground almonds.

Home-made Wholewheat Pasta

Enough for 4

6 oz (175 g) wholewheat flour
1 egg
2 tablespoons sunflower oil
Cold water to mix

Method

Put the flour into a large bowl. Mix the egg and oil in a cup and pour into the flour. Use a fork to mix and then add about 2 tablespoons of cold water. Now pull it into a ball by hand. Knead on a floured worktop until the dough is tough and shiny. This will take at least 5 or 6 minutes. Divide into three or four pieces and roll out thinly until it is almost like paper. Cut into thin strips with a sharp knife and leave to dry on a clean tea towel over the back of a kitchen chair. Alternatively, cut into flat strips for lasagne, or use for ravioli as required.

Wheat-free and Gluten-free Pasta

Makes about 10 oz (280 g) dough: enough for 2–3 servings

 Avoid salt

8 oz (225 g) Trufree No. 4 flour
3 pinches salt (optional)
2 tablespoons sunflower oil
1 egg, beaten
3 tablespoons cold water

Method

Mix the flour and salt in a bowl. Sprinkle in the oil and rub in with the fingers. Add the egg and mix. Put in the water and mix to a sticky paste. Knead, adding a little more of the No. 4 flour if necessary. Knead on a floured worktop until smooth. Divide the dough into four portions. Roll out each portion on a floured worktop as thinly as possible, then cut into thin strips.

To cook this pasta, drop into boiling water and cook steadily for about 12 minutes until tender but still a little firm. Drain in a colander and serve with a suitable sauce.

For cannelloni roll out the dough and cut into 3 × 4 in. (7.5 × 10 cm) rectangles. Cook in boiling water for 12 minutes. Drain and pat dry on a clean tea towel. Fill and bake in the usual way (see recipe on p. 168).

Green Pasta

This is rather more difficult to handle than plain wholewheat pasta, but is well worth the effort.

Enough for 4

10–12 spinach leaves, thoroughly washed
6 oz (175 g) wholewheat flour
1 egg
2 tablespoons sunflower oil
Cold water to mix

Method

Put the spinach into a saucepan with 2 tablespoons of water. Put the lid on and bring to the boil. Cook steadily for about 15 minutes or until the spinach is tender. Strain in a colander, squeezing out all the water you can with the back of a wooden spoon. Chop the spinach very finely and allow it to cool. Put the flour into a large bowl. In a small basin mix the egg, oil and chopped spinach with a fork. Add to the flour and stir well. Put in a little water – about 1 tablespoon to start – and pull together by hand into a ball. Knead well for 5 minutes until the dough is smooth and shiny. Roll out as thinly as you can on a floured worktop and cut into thin strips with a sharp knife. Use immediately.

Herb Butter for Pasta

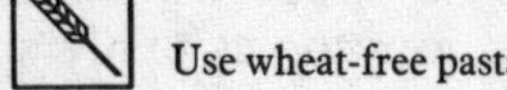 Use wheat-free pasta

 Use egg-free pasta

 Use gluten-free pasta

 Use home-made salt-free pasta

For each portion of hot, cooked pasta you will need:

½ oz (15 g) butter or polyunsaturated margarine
½ clove garlic
1 tablespoon freshly chopped parsley
Freshly ground black pepper, to taste
1 slightly heaped tablespoon finely grated Parmesan or Cheddar cheese

Method

Use a small saucepan to melt the butter or margarine gently. Crush in the garlic through a garlic press and stir in the parsley. Pour over the hot pasta and toss to combine. Season with the black pepper, and serve with the cheese sprinkled on the top.

SAUCES FOR PASTA

Tomato and Tuna Sauce

 Use wheat-free pasta

 Use ground almonds instead of cheese

 Use gluten-free pasta

 Use egg-free pasta

For each portion of hot cooked pasta you will need:

3 canned tomatoes
1 teaspoon sunflower oil
Freshly ground black pepper, to taste
½ small tin tuna fish, drained
1 heaped tablespoon finely grated Cheddar cheese, or 1 level tablespoon finely grated Parmesan cheese

Method

Chop the tomatoes and put into a saucepan oiled with the sunflower oil. Season to taste with the pepper and flake in the tuna. Heat through for 3 minutes and stir into hot pasta. Serve immediately, with the cheese sprinkled on the top.

Pepper Sauce

 Use wheat-free pasta

 Use egg-free pasta

 Use gluten-free pasta

 Avoid cheese and use home-made salt-free pasta

 Use ground almonds instead of cheese

For each portion of hot, cooked pasta you will need:

¼ medium onion, chopped finely
2 teaspoons sunflower oil
½ clove garlic, peeled
½ red, green or yellow pepper, deseeded and cut into fine strips
1 canned tomato, chopped
Freshly ground black pepper, to taste
Parmesan cheese for sprinkling

Method

Fry the onion in the oil while you stir for 3 or 4 minutes. Crush in the garlic through a garlic press and stir. Add the pepper strips and the tomato. Stir/fry until the pepper is tender, for about 5–6 minutes. Season to taste with black pepper and stir into the hot pasta. Serve sprinkled with Parmesan cheese.

Variations

Add 2 good pinches of dried basil and stir in just before serving.
Add 1 heaped teaspoon freshly chopped parsley and stir in just before serving.

Onion Sauce

Use wheat-free soy sauce and pasta

Use egg-free pasta

Use gluten-free soy sauce and pasta

Avoid soy sauce

Use ground almonds or walnuts instead of cheese

Avoid soy sauce

For each portion of hot, cooked pasta you will need:

½ tablespoon sunflower oil
½ small clove garlic, peeled
1 medium onion, sliced thinly
2 tablespoons water
2 teaspoons thin soy sauce, or ½ teaspoon yeast extract
1 tablespoon water
1 teaspoon tomato purée
Freshly ground black pepper to taste
1 heaped teaspoon freshly chopped parsley
Finely grated Cheddar cheese for sprinkling

Method

Put the oil into a saucepan with the garlic, crushed in through a garlic press, the onion slices and the 2 tablespoons of water. Begin to cook very gently, stirring occasionally. Continue to cook for about 20 minutes with the lid on or until the onion is transparent and soft. Mix the stock of your choice, 1 tablespoon of water and the tomato purée in a cup. Add to the onions, season with black pepper and stir well. Mix into the cooked pasta and sprinkle with the parsley and cheese.

Mushroom Sauce

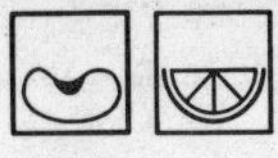   

 Use wheat-free pasta

 Use egg-free pasta

 Use gluten-free pasta

 Use home-made salt-free pasta

For each portion of hot, cooked pasta you will need:

¼ medium onion, chopped finely
2 teaspoons sunflower oil
½ small clove garlic, peeled
2 oz (50 g) fresh mushrooms, washed well and chopped
1 slightly rounded tablespoon low fat dried milk granules
2 tablespoons water
1 heaped teaspoon freshly chopped parsley
Freshly ground black pepper, to taste

Method

Gently fry the onion in the oil for 4 minutes while you stir. Crush in the garlic through a garlic press and stir well. Add the chopped mushrooms and put the lid on the pan to let them sweat over a low heat: this should take about 7 or 8 minutes, less if they are button mushrooms. Give them an occasional stir while they are cooking. Mix the dried milk with the water and add to the mixture. Sprinkle in the parsley and season with the black pepper. Combine with the hot pasta and serve immediately.

Courgette Sauce

 Use wheat-free pasta

 Use egg-free pasta

 Use gluten-free pasta

 Avoid cheese, and use home-made salt-free pasta

 Use ground almonds instead of cheese

For each portion of hot, cooked pasta you will need:

2 teaspoons sunflower oil
½ clove garlic, peeled
2 small courgettes, trimmed and cut into thin slices
1–2 tablespoons water
1 heaped teaspoon freshly chopped parsley
Freshly ground black pepper, to taste
About 1 tablespoon cheese for sprinkling – Parmesan or Cheddar

Method

Heat the oil in a saucepan and crush in the garlic through a garlic press. Stir while you fry gently to brown the garlic. Add the courgettes and water and stir/fry for about 8–10 minutes, until the courgettes are softened but still a little crisp. Combine with the cooked pasta and add the parsley, seasoning and cheese. Mix carefully and serve immediately.

Prawn and Tomato Sauce

 Use wheat-free pasta

 Use artificial sweetener to taste

 Use gluten-free pasta

 Use fresh tomatoes and water, and home-made salt-free pasta

 Use egg-free pasta

For each portion of hot, cooked pasta you will need:

3 canned tomatoes, with 2 tablespoons of their juice
¼ medium onion, chopped
½ clove garlic, peeled
½ small carrot, sliced thinly
¼ stick celery, chopped finely
2 teaspoons sunflower oil
1 teaspoon brown sugar
Water
Freshly ground black pepper, to taste

Good pinch dried basil or oregano
2 oz (50 g) shelled, cooked prawns (defrosted, if frozen ones are used)

Method

Put the tomatoes into a saucepan and chop into smaller pieces. Add the onion and crush in the garlic through a garlic press. Put in the carrot, celery, sunflower oil and brown sugar. Bring to the boil and simmer with the lid on for about 15 minutes. Add a little water (about 4 tablespoons) and transfer to a liquidizer goblet. Blend and return to the pan. Season with the black pepper and add the herb of your choice. Put in the prawns, stir and gently heat until the prawns are hot right through. Stir into the cooked pasta and serve immediately.

Pea and Ham Sauce

 Use wheat-free pasta

 Use egg-free pasta

 Use gluten-free pasta

 Use potato flour instead of cornflour

For each portion of hot, cooked pasta you will need:

2 teaspoons sunflower oil
¼ medium onion, chopped finely
About ½ cup skimmed milk mixed with 1 teaspoon cornflour
2 oz (50 g) peas, fresh cooked or defrosted
1 slice ham, trimmed of all fat and chopped
Freshly ground black pepper, to taste
Parmesan or Cheddar cheese for sprinkling, finely grated

Method

Heat the oil in a saucepan and fry the onion for 2 or 3 minutes while you stir. Add the milk/cornflour mixture and bring to the boil, still stirring. Cook for about 1 minute to thicken, then add the peas. Simmer while they heat through. Add the ham and season to taste. Heat for another minute and then stir into the cooked pasta. Serve with a light sprinkling of cheese.

Wine and Rosemary Sauce

 Use wheat-free pasta

 Use egg-free pasta

 Use gluten-free pasta

For each portion of hot, cooked pasta you will need:

¼ medium onion, sliced thinly
Lean from 2 rashers unsmoked back bacon, chopped
2 teaspoons sunflower oil
1 tablespoon white wine (a dry one is best)
3 canned tomatoes
Freshly ground black pepper, to taste
¼ teaspoon fresh chopped rosemary, or 1 good pinch dried rosemary
1 tablespoon finely grated Parmesan cheese

Method

Fry the onion and bacon in the oil while you stir for about 4 minutes. Add the wine, tomatoes and black pepper to taste. Simmer for about 10 minutes, giving the mixture an occasional stir. Sprinkle in the rosemary and stir into the hot pasta. Serve sprinkled with the Parmesan cheese.

Bolognese Sauce

This meat sauce is the basis of many Italian-type dishes – Spaghetti Bolognese, ravioli filling and for cannelloni. While traditional recipes will be high in fat, this version is a much healthier one.

Serves 4

 Use wheat-free soy sauce

 Avoid soy sauce

 Use gluten-free soy sauce

 Use home-made salt-free stock, use fresh tomatoes and avoid purée, and use home-made salt-free pasta

 Use ground almonds instead of cheese

 Avoid soy sauce

1 medium onion, chopped
1 tablespoon sunflower oil
4 oz (110 g) extra lean raw minced beef
2 oz (50 g) chicken livers, chopped (optional)
1 small carrot, diced or grated coarsely
½ stick celery, diced
2 slices ham, trimmed of fat and chopped
2 level teaspoons tomato purée
3 tablespoons white wine
1 tablespoon thin soy sauce, or 2 teaspoons yeast extract, or home-made stock to taste
¼ pint (150 ml) water (approx)
Freshly ground black pepper, to taste
3 good pinches freshly grated nutmeg

Method

Fry the onion in the oil for 3 minutes while you stir. Add the beef and stir/fry for 2 minutes, or until the meat is no longer red. Add the livers and stir/fry for another 2 minutes. Now put in all the other ingredients and bring to the boil. Turn down the heat and simmer, for about 30–35 minutes, giving an occasional stir. The sauce should be both thick and rich.

Use for Spaghetti Bolognese with 1 lb (450 g) of cooked spaghetti and a little Parmesan cheese sprinkled over. Use as a filling for cannelloni (see the recipe on p. 170).

Tomato and Herb Sauce

Makes enough for 4–5 portions of pasta

 Use wheat-free pasta

 Use egg-free pasta

 Use gluten-free pasta

 Avoid sugar

2 teaspoons sunflower oil
2 cloves garlic, peeled
1 medium can tomatoes, chopped
1 heaped teaspoon tomato purée
2 level teaspoons dried basil

1 tablespoon freshly chopped parsley
Freshly ground black pepper, to taste
½ teaspoon dried oregano
Few pinches sugar (optional)

Method

Heat the oil in a saucepan and crush in the garlic through a garlic press. Fry lightly for a minute while you stir. Add the tomatoes, tomato purée, basil and parsley. Bring to the boil and then turn down the heat to simmer the sauce for about 20 minutes, giving it an occasional stir. Taste and season with the black pepper and oregano. Taste again and adjust the seasoning with sugar, a pinch at a time until the sauce tastes right (i.e. it should not taste sour). Serve on hot pasta.

Parsley and Nut Sauce

This is a kind of paste rather than a sauce.

 Use wheat-free pasta

 Use egg-free pasta

 Use gluten-free pasta

 Use home-made salt-free pasta

 Use ground almonds instead of cheese

For each portion of hot, cooked pasta you will need:

1 heaped tablespoon freshly cooked parsley
2 grinds black pepper
½ small clove garlic, peeled and put through a garlic press
1 tablespoon freshly grated Parmesan cheese
4 walnut halves, finely chopped
2 teaspoons sunflower oil

Method

Put the parsley, pepper, garlic, cheese and nuts into a pestle and mortar. Pound to a paste, adding the oil gradually. Stir into cooked pasta that is moist and not too well drained. (For larger amounts blend the mixture in a liquidizer.)

Bacon and Egg sauce

 Use wheat-free pasta

 Use gluten-free pasta

For each portion of hot, cooked pasta you will need:

1 teaspoon sunflower oil
1 rasher back bacon (unsmoked), trimmed of fat and chopped
1 small egg
1 tablespoon Parmesan cheese
1 tablespoon skimmed milk
Freshly ground black pepper, to taste

Method

Heat the oil in a frying pan and fry the bacon pieces until they are crisp. Beat the egg in a small basin and add half the cheese and the milk. After draining the pasta put it back into the pan. Sprinkle in the bacon pieces and pour in the egg mixture. Heat gently while you stir to let the egg cook. As it scrambles it will make a creamy sauce for the pasta. Season to taste with the black pepper and serve right away, sprinkled with the remainder of the cheese.

Vegetable Sauce

A flexible dish, suitable for vegetarian diets.

 Use wheat-free pasta and soy sauce

 Use egg-free pasta

 Use gluten-free pasta and soy sauce

 Use potato flour, instead of cornflour, and avoid soy sauce

 Avoid cheese

For each portion of hot, cooked pasta you will need:

¼ medium onion, chopped finely
2 teaspoons sunflower oil
2 canned tomatoes with 2 tablespoons of their juice
1 baby carrot
1 heaped tablespoon raw or defrosted peas
2 stringless beans, cut into short lengths
4 spinach leaves, well washed and shredded
2 teaspoons thin soy sauce, or ½ teaspoon yeast extract
1 level teaspoon tomato purée
1 level teaspoon cornflour mixed with 2 tablespoons water
Freshly ground black pepper, to taste
1 tablespoon single cream
Parmesan cheese for sprinkling (optional)

Method

Fry the onion in the oil for 3 or 4 minutes while you stir. Add all the other ingredients except the black pepper, cream and cheese. Stir well and bring to the boil. Simmer with the lid on for about 10 minutes, or until all the vegetables are tender. Take off the heat and season with black pepper. Stir in the cream and mix into the cooked pasta. Serve immediately, sprinkled with a little cheese if you wish.

Variations

Use any of these instead of the carrot, peas, beans or spinach: 1 mushroom, chopped; ¼ courgette, chopped; ¼ green, red or yellow pepper, chopped; 2 sprouts, trimmed and finely shredded; 1 slightly heaped tablespoon cooked sweetcorn.

Almond Sauce

 Use wheat-free pasta

 Use egg-free pasta

 Use gluten-free pasta

 Use chopped fresh tomatoes, avoid purée, and use home-made salt-free pasta

For each portion of hot, cooked pasta you will need:

¼ medium onion, chopped
2 teaspoons sunflower oil
½ clove garlic, peeled
2 canned tomatoes with 2 tablespoons of their juice
1 teaspoon tomato purée
¼ green pepper, deseeded and chopped
2 mushrooms, chopped
1 heaped tablespoon freshly ground almonds
Freshly ground black pepper, to taste

Method

Fry the onion in the oil while you stir for about 3 minutes. Crush in the garlic through a garlic press and add all the other ingredients except the almonds and black pepper. Stir and bring to the boil. Turn down the heat and simmer for about 8 minutes, giving an occasional stir. Mix in the ground almonds. Taste and season with black pepper. Stir into the hot pasta and serve.

Cheese Sauce with Vegetables

This makes a creamy but low fat sauce. Be careful that the dish does not continue cooking after the cheese has been added or it will spoil. As the vegetables are generous in this recipe, use with less pasta than a normal portion, and there is no need to add more cheese when serving.

 Use wheat-free pasta

 Use egg-free pasta

 Use gluten-free pasta

For each small portion of hot, cooked pasta you will need:

¼ medium onion, chopped finely
1 teaspoon sunflower oil
½ small clove garlic
2–3 canned tomatoes with 2 tablespoons of their juice
1 mushroom, chopped
½ courgette, trimmed and diced, or 1 heaped tablespoon cooked peas

¼ green or red pepper, deseeded and chopped finely
2 good pinches dried basil or oregano
1 heaped teaspoon tomato purée
Freshly ground black pepper, to taste
2 oz (50 g) low fat cottage cheese

Method

Fry the onion in the oil while you stir for 3 or 4 minutes. Crush in the garlic through a garlic press. Chop the tomatoes and add to the pan with the juice, mushroom, courgette or peas, pepper and dried herb of your choice. Stir well and add the purée, and a little water if the mixture looks too thick. Bring to the boil and simmer for about 8 minutes, or until the vegetables are tender, giving an occasional stir. Taste and season with black pepper. Take off the heat and spoon in the cottage cheese. Mix well. Stir in the cooked pasta and serve immediately.

CANNELLONI

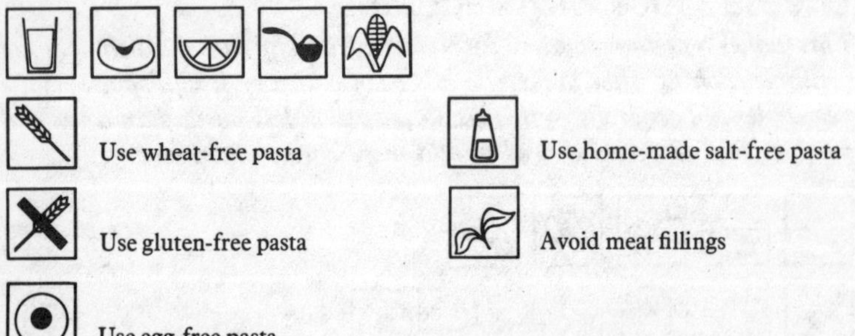

These are pasta tubes or rolled pieces of flat pasta. They are filled, covered in a sauce and baked in the oven. For each portion you will need 2 or 3 pasta tubes or pieces of flat pasta (about 3 × 4 in./7.5 × 10 cm). Some commercial brands of (large) pasta tubes do not need to be cooked before filling. Home-made and commercial brands of flat pasta sheets definitely need to be cooked to soften them enough to be rolled up. Put them into plenty of boiling water and cook until tender but not soft. Drain in a colander and pat dry with a clean tea towel.

Tubes should be filled with a teaspoon. Flat pieces should have filling arranged across them, about a third of the way along, and then be rolled up. Place in a greased ovenproof dish and cover with a suitable sauce. Bake in a preheated oven, above the centre, at Gas Mark 6, 200°C or 400°F, for about 20 minutes. Serve hot from the oven, still bubbling.

Beef and Spinach Filling for Cannelloni

This goes well with white sauce flavoured with a pinch of nutmeg.

Serves 2–3 and will fill about 6 or 8 tubes or 6 pasta sheets

 Use wheat-free pasta and yeast extract

 Use egg-free pasta

 Use gluten-free pasta and yeast extract

 Use potato flour instead of cornflour

1 small onion, chopped finely
1 tablespoon sunflower oil
½ clove garlic, peeled
6 oz (175 g) extra lean beef, finely minced
2 portions cooked, well-drained (squeeze out by hand) spinach, chopped finely
1 heaped teaspoon tomato purée
1 level teaspoon cornflour stirred into 3 tablespoons water
1 teaspoon thin soy sauce, or ½ teaspoon yeast extract
Freshly ground black pepper, to taste

Method

Fry the onion in the oil while you stir for 2 minutes. Crush in the garlic through a garlic press and stir in the minced beef. Stir/fry for about 2 minutes or until the meat changes colour. Add the spinach, tomato purée, cornflour/water mixture and stock of your choice. Season with black pepper and mix well. Bring to the boil and simmer while you stir for about 1 minute, or until the mixture thickens and binds together. Fill and cook as above.

Spinach and Cheese Filling for Cannelloni

Serves 2 and will fill 4–6 pasta tubes or flat pasta sheets

 Use wheat-free pasta

 Use egg-free pasta

 Use gluten-free pasta

2 portions cooked spinach, drained and squeezed dry
4 oz (110 g) cottage cheese
2 pinches freshly grated nutmeg
Freshly ground black pepper, to taste

Method

Mix all the ingredients together in a bowl. Use to fill cannelloni and cover with a tomato-based sauce and a sprinkling of Parmesan cheese before baking in the oven. (See the recipe for Tomato and Herb Sauce on p. 163).

Bolognese Filling for Cannelloni

 Use wheat-free pasta

 Use gluten-free pasta

The recipe for Bolognese Sauce on p. 162 can also be used for filling cannelloni. A half recipe will fill 8–10 tubes or flat pasta sheets. Top with white sauce and sprinkle with Parmesan cheese before baking.

Almond Sauce Filling for Cannelloni

 Use wheat-free pasta

 Use gluten-free pasta

The recipe for Almond Sauce on p. 166 can also be used for filling cannelloni, making a nourishing vegetarian dish. Cover with white sauce and sprinkle with Parmesan cheese before baking.

Macaroni Cheese

Serves 2

5 oz (150 g) wholewheat macaroni
1 tablespoon low fat dried milk granules
½ pint (300 ml) skimmed milk
1 generous knob polyunsaturated margarine
1 heaped tablespoon fine plain wholewheat flour
2 pinches nutmeg (preferably freshly grated)
2 oz (50 g) mature Cheddar cheese, finely grated
Freshly ground black pepper, to taste
1 heaped tablespoon wholewheat breadcrumbs

Method

Cook the wholewheat macaroni in boiling water (without salt) until just undercooked. Drain and put back into the pan with the lid on. Keep warm an ovenproof dish, greased with margarine. Quickly make the cheese sauce. Mix the milk granules into the skimmed milk. Melt the margarine in a heavy based saucepan and add the flour. Stir while you heat for a minute. Gradually add the milk, a little at a time, over a medium heat, stirring well all the time so that the flour mixture absorbs the milk. Put in the nutmeg and grated cheese and season with black pepper. Stir over a very low heat to melt the cheese. When the sauce is smooth stir in the partly cooked macaroni. Sprinkle the greased dish with half the breadcrumbs and spoon in the macaroni and sauce. Cover the top with the remaining breadcrumbs and bake on the top shelf of a preheated oven at Gas Mark 7, 220°C or 425°F for about 20 minutes. Serve hot with a green salad or green vegetables such as broccoli or peas. For colour serve with grilled tomatoes.

COLD PASTA FOR SALADS

When using pasta cold for salads it is best to slightly undercook it and rinse it under the cold tap. Leave it to drain well in a colander or fine mesh wire sieve. The pasta must be absolutely cold before using. The best types of pasta for salads are shapes such as bows, spirals or short tubes. If using flat noodles or spaghetti, break it into short lengths before cooking. As for hot pasta, wholewheat shapes will be the tastiest and the healthiest.

Pasta Salad with Pepper and Celery

 Use wheat-free pasta

 Avoid lemon dressing

 Use gluten-free pasta

 Use home-made salt-free pasta

 Use egg-free pasta

 Serve with nuts

For each person you will need:

About 3 heaped tablespoons cold, cooked pasta shapes
1 small stick celery, including leaves, chopped
¼ red pepper, deseeded and chopped
1 tablespoon lemon or French dressing (see recipes on pp. 269, 270)
Freshly ground black pepper, to taste

Method

Put the pasta into a bowl with the celery and red pepper. Spoon over the dressing and season with black pepper. Toss lightly to combine and serve with cold meat or fish and a green salad.

Pink Pasta Salad

 Use wheat-free pasta

 Use home-made salt-free pasta

 Use gluten-free pasta

 Serve with nuts

 Use egg-free pasta

For each person you will need:

About 3 heaped tablespoons cold, cooked pasta shapes or small tubes
1 small cooked beetroot, diced
¼ eating apple, chopped
2 small celery sticks with leaves, chopped
1 tablespoon French dressing (see recipe on p. 269)
Freshly ground black pepper, to taste

Method

Put the pasta into a bowl with the beetroot, apple and celery. Pour on the dressing and season with black pepper. Toss to combine and serve with cold meat or fish and green salad.

Pasta Salad with Prawns

 Use wheat-free pasta

 Use egg-free pasta

 Use gluten-free pasta

 Use home-made salt-free pasta

For each person you will need:

About 3 heaped tablespoons cold, cooked pasta shapes
1 heaped tablespoon defrosted prawns
1 small tomato, chopped
¼ green pepper, deseeded and chopped
1 heaped teaspoon freshly chopped parsley
1 tablespoon lemon dressing (see recipe on p. 270)
Freshly ground black pepper, to taste
¼ lettuce heart (cos, flat, etc.)
Slice of lemon for garnish

Method

Put the pasta into a bowl with the prawns and vegetables. Pour on the dressing and season with black pepper. Toss lightly to combine. Cover a plate with lettuce leaves and pile the salad in the centre. Garnish with the slice of lemon and serve.

Pasta Salad with Cheese and Tomato

 Use wheat-free pasta  Use egg-free pasta

 Use gluten-free pasta

For each person you will need:

About 3 heaped tablespoons cold, cooked pasta shapes
1 tomato, chopped
1 heaped tablespoon cottage cheese
Few raisins or 1 chopped, stoned date
½ stick celery, chopped
Freshly ground black pepper, to taste
Lettuce or watercress

Method

Put the pasta into a bowl with the tomato, cottage cheese, dried fruit and celery. Season with black pepper and toss lightly to combine. Serve on a bed of lettuce or watercress.

Pasta Salad with Ham and Peas

 Use wheat-free pasta  Use egg-free pasta

 Use gluten-free pasta

For each person you will need:

About 3 heaped tablespoons cold, cooked pasta shapes
1 slice ham, trimmed of fat and chopped
2 heaped tablespoons cooked peas
2 raw button mushrooms, chopped
1 tablespoon French dressing (see recipe on p. 269)
Freshly ground black pepper, to taste
1 teaspoon freshly chopped parsley or chives

Method

Put the pasta into a bowl with the ham, peas and mushrooms. Pour on the dressing and season with black pepper and the herb of your choice. Toss to combine and serve with a green salad.

Pasta Salad with Chicken and Pineapple

 Use wheat-free pasta

 Use egg-free pasta

 Use gluten-free pasta

 Use home-made salt-free pasta

For each person you will need:

About 3 heaped tablespoons cold, cooked pasta shapes
About 2 oz (50 g) cooked chicken meat, fat removed, chopped into small pieces
¼ pineapple ring, chopped
3 radishes, sliced
1 tablespoon lemon dressing (see recipe on p. 270)
Freshly ground black pepper, to taste
3 lettuce leaves
Few watercress sprigs
Few flaked almonds

Method

Put the pasta into a bowl with the chicken, pineapple and radishes. Spoon over the dressing and season with black pepper. Toss lightly to combine. Tear the lettuce in pieces and lay on a plate. Pile the pasta salad in the centre and lay the watercress sprigs around the edge. Sprinkle the salad with the flaked almonds and serve.

EASY PASTA DISHES

It is not always necessary to make a sauce for hot pasta. A mixture of cooked vegetables, meat, fish, etc. can be stirred into the pasta with a knob of polyunsaturated margarine and a seasoning of freshly ground black pepper. Topped with a sprinkle of cheese this makes an excellent hot dish that is very little trouble to make, and is particularly useful for people who live on their own and only need to make single portions at a time. Here are a few suggested combinations. Allow 4 oz (110 g) of raw pasta per portion.

Broccoli and Potato with Pasta

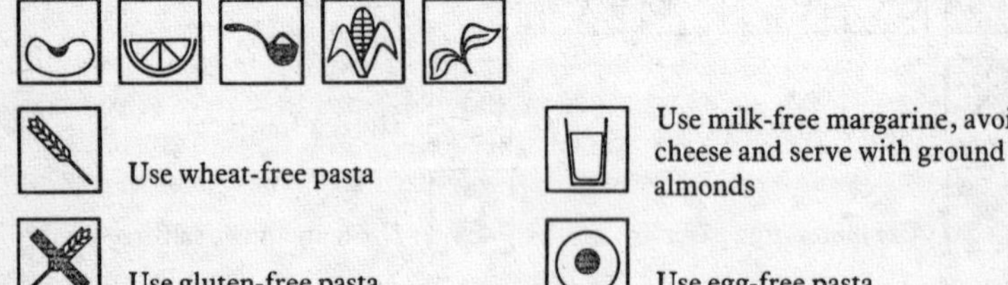

For each person you will need 1 portion of hot, cooked pasta, about 2 oz (50 g) of cooked broccoli florets and a small boiled potato. Chop the potato into small pieces. Stir into the pasta with a knob of polyunsaturated margarine and a grind of black pepper. Stir in the broccoli and serve sprinkled with finely grated Cheddar or Parmesan cheese. Serve immediately.

Prawn and Tomato with Pasta

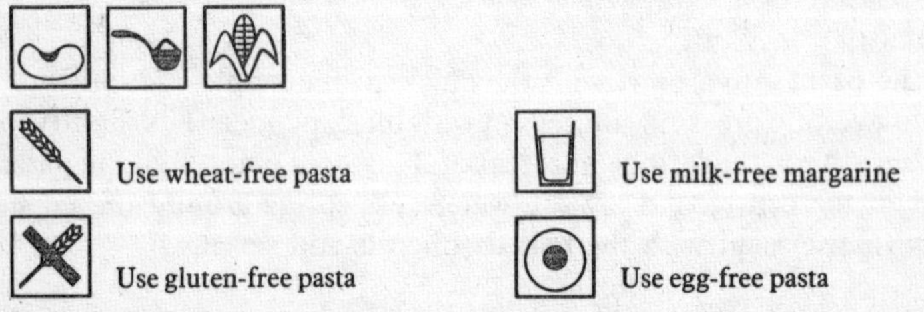

For each person you will need 1 portion of hot, cooked pasta (preferably shapes), 1 heaped tablespoon defrosted, cooked prawns and 1 small tomato. Put the prawns in a small basin and cover with boiling water. Leave for 3 minutes and then drain. Add to the pasta with a knob of polyunsaturated margarine, a squeeze of fresh lemon juice, the chopped tomato, and a grind of black pepper. Serve immediately.

Bacon and Mushrooms with Pasta

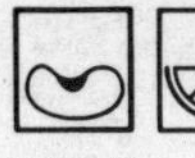   

 Use wheat-free pasta

 Use milk-free margarine

 Use gluten-free pasta

 Use egg-free pasta

For each person you will need 1 portion of hot, cooked pasta, 2 mushrooms and 1 slice unsmoked back bacon, trimmed of fat and chopped. Put a knob of polyunsaturated margarine into a small frying pan and stir/fry the bacon and mushrooms. Add to the pasta and stir in with a grind of black pepper. A tablespoon of single cream can also be used. Serve immediately.

Chicken and Mushrooms with Pasta

 Use wheat-free pasta

 Use sunflower oil instead of margarine

 Use gluten-free pasta

 Use egg-free pasta

For each person you will need 1 portion of hot, cooked pasta, 1 mushroom, chopped, about 2 oz (50 g) cooked, lean chicken meat and 1 spring onion, trimmed and chopped. Heat a knob of polyunsaturated margarine in a small frying pan and gently fry the spring onion for 1 minute. Add the chopped chicken and stir/fry for 1 minute to heat through with the mushroom. Stir into the pasta and season with black pepper to taste. Serve immediately.

CHINESE-STYLE DISHES

Chow Mein with Beef

This dish goes well with a salad of raw grated root vegetables.

Serves 1

 Use wheat-free soy sauce and pasta

 Use egg-free pasta

 Use gluten-free soy sauce and pasta

 Avoid soy sauce

 Avoid sugar

4 oz (110 g) wholewheat pasta noodles
2 teaspoons sunflower oil
¾ clove garlic, peeled
1 spring onion
½ small stick celery, chopped
1 small cabbage leaf, or 2 sprouts, shredded finely
About 2 oz (50 g) very lean frying steak or raw beef for beef olives cut into matchstick strips
1 mushroom, sliced
2 teaspoons sherry
3 pinches sugar
1 teaspoon thin soy sauce
About 4 tablespoons water
1 tablespoon defrosted prawns

Method

Cook the noodles in boiling water until tender but still firm. Drain in a colander and rinse under the cold tap. Heat the oil in a shallow-sided pan, crush in the garlic through a garlic press and put in the spring onion. Stir/fry for about 1 minute. Add the celery and greens. Stir/fry for another minute and remove to a warmed plate. Keep warm. Next stir/fry the meat with the mushrooms, over a high heat, until the meat has turned colour. Remove the meat and mushrooms with a slotted spoon and add to the warmed dish. Take the pan off the heat and add the sherry, sugar and soy sauce. Add a little water and then stir well over a gentle heat. Put the prawns into this gravy and heat through for 1 minute. Add the cooked pasta and continue heating. Stir in the mixture from the warmed plate and mix everything together. Serve immediately, with a spoon and fork.

Chow Mein with Chicken

Serves 1

 Use wheat-free pasta and soy sauce

 Use artificial sweetener

 Use gluten-free soy sauce and pasta

 Avoid soy sauce

 Use egg-free pasta

3 oz (75 g) wholewheat pasta noodles
½ skinned chicken breast, cut into matchsticks
2 teaspoons sherry
2 teaspoons sunflower oil
¼ clove garlic, peeled
1 spring onion, trimmed and chopped finely
2 oz (50 g) defrosted peas
2 teaspoons soy sauce
3 pinches sugar

Method

Cook the noodles in boiling water until tender. Drain and rinse under the cold tap. Put the chicken in a small bowl and sprinkle with the sherry. Leave to marinate for a few minutes. Heat the oil in a frying pan and crush in the garlic. Add the marinated chicken and stir/fry for about 3 minutes, or until the chicken has changed colour. Take out of the pan with a slotted spoon and keep warm on a plate. Stir/fry the spring onion and peas for 1 minute, adding a little water if they start to stick. Put in the soy sauce and sugar and stir. Add the noodles and turn them over while you heat through. Stir in the cooked chicken and serve at once.

Variation

If you want to add more protein, put in a slice of ham, trimmed of all fat and chopped, when you add the noodles.

Pasta with Ham and Beansprouts

Serves 1

 Use wheat-free pasta and soy sauce

 Use egg-free pasta

 Use gluten-free pasta and soy sauce

4 oz (110 g) wholewheat pasta noodles
3 teaspoons thin soy sauce
3 teaspoons sherry
1 spring onion, trimmed and very finely chopped
¼ clove garlic, peeled
3 tablespoons water
4 oz (110 g) fresh beansprouts (mung beans)
½ slice lean ham, cut into matchsticks

Method

Cook the noodles in boiling water until tender. Drain in a colander and rinse under the cold tap. Put the soy sauce, sherry, chopped onion, garlic (crushed in through a garlic press) and water into a small basin. Stir and pour into a large saucepan. Bring to the boil. Add the bean sprouts and ham and stir/fry for about 3 minutes. Stir in the noodles and heat through. Serve immediately.

RICE DISHES

Rice is grown in many countries of the world. There are a number of different types of rice on sale, some partly processed to remove the outer husk, others further processed to polish the grains and, even more popular, rice which has been partly cooked too, to cut down on home cooking time. Brown rice is generally considered to be the healthiest kind, being the least processed and with more taste than the blander, white varieties. Most supermarkets will sell several kinds. The husks which are removed are ground into a bran useful for people on wheat-free and gluten-free diets who cannot tolerate the more usual types of bran such as wheat bran.

The length of rice grains varies from region to region in the countries where it is grown. They can be short (as is Basmati rice), medium (as is Carolina) or long grain (as is Patna). Short grain rice is sometimes called 'pudding rice' and, as its name suggests, it is popular for making puddings.

Both savoury and sweet dishes can be made with rice. In most recipes it is used as the starch part of a meal, being very high in carbohydrate. Cooking times vary with the type and brand of rice, and instructions are always put on packets for this reason. Brown rice, being less processed, requires longer cooking time than white rice.

Most people in the western world prefer to eat rather dry rice. A few dishes, such as rice pudding with milk, and Italian risottos, call for rather more moist rice. Some types of rice go very sticky after cooking and these are generally better rinsed under a hot tap to separate the grains. Cheaper rice may need to be washed before cooking.

Rice will keep well after cooking, for up to 24 hours in the fridge, and can be reheated easily by being placed in a colander over a pan of boiling water: put a saucepan lid on the colander and the steam from the boiling water will gently heat the rice. Uncooked rice will keep indefinitely in good conditions.

Rice can be ground to make a coarse or fine flour. This is known as ground rice (coarse) or rice flour (fine).

Vegetable and Ham Risotto

Serves 1 (substantially) or 2

 Use wheat-free soy sauce

 Avoid soy sauce

 Use gluten-free soy sauce

 Avoid soy sauce

 Avoid cheese

3 teaspoons sunflower oil
½ stick celery, including leaves, chopped
¼ red or green pepper, deseeded and chopped
1 small onion, sliced thinly
1 small courgette, sliced thinly, or 4 stringless beans, chopped
1 heaped tablespoon defrosted peas or sweetcorn
About 3 oz (75 g) rice, half cooked and drained (start with 2 slightly heaped tablespoons raw rice)
½ pint (300 ml) water
2 teaspoons thin soy sauce, or 1 teaspoon yeast extract, or home-made stock to taste
1 slice cooked ham, trimmed of fat and cut into small pieces
1 tablespoon Parmesan or Cheddar cheese, finely grated
Freshly ground black pepper, to taste

Method

Heat the oil in a heavy based saucepan and stir/fry the celery, pepper and onion for about 4 minutes. Put in the courgette or beans and the peas or sweetcorn. Add the partly cooked rice and about half the water. Stir and spoon in the stock of your choice. Stir while you cook until the rice is tender, adding more of the water as required. When the rice is creamy add the ham. Heat for another minute, stir in the cheese and season to taste with the black pepper. Serve hot, immediately.

SAVOURY RICE

For each portion you will need 2 oz (50 g) long grain rice, boiled in water and drained in a colander. Stir the rice into any of the sauces which follow, heat through and serve. Dishes of this type, which include high protein ingredients such as meat, fish or cheese, can be served with a green salad. Others, with just a vegetable base, can be used instead of vegetables for serving with grilled meat or fish.

All the sauces start with onion fried in a little oil. The remaining ingredients are added with a liquid and cooked for a few minutes until tender. Recipes can be varied according to what is available or in season. Always try to add one or two colourful vegetables to make the dishes look attractive.

Savoury Rice with Peas and Ham

This goes well with a green salad.

 Avoid cheese, use ground almonds instead

For each portion you will need:

1 portion hot, cooked rice
¼ medium onion or 1 shallot, finely chopped
2 teaspoons sunflower oil
2 heaped tablespoons defrosted peas
1 slice lean ham, trimmed of fat and cut into small squares
1 heaped tablespoon grated cheese

Method

Fry the onion in the oil for 3 minutes, but do not let it brown. Add the peas and stir/fry for 2 minutes. Put in the ham and heat through while stirring. Mix into the hot rice and serve sprinkled with the cheese.

Savoury Rice with Vegetables

This savoury rice is especially good with baked or grilled fish and with chicken. If serving with other meats leave out the lemon juice.

 Use wheat-free soy sauce

 Use salt-free home-made stock

 Use gluten-free soy sauce

 Avoid soy sauce

 Omit lemon juice

For each person you will need:

1 portion hot, cooked rice
¼ medium onion, or 1 small shallot, finely sliced
2 teaspoons sunflower oil
1 finger carrot or equivalent, finely sliced
2 tablespoons water
1 heaped tablespoon defrosted peas
¼ green or red pepper, deseeded and chopped
1 medium mushroom, chopped
Few cauliflower or broccoli florets, chopped (optional)
1 teaspoon thin soy sauce, or ½ teaspoon yeast extract
Freshly ground black pepper, to taste
Squeeze fresh lemon juice

Method

Fry the onion in the oil for about 3 minutes. Add the carrot and stir/fry for another 3 minutes, adding the 2 tablespoons of water to stop the vegetables sticking. Put in the peas, pepper, mushroom and the florets. Stir/fry for about 5 minutes, or until the vegetables are tender but still a little crisp. Stir in the stock of your choice, season with the black pepper and sprinkle with the lemon juice. Mix into the hot rice and serve immediately with grilled meat or fish.

Savoury Rice with Nuts

The best rice to use for this recipe is brown long grain rice. The protein content of this dish is not sufficient for a main meal so follow it with a low fat milk-based sweet. (See recipes on pp. 333, 335 for some suggestions.

For each person you will need:

1 portion hot, cooked brown rice
¼ medium onion, finely sliced
2 teaspoons sunflower oil
¼ red or green pepper, deseeded and chopped
1 mushroom, sliced
1 heaped tablespoon chopped cashews or walnuts
2 canned tomatoes, chopped finely
½ small clove garlic, peeled
Freshly ground black pepper, to taste

Method

Fry the onion in the oil for 3 minutes, letting it brown and stirring from time to time. Add the pepper and mushroom with the nuts and stir/fry for another 5 minutes over a medium heat. (If the mixture begins to get dry add 1 tablespoon of water.) Stir in the tomatoes and crush in the garlic through a garlic press. Heat through while you stir and season with the black pepper. Mix in the hot rice and serve immediately with either green vegetables or a green salad.

Savoury Rice with Chicken and Mushrooms

This tastes good with a mixed green salad or green vegetables such as peas, broccoli, leeks or spring greens, plain boiled.

 Use wheat-free soy sauce

 Use yeast extract

 Use gluten-free soy sauce

 Use yeast extract

For each person you will need:

1 portion hot, cooked rice
¼ medium onion, sliced, or 2 spring onions, chopped finely
3 teaspoons sunflower oil
2 mushrooms, chopped
1 portion cooked chicken meat, skinned and boned, chopped into small pieces
2 teaspoons thin soy sauce, or ½ teaspoon yeast extract
Freshly ground black pepper, to taste
1 heaped teaspoon finely chopped fresh parsley (optional)

Method

Fry the onion in the oil while you stir for 2 minutes. Add the mushrooms and stir/fry for another 2 minutes. Add all the other ingredients except the parsley and heat through. Stir and sprinkle in the parsley. Serve immediately.

Rice with Eggs and Lemon

Use milk-free margarine and avoid cheese

For each person you will need:

1 portion hot, cooked long grain rice
1 egg
1 tablespoon Parmesan cheese, finely grated
1 tablespoon freshly squeezed lemon juice
Freshly ground black pepper, to taste
Small knob margarine

Method

Boil the rice in water until just tender. Drain in a colander and keep warm. Beat the egg with a fork in a small basin. Add the cheese, lemon juice and black pepper. Beat to combine. Melt the margarine in a saucepan and add the hot rice. Stir in the egg mixture and heat while you stir for about 3–4 minutes, until the egg has set but is still creamy. Serve hot immediately with a green salad or a cooked green vegetable such as broccoli or spinach.

Risotto with Prawns

Serves 1

3 oz (75 g) rice
1 shallot, chopped finely
2 teaspoons sunflower oil
½ small clove garlic, peeled
Pinch powdered bay leaves
1 small carrot, coarsely grated
3 oz (75 g) defrosted prawns
1 tablespoon dry white wine
Freshly ground black pepper, to taste
1 teaspoon freshly chopped parsley

Method

Boil the rice in water until tender. Drain in a colander and keep warm. Fry the shallot in the oil for 2 minutes, then crush in the garlic through a garlic press. Add the herb and the carrot. Stir/fry for another 2 minutes. Add the prawns and white wine. Heat gently while stirring until the prawns are hot. Stir in the rice and season with black pepper. Serve immediately, sprinkled with the parsley.

Paella

A savoury rice dish with meat, seafood and saffron.

For each person you will need:

1 portion hot, cooked rice, flavoured with a good pinch powdered saffron
1 shallot or ¼ medium onion, finely chopped
2 teaspoons sunflower oil
½ small clove garlic, peeled
2 canned tomatoes (or 1 fresh tomato, peeled)
¼ green or red pepper, deseeded and chopped
Good pinch paprika pepper
1 heaped tablespoon defrosted peas, or cooked fresh peas
½ portion cooked chicken, boned and skinned, meat cut into small pieces

½ slice ham, trimmed of all fat and cut into small squares
1 heaped tablespoon defrosted prawns
Juice ½ small lemon

Method

Fry the onion in the oil while you stir for 3 minutes, but do not let it brown. Crush in the garlic, through a garlic press. Chop the tomatoes and add to the mixture with the pepper, paprika, peas, cooked rice and chicken. Stir/fry for 3 minutes. Now add the ham and prawns. Heat through and then stir, adding the lemon juice at the last minute. Serve hot, right away, with an optional garnish of parsley and slices of lemon.

Fried Rice

This dish is very popular in Chinese restaurants where large quantities of lard are used. However, sparing use of sunflower oil is even more palatable, and much healthier and in no way spoils the dish. It is good with stir/fry vegetables, broccoli or stir/fry beansprouts.

 Use wheat-free soy sauce

 Avoid soy sauce

 Use gluten-free soy sauce

For each person you will need:

1 portion hot, cooked rice
1 spring onion, chopped finely including the green parts
2 teaspoons sunflower oil
1 mushroom, sliced finely
1 heaped tablespoon frozen prawns, defrosted
1 egg, beaten lightly
2 teaspoons thin soy sauce

Method

Fry the onion in the oil while you stir for 1 minute. Add the mushroom slices and peas. Stir/fry for another 2 minutes. Put in the prawns and heat through. Stir into the hot rice. Now put the beaten egg and soy sauce into the saucepan. Scramble lightly, taking the pan off the heat as soon as the eggs have set but are still creamy. Stir into the rice mixture and serve at once.

Chinese Style Rice with Vegetables

 Avoid serving with fish

For each person you will need:

1 portion, hot cooked rice
1 small leek, sliced finely
2 teaspoons sunflower oil
1 thumbnail-size piece of fresh ginger, peeled and chopped very finely
½ small clove garlic, peeled
2 oz (50 g) fresh green vegetables such as sprouts or spring greens, shredded
Water
Few sprigs watercress for garnish (optional)

Method

Fry the leek in the oil for a few seconds with the ginger. Crush in the garlic through a garlic press and add the shredded greens. Spoon in a tablespoon or two of water to prevent the vegetables sticking and stir/fry for 4 or 5 minutes until the vegetables are tender but still crisp. Stir into the cooked rice and garnish with the watercress. Serve immediately with grilled white fish or other kinds of Chinese-style dishes.

See also the Salads section in this book for dishes made with cold rice.

Cracked Wheat

For people who cannot eat rice, cracked wheat is a tasty substitute. It has other names – bulgar wheat, burghul wheat or bulghur wheat – and is whole wheat that has been cooked (or partly cooked), dried and then cracked. Small, medium and large grains are obtainable. The smallest grains are best used for salads and only need soaking (for at least an hour, if not more) to let them swell. The larger grains need to be brought to the boil in water, then simmered gently (as for rice).

Cooking times vary with the size of the grains, so follow the instructions on the packet. The larger grains are ideal for adding to soups and casseroles.

All sizes of grain should be squeezed dry before eating cold, as they hold a good deal of water. The best way to get the water out is to put a single thickness of clean tea towel into a colander and put the cooked grains in the centre. Draw the edges of the tea towel together and pull tightly, squeezing the resulting ball to remove the water.

MAIN MEALS WITH FISH

It is sad that as a nation we do not eat enough fish, because it can be a valuable part of the diet. Fish is a high protein food and is widely available in both fresh and frozen form. While some people find fish rather tasteless, it goes very well with herbs, tart fruits such as lemon, and tasty vegetables such as mushrooms and peppers.

Poaching Liquid for Fish

    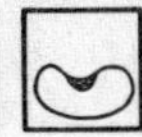     

Enough to poach 2 portions of salmon or white fish:

1 pint (600 ml) water
4 tablespoons white wine vinegar, or cheap, dry white wine
1 small onion, sliced
1 stick celery (½ stick if the flavour is strong)
1 bay leaf
1 small carrot, thinly sliced
Handful chopped parsley
1 heaped teaspoon peppercorns

Method

Put all the ingredients into a saucepan and bring to the boil. Simmer on a reduced heat for about 15–20 minutes, by which time the liquid will have reduced. Strain and use the clear liquid to poach fish.

Fish Cakes (with Fresh Fish)

These fish cakes will keep in the fridge for up to 24 hours before frying. Grilled tomatoes, peas and brown bread and butter go well with them: serve them for breakfast (without the peas), or for a light lunch or snack.

Makes 6

 Use potato flour for coating

 Use milk-free margarine

 Use potato flour for coating

 Omit lemon juice

8 oz (225 g) cod, haddock or coley fillets
3 medium potatoes, boiled and mashed
1 generous knob polyunsaturated margarine
2 heaped tablespoons freshly chopped parsley
Squeeze lemon juice
Wholewheat flour for coating
Sunflower oil for frying
Parsley for garnishing

Method

Poach the fish in water for about 15 minutes. Remove the skin and bones, flake the fish and put it into a basin with the mashed potatoes, margarine, parsley and lemon juice. Mix well to combine, using a wooden spoon. Shape into six balls. Flatten each one into a cake shape and roll in flour to coat. Heat a little vegetable oil in a heavy based frying pan and fry the fish cakes on both sides, turning them two or three times during cooking. (They should take about 6–8 minutes altogether.) Serve on hot plates, garnished with a sprig of parsley.

Fish Cakes (with Canned Fish)

Serve with salad for a main meal, or with brown bread and butter for breakfast or as a snack. The inclusion of the bones makes these a high calcium food.

Serves 1

 Use potato flour or ground rice for coating

 Use potato flour or ground rice for coating

1 small can (3½ oz/99 g) fish – tuna in oil or salmon in water
1 medium potato, boiled and mashed
1 heaped teaspoon freshly chopped parsley
Wholewheat flour for coating
Sunflower oil for frying

Method

Drain the fish of oil or water. Turn into a basin and flake/mash with a fork, including the bones and skin. Add the mashed potato and parsley. Mix with the fork to combine. Form into two or three cakes and roll in flour to coat. When required, fry in a little sunflower oil, turning the fish cakes over two or three times while cooking for 5 minutes. Eat freshly made.

Trout with Almonds

Serves 1

 Serve with potatoes

 Use oil instead of butter or margarine

 Serve with potatoes

 Avoid cornflour

 Avoid butter, use milk-free margarine

1 cleaned trout, fresh or defrosted
Cornflour, potato flour or ground rice for coating
1 tablespoon sunflower oil
1 knob butter or margarine
1 tablespoon flaked almonds
½ small lemon
Freshly ground black pepper, to taste

Method

Coat the trout with the flour of your choice. Heat the oil in a heavy based frying pan and fry the fish on both sides for 5–6 minutes, turning it with a spatula. Put the cooked fish on to a warm plate and keep warm. Clean out the pan with kitchen paper. Melt the butter or margarine and sprinkle in the almonds. Fry for a few seconds, until they begin to brown. Squeeze the lemon juice over the fish, season with pepper and sprinkle with the almonds. Serve immediately with brown bread and butter and a green side salad.

Fried Trout with Herbs

Serve with brown bread and butter, plain boiled potatoes or brown rice and broccoli or peas.

Serves 1

 Serve with rice or potatoes

 Serve with rice or potatoes

 Avoid butter or margarine, use oil instead

 Avoid butter, use milk-free margarine

 Avoid cornflour

1 cleaned trout, fresh or defrosted
Cornflour, potato flour or ground rice for coating
1 tablespoon sunflower oil
1 knob butter or margarine
½ small lemon
½ level teaspoon mixed herbs
Freshly ground black pepper, to taste
Lemon slices, for garnishing
Parsley, for garnishing

Method

Coat the trout with the flour of your choice. Heat the oil in a heavy based frying pan and fry the fish for 5 or 6 minutes on each side, turning it over carefully with a spatula. Put on to a plate and keep warm. Clean out the pan with kitchen paper, then melt the butter or margarine. Squeeze in the lemon juice and sprinkle in the herbs. Stir and pour over the trout. Serve immediately, seasoned with the pepper and garnished with lemon twists and parsley.

Baked Trout with Tarragon

Good with new boiled potatoes and a green side salad.

Serves 1

Sunflower oil
1 cleaned trout, fresh or defrosted
3 pinches dried tarragon
2 tablespoons dry white wine

Method

Preheat the oven to Gas Mark 4, 180°C or 350°F. Oil a shallow ovenproof dish with sunflower oil. Lay the washed fish in the dish and sprinkle with the herb and wine. Bake for about 30 minutes, above the centre of the oven, and serve hot with the juices.

Grilled Trout

Brown bread and butter, brown rice or new boiled potatoes and peas are good accompaniments.

Serves 1

  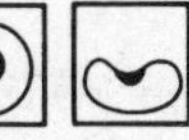   

 Serve with rice or potatoes  Avoid lemon wedges

 Serve with rice or potatoes

Sunflower oil
1 cleaned trout, fresh or defrosted
Lemon wedges
Parsley sprigs for garnish

Method

Oil the grill pan lightly with sunflower oil. Lay the fish in it and grill for 8–10 minutes. Turn the fish over carefully with a spatula and grill on the other side for another 8–10 minutes. Serve hot with lemon wedges and garnished with parsley.

Grilled Fish

Serves 1

Avoid serving with wholewheat or brown bread

Avoid butter, use milk-free margarine

Avoid serving with wholewheat or brown bread

Avoid brown bread and butter

1 portion suitable fish (see list below)
Sunflower oil for brushing

Method

Oil the grill pan lightly. Lay the fish in it and brush with oil. Grill for 5 minutes or more (depending on the thickness of the fish). Turn over carefully with a spatula and grill on the other side. Serve hot with a sauce. (See recipes for sauces on pp. 404–5).

Suitable fish

Cod steak or fillet; haddock; whiting; halibut; trout; mackerel; salmon.

Accompaniments

Boiled new potatoes with parsley; brown rice; buckwheat (boiled); wholewheat; brown bread and butter; and green salad or green vegetables such as peas, mangetout, broccoli.

Fish in Breadcrumbs

Much, much lower in fat than deep fried fish. For gluten-free and wheat-free diets use home-made special breadcrumbs or breadcrumbs made from Trufree Nos 1, 3, 4 and 5 flours – all are suitable.

Serves 1

  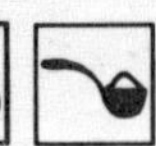 

Use wheat-free bread

Do not serve with lemon wedges

Use gluten-free bread

Avoid cornflour

1 portion filleted fish – cod, haddock, plaice or halibut
Cornflour, potato flour or rice flour
1 small egg, beaten
½ slice wholewheat bread made into fine crumbs
1 tablespoon sunflower oil
Lemon wedges

Method

Preheat the oven to Gas Mark 6, 200°C or 400°F. Oil a baking tin and put into the oven to heat. Wash the fish and dry with kitchen paper. Rub in a little flour of your choice, all over. Dip in the egg and lastly in the breadcrumbs to coat. Place the prepared fish on the baking tin and sprinkle with oil. Bake, uncovered, for 12–20 minutes, depending on the thickness of the fish. Serve immediately with wedges of lemon or tomato sauce, peas, carrots and potatoes.

Herrings in Oatmeal or Millet

Rolled porridge oats can be used instead of oatmeal. Gluten-free dieters should use millet flakes only.

Serves 1

 Use millet flakes and wheat-free bread

 Avoid butter, use milk-free margarine

 Use millet flakes and gluten-free bread

 Serve with rice or potatoes, unsalted, and use unsalted butter

2 heaped tablespoons oatmeal or millet
Freshly ground black pepper, to taste
1 herring, cleaned and filleted, head removed
Sunflower oil for frying
½ lemon

Method

Put the oatmeal or millet on to a plate and season to taste with pepper. Wash the fish in water and press into the coating to cover it all over. Heat a little sunflower oil in a heavy based frying pan and put in the fish, skin side down, to fry for about 2–3 minutes. Turn over and fry on the other side. Serve hot with grilled or stewed tomatoes and brown bread and butter or polyunsaturated margarine.

Mackerel Stuffed with Fruit

Serves 1

 Serve with wheat-free bread, or rice

 Use artificial sweetener or naturally sweet fruit

 Serve with gluten-free bread, or rice

1 fresh mackerel
About 2 oz (50 g) tart stewing fruit – gooseberries, blackberries, apricots, stoned cherries, etc.
Freshly ground black pepper, to taste
Brown sugar or fructose, to taste

Method

Get the fishmonger to fillet the mackerel from the back, leaving it still joined at the belly. Stew the fruit in a little water until it can be mashed to a purée. Season with the pepper and sugar, but do not make it too sweet. Open out the fish and spread one side with the purée, generously. Close it up again and put into a greased pie dish. Cover with a piece of greased, greaseproof paper and bake in a preheated oven, above the centre, at Gas Mark 4, 180°C or 350°F for about 30–35 minutes or until the fish is cooked. Serve with brown bread and butter.

Variation

Use a mashed kiwi fruit for the stuffing but do not stew it or add sugar.

Poached Salmon

Leaving the fish in the poaching liquid prevents it from becoming dry.

Serves 1

Poaching liquid for fish (see p. 191)
1 fresh salmon steak

Method

Put the poaching liquid into a saucepan. Warm it and then carefully lay the salmon steak in it. Bring slowly to the boil and turn down the heat to let the fish simmer for about 3 minutes. Turn the fish over with a spatula. Simmer for another 3 minutes and then remove the pan from the heat. Leave the fish to cook slowly in the liquid for a few hours. When required, lift it out carefully with a fish slice, drain and put on to a serving plate. Serve with a thick dressing from the sauces section, e.g. mayonnaise. New, boiled potatoes with parsley and salad are the traditional accompaniments for this fish.

Sole Baked in Cider

Serves 1

 Avoid wholewheat flour

 Use 1 scant tablespoon oil instead of butter or margarine

 Avoid wholewheat flour

 Avoid cornflour

 Avoid butter, use milk-free margarine

1 sole fillet
1 spring onion, chopped finely
Freshly ground black pepper, to taste
6 tablespoons cider
1 generous knob butter or polyunsaturated margarine
2 teaspoons fine wholewheat flour, corn flour or rice flour
1 teaspoon freshly chopped parsley

Method

Preheat the oven to Gas Mark 4, 180°C or 350°F. Grease an ovenproof casserole and lay the fish in it. Sprinkle with the spring onion and season to taste. Pour in the cider. Bake above the centre of the oven for about 20 minutes. Carefully lift the fish on to a warm plate and keep warm while you make the sauce. Melt the butter or margarine in a small saucepan and stir in the flour. Heat while you stir and add the cooking liquid from the casserole. The sauce will thicken and then can be beaten smooth. Stir in the parsley and pour over the fish. Serve at once with grilled tomatoes, peas or broccoli.

Whiting with Mushrooms

This is good with grilled tomatoes, peas or broccoli, and brown rice, boiled potatoes or brown bread and butter.

Serves 2

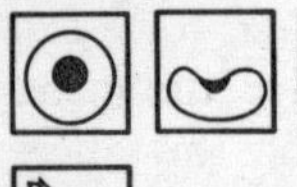 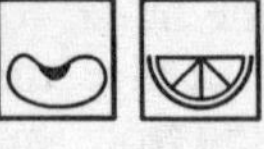  

 Serve with potatoes

 Avoid butter, use milk-free margarine

 Serve with potatoes

 Use 3 teaspoons oil

2 spring onions or shallots, finely chopped
1 tablespoon freshly chopped parsley
2 heaped teaspoons butter or polyunsaturated margarine
2 whiting, cleaned
Freshly ground black pepper, to taste
2 oz (50 g) mushrooms
Pinch powdered bay leaves
6 tablespoons white wine

Method

Mix half the onions with half the parsley and 1 teaspoon of the butter. Use to stuff the whiting. Sprinkle the remaining parsley and onions into a greased ovenproof casserole and lay the fish on top. Season with black pepper. Use the remaining butter or margarine to fry the onions. Add the mushrooms and the pinch of bay leaves and add to the casserole. Pour the wine over the fish and bring to the boil on the hob. Transfer to the oven, preheated to Gas Mark 4, 180°C or 350°F and bake for about 20 minutes. Baste with the cooking liquid every few minutes to keep the fish nice and moist. Serve in the casserole.

Prawns with Lettuce and Ginger

Serves 2

 Use potato flour instead of cornflour

4–6 oz (110–175 g) peeled prawns, defrosted
2 small pieces fresh ginger, peeled and chopped finely
1 teaspoon cornflour
2 teaspoons sunflower oil
1 small clove garlic, peeled
½ lettuce – crisp varieties such as Cos, Little Gem or Webb's Wonder, shredded coarsely
Freshly ground black pepper, to taste
About 6 tablespoons water

Method

Put the prawns on a plate and sprinkle with the ginger and cornflour. Heat the oil in a heavy based frying pan and crush in the garlic through a garlic press. Stir and add the prawns. Fry, turning them over constantly for about 2 minutes. Add the lettuce, and stir/fry for another minute. Season with black pepper and add the water. Bring to the boil and serve with plain boiled rice and stir/fry vegetables.

Fish Kebabs

Serves 1

4 oz (110 g) cod fillet, cut into cubes
½ small red, green or yellow pepper, deseeded and cut into squares
2 oz (50 g) button mushrooms, washed
1 small onion, quartered
2 bay leaves
½ small lemon, quartered

Marinade

4 tablespoons dry white wine
3 pinches paprika
Good pinch powdered bay leaves
1½ tablespoons sunflower oil
Freshly ground black pepper, to taste

Garnish

Bay leaves
Lemon wedges

Method

Thread the fish, pepper, mushrooms and onion wedges on to two long skewers, alternating them. Mix the marinade ingredients. Pour over the kebabs and leave to marinade for at least an hour, turning occasionally. When ready to cook, take the kebabs out of the marinade and put on the grill pan, under a high heat. Keep turning them until the fish starts to flake and is cooked – 5 or 6 minutes. Serve right away on a bed of rice. Put a bay leaf and a wedge of lemon on the end of each skewer as a garnish.

Marinaded Cod

Serves 1

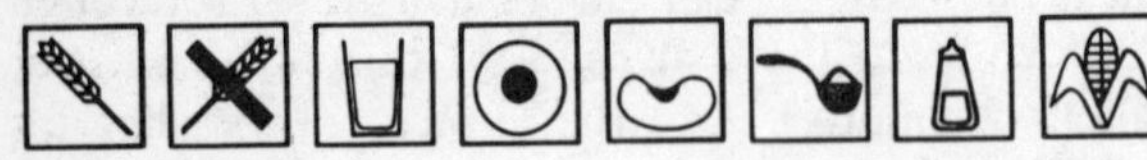

Juice ½ lemon
1 tablespoon olive oil
4 peppercorns
1 small bay leaf or pinch powdered bay leaf
½ small clove garlic, peeled
1 portion cod fillet or steak
Parsley

Method

Mix the lemon juice, oil, peppercorns and bay leaf in a small basin. Crush in the garlic through a garlic press and stir well. Spoon a little on to a plate and place the cod in it. Pour the remainder over the fish and leave to marinade for 30 minutes, turning once. Drain and put the cod into a greased casserole. Cover and bake in a preheated oven at Gas Mark 4, 180°C or 350°F, above the centre, for about 25–30 minutes. Serve hot with tomato sauce and garnished with parsley.

Baked Cod with Vegetables

Plain boiled potatoes, brown rice or buckwheat are suitable accompaniments, with broccoli or peas.

Serves 1

     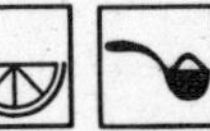 

 Use milk-free margarine

 Use sunflower oil instead of margarine

1 cod steak or fillet
1 tomato
1 small onion, chopped and fried in a little sunflower oil
Freshly ground black pepper, to taste
Butter or polyunsaturated margarine
Parsley

Method

Preheat the oven to Gas Mark 4, 180°C or 350°F. Butter a small ovenproof casserole. Put the fish into the casserole and cover with the tomato and onion. Season to taste with the pepper and dot with butter or margarine. Bake, uncovered, above the centre of the oven for about 25–30 minutes, or until the fish is cooked. Serve hot, sprinkled with the parsley.

Cod Creole

Crusty bread and a green salad are the best accompaniment.

Serves 2

 Serve with wheat-free bread

 Avoid cheese topping

 Serve with gluten-free bread

 Avoid cheese topping

8 oz (225 g) cod fillets

Marinade

Juice ¼ lemon
1 tablespoon olive oil
1 tablespoon vinegar

Sauce

Small tin tomatoes, chopped
½ small green pepper, chopped
1 small clove garlic, peeled
Freshly ground black pepper, to taste

Topping

1 tablespoon finely grated Cheddar cheese

Method

Put the fish on to a plate. Mix the lemon, oil and vinegar in a cup. Pour over the fish and leave to marinade for at least an hour, turning once. To make the sauce, put the tomatoes and green pepper into a small pan. Crush in the garlic through a garlic press. Bring to the boil and cook over a steady heat for 3 or 4 minutes while you stir. Turn down the heat and simmer for another 12–15 minutes. Grease an ovenproof casserole and put the fillets into it. Spoon in the marinade from the plate and cover with the sauce mixture. Season with black pepper and bake, covered, in a preheated oven at Gas Mark 4, 180°C or 350°F on the centre shelf. Take off the cover and sprinkle with the cheese. Put under a hot grill for 2 minutes to melt the cheese and serve at once.

Fish Pie

Serves 2

  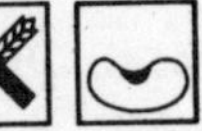  

 Avoid milk, use water and milk-free margarine

 Use potato flour instead of cornflour

 Avoid margarine

8–10 oz (225–280 g) fresh haddock or cod fillet
Pinch powdered bay leaves (optional)
1 tablespoon cornflour
¼ pint (150 ml) water
1 heaped tablespoon low fat skimmed milk powder
Few drops wine vinegar
Freshly ground black pepper to taste
1 hard boiled egg, chopped
1 heaped teaspoon freshly chopped parsley
3 medium potatoes, boiled and mashed with skimmed milk and 1 generous knob butter or polyunsaturated margarine

Method

Preheat the oven to Gas Mark 5, 190°C or or 375°F. Poach the fish in enough water to cover, with the bay leaves, for about 15 minutes on the hob. Remove the fish skin and any bones, flake and put to one side. Put the cornflour, water and milk powder into a basin. Stir until smooth. Heat in a heavy based saucepan, while you stir, until thickened. Stir in the vinegar, black pepper, egg and parsley. Mix the sauce with the fish and put into a greased pie dish. Cover with the mashed potatoes, forking to make a textured top. Bake on the top shelf until brown – about 25 minutes – and serve hot with peas and grilled tomatoes.

Fish in White Sauce

Be careful not to let the fish get dry while you are keeping it warm.

Serves 1

1 portion cod, haddock or halibut, poached in milk and flaked

Sauce

1 generous knob polyunsaturated margarine
2 heaped teaspoons wholewheat flour
About 5 tablespoons skimmed milk
Freshly ground black pepper, to taste
1 tablespoon grated Parmesan cheese
1 heaped tablespoon fresh wholewheat breadcrumbs

Method

Remove all the bones from the flaked fish. Put into a small, greased casserole and keep warm. Use a small saucepan to melt the margarine. Remove from the heat and stir in the flour. Gradually add the milk, stirring all the time. Bring to the boil and cook for 3 minutes over a lower heat, until the sauce has thickened. (Taste to see if the flour is cooked.) Season to taste and pour over the fish. Mix the cheese and breadcrumbs and sprinkle over the fish. Put under a hot grill for 3 or 4 minutes, until the top is golden and bubbling. Serve immediately with grilled tomatoes and a green vegetable, and either potatoes or rice.

Fish Casserole with Leeks

Serves 1

 Use milk-free margarine

1 knob polyunsaturated margarine
1 small leek, washed well and cut into pieces
¼ green pepper, cut into thin strips
1 heaped teaspoon tomato purée
½ cup water
Freshly ground black pepper, to taste
1 tomato
4 oz (110 g) cod or haddock fillet
2 teaspoons lemon juice
1 heaped teaspoon freshly chopped parsley

Method

Preheat the oven to Gas Mark 4, 180°C or 350°F. Melt the margarine in a small saucepan and put in the leek and green pepper. Stir/fry for about 4 minutes. Mix the tomato purée into the water and pour over the leek mixture. Continue to cook while you stir for another 3 or 4 minutes. Season to taste and put into a warmed casserole. Slice the tomatoes and stir in. Lay the fish on top and sprinkle with the lemon juice and parsley. Put a lid on and bake for about 15 minutes, above the centre of the oven. Serve hot from the oven with thick slices of wholewheat bread or brown rice.

Fish Hotpot

Serves 1

 Use milk-free margarine

2 medium old potatoes, peeled
1 generous knob butter or polyunsaturated margarine
½ small clove garlic
About 6 oz (175 g) cod, haddock or plaice, filleted
Freshly ground black pepper, to taste
1 small onion, sliced thinly
1 heaped teaspoon freshly chopped parsley

Method

Parboil the potatoes for about 10 minutes. Drain well and cut into thin slices. Grease a small ovenproof dish with a little of the butter or margarine. Rub the cut end of the garlic clove over the greased area. Put in the fish, skinned and cut into pieces. Season to taste with pepper. Cover first with the onion slices and then the potato slices, overlapping them neatly. Dot with what is left of the butter or margarine and bake in a preheated oven at Gas Mark 4, 180°C or 350°F, above centre, for about 35 minutes. Sprinkle with the parsley and serve with peas and tomatoes.

White Fish Stew

Serves 2

 Serve with wheat-free bread  Serve with gluten-free bread

8 oz (225 g) cod or haddock fillets
Water
¼ pint (150 ml) water mixed with 1 heaped tablespoon low fat dried milk granules
1 onion, chopped finely
3 medium potatoes, peeled and cut into thick slices
1 small can tomatoes
1 heaped teaspoon freshly chopped parsley
Freshly ground black pepper, to taste

Method

Poach the fish in water to cover for about 15 minutes, over a gentle heat. Lift out with a spatula and put on to a plate, removing the skin and any bones. Strain the cooking liquid into a large saucepan. Add the milk and the vegetables. Season with black pepper and add more water, if required, to cover the vegetables. Bring to the boil, cover and simmer on a lower heat for about 20 minutes, or until the vegetables are tender. Flake the fish and add to the stew. Sprinkle in the parsley and serve hot with thickly sliced wholewheat bread.

White Fish with Parsley Sauce

Serves 1

4–6 oz (110–175 g) fresh haddock fillets (preferably tail end)
1 small onion, thinly sliced into rings
Under ¼ pint (150 ml) water
1 heaped tablespoon low fat dried milk granules
1 generous knob butter or polyunsaturated margarine
2 heaped teaspoons wholewheat flour
Freshly ground black pepper, to taste
1 slightly heaped tablespoon freshly chopped parsley

Method

Put the fish into a heavy based pan, cutting it in half if it does not fit. Cover with the onion rings. Mix the water and milk granules and whisk until absorbed. Pour over the fish and slowly heat until the liquid is almost boiling. Reduce the heat so that the fish simmers and continue cooking for about 12–15 minutes, until the fish is done. Remove the fish and onion with a fish slice and put on to a warmed serving plate. Keep warm while you make the sauce. Pour the cooking liquid into a jug. Melt the butter or margarine in the pan and stir in the flour. Take off the heat. Mix to a paste and gradually add the liquid from the jug while you stir. Put back over a moderate heat, stirring all the time, and cook until thickened – about 2 or 3 minutes. Season with pepper and stir in the parsley. Pour over the fish and serve with grilled tomatoes and peas, rice or potatoes.

MAIN MEALS WITH MEAT

MEAT ROASTING TABLES

Quick Roasts

The following meats can be quick roasted, starting with an oven temperature of Gas Mark 8, 230°C or 450°F for the first 15 minutes (this will seal the meat), and lowering the heat after 15 minutes to Gas Mark 5, 190°C or 375°F for the remaining cooking time.

Beef (rare)
15 minutes to the pound and 15 minutes extra.

Beef (well done)
20 minutes to the pound and 20 minutes extra.

Chicken
20 minutes to the pound and 20 minutes extra.

Lamb
25 minutes to the pound and 25 minutes extra.

Veal
30 minutes to the pound and 30 minutes extra.

Pork
35 minutes to the pound and 35 minutes extra. (Pork must always be well cooked, never underdone.)

Slow Roasts

The following meats can be slow roasted at a temperature of Gas Mark 3, 170°C or 325°F.

Beef
40 minutes to the pound and 45 minutes extra.

Chicken
Large birds (over 4 lb) – 25 minutes to the pound and 25 minutes extra.

Lamb
45 minutes per pound and 45 minutes extra.

Veal
50 minutes to the pound and 50 minutes extra.

Pork
Unsuitable for slow roasting: see quick roasting chart.

Calculating the Cooking Time
Weigh the meat and multiply by the number of minutes suggested, e.g. to quick roast a 3 lb chicken = 3 × 20 minutes (= 60 minutes) plus 20 minutes over (60 + 20 = 80 minutes), making the total cooking time 1 hour and 20 minutes. Where the joint does not work out exactly to the pound, use your common sense to calculate to the nearest part measurement (e.g. suppose the chicken weighed 2½ lb and the allowance is 20 minutes to the pound, then the ½ lb would only require 10 minutes. The 2 lb would mean a calculation of 40 minutes and the extra ½ lb 10 minutes, making a sub total of 50 minutes. With the extra 20 minutes this would make a total of 70 minutes (or 1 hour and 10 minutes).)

Meat that has a bone through the middle, such as a leg of lamb, will not need the extra cooking time. Just calculate how much it weighs and multiply by the number of minutes required. Do not add on the extra. Extra large joints will cook better with a metal skewer put through the biggest part to conduct the heat. This will prevent the outside of the joint being cooked while the inside is still raw.

Allow several hours to defrost meat that has been frozen, and up to a day for large joints.

Liver with Orange
Serve with boiled or mashed potatoes, brown rice or buckwheat, peas and carrots or a green vegetable. Also good with stir/fry mixed vegetables.

Serves 2

 Avoid wholewheat flour and use wheat-free soy sauce

 Avoid soy sauce

 Use gluten-free soy sauce

 Avoid cornflour and soy sauce

4 oz (110 g) lambs' liver, prepared and sliced
Cornflour, wholewheat flour, potato flour or rice flour for coating
2 tablespoons sunflower oil
Lean only from 2 rashers unsmoked back bacon, cut into small squares
2 oranges – 1 made into juice and the other peeled and cut into round slices
3 teaspoons thin soy sauce, or 1 teaspoon yeast extract dissolved in a little hot water
Freshly ground black pepper, to taste
Water or vegetable strainings

Method

Dip the liver in the flour of your choice to coat the slices all over. Heat the oil in a frying pan. Put in the liver and bacon and fry gently, turning them over, for 4 or 5 minutes. Add the orange juice, orange slices and stock. Season with pepper and heat through gently, adding a little water or vegetable strainings to make the gravy. Serve at once.

Liver Casserole

Serves 2

 Use wheat-free soy sauce

 Avoid soy sauce

 Use gluten-free soy sauce

1 medium onion, sliced thinly
1 cooking apple, peeled, cored and sliced thinly
2 oz (50 g) button mushrooms (or 1 large mushroom, sliced)
8 oz (225 g) lambs' liver, sliced
1 slice lean ham, fat removed and lean chopped
2 tomatoes, sliced
2 heaped teaspoons tomato purée
About ¼ pint (150 ml) hot water
3 teaspoons thin soy sauce
Freshly ground black pepper, to taste
2 heaped teaspoons freshly chopped parsley

Method

Preheat the oven to Gas Mark 4, 180°C or 350°F. Grease an ovenproof casserole and spread a little of the onion over the base. Cover with a few of the apple slices and mushrooms and half the liver and ham. Continue with more layers in this way. Top with tomato slices. Mix the tomato purée into the hot water and add the soy sauce. Stir well and pour over the casserole. Season to taste with black pepper and put on the lid. Cook above the centre shelf for about 1¼ hours and serve sprinkled with the parsley. Mashed potatoes and a green vegetable are good accompaniments.

Beefburgers

Use wheat-free and gluten-free bread, flour and soy sauce for special diets.

Makes 4

 Use wheat-free bread, flour and soy sauce

 Use gluten-free bread, flour and soy sauce

8 oz (225 g) lean stewing beef
1 slice wholewheat bread or granary bread, made into breadcrumbs
½ medium onion, chopped finely
1 small egg (or ½ large), beaten
Freshly ground black pepper, to taste
Pinch dried, mixed herbs
2 teaspoons thin soy sauce
Wholewheat flour for coating
Sunflower oil or similar for frying

Method

Cut off and discard all the visible fat from the meat. Mince the meat finely and put into a basin with the breadcrumbs, onion, egg, seasoning, herbs and soy sauce. Mix well and shape into flat cakes. Dip in flour to coat all over and fry in a little oil, first on one side for about 3 minutes and then on the other. Serve instead of slices of meat with a gravy and vegetables, or serve inside a split wholewheat bap with lettuce and tomato.

Meatballs

Serves 4

 Use wheat-free bread, flour and soy sauce

 Use gluten-free bread, flour and soy sauce

Use the recipe for Beefburgers but instead of the egg use half a finely grated cooking apple. Shape into balls, roll in flour and fry in a little sunflower oil, turning them to cook evenly for 5–6 minutes. Serve with gravy and vegetables.

Chilli con Carne Casserole

Serves 2

 Avoid wholewheat flour and use wheat-free soy sauce

 Use artificial sweetener to taste, and use home-made beans

 Avoid wholewheat flour and use gluten-free soy sauce

 Avoid soy sauce

 Avoid soy sauce

1 medium onion, sliced
1 tablespoon sunflower oil
8 oz (225 g) lean stewing beef, trimmed of all fat and cut into pieces
1 small clove garlic, peeled
1 tablespoon flour – wholewheat, cornflour, potato flour or rice flour
1 level teaspoon chilli powder
¼ pint (150 ml) water
1 tablespoon thin soy sauce, or 2 teaspoons yeast extract
1 small can tomatoes, chopped, with their juice
3 or 4 good pinches brown sugar
1 small can cooked red kidney beans

Method

Preheat the oven to Gas Mark 3, 170°C or 325°F. Use a flameproof casserole to fry the onions in the oil, for 4 minutes, while you stir. Add the meat and crush in the garlic through a garlic press. Fry, turning the meat over to brown, for another 3 or 4 minutes. Sprinkle in the flour and the chilli powder. Take off the heat and stir well. Put back on the heat and gradually add the water, stirring all the time. Add the soy sauce, tomatoes and sugar. Bring to the boil and transfer to the oven, on the centre shelf. Cook for about 3 hours or until the meat is tender. Just before serving heat the beans in their juice. Drain and add to the casserole. Serve with brown rice and a green vegetable.

Beef Casserole with Prunes

Look at the casserole after an hour. If it seems too dry, add a little boiling water.

Serves 2

 Avoid wholewheat flour and use wheat-free soy sauce

 Avoid soy sauce

 Avoid wholewheat flour and use gluten-free soy sauce

 Avoid soy sauce

2 tablespoons flour – wholewheat, cornflour, rice flour or potato flour
8 oz (225 g) lean stewing beef, trimmed of fat and cut into small pieces
2 tablespoons sunflower oil
1 medium onion, sliced
About ½ pint (300 ml) water
5 small carrots or 2 medium old carrots, sliced
3 teaspoons thin soy sauce, or 1 generous teaspoon yeast extract dissolved in 3 teaspoons boiling water
1 generous teaspoon tomato purée
Freshly ground black pepper, to taste
6 unsoaked prunes, stones removed
1 tablespoon freshly chopped parsley

Method

Preheat the oven to Gas Mark 2, 150°C or 300°F, and put in a flame-proof casserole to warm. Put the flour of your choice on to a plate and roll the meat in it to coat it all over. Heat 1 tablespoon of the oil in a saucepan and fry the meat, turning the pieces over to brown them. Remove with a slotted spoon to the warmed casserole. Add the remaining tablespoon of oil to the pan and fry the onion while you stir for 4 minutes. Take out with a slotted spoon and transfer to the casserole. Keep warm. Use the flour left on the plate to sprinkle into the pan. Stir and gradually add the water. Add the carrots, soy sauce, tomato purée, pepper to taste, and the prunes. Bring to the boil while you stir. Spoon into the casserole and stir. Put back into the oven on the shelf above centre and cook for about 2½ hours. Sprinkle with chopped parsley and serve with jacket potatoes or brown rice and a green vegetable.

Beef Stew with Vegetables

Serves 3 and can be reheated

Avoid wholewheat flour and use wheat-free soy sauce

Avoid soy sauce, use 2 level teaspoons yeast extract

Avoid wholewheat flour and use gluten-free soy sauce

Avoid cornflour and soy sauce (use 2 level teaspoons yeast extract)

8 oz (225 g) lean braising steak
Wholewheat flour, potato flour, rice flour or cornflour for coating the meat
2 medium onions, sliced
3 teaspoons sunflower oil
About 4 oz (110 g) swede, cut into cubes
2 large potatoes, cut into cubes
2 medium carrots, sliced thickly
1 medium parsnip, sliced thickly
1 small turnip, cubed
2 oz (50 g) mushrooms, sliced
Water
1 clove garlic, peeled
1 tablespoon soy sauce

More wholewheat flour, potato flour, rice flour or cornflour for thickening the gravy
Freshly ground black pepper, to taste

Method

Trim and discard all the fat from the meat. Cut the meat into cubes, put a little flour of your choice on to a plate and roll the meat cubes in it to coat them all over. Preheat the oven to Gas Mark 6, 200°C or 400°F. Use a flameproof casserole to fry the onion in the oil for 3 or 4 minutes, while you stir. Push to one side of the casserole, tipping it to let the oil run over the base. Put in the coated meat cubes and fry, turning them over to seal. Put in the vegetables and enough water to cover. Stir and bring to the boil. Crush in the garlic through a garlic press and add the soy sauce. Give the stew a good stir and bring back to the boil. Put on the lid and transfer to the middle shelf of the oven. Cook for about 45 minutes, then put back on the hob. Stir a tablespoon of the flour of your choice into 4 tablespoons of water. Mix into the stew and bring back to the boil. Cook while you stir until the gravy has thickened. Put the lid on and put the casserole back into the oven to finish cooking for another 10–20 minutes, until the meat is tender. Season to taste with black pepper and serve hot with thick slices of wholewheat bread.

Beef Stew with Oatmeal

Serves 2

Use wheat-free soy sauce and serve with wheat-free bread

Avoid soy sauce, use 2 level teaspoons yeast extract

Avoid soy sauce, use 2 level teaspoons yeast extract

1 tablespoon sunflower oil
Lean only from 2 slices back bacon, chopped
8 oz (225 g) stewing beef, trimmed of fat and cubed
2 medium potatoes, peeled and sliced
1 carrot, sliced
1 small parsnip, sliced
¼ small cabbage, shredded
Freshly ground black pepper, to taste

Good pinch powdered bay leaves
¼ teaspoon dried thyme
¼ pint (150 ml) water
1 tablespoon soy sauce
2 young leeks, chopped finely
1 tablespoon fine oatmeal

Method

Heat the oil in a heavy based saucepan with a well-fitting lid. Fry the bacon and meat, turning the pieces over until evenly browned – about 6 minutes. Add all the other ingredients except the leeks and oatmeal. Bring to the boil and simmer gently with the lid on for about 1¾ hours. Add the leeks and oatmeal and bring back to the boil. Simmer with the lid on for another 25 minutes. Serve with thick slices of wholewheat bread.

Beef and Bean Casserole

Serves 2

 Avoid wholewheat flour, use wheat-free soy sauce

 Avoid wholewheat flour, use gluten-free soy sauce

 Avoid soy sauce, use 1 level teaspoon yeast extract

 Use home-made, sugar-free beans

 Avoid cornflour and soy sauce, use 1 level teaspoon yeast extract

1 medium onion, sliced
2 teaspoons sunflower oil
Flour for coating – wholewheat, rice, potato or cornflour
6 oz (175 g) lean braising beef, trimmed of fat and cut into small pieces
2 canned tomatoes, chopped
1 medium carrot, sliced
2 mushrooms, chopped
2 teaspoons soy sauce
½ clove garlic, peeled
Water

Flour for thickening the gravy, as above
3 heaped tablespoons cooked haricot beans – red, green or white
Freshly ground black pepper, to taste

Method

Preheat the oven to Gas Mark 3, 170°C or 325°F. Use a flameproof casserole to fry the onion in the oil, while you stir. Put a little of the flour of your choice on a plate and use it to coat the meat. Add the meat to the casserole and stir/fry for 3 minutes to seal. Add the tomatoes, carrot, mushrooms, soy sauce and the garlic crushed through a garlic press. Put in enough water to cover and bring to the boil. Put the lid on and simmer for a minute. Transfer to the oven, above the centre shelf. Cook for 50 minutes and then put back on the hob. Mix 2 teaspoons of the flour of your choice with 2 tablespoons of water. Stir into the casserole and cook while you stir until the gravy has thickened. Put in the drained haricot beans and bring back to the boil. Put the lid on and put the casserole back in the oven for another 10 minutes or until the meat is tender. Season to taste with pepper and serve hot with potatoes or rice and a green vegetable.

Beef Casserole with Carrots

Serves 2

Avoid wholewheat flour and use wheat-free soy sauce

Avoid soy sauce, use 1 teaspoon yeast extract

Avoid wholewheat flour, and use gluten-free soy sauce

Avoid cornflour and soy sauce, use 1 teaspoon yeast extract

2 teaspoons sunflower oil
1 medium onion, sliced
Flour for coating – wholewheat, rice, cornflour or potato
8 oz (225 g) very lean braising beef, trimmed of fat and cut into small pieces
2 teaspoons soy sauce
2 medium carrots, sliced
2 mushrooms, chopped
½ clove garlic, peeled

Freshly ground black pepper, to taste
Water
Flour for thickening the gravy, as above

Method

Preheat the oven to Gas Mark 3, 170°C or 325°F. In a flameproof casserole fry the onion in the oil while you stir for about 4 minutes. Put a little of the flour of your choice on to a plate and use to coat the meat. Put into the casserole and stir/fry, turning the meat over to seal for about 4 minutes. Pour in a little water, the soy sauce, and the carrots and mushrooms. Crush in the garlic through a garlic press and stir well. Season with black pepper and bring to the boil, adding enough water to cover. Put on the lid and transfer to the oven, above the centre shelf. Cook for about 60–70 minutes, depending on the meat. Put the casserole back on the hob. Mix 2 teaspoons of the flour of your choice with 2 tablespoons of water and add to the casserole. Stir while you cook for 3 minutes, until the gravy has thickened. Serve hot with jacket potatoes and peas, broccoli, mangetout, spring greens or sprouts.

Beef Casserole with Ginger

Serves 2

 Use artificial sweetener

 Avoid wholewheat flour, use wheat-free soy sauce

 Avoid soy sauce, use 1 heaped teaspoon yeast extract

 Avoid wholewheat flour, use gluten-free soy sauce

 Avoid cornflour and soy sauce, use 1 heaped teaspoon yeast extract

2 teaspoons sunflower oil
Small piece fresh ginger, peeled and chopped very finely
1 medium onion, sliced
8 oz (225 g) lean braising beef, trimmed of fat and cut into small pieces
Flour for coating – rice, potato, wholewheat or cornflour
1 small can tomatoes, chopped
2 heaped teaspoons tomato purée
3 teaspoons soy sauce
Water

½ clove garlic, peeled
Freshly ground black pepper, to taste
Flour for thickening, as above
Sugar, if necessary
Freshly chopped parsley for garnish

Method

Heat the oil in a flameproof casserole. Fry the ginger for a few seconds, and then put in the onion. Stir/fry for 3 minutes and push to one side of the casserole. Coat the beef in the flour of your choice and add to the casserole. Stir/fry, turning the meat over to seal it. Stir in the tomatoes, purée, soy sauce and enough water to cover. Crush in the garlic through a garlic press. Season with black pepper and put on the lid. Bring to the boil then transfer to an oven preheated to Gas Mark 3, 170°C or 325°F, above the centre shelf. After 50 minutes, take out of the oven. Mix 2 teaspoons of the flour of your choice with 2 tablespoons of water and add to the casserole. Bring to the boil and cook while you stir for 2 minutes, until the gravy has thickened. Taste and add a few pinches of sugar if you think it necessary to round off the flavour. Put the lid on and put the casserole back in the oven for another 20–30 minutes, or until the meat is tender. Garnish with parsley and serve with brown rice and a green vegetable.

Beef Cooked in Stout

Serves 2

Avoid soy sauce, use 1 teaspoon yeast extract

Avoid cornflour and soy sauce, use 1 teaspoon yeast extract

Use artificial sweetener

8 oz (225 g) lean braising beef, trimmed of all fat and cut into small cubes
1 tablespoon sunflower oil
1 medium onion, sliced
Flour – rice, potato, wholewheat or cornflour
2 teaspoons soy sauce or other stock

¼ pint (150 ml) stout
About ¼ pint (150 ml) water
Freshly ground black pepper, to taste
Good pinch dried mixed herbs
Pinch grated nutmeg
Pinch sugar
1 generous teaspoon wine vinegar

Method

Stir/fry the meat in the oil in a flameproof casserole. Take out after about 4 minutes, using a slotted spoon, and keep warm on a plate. Put in the onions and fry until brown. Sprinkle in 2 teaspoons of the flour of your choice and cook/stir for 1 minute. Now add the soy sauce and the stout. Stir and add the water. Season with black pepper and bring to the boil. Put in the herbs, spice, sugar and vinegar. Stir and add the meat from the plate. Add more water to cover if needed. Bring to the boil, put on the lid and bake on the centre shelf for up to 1½ hours. Serve hot with peas and boiled potatoes.

Veal with Mushrooms

Serves 1

 Use wheat-free soy sauce

 Avoid soy sauce, use 1 teaspoon yeast extract

 Use gluten-free soy sauce

2 teaspoons sunflower oil
2 spring onions, chopped
2 oz (50 g) mushrooms, sliced
1 small fillet of veal (escalope), cut into slivers
2 slightly heaped tablespoons low fat dried milk granules
¼ pint (150 ml) water
2 teaspoons soy sauce or other stock
2 teaspoons cornflour mixed into 2 tablespoons water
3 pinches paprika
2 pinches grated nutmeg
Pinch freshly ground black pepper

Method

Heat the oil in a heavy based frying pan and fry the onions for about 30 seconds, while you stir. Put in the mushrooms and stir/fry for a minute, turning them over. Push to one side and tip the pan to let the juices run over the base. Put in the veal strips and stir/fry over a high heat for 2 or 3 minutes, until the meat has turned white. Take everything out of the pan with a slotted spoon and keep it warm. Mix the milk granules into the water, soy sauce and cornflour, and stir to combine. Pour into the pan and bring gently to the boil. Lower the heat and simmer gently, stirring, for 1½–2 minutes until it thickens. Add the paprika, nutmeg and black pepper. Stir and add the meat mixture. Mix lightly and serve right away with a green vegetable and mashed potato or brown rice.

Spiced Pork Casserole with Plums

Serves 2

 Use artificial sweetener

1 tablespoon sunflower oil
Lean meat from 2 pork chops or fillets
4–6 plums
Brown sugar or fructose, to taste
4 good pinches allspice
5 tablespoons cheap red wine
Freshly ground black pepper, to taste

Method

Preheat the oven to Gas Mark 4, 180°C or 350°F. Put a shallow casserole in to warm. Heat the oil in a frying pan and fry the pork, turning the pieces over to seal them. Transfer to the warmed casserole. Stew the plums in a little water with sugar to taste and the spice. Allow to cool slightly, then remove the stones and purée in a blender or mash/chop finely. Stir into the red wine and add the black pepper to taste. Pour over the pork, adding hot water if needed to make the liquid cover the meat. Put on the lid and bake above the centre of the oven for about 45 minutes or until the pork is tender. Serve with green and root vegetables, jacket potatoes or brown rice.

Ham in Cider

Serve hot with boiled root vegetables and Parsley Sauce (see recipe on p. 404). Ham is also good served cold, sliced very thinly, with jacket potatoes and mixed salads.

Serves 8–10

3½ lb (1.5 kg) unsmoked gammon
2 pints (1.2 l) cider
1 onion
Pinch powdered cloves
Few sprigs parsley
Pinch powdered bay leaves
2 pinches dried thyme
3 tablespoons brown sugar
Cloves

Method

Soak the gammon overnight in a large bowl of cold water. (The joint should be tied tightly with string around the middle in two or three places.) Put the gammon into a large saucepan and cover with the cider. Put in the onion, powdered cloves, parsley, bay leaf and thyme. Bring to the boil and simmer for about 1½ hours. Remove the joint from the saucepan and place in a roasting tin. Preheat the oven to Gas Mark 7, 220°C or 425°F. Carefully cut away the rind, leaving only a thin layer of fat on the joint. Spread the brown sugar over the fat and stud with the cloves in a neat pattern. Roast in the oven, above the centre, for about 1 hour.

Chicken with Tarragon

Serves 2

 Use wheat-free soy sauce

 Use gluten-free soy sauce

 Avoid soy sauce, use 1 teaspoon yeast extract

 Avoid soy sauce, use 1 teaspoon yeast extract, and use potato flour instead of cornflour

1 spring onion
1 tablespoon sunflower oil
1 clove garlic, peeled and put through a garlic press
2 chicken breasts, skinned and cut into slivers
2 teaspoons cornflour
2 teaspoons soy sauce
2 tablespoons water
¼ pint (150 ml) vegetable strainings or water
1 teaspoon freshly chopped tarragon, or ½ teaspoon dried
Freshly ground black pepper, to taste

Method

Chop the spring onion and fry in the oil for 1 minute. Crush in the garlic and fry for a few seconds while you stir. Put in the slivers of chicken and stir/fry for about 3 minutes. Take off the heat. In a small basin mix the cornflour, soy sauce and 2 tablespoons of water. When blended stir in the vegetable strainings. Mix well. Take the chicken mixture out of the pan with a slotted spoon and put on to warmed serving plates. Keep warm. Pour the cornflour mixture into the pan, sprinkle in the tarragon and bring to the boil. Stir well with a wooden spoon while you simmer for 2 minutes. Season with pepper. Pour this hot gravy over the chicken mixture and serve with vegetables and either potatoes or rice.

Chicken and Mushroom Casserole

Serves 2

 Avoid wholewheat flour and use wheat-free soy sauce

 Avoid soy sauce

 Avoid wholewheat flour and use gluten-free soy sauce

 Avoid cornflour and soy sauce

2 chicken portions, breast or legs, skinned
2 tablespoons flour – wholewheat, cornflour, rice or potato flour
2 tablespoons sunflower oil
½ medium onion, sliced
3 oz (75 g) mushrooms, sliced

1 small tin tomatoes, chopped, with their juice
¼ pint (150 ml) water
2 teaspoons thin soy sauce, or 1 teaspoon yeast extract
Freshly ground black pepper, to taste
2 tablespoons sherry
1 tablespoon freshly chopped parsley, for garnish

Method

Preheat the oven to Gas Mark 3, 170°C or 325°F. Put in a casserole to warm. Rub the chicken with the flour of your choice. Heat 1 tablespoon of the oil in a frying pan and fry the onion while you stir for 3 or 4 minutes. Remove with a slotted spoon and keep warm in the casserole. Add the remaining tablespoon of oil and fry the coated chicken, turning the meat over to brown it. Add to the onions in the casserole. Put the mushrooms and tomatoes into the pan and cook for 3 minutes. Pour in the water and soy sauce. Season to taste with black pepper and bring to the boil. Pour over the chicken and onions and put on the casserole lid. Bake on the centre shelf for about 1 hour. Spoon in the sherry and put back in the oven for another 10–15 minutes. Serve with the parsley sprinkled over the top; good with brown rice or potatoes and a green vegetable.

Cold Chicken

A chicken cooked this way will be nice and moist. Leftover meat can be used to make risottos, sandwiches, pies, etc.

Serves 6

   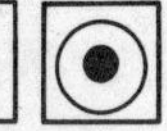    

1 oven ready fresh chicken, about 3 lb (1.5 kg) weight
About 1 pint (600 ml) water
½ lemon, chopped
Handful parsley sprigs
3 grinds black pepper
Small pinch powdered bay leaves
1 stalk celery, cut into pieces
Pinch celery seeds
1 carrot, sliced
4 pickling onions, peeled (use ½ medium onion, peeled, if these are not available)

Method

Wash the chicken, removing the giblets from the inside. Choose a saucepan that has a tightly fitting lid. Pour in the water and then add all the remaining ingredients except for the chicken. Bring to the boil and put in the chicken. Put the lid on firmly and simmer for about 1 hour. Leave the chicken in the saucepan with the vegetables and let it cool down overnight. When ready to eat take out the chicken and put on to a carving dish. Serve cold with salads and new potatoes or jacket potatoes.

Casserole of Chicken in Red Wine

Serves 2

 Avoid cornflour, use potato or rice flour

2 teaspoons sunflower oil
½ medium onion, sliced
Lean from 1 rasher unsmoked back bacon, cut into strips
2 chicken portions, breast or leg, skinned
2 oz (50 g) mushrooms, sliced
1 clove garlic, peeled
About 6 tablespoons red wine – a cheap one will do
Pinch dried mixed herbs
Small pinch powdered bay leaves
Freshly ground black pepper, to taste
Water
2 teaspoons cornflour or other thickener

Method

Preheat the oven to Gas Mark 4, 180°C or 350°F. Heat the oil in a flameproof casserole and fry the onion. Put in the bacon and chicken. Fry, turning them over to seal, for about 3 minutes. Add the mushrooms and crush in the garlic through a garlic press. Put in the wine, herbs and black pepper and top up with enough water to cover. Bring to the boil, put on the lid and put in the oven, above the centre, to cook for 35–40 minutes. When ready to serve put back on the hob. Mix the cornflour with 2 tablespoons of water and add to the casserole. Bring to the boil and then turn down the heat while stirring. When the gravy has thickened – after about 1½–2 minutes – remove from the heat and serve with green vegetables and either potatoes or brown rice.

Plain Roast Chicken with Herb Gravy

This is a low fat method of roasting chicken. The carcass can be boiled to make stock for soup.

Serves 4 (or 2 hot servings and 2 cold)

 Avoid wholewheat flour and use wheat-free soy sauce

 Avoid soy sauce, use 2 level teaspoons yeast extract

 Avoid wholewheat flour and use gluten-free soy sauce

 Avoid cornflour and soy sauce

1 fresh chicken, 2½–3 lb (1.25–1.5 kg)
3 rashers unsmoked streaky bacon
1 level tablespoon cornflour, fine wholewheat flour or potato flour
1 tablespoon thin soy sauce
½ level teaspoon dried mixed herbs
½ pint (300 ml) vegetable strainings

Method

Wash out the chicken. Lay breast upwards in a roasting tin and put the rashers over the breast to keep it moist. Put on the middle shelf of an oven preheated to Gas Mark 8, 230°C or 450°F for about 15 minutes. After that reduce the heat to Gas Mark 5, 190°C or 375°F for the remainder of the cooking time. (Calculate the total cooking time, allowing 20 minutes to the pound and 20 minutes extra.) Five minutes before the end of the cooking time take a sharp knife and prick the skin, remove the bacon and put back into the oven. The fat will run out of the meat. Then take the chicken out of the roasting tin and keep hot in the oven on a carving dish. Mix the flour of your choice, soy sauce and herbs. Add a little of the vegetable strainings and stir well. Gradually add the remaining liquid and stir again. Pour the fat out of the roasting tin and wipe out with kitchen paper, taking care not to disturb the brown juices. Add the gravy mixture and rub the base of the tin with a wooden spoon to release the juices. Bring to the boil and cook briskly while you stir for 1 minute until the gravy has thickened. Serve hot with the chicken, green vegetables and roast potatoes. (See the recipe on p. 263 for Dry Roast Potatoes.)

Chicken Casserole

Serves 2

 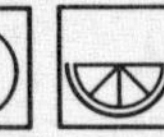 

 Use wheat-free soy sauce

 Avoid soy sauce

 Use gluten-free soy sauce

 Avoid soy sauce, use 1 teaspoon yeast extract

1 tablespoon sunflower oil
2 spring onions, chopped
2 portions raw chicken, skinned
Lean from 2 slices unsmoked back bacon, cut into strips
2 mushrooms
2 tomatoes
8 oz (225 g) new potatoes, unpeeled
Freshly ground black pepper, to taste
¼ pint (150 ml) hot water
2 teaspoons thin soy sauce
1 heaped teaspoon freshly chopped parsley

Method

Preheat the oven to Gas Mark 4, 180°C or 350°F. Heat the oil in a heavy based frying pan and brown the onion, chicken and bacon. Put into a warmed casserole. Chop the mushrooms, slice the tomatoes and the new potatoes, and add all three to the casserole. Season with black pepper to taste and pour in the water, mixed with the soy sauce. Sprinkle with the parsley and put on the lid. Bake above the centre of the oven for about 1 hour, or until the chicken is cooked. Serve with green vegetables and carrots.

Chicken Casserole with Leeks

Serves 2

 Use wheat-free bread

 Use gluten-free bread

2 medium leeks, halved lengthways and washed well
1½ portions cooked chicken meat, skin removed, cut into pieces
½ pint (300 ml) Cheese Sauce with Mustard (see recipe on p. 404)
Freshly ground black pepper, to taste
1 slice wholewheat bread made into fine breadcrumbs

Method

Preheat the oven to Gas Mark 4, 180°C or 350°F. Grease an ovenproof casserole. Cut the leeks into short lengths and cover the base of the casserole. Lay the chicken pieces on top. Cover with the hot cheese sauce, season to taste with black pepper and top with the breadcrumbs. Bake for about 25–30 minutes, above the centre of the oven. Serve hot with plain boiled potatoes, jacket potatoes or brown rice and grilled tomatoes.

Chicken Baked in Fruit Juice

Serves 2

1 lemon
2 skinned chicken breasts rubbed with a few pinches cinnamon
Freshly ground black pepper, to taste
1 orange
1 tablespoon sunflower oil

Method

Preheat the oven to Gas Mark 5, 190°C or 375°F. Grease a casserole that has a tightly fitting lid. Peel half the lemon and chop the flesh. Put into a basin. Squeeze the juice from the other half. Put the chicken breasts into the casserole and pour the lemon juice over them. Season with black pepper to taste. Grate the rind from half the orange and add to the basin. Peel the orange, chop the flesh, and add that to the basin too. Stir well and spoon into the casserole. Spoon the sunflower oil over the chicken and bake, with the lid on, for about ½ hour on a shelf above centre, or until the chicken is tender. (Inspect the casserole half way through the cooking. If it looks too dry add a little hot water.) Serve with green vegetables and either rice or potatoes.

Chicken with Yoghurt and Ginger

Serves 2

 Use wheat-free chappatis or flatbreads

 Use gluten-free chappatis

1 medium onion, sliced thinly
1 tablespoon sunflower oil
1 small clove garlic, peeled
Small piece fresh ginger, peeled and chopped finely
1 large chicken breast, cut into slivers
1 small carton plain, low fat yoghurt
2 tablespoons water
Good pinch cayenne pepper

Method

Fry the onion in the oil for 3 minutes, while you stir. Crush in the garlic and put in the ginger. Stir/fry for another 2 minutes and then remove to a warm plate. Keep warm. Put the chicken into the pan and stir/fry for about 3 minutes, turning the slivers over to cook evenly. Remove from the heat. Put the yoghurt into a basin and gradually beat in 2 tablespoons of water. Spoon into the pan with the chicken and transfer the onion mixture to the pan as well. Add the pepper. Stir to combine, heat through and serve immediately with either chappatis or suitable flatbreads or brown rice, fresh tomato or fruit chutney and a green vegetable such as peas or French beans.

Turkey with Chestnuts and Apples

Serves 2

 Use wheat-free soy sauce

 Use artificial sweetener

 Use gluten-free soy sauce

 Avoid cornflour, use potato flour instead, and avoid soy sauce, use 1 teaspoon yeast extract

 Avoid soy sauce, use 1 teaspoon yeast extract

5 chestnuts
1 tablespoon sunflower oil
½ medium onion, chopped finely
¼ cooking apple, peeled and sliced thinly
1 small turkey breast, cut into slivers
2 teaspoons cornflour
2 teaspoons soy sauce
2 tablespoons water
Freshly ground black pepper, to taste
2 tablespoons white wine
1 teaspoon soft brown sugar
Vegetable strainings or water

Method

Cook the chestnuts in boiling water for about 15 minutes. Drain in a colander, leave to cool, skin and then chop finely. Heat half the oil in a heavy based frying pan and fry the onion while you stir for 3 minutes. Add the apple slices and stir/fry for 3 minutes. Put them into a hot dish and keep warm. Put the remaining oil in the pan and add the slices of turkey. Stir/fry until the meat is opaque – about 3 minutes. Transfer to the hot dish and keep warm while you make the sauce. Mix the cornflour, soy sauce and water in a small basin. When blended add the black pepper, wine, sugar and a cup of vegetable strainings or water. Stir well and pour into the pan. Heat to boiling point, while you stir, then turn down the heat and simmer, still stirring, for another 2 minutes. Remove from the heat and stir in the chestnuts and the turkey mixture. Serve hot with a green vegetable and potatoes or rice.

Lamb with Apples

Serves 1

 Use wheat-free soy sauce

 Use artificial sweetener to taste

 Use gluten-free soy sauce

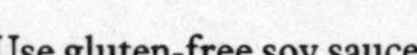

 Avoid soy sauce, use 1 level teaspoon yeast extract

 Avoid soy sauce, use 1 teaspoon yeast extract

2 teaspoons sunflower oil
½ medium onion, sliced thinly
Lean only from 2 lean, loin lamb chops or 1 lean chump chop, cut into thin slices
½ cooking apple, peeled, cored and sliced thinly
1 level teaspoon brown sugar, or fructose
Freshly ground black pepper, to taste
About 8–10 raisins
2 teaspoons soy sauce
Water
Few drops fresh lemon juice

Method

Heat the oil in a heavy based frying pan. Stir/fry the onion for 3 minutes. Remove with a slotted spoon and transfer to a warm plate. Keep warm. Stir/fry the lamb for about 3–4 minutes. Transfer to the plate and keep warm. Put the apple into the pan and sprinkle with the sugar. Season with black pepper. Add the raisins, soy sauce and enough water to stew the apples. Stir while you cook for about 5 minutes. Add the onions and lamb from the plate, and the lemon juice. Mix everything together and serve immediately with peas or a green vegetable, and potatoes or brown rice.

Lancashire Hot Pot

This is a much less salty and fatty version than the traditional one.

Serves 2

 Use wheat-free soy sauce

 Avoid soy sauce, use 1 teaspoon yeast extract

 Use gluten-free soy sauce

 Avoid soy sauce, use 1 teaspoon yeast extract

3 medium potatoes, peeled and sliced thickly
Lean only from 3–4 loin lamb chops
1 medium onion, sliced

2 oz (50 g) mushrooms, sliced
2 lambs' kidneys, prepared and sliced
3 good pinches dried thyme
Freshly ground black pepper, to taste
¼ pint (150 ml) water
2 teaspoons thin soy sauce

Method

Preheat the oven to Gas Mark 4, 180°C or 350°F. Use an old fashioned earthenware casserole and put half the potatoes in the bottom. Cover with the lamb, onion, mushrooms and slices of kidney. Sprinkle with the thyme and black pepper. Arrange the remaining potato slices on top, in circles of overlapping slices. Mix the water and soy sauce and pour over the casserole. Put the lid on and cook in the centre of the oven for about 1½ hours. Remove the lid and turn up the heat to Gas Mark 6, 200°C or 400°F for about 25 minutes, or until the potatoes are crisp and golden. Serve with a green vegetable.

Roast Leg of Lamb with Garlic and Rosemary

This cuts very well cold or hot.

Serves 5–6 (hot or cold)

1 leg of lamb, washed
5 or 6 cloves garlic, peeled
1 teaspoon dried rosemary, or a few small sprigs of the fresh herb

Method

Weigh the leg of lamb and calculate the cooking time, allowing 20 minutes per pound. Preheat the oven to Gas Mark 8, 230°C or 450°F. Put the leg of lamb into a roasting tin. Stab with a knife through the thin layer of fat into the lean and insert ½ clove of garlic into each cut. Sprinkle with the herb and put into the oven on the centre shelf to cook. After 15 minutes turn down the heat to Gas Mark 5, 190°C or 375°F for the remainder of the cooking time. Take the joint out of the tin and keep warm on a carving plate. Drain off all the fat from the pan before making the gravy as described in the recipe on p. 407.

Irish Stew

Serves 2

 Avoid wholewheat flour and use wheat-free soy sauce

 Avoid soy sauce, use 1 slightly heaped teaspoon yeast extract

 Avoid wholewheat flour and use gluten-free soy sauce

 Avoid soy sauce, use 1 slightly heaped teaspoon yeast extract

4 lean loin lamb chops, or 2 chump lamb chops
1 tablespoon sunflower oil
2 medium onions, sliced
2 teaspoons wholewheat flour, cornflour or potato flour
3 teaspoons thin soy sauce
Water
Freshly ground black pepper, to taste
4 medium potatoes, peeled and cut into pieces

Method

Preheat the oven to Gas Mark 4, 180°C or 350°F. Trim all fat, bone, etc. from the chops, just leaving the lean. Heat the oil in a flameproof casserole and brown the meat on both sides. Put into a warmed dish and keep warm. Fry the onions in the casserole while you stir for 4 or 5 minutes. Spoon into the casserole and sprinkle with the flour of your choice. Stir and add the meat and soy sauce. Cover with water, season to taste and bring to the boil. Cover and put into the oven, above the centre shelf, for about 1 hour. Take the casserole out of the oven and put back on the hob. Add the potatoes and more water if required. Stir, bring back to the boil and cover. Put back in the oven for another 35–45 minutes, until the potatoes are tender. Serve hot with hunks of suitable bread and a green vegetable.

Meat Pasties

To give a shiny finish to the pasties, brush with beaten egg before putting in the oven.

Makes 4

 Use milk-free margarine

 Avoid soy sauce, use 1 teaspoon yeast extract

 Avoid egg glaze

 Avoid soy sauce, use 1 teaspoon yeast extract

Pastry

4 oz (110 g) wholewheat flour (plus extra)
2 oz (50 g) polyunsaturated margarine
Water

Filling

2 portions lean cold meat – chicken, beef or lamb – minced or chopped coarsely
½ medium onion, chopped finely
1 medium potato, grated coarsely
2 teaspoons thin soy sauce
Freshly ground black pepper, to taste

Method

Preheat the oven to Gas Mark 6, 200°C or 400°F. Put the flour and margarine into a bowl and rub in with the fingers until the mixture resembles breadcrumbs. Add enough water to make a sticky paste and then add more flour to make a workable dough. Roll out on a floured worktop into four circles. Mix the filling ingredients in a bowl and divide among the pastry circles, putting it over half of each one and leaving a margin all round. Brush the margin with water. Fold the pastry over to cover the filling and press around the margins to join. Turn them so that the pastry seam is on top and flute with the fingers. Cut a hole each side to let out the steam and put on to a baking sheet. Bake above the centre of the oven for about 25 minutes and serve either hot or cold, with vegetables or salad.

Ham and Egg Casserole

Serves 2

2 medium potatoes
2 slices lean ham, trimmed of fat and chopped
2 hard boiled eggs
1 heaped tablespoon grated cheese

2 spring onions, chopped finely
Freshly ground black pepper, to taste
1 heaped tablespoon low fat dried milk granules
¼ pint (150 ml) water
2 tomatoes, sliced
1 heaped teaspoon freshly chopped parsley

Method

Boil the potatoes in water and drain. Leave to cool a little, then cut into slices. Preheat the oven to Gas Mark 4, 180°C or 350°F. Grease a small casserole and cover the base with the potato slices. Top with layers of ham, sliced egg and a little cheese. Sprinkle with the chopped onions and black pepper to taste and top with potato slices. Stir the milk granules into the hot water and pour over the casserole. Top with tomato slices and bake, uncovered, above the centre shelf, for about 25 minutes. Serve hot, garnished with the parsley. A green side salad makes a good accompaniment.

DINNERS FOR ONE

Often people on special diets need to have a meal cooked just for them. Others living on their own long for the flavours of a larger joint of meat or poultry but would find this kind of cooking uneconomical. The following recipes are for one person, but offer all the flavours desired and are designed to be cooked very quickly.

Chicken Dinner for One

This replaces the traditional roast chicken with sage and onion stuffing and gravy. A dish of baked bananas or a baked apple can be cooked in the oven at the same time for a complete meal.

Serves 1

 Avoid wholewheat flour, use wheat-free bread and soy sauce

 Avoid soy sauce

 Avoid wholewheat flour, use gluten-free bread and soy sauce

 Avoid soy sauce

½ medium onion, chopped
1 tablespoon sunflower oil
1 chicken breast, skinned
½ slice bread made into crumbs (use gluten-free or wheat-free bread as appropriate)
3 good pinches dried sage, or 1 fresh sage leaf, chopped
1 teaspoon cornflour, wholewheat flour, potato flour or rice flour mixed with 1 tablespoon water
Grated rind ¼ lemon
1–2 teaspoons thin soy sauce, or ¼ teaspoon yeast extract
1 cup vegetable strainings
Freshly ground black pepper, to taste

Method

Put the onion into a frying pan with the oil and fry while you stir for 2 minutes. Cut the chicken into thin strips and put into the pan. Stir/fry, turning the meat over to cook evenly for about 3–4 minutes. Remove with a slotted spoon and keep warm on a plate. Put in the breadcrumbs and fry for 2 minutes. Stir in the sage, then add to the chicken mixture. Pour the flour mixture into the pan and add the lemon rind, stock and vegetable strainings. Season to taste with the pepper. Stir well and bring to the boil. Stir/cook for 2 minutes and pour over the mixture on the warm plate. Serve with a green vegetable (to make the strainings) and roast potatoes and parsnip (see recipe on p. 264).

Pork Dinner for One

To replace roast, stuffed pork with apple sauce and gravy.

Serves 1

Use wheat-free soy sauce

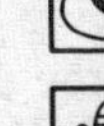
Avoid soy sauce

Use gluten-free soy sauce

Avoid soy sauce

2 teaspoons sunflower oil
¼ medium onion, chopped
¼ cooking apple, peeled and chopped finely, or grated coarsely
1 small fillet or 1 pork chop, lean meat only
3 good pinches dried sage
1–2 teaspoons thin soy sauce, or ¼ teaspoon yeast extract
Vegetable strainings
Freshly ground black pepper, to taste

Method

Put the oil into a frying pan and heat. Add the onion and fry while you stir for 3 minutes. Put in the apple and continue to stir/fry until the apple is soft. Remove with a slotted spoon and put on to a warm plate. Keep warm. Cut the pork into thin strips and stir/fry for about 3 minutes or until you are sure the meat is cooked right through. Add the sage and the soy sauce. Put in the mixture from the warm plate and add about 5 tablespoons of vegetable strainings. Season to taste with pepper. Heat through (do not boil or you will make the meat tough). Serve hot with vegetables and boiled potatoes.

Chicken in Red Wine Dinner for One

This makes a very tasty dish, rather like Coq au Vin.

Serves 1

    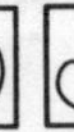   

2 spring onions, chopped
2 teaspoons sunflower oil
½ clove garlic, peeled
Very small pinch dried mixed herbs
1 rasher unsmoked back bacon, trimmed of fat and chopped
1 small skinned chicken breast, cut into slivers
2 mushrooms, chopped
2 tablespoons red wine (cheap)
Freshly ground black pepper, to taste

Method

Put the spring onions into a frying pan with the oil and stir/fry for 30 seconds. Crush in the garlic through a garlic press and add the herbs. Stir/fry for another few seconds. Push to one side of the pan and add the bacon with the chicken. Fry, turning the meats over, for 2 or 3 minutes until the chicken is cooked. Add the mushrooms and mix all the pan contents together. Stir/fry for 1 minute, then pour in the wine. Season to taste with black pepper and stir well. Serve with a green vegetable and plain boiled rice or potatoes.

Steak Dinner for One

Serves 1

 Avoid wholewheat flour, use wheat-free soy sauce

 Avoid soy sauce, use 1 teaspoon yeast extract

 Avoid wholewheat flour, use gluten-free soy sauce

 Avoid soy sauce, use 1 teaspoon yeast extract

3 teaspoons sunflower oil
1 medium onion, sliced thinly
1 tablespoon water
About 3 oz (75 g) lean grilling steak, trimmed of fat and cut into slivers
2 mushrooms, sliced
2 teaspoons thin soy sauce
1 teaspoon cornflour, wholewheat flour, potato flour or rice flour mixed with 1 tablespoon water
½ cup or more of vegetable strainings
Freshly ground black pepper, to taste

Method

Heat the oil in a frying pan and put in the onions. Stir/fry, adding a tablespoon of water after 5 minutes. Let the onions brown by turning up the heat while you stir. Push to the side of the pan and tip the pan so that the juice/oil runs out of the onions and over the base of the pan. Put in the meat and mushrooms. Continue to stir/fry over a moderate heat until the steak has changed colour. This should only take about 3 minutes. Remove to a warmed plate and keep warm. Stir the soy sauce into the flour mixture and add the vegetable strainings. Stir and add to the pan. Bring to the boil, still stirring, and simmer for 2 minutes or until the gravy has thickened. Season to taste. Pour over the steak mixture and serve with greens and potatoes.

VEGETARIAN MAIN MEALS WITH NUTS, CHEESE, PULSES, TVP AND GRAINS

As meat-eating is on the decline there is a greater interest in vegetarian cooking and this section offers alternative sources of protein for main meals from a variety of ingredients.

A number of the recipes use breadcrumbs. For gluten-free and wheat-free diets use appropriate bread to make the crumbs, such as from Trufree flours Nos 4 or 5.

Roast Walnuts

Serves 2–3

 Use wheat-free bread and soy sauce

 Avoid soy sauce

 Use gluten-free bread and soy sauce

 Avoid soy sauce

1 medium onion, chopped finely
1 tablespoon sunflower oil
½ clove garlic, peeled
2 slices bread, made into crumbs (preferably brown) (for gluten-free/wheat-free diets use appropriate bread, such as Trufree Nos 4 or 5)
1 small tin tomatoes, chopped
4 oz (110 g) walnuts, ground
2 oz (50 g) mushrooms
1 tablespoon thin soy sauce, or 2 teaspoons yeast extract
½ teaspoon dried mixed herbs
Freshly ground black pepper, to taste

Method

Preheat the oven to Gas Mark 4, 180°C or 350°F. Fry the onion in the oil while you stir for 3 minutes. Crush in the garlic through a garlic press. Stir/fry for another 30 seconds and take off the heat. Add all the other ingredients, stir well, and put back over the heat. Heat through while you stir, then turn into a pie dish, oiled with sunflower oil. Bake on the top shelf of the oven for about an hour. Serve with potatoes or brown rice, a green vegetable and carrots.

Marrow Stuffed with Nuts

Serves 2

 Use rice for stuffing and wheat-free soy sauce

 Avoid soy sauce

 Use rice for stuffing and gluten-free soy sauce

 Avoid soy sauce

4 thick slices from a medium marrow

Stuffing

½ medium onion, chopped and fried in 1 tablespoon of sunflower oil
2 oz (50 g) walnuts, finely ground
1 heaped tablespoon fresh wholewheat breadcrumbs or cooked brown rice
½ clove garlic, peeled
2 teaspoons thin soy sauce, or 1 teaspoon yeast extract dissolved in a little hot water
3 canned tomatoes, chopped
Freshly ground black pepper, to taste

Gravy

1 tablespoon tomato purée
¼ pint (150 ml) hot water
1 teaspoon thin soy sauce, or ½ teaspoon yeast extract

Method

Preheat the oven to Gas Mark 5, 190°C or 375°F. Cut out the centres of the marrow containing the seeds and put the resulting rings into boiling water for 5 minutes to parboil them. Mix the stuffing ingredients in a basin. Grease a shallow ovenproof dish with a little sunflower oil. Carefully lift out the marrow rings with a slotted spoon and place in the dish. Pile the stuffing into the centre cavities. Bake above the centre shelf with the gravy ingredients mixed and poured around the marrow. Serve hot with mashed potato and greens.

Nut Roast

Serves 1

 Use wheat-free soy sauce and breadcrumbs

 Avoid soy sauce

 Use gluten-free soy sauce and breadcrumbs

 Avoid soy sauce

1 pinch dried mixed herbs
1½ oz (40 g) ground nuts – almonds, hazelnuts, cashews, brazils or walnuts
½ eating apple, grated finely, including the skin
2 canned or 1 fresh tomato, chopped
1 teaspoon tomato purée
½ medium onion, chopped finely
½ slice bread, made into crumbs (preferably wholewheat)
1½ teaspoons thin soy sauce, or ½ teaspoon yeast extract dissolved in a little hot water
Freshly ground black pepper, to taste

Method

Preheat the oven to Gas Mark 7, 220°C or 425°F. Grease an ovenproof dish with sunflower oil. Mix all the ingredients together in a bowl and turn into the dish. Bake above the centre of the oven for about 30 minutes. Serve with green vegetables, carrots and potatoes or brown rice.

Vegetable and Nut Curry

The nuts can be roasted by putting on to a baking sheet and toasting under the grill for a few minutes, turning them once.

Serves 2–3

1 tablespoon sunflower oil
1 medium onion, sliced
1 level teaspoon mild curry powder
½ teaspoon ground coriander

1 clove garlic, peeled
1 small piece root ginger, chopped finely
2 medium carrots, sliced
1 small parsnip, diced
1 small turnip, diced
Water
2 teaspoons thin soy sauce, or 1 teaspoon yeast extract
1 small courgette, sliced
2 heaped tablespoons frozen peas, defrosted
3 heaped tablespoons lightly roasted nuts – cashews, hazelnuts or walnuts
2 heaped tablespoons natural, low fat yoghurt

Method

Heat the oil in a saucepan. Fry the onions while you stir for 4 minutes. Put in the curry powder and coriander, crush in the garlic through a garlic press and sprinkle in the ginger. Continue to stir/fry for another 30 seconds. Add the carrots, parsnip and turnip, enough water to cover and the soy sauce. Bring to the boil and simmer with the lid on for 15 minutes. Put in the courgettes and peas and bring back to the boil. Simmer for another 4–5 minutes, then stir in the nuts and yoghurt. Heat gently to warm through and serve with brown rice or chappatis, chutney and a green salad.

Nut Rissoles (without Egg)

For gluten-free and wheat-free diets use 2 heaped tablespoons cooked brown rice instead of bread.

Serves 2

 Use wheat-free soy sauce and bread, and avoid wholewheat flour

 Avoid soy sauce

 Use gluten-free soy sauce and bread, and avoid wholewheat flour

 Avoid cornflour and soy sauce

1 onion, peeled and finely chopped
3 oz (75 g) almonds, walnuts or cashews, ground finely
½ cooking apple, grated finely
2 tomatoes, chopped

1 heaped tablespoon freshly chopped parsley
3 teaspoons thin soy sauce, or 1 teaspoon yeast extract dissolved in a little hot water
1 slice wholewheat bread, made into crumbs
Freshly ground black pepper, to taste
Flour for coating – wholewheat, rice flour, potato flour or cornflour
Sunflower oil for frying

Method

Put the onion, nuts, apple, tomatoes, parsley, stock and breadcrumbs into a bowl. Mix well with a fork and season to taste. Shape by hand into four flat cakes and roll in the flour of your choice. Put a little oil into a frying pan and heat. Put in the rissoles and fry gently for 3 minutes. Turn over carefully with a spatula and fry on the other side for 3 minutes. Serve hot with mashed potato and salad or hot vegetables and a gravy.

Nut Rissoles (with Egg)

Use cooked rice or buckwheat for gluten-free or wheat-free diets, instead of the bread.

Serves 2

 Avoid breadcrumbs and wheat flour, and use wheat-free soy sauce

 Avoid soy sauce

 Avoid breadcrumbs and wheat flour, and use gluten-free soy sauce

 Avoid soy sauce and cornflour

1 medium onion, chopped finely
1 slice wholewheat bread, made into crumbs
3 teaspoons thin soy sauce, or 1 teaspoon yeast extract dissolved in a little hot water
1 heaped tablespoon tomato purée
1 egg, beaten
2 tomatoes, chopped
3 oz (75 g) finely ground nuts – walnuts, almonds, cashews or brazils
¾ level teaspoon dried mixed herbs
Freshly ground black pepper, to taste
Flour for coating – wholewheat, cornflour, rice flour or potato flour
Sunflower oil for frying

Method

Put all the ingredients except the flour and the sunflower oil into a bowl and mix with a fork. Shape into four or five flat cakes by hand, flouring the hands first with the flour of your choice. Use more flour to coat the rissoles, then fry them in a little hot oil for 4 minutes. Turn them over carefully with a spatula and fry for another 4 minutes on the other side. Serve hot with potatoes and salad or hot vegetables and gravy.

Spicy Nut Rissoles

Serves 2

 Avoid wholewheat flour, use wheat-free soy sauce

 Avoid soy sauce

 Avoid wholewheat flour, use gluten-free soy sauce

 Avoid cornflour and soy sauce

¼ teaspoon mild curry powder
2 spring onions, finely chopped
4 good pinches ground coriander
3 pinches ground ginger
½ clove garlic, peeled and put through a garlic press
½ cooking apple, finely grated
3 oz (75 g) cashews or walnuts, finely ground
5 thin slices cucumber, chopped finely
2 teaspoons thin soy sauce, or 1 teaspoon yeast extract mixed with 2 teaspoons boiling water to dissolve it
2 heaped tablespoons cooked brown rice
Flour for coating – wholewheat, cornflour, rice flour or potato flour
Sunflower oil for frying

Method

Put the first ten ingredients into a basin and mix well to distribute the spices. Form into four flat cakes by hand. Coat with the flour of your choice and fry in a little sunflower oil for 4 minutes. Turn over carefully with a spatula and cook on the other side for another 4 minutes. Serve hot with a green salad and chutney.

Grilled Nutburgers

Serves 2

 Use wheat-free soy sauce  Use gluten-free soy sauce

3 spring onions, chopped finely
1 tablespoon sunflower oil
2 oz (50 g) ground almonds
2 heaped tablespoons cooked rice or buckwheat
½ cooking apple, finely grated
¼ teaspoon dried herbs – sage or thyme – or 1 tablespoon freshly chopped parsley
2 teaspoons thin soy sauce, or 1 teaspoon yeast extract mixed with 2 teaspoons boiling water
Freshly ground black pepper, to taste
2 medium tomatoes, chopped

Method

Fry the onion in the oil for 4 minutes while you stir. Put into a bowl with all the other ingredients and combine with a fork. Shape by hand into rissoles. Put into the grill pan and brush with a little sunflower oil. Grill under a high heat for 4–5 minutes. Turn the rissoles over carefully and brush with a little more oil. Grill on the second side and serve hot with potatoes and either vegetables or a green salad.

High Protein Burgers

Makes 4 large or 8 small burgers: serves 4

4 medium potatoes, boiled and mashed with a pinch of nutmeg
4 tablespoons cooked haricot beans
1 heaped tablespoon chopped nuts
1 heaped tablespoon finely grated Parmesan cheese
Milk to mix
1 egg white
Rolled oats or medium oatmeal for coating
Sunflower oil for frying

Method

Mix the mashed potato, beans, nuts and Parmesan cheese, adding a little milk if the mixture is too stiff. Lightly whisk the egg white and put in a shallow bowl. Shape the mixture into flat cakes. Dip each one in the egg white and roll in the oats to cover. Fry in a little oil, turning once until each one is crisp and golden. Drain on kitchen paper and serve hot with green vegetables or a salad.

Boston Baked Beans

Can be stored for up to three days in the fridge.

Serves 4

8 oz (225 g) dried haricot beans, white or red
1 medium onion
1 small can tomatoes, chopped
1 teaspoon French mustard
1 generous tablespoon black treacle
3 good pinches dried mixed herbs
2 heaped teaspoons tomato purée
Freshly ground black pepper, to taste

Method

Soak the beans overnight in plenty of water. Drain and put into a pan with fresh water. Bring to the boil and boil steadily for 10 minutes (this is very important), then turn down the heat and simmer for about 30 minutes. The beans should be softened but not completely cooked. Drain, but save the liquid for later. Preheat the oven to Gas Mark 3, 170°C or 325°F. Put all the ingredients into a casserole and add about ½ cup of the liquid from the beans. Stir well and put on the lid. Bake on the centre shelf for about 2½–3 hours, topping up the liquid as necessary.

Quick Boston Baked Beans

Serves 1

      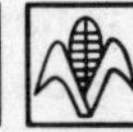 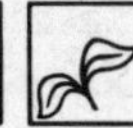

¼ medium onion, chopped finely
2 teaspoons sunflower oil
1 tomato, chopped
1 heaped teaspoon black treacle
¼ teaspoon French mustard
1 small pinch dried mixed herbs
1 teaspoon tomato purée
Freshly ground black pepper, to taste
Water
1 small can cooked haricot beans, drained

Method

Fry the onion in the oil while you stir for 3 minutes. Add all the other ingredients except the beans and enough water to make a sauce – about 3 tablespoons. Stir while you heat, then add the drained beans. Heat through and serve immediately.

Vegetarian Pâté

This high protein, low fat pâté replaces cold meat and fish pâtés. It can be stored in the fridge for up to 48 hours and used as required.

Serves 2

  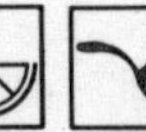  

 Use wheat-free soy sauce

 Use gluten-free soy sauce

1 small onion, finely chopped
1 clove garlic, peeled and put through a garlic press
1 tablespoon sunflower oil
2 teaspoons soy sauce
2 oz (50 g) natural flavour TVP mince, ground to a powder in a coffee grinder
Freshly ground black pepper, to taste
1 small tin tomatoes, chopped
½ teaspoon dried mixed herbs
1 tablespoon ground almonds

Method

Fry the onion and garlic in the oil for 2 or 3 minutes. Put the soy sauce, TVP, black pepper to taste and tomatoes into a basin and stir. Turn into the pan with the onions and heat while you stir for about 2 minutes. Add the herbs and nuts and mix well. Spoon into a flat dish and leave to cool. Serve with salads and jacket or mashed potatoes, or eat with a rice-based salad or cracked wheat salad, and a green salad.

Cauliflower Cheese

Serves 2

 Serve with wheat-free bread  Serve with gluten-free bread

1 small cauliflower
½ pint (300 ml) Cheese Sauce or Cheese and Onion Sauce (see recipes on pp. 404 and 405)
1 tablespoon Parmesan cheese, finely grated

Method

Prepare and cook the cauliflower, cut into quarters, in boiling water for 10 minutes. Drain and put into a warmed flameproof dish. Make the sauce and pour over the cauliflower. Sprinkle with the cheese and put under a hot grill until the top is golden and bubbling – about 5 minutes. Serve hot with brown bread.

Leeks in Cheese Sauce

Serves 2

4 leeks, cut lengthways, washed thoroughly and chopped
1 hard boiled egg, peeled and chopped
½ pint Cheese Sauce (see recipe on p. 404)

Method

Cook the leeks in boiling water for about 15 minutes or until tender. Put into a warmed flameproof dish and keep warm. Make the sauce. Sprinkle the leeks with the egg and cover with the sauce. Put under a hot grill for 2 minutes and serve hot with brown bread.

Cheese and Vegetable Pie

If serving to a vegetarian make sure the cheese is a vegetarian one. Your local health store will have suitable brands.

Serves 2

Base

1 tablespoon sunflower oil
1 medium onion, sliced
2 courgettes, sliced
1 small can tomatoes
1 teaspoon tomato purée
1 clove garlic, peeled
2 heaped tablespoons frozen peas, defrosted
Freshly ground black pepper, to taste

Topping

4 medium potatoes, boiled and mashed
1 generous knob polyunsaturated margarine
Little skimmed milk to mix
2 spring onions, finely chopped
2 heaped tablespoons grated Cheddar cheese
1 heaped tablespoon freshly chopped parsley

Method

Preheat the oven to Gas Mark 6, 200°C or 400°F, after boiling the potatoes. Heat the oil in a saucepan and fry the onion and courgettes while you stir for 4 minutes. Add all the other ingredients for the base, crushing in the garlic through a press, and bring to the boil. Simmer for 5 minutes to reduce the liquid, then turn into a warmed ovenproof dish. Make the topping. Beat the potatoes with a wooden spoon to make them smooth. Add the margarine and a little milk to make them creamy. Stir in the spring onions, cheese and parsley. Spread over the vegetable base and pattern with a fork. Put into the oven on a shelf above centre and bake for about 30 minutes. The top should be crisp and golden. Serve with a green salad.

Onions with Cheese Stuffing

Serves 2

2 medium onions, peeled
2 tablespoons wholewheat breadcrumbs
2 slightly heaped tablespoons finely grated Parmesan cheese
Freshly ground black pepper, to taste
1 heaped tablespoon finely chopped fresh parsley

Sauce

½ oz (15 g) polyunsaturated margarine
½ oz (15 g) wholewheat flour
¼ pint (150 ml) water
2 slightly heaped tablespoons low fat dried milk granules

Method

Preheat the oven to Gas Mark 4, 180°C or 350°F. Put in a shallow ovenproof dish to warm. Parboil the onions for 15 minutes, then drain. Remove the centres with a teaspoon and chop finely. Mix with the breadcrumbs and half the cheese. Season to taste and stir in the parsley. Stuff the onions with this mixture, put into the dish and sprinkle with the rest of the cheese. Keep warm in the oven while you make the white sauce. Mix the dried granules into the water to make milk. In a small saucepan melt the margarine, stir in the flour, then add the milk and gently bring to the boil, stirring all the time, until thickened. Pour around the onions. Bake above the centre of the oven for about 30 minutes. Eat hot with a green vegetable and grilled tomatoes.

TVP and Bean Loaf

A vegetarian/vegan substitute for meat loaf. Split pea flour is best for this recipe, if you can get it. Try Asian stores or health food stores.

Serves 4, or makes 8 slices

Avoid wholewheat flour and use wheat-free soy sauce

Use home-made, sugar-free beans

Avoid wholewheat flour and use gluten-free soy sauce

Avoid soy sauce and cornflour

Avoid soy sauce

2 oz (50 g) natural flavour TVP mince
About 12 fluid oz (350 ml) water
1 heaped tablespoon tomato purée
2 tablespoons sunflower oil
1 heaped tablespoon onion, finely chopped
1 oz (25 g) flour – split pea, bean, cornflour, wholewheat or potato flour
2 teaspoons thin soy sauce, or ½ teaspoon yeast extract mixed with 3 teaspoons hot water
1 small can cooked haricot beans, mashed to a paste with a fork
2 or 3 pinches dried mixed herbs
Freshly ground black pepper, to taste
1 tablespoon cooked rice (optional)

Method

Grind the TVP to a powder in a coffee grinder. Put into a basin with the water and the tomato purée. Stir to combine. Heat the oil in a saucepan and fry the onion while you stir for 2 minutes. Put in the flour and stir/cook for 3 minutes until the oil has been absorbed by the flour. Take off the heat and put in the TVP mixture, soy sauce and bean paste. Put back on the heat and cook steadily while you stir for 2 minutes, until you have a stiff paste. Stir in the herbs, black pepper and rice. Mix well and turn into a rectangular dish or loaf tin. Allow to cool, then turn out on to a plate. Serve in slices with salads and jacket potatoes.

Vegetable Casserole with TVP

Serves 3

 Use wheat-free soy sauce, and serve with wheat-free bread

 Avoid soy sauce

 Use gluten-free soy sauce, and serve with gluten-free bread

 Avoid soy sauce

2 medium onions, sliced thinly
1 tablespoon sunflower oil
¼ medium swede, cut into small pieces
2 medium carrots, sliced thickly
3 medium potatoes, sliced thickly
1 teacup natural flavour TVP mince soaked for 3 minutes in 1 cup of water
1 tablespoon thin soy sauce, or 2 teaspoons yeast extract
Herbs – choose from ¼ teaspoon dried mixed herbs, ½ teaspoon dried basil or dried sage, or 1 level teaspoon dried tarragon
1 medium can tomatoes, chopped, with their juice
1 heaped teaspoon tomato purée
Freshly ground black pepper, to taste
4 oz (110 g) frozen peas, defrosted

Method

Preheat the oven to Gas Mark 7, 220°C or 425°F. Fry the onion in the oil for 3 minutes while you stir, using a large saucepan. Add all the other ingredients except the peas and bring to the boil. Simmer for 2 minutes then transfer to a warmed casserole. Put on the lid and cook on the centre shelf for 20 minutes. Add the peas and cook for another 20 minutes. Serve with thickly sliced wholewheat bread and a leafy green vegetable.

Goulash with TVP

Serves 2

 Use wheat-free soy sauce

 Use artificial sweetener and home-cooked sugar-free beans

 Use gluten-free soy sauce

 Avoid soy sauce

 Avoid soy sauce

1 tablespoon sunflower oil
1 medium onion, chopped
1 small can tomatoes, chopped, with their juice
1 small can drained, cooked haricot beans
1 heaped teaspoon tomato purée
1 teaspoon sugar
1 good pinch powdered bay leaves
¼ level teaspoon paprika
1 teacup natural flavour TVP mince, soaked in 1 teacup water
2 oz (50 g) mushrooms, chopped
1 tablespoon thin soy sauce, or 2 teaspoons yeast extract

Method

Heat the oil in a saucepan and fry the onion while you stir for 2 minutes. Add all the other ingredients and stir while you cook steadily for about 5–6 minutes. Serve with plain boiled rice or buckwheat.

Curried TVP with Vegetables

This reheats well.

Serves 4

 Avoid wholewheat flour and use wheat-free soy sauce

 Use artificial sweetener and home-cooked sugar-free beans

 Avoid wholewheat flour and use gluten-free soy sauce

 Avoid soy sauce

 Avoid soy sauce

1 onion, sliced
2 slightly heaped teaspoons mild curry powder
1 slightly heaped teaspoon ground coriander
1 tablespoon sunflower oil
2 slightly heaped teaspoons thickener – choose from wholewheat flour, ground rice, potato flour or cornflour
½ pint (300 ml) cold water
1 tablespoon tomato purée
1 tablespoon thin soy sauce, or 2 teaspoons yeast extract
1 teaspoon brown sugar, or fructose
1 heaped tablespoon sultanas

1 can cooked haricot beans, drained
1 teacup natural flavour TVP mince, soaked in 1 teacup water
About 1 lb (450 g) diced fresh vegetables in season – potato, carrot, swede, parsnip, turnip, celery, etc.
1 small can tomatoes, chopped, with their juice

Method

Use a large saucepan to fry the onion, curry powder and coriander in the oil. Stir while you fry. Mix the thickening of your choice into a little of the water. Stir into the remaining water with the tomato purée and soy sauce. Add to the pan with all the remaining ingredients and bring to the boil while you stir. Turn down the heat and simmer for 2 or 3 minutes until thickened. Put the lid on and continue to simmer for 20 minutes or until the vegetables are cooked. Serve hot with plain boiled brown rice and chutney. Chappatis and thin slices of cucumber can also be served with the curry.

Stewed Lentils

Most lentils have a peppery taste and should not need the addition of black pepper.

Serves 2

   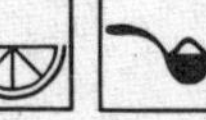 

 Use wheat free soy sauce and serve with wheat-free bread

 Avoid soy sauce

 Use gluten-free soy sauce and serve with gluten-free bread

 Avoid soy sauce

1 tablespoon sunflower oil
1 stick celery, chopped
1 medium onion, chopped
1 medium carrot, sliced
1 clove garlic, peeled
1 heaped teaspoon tomato purée
About 1 pint (600 ml) water
2 teaspoons thin soy sauce, or 1 teaspoon yeast extract dissolved in a little boiling water
4 oz (110 g) red lentils, soaked for 1 hour in water and drained
1 tablespoon freshly chopped parsley, or ¼ teaspoon dried sage, thyme or basil

Method

Heat the oil in a large saucepan and stir/fry the celery, onion and carrot for a few minutes to tenderize them. Add all the other ingredients, crushing the garlic in through a garlic press, and bring to the boil. Put the lid on and simmer for about 1 hour, stirring from time to time. Serve with a green salad and thick slices of wholewheat bread.

Vegetable Stew with Barley

This stew can be served instead of a selection of vegetables or instead of soup. Serve with thickly sliced wholewheat bread and slices of cheese, followed by fresh fruit for a nourishing vegetarian meal.

Serves 2–3

 Avoid wholewheat flour and use wheat-free soy sauce

 Avoid soy sauce and cornflour

 Avoid soy sauce

1 medium onion, sliced
1 tablespoon sunflower oil
1 clove garlic
1 medium potato, cubed
1 small parsnip, sliced
2 medium carrots, sliced
2 small turnips, sliced
Small piece of swede, cubed
2 heaped tablespoons fresh peas or frozen peas, defrosted
1 heaped tablespoon pot barley, soaked for at least 12 hours
1 tablespoon thin soy sauce, or 2 teaspoons yeast extract
Good pinch of thyme
Freshly ground black pepper, to taste
2 heaped teaspoons wholewheat flour, cornflour, rice flour or potato flour for thickening
2 tablespoons water

Method

In a saucepan, fry the onion in the oil for 3 minutes while you stir. Crush in the garlic, through a garlic press. Add all the remaining vegetables and the barley. Put in the soy sauce, herb and black pepper, and add water to cover. Stir well and bring to the boil. Turn down the heat and simmer with the lid on for about 20 minutes or until the vegetables are tender. Put the thickening of your choice in a cup with 2 tablespoons of water. Stir well and add to the stew. Bring to the boil and turn down the heat to let it simmer while you stir for 2 minutes to thicken the gravy. Serve hot.

COOKED VEGETABLES

BOILED VEGETABLES

Boiling is probably the most widely used method of cooking vegetables as it is very easy, the vegetables being cooked in a saucepan with water. Unfortunately, some of the nutrients in the vegetables will leach out into the water and then be thrown down the drain when they are strained. The solution to this is not to use too much water and to save these vegetable strainings for gravy or soup, as suggested in many of the recipes in this book.

Greens: Brussels Sprouts, Sprout Tops, Cabbage, Kale, Spring Greens

Wash the greens well, allowing about 1 lb (450 g) for 3–4 servings. Remove any yellow or discoloured parts and on tougher leaves cut out and discard the coarser stems. Sprouts should be trimmed and have a cross cut in the base to ensure thorough cooking. Put into a saucepan with 2 or 3 cups of boiling water. Poke them down with a wooden spoon and bring to the boil. Put on the lid and simmer for about 10 minutes for young tender greens to as much as 25 minutes for older and tougher varieties such as kale. Strain in a colander, catching the strainings for use in gravy, soups, etc.

Spinach

Allow about 8 oz (225 g) raw leaves per person before preparing. Spinach is cooked differently from other greens as it contains a good deal of water. Fill the sink and wash well in lots of cold water, removing the coarser stems. Use only green leaves, discarding any yellowing or discoloured ones. Put into a large saucepan with 2 or 3 tablespoons of water. Heat and poke the leaves down with a wooden spoon until the juices start to run out. Put on the lid and cook for 7–10 minutes. If the saucepan starts to dry add a little more water, but this is not usually necessary. When the spinach is cooked strain in a colander, pressing with the back of a wooden spoon and catching the strainings for soup, gravy, etc. Chop with kitchen scissors if preferred.

Cauliflower

A medium cauliflower will serve 4 people. Trim off the base and outer leaves. Wash and cut into portions. Bring 1 or 2 cups of water to the boil in a saucepan and put in the cauliflower. Bring back to the boil, then put on the lid and cook for about 10 minutes or until the cauliflower is tender but still crisp. (Test with a knife.) Strain in a colander, saving the strainings if they are to be used immediately. If not, throw them away as they will develop an unpleasant aroma.

Broccoli and Calabrese

     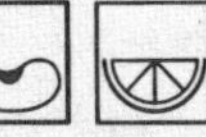    

Allow about 4 oz (110 g) of these per serving. Wash and cut into florets. Cook as for cauliflower.

Leeks

Trim off the coarser parts and root base, allowing 2 medium leeks per person. Cut lengthways and wash really well between the layers. Chop and cook as for spinach. Tougher leeks may need up to 20 minutes cooking. Strain as for spinach.

Runner Beans (Stick Beans)

Allow about 8 oz (225 g) raw beans per portion. Wash, top and tail, and trim off the strings each side with a sharp kitchen knife. Discard beans which are too tough. Cut in slices at an angle, making sure you cut through the beans inside the green pods. Cook in boiling water, enough to come half way up the beans, for anything from 10 minutes for young beans to 25 minutes for older, tougher ones. Strain in a colander and save the strainings for gravy.

French Beans

Cook as for runner beans but prepare by just topping and tailing. These are sometimes called stringless beans.

Peas

Allow 8 oz (225 g) peas in the pod per person. Shell and cook in boiling water with the lid on for about 10 minutes, or more if the peas are old.

Carrots

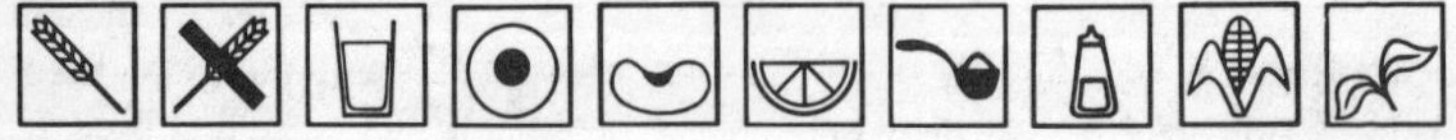

Trim off the tops and roots, allowing about 2 medium carrots per portion. Quarter lengthways if large, or slice. Baby or finger carrots can be left whole. Boil in water for anything from 10 minutes for young baby carrots to 25 minutes for old carrots. Strain in a colander and save the strainings for gravy.

Onions

Not a very popular boiled vegetable and best served with a sauce such as Parsley Sauce (see recipe on p. 404). Peel 2 medium or 4 small onions per person, cutting off the top shoot and the roots. Put in enough boiling water to cover and boil with the lid on for 20–30 minutes, depending on size. Strain, saving the strainings for gravy or soup.

Beetroot

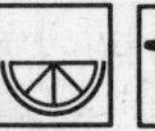

These are rarely eaten hot but are a popular and sweet-tasting salad vegetable. Wash the beetroot, allowing 1 medium per person, but do not trim off the stalk or long root. Put in a large saucepan, with enough boiling water to cover, and bring to the boil. Simmer with the lid on for up to 30 minutes. Strain in a colander and leave to cool. The skin will peel off easily. (NB There is no need to steep the cooked beetroot in vinegar.)

Potatoes

Peel old potatoes but leave the skins on new ones, allowing 2 medium per person. Wash well. Cut the larger potatoes in half and the very large ones into quarters. Put into enough boiling water to cover and put on the lid. Boil for about 10 minutes for young potatoes, and up to 25 minutes for old ones. Strain in a colander.

Turnips

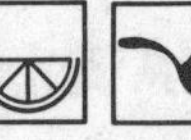

Wash and trim off the tops and bottoms, allowing 1 medium or 2 small turnips per serving. Older turnips will need to be peeled. Cut into pieces if large, or leave whole if they are small and young. Put into enough boiling water to cover and cook with the lid on for 15–25 minutes, until tender. Strain in a colander and use the strainings for gravy.

Swedes

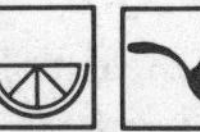

A tough, fibrous vegetable. Trim off the top and peel. Cut into pieces, allowing about a quarter of a medium swede per person, and cook in enough boiling water to cover. Cook for up to 25 minutes, or until tender, with the lid on. Strain and save the strainings for gravy.

Parsnips

    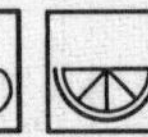    

Trim off the top and the long root allowing 1 medium parsnip per person. Scrub and cut in half lengthways or into four if large. Cut out the central core if it is tough and woody. Put into enough boiling water to cover and put on the lid. Cook for up to 25 minutes, depending on how old the parsnips are. Strain in a colander and save the strainings for gravy.

Mixed Vegetables

For each person make up a selection of about 6–8 oz (175–225 g) of prepared root vegetables – carrot, swede, parsnip and turnip – and onion. Put into enough boiling water to cover and cook with the lid on for up to 25 minutes, until all the vegetables are tender. Strain and serve with White Sauce or Parsley Sauce (see recipes on pp. 403 and 404). This is very good with boiled bacon.

MASHED VEGETABLES

Good mixtures of mashed vegetables are swede and potato, carrot and parsnip, and carrot and potato. Allow 6–8 oz (175–225 g) per serving.

Avoid milk, use water instead, and use milk-free margarine

Prepare the vegetables in the usual way, then boil and strain. Put them back into the saucepan, with a knob of butter or polyunsaturated margarine, and mash with a potato masher. Then add a little skimmed milk and beat with a wooden spoon. A little freshly ground black pepper, to taste, can also be added. Mashed potatoes also taste good with a pinch or two of freshly ground nutmeg.

STEAMED VEGETABLES

For some vegetables, steaming is a far superior method of cooking to boiling in water. Carrots, cauliflower and broccoli are particularly suitable, as are sprouts. The cheapest gadget for steaming is a perforated rack which opens up like the petals of a flower, to fit several sizes of saucepan. The water remains under the rack and sends steam up through the holes to cook the vegetables on top. Put the saucepan lid on firmly to keep the steam in.

Prepare the vegetables and cut into slices or pieces. (Baby carrots and stringbeans can be left whole.) Put the rack into the pan and add water. Put the vegetables into the rack and put on the lid. Bring to the boil and steam for half the usual cooking time. Use the water for gravy or stock.

BAKED AND ROAST VEGETABLES

Baked Potatoes

Use 2 medium old potatoes per person but do not peel them: scrub well, removing any 'eyes' or discoloured parts. Prick all over with a knife to prevent them bursting during baking. Put at the top of a hot oven, Gas Mark 7, 220°C or 425°F for 50–60 minutes, or cook more slowly at Gas Mark 4, 180°C or 350°F for about 1 hour 20 minutes. Large potatoes will cook better with a metal meat skewer pushed right through lengthways. The skin, as well as the flesh, should be eaten.

Dry Roast Potatoes

        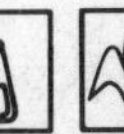 

Allow 2 medium potatoes per person and use old potatoes. Peel and halve, then put into enough boiling water to cover. Bring to the boil and parboil for about 10 minutes. Preheat the oven to Gas Mark 7, 220°C or 425°F. Take a screw of kitchen paper and dip in sunflower oil. Lightly grease a roasting tin and put into the oven to heat. As soon as the potatoes have been parboiled and strained, put into the roasting tin and brush each one with a little sunflower oil (or dab with oil on kitchen paper). This small amount of oil is all that is required for crisp golden roast potatoes. Bake on the top shelf for up to an hour.

Roast Parsnips

Prepare and roast as for potatoes, but parboil for only 5 minutes. Roast parsnips can be cooked at the same time as roast potatoes, in the same dish. Allow 3 small parsnips per serving.

STIR/COOK VEGETABLES

  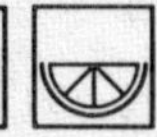  

 Use wheat-free soy sauce

 Avoid soy sauce

 Use gluten-free soy sauce

 Avoid soy sauce

Lightly cooked vegetables, served in their own juices, make colourful and healthy eating. They are cooked on top of the stove in a big frying pan or large shallow saucepan, enabling a wide variety of vegetables to be cooked in the one utensil. The gravy accumulates in the bottom of the pan and does not need to be made separately.

Always start with onion – spring onion or ordinary onion, sliced – and a little sunflower oil. Fry the spring onion for a few seconds or the other kind for 2 or 3 minutes while you stir. Next put in prepared and thinly sliced root vegetables – potato, carrot, swede, parsnip and turnip. Add a tablespoon or two of water and stir while you cook, turning the vegetables over. After 3 or 4 minutes put in the less hard vegetables – peppers (sliced), peas, green beans (chopped), celery (chopped), courgette (sliced) and shredded green leaves or sprouts. Put in a little more water and continue to stir/cook. Finally put in the softer vegetables – sliced mushrooms, tomatoes and cucumber, beansprouts. Add 2–3 teaspoons of thin soy sauce or other suitable stock and you will have an enriched gravy at the bottom of the pan. Serve immediately.

Good Combinations for Stir/Cook Vegetables

Onion, potato, spinach and mushrooms.
Onion, celery, carrot and greens.
Onion, green beans (stringless), tomato and mushroom.
Onion, carrot, swede, turnip or parsnip and sprouts.
Onion, greens, sprouts and leeks.

COOKING DRIED BEANS

These need careful cooking as, in their dried state, they contain toxins which can only be rendered harmless by proper cooking methods. Haricot beans (the kidney-shaped beans which can be white, red or green) should all be cooked in the same way. Soak overnight in plenty of cold water. The following day bring to the boil in fresh water. Continue to boil steadily for 10 minutes – this is **very important** – then turn down the heat and simmer until the beans are tender. Depending on the beans this will take 1–1½ hours. Drain and use with a sauce or add to soups, casseroles or vegetarian dishes. Cold cooked beans can also be added to salads.

Provençale Potatoes

Serve with hot or cold meat.

Serves 4

½ teaspoon dried mixed herbs
2 cloves garlic, peeled and put through a garlic press
½ pint (300 ml) water
8 old potatoes, sliced thickly after peeling
6 tomatoes, sliced
Freshly ground black pepper, to taste
1 heaped tablespoon freshly chopped parsley for garnish

Method

Put the herbs, garlic and water into a saucepan. Bring to the boil and simmer with the lid on for about 10 minutes. Pour a little of this liquid into an ovenproof dish. Arrange the potatoes and tomatoes in the dish, in layers. Season to taste with the pepper, and pour the remaining liquid over. Put on a lid and bake for about 1¼ hours, or until the potatoes are tender, in a preheated oven, Gas Mark 4, 180°C or 350°F. Serve hot, garnished with the parsley.

Potatoes with Cheese and Bacon

This makes a tasty snack.

Serves 3, or 2 generously

1 scant tablespoon sunflower oil
2 slices unsmoked back bacon, trimmed of fat and chopped
3 medium potatoes, peeled and cut into thin slices
2 oz (50 g) grated cheese
1 clove garlic, peeled and put through a garlic press
Freshly ground black pepper, to taste
1 generous tablespoon freshly chopped parsley
2 tablespoons water mixed with 2 tablespoons low fat dried milk granules

Method

Use a heavy based frying pan to heat the oil. Fry the bacon pieces until crisp and brown. Grease an ovenproof dish with sunflower oil. Arrange half the potatoes in a layer. Sprinkle with half the cheese and bacon. Add another layer of potatoes and top with the remaining cheese and bacon. Sprinkle the garlic, black pepper and parsley over the top and put on a cover. Bake in a preheated oven at Gas Mark 5, 190°C or 375°F for about 40–45 minutes. Heat the milk and pour over the top. Serve immediately.

Potatoes Lyonnaise

Serves 2–3

1 medium onion, sliced finely
1 tablespoon sunflower oil
3 medium old potatoes, peeled and cut into thin slices
Freshly ground black pepper, to taste
1 heaped tablespoon freshly chopped parsley

Method

Preheat the oven to Gas Mark 4, 180°C or 350°F. Fry the onions in the oil for 3 or 4 minutes until they start to brown. Grease an ovenproof dish with a little oil and arrange half the potatoes in a layer. Sprinkle with black pepper and parsley and distribute half the onions. Cover with the remaining potatoes and finish off with pepper, parsley and onions. Put on a lid and bake on a shelf above centre for about 1 hour. Serve hot with hot or cold meat.

SALADS AND SALAD DRESSINGS

SALADS

In Britain there is still a stronghold of opinion, especially among older people, that salad is 'rabbit's food' and not really a worthwhile addition to the diet. There is also a feeling that salad is a hot weather food and is unsuitable for winter. This attitude is not found in other European countries such as France, Italy and Spain, where salad is a staple part of the diet. (By coincidence, these are countries which enjoy long, hot summers, so perhaps the British weather must take some of the blame?) Salads are an extremely valuable source of vitamins and minerals, and their regular use in the diet cannot be too strongly recommended, to the extent of everyday eating. For this reason the number of salad recipes in this book may seem a little extravagant to most people, even vegetarians.

Failure to introduce regular eating of salads into the diet can be caused not just by the attitude already mentioned but by a lack of knowledge concerning the preparation of such a simple dish for the intended eater. For instance, some people have difficulty in chewing, especially older people or those with ill-fitting dentures, and this tends to put such people off salads altogether. However, the problem is easily solved by very finely grating the chewier kind of vegetables. Cold, cooked vegetables can also be used, and these are usually easier to eat than raw ingredients. Lightly coating the salad with dressing rather than serving it with a mound of salad cream or mayonnaise offers an easier solution for eating too. As to variety, the winter offers an even wider selection of salad ingredients than the summer. Dried and fresh fruit can also be used as well as sprouting seeds, dried seeds, nuts, cooked vegetables and fresh herbs.

SALAD DRESSINGS

Although raw vegetables and other salad ingredients are generally moist it is difficult to eat a mixture of them without some kind of dressing to moisten them further. Commercial salad dressings tend to be very high in oil/fat as well as the usual additives for preserving, colouring and flavouring. Advertising tends to show large quantities of dressing being applied to the minimum amount of salad, and this tends to make the dressing seem more important than the raw vegetables. Dressing is primarily to make the salad moist and easy to eat and should not be regarded as a base in which to mix the salad.

Dressings made at home offer more control over the oil/fat than commercial dressings, especially the thick cream types. Unnecessary additives can be left out and a wider variety of dressings enjoyed, with several bottled and stored in the fridge for convenience. Herbs, flavourings, etc. can be added to basic dressings as required, to give variety and maintain interest in this kind of food.

Basically there are two kinds of dressing – the thick cream type known as 'salad cream' or 'mayonnaise', and the thinner, transparent kind with an oil base called 'salad dressing'. Raw egg yolks are often used for the thick cream types, making them a high cholesterol food. A variety of oils can be used for the thinner dressings, ranging from the rather heavy olive oil to lighter oils such as sunflower, safflower, corn and soya. These last four are high in polyunsaturates. Ground nut oil and some mixed vegetable oils tend to pose as polyunsaturated oils, being transparent, but they can be very high in saturated fat. (Most users will be unaware of this fact, such is the widespread belief that transparency indicates high concentrations of polyunsaturates.)

BASIC DRESSINGS

Except where indicated the following recipes are for small amounts that can be stored in the fridge and used as required. You will find salad recipes refer back to these basic recipes for dressings rather than repeating the same information.

Basic Vinaigrette (French Dressing)

Suitable oils are sunflower, safflower (the two healthiest), olive, corn and soya. (A mixture of half olive and one of the others makes a thinner dressing than all olive oil.)

5 tablespoons oil
2 tablespoons wine vinegar
Freshly ground black pepper, to taste

Method

Put all three ingredients into a screwtop jar. Put the lid on firmly and shake well to combine before use.

Sweet vinaigrette

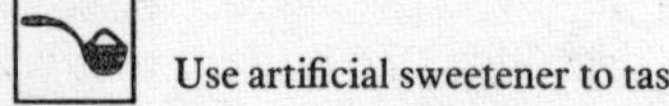
Use artificial sweetener to taste

Use the Basic Vinaigrette recipe and add a little sugar to taste. Soft brown sugar, fructose or caster sugar are suitable.

Vinaigrette with mustard

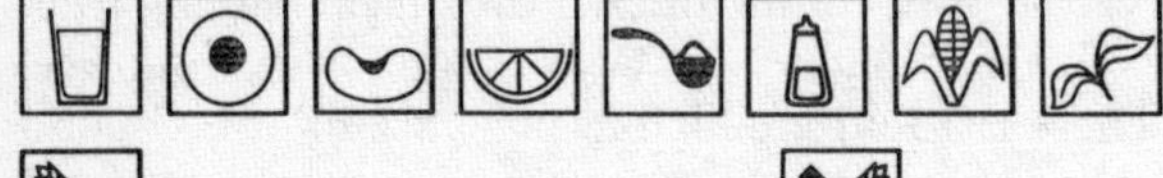

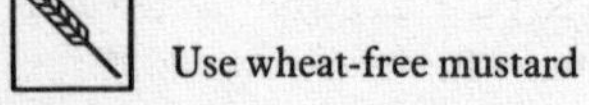
Use wheat-free mustard

Use gluten-free mustard

A useful dressing for salads with the minimum of ingredients, such as a green salad. Use the Basic Vinaigrette recipe but add 1 teaspoon of real French mustard. Shake really well before using.

Vinaigrette with herbs

Use the Basic Vinaigrette recipe but add 1 tablespoon of any of the following herbs, which should be fresh and chopped very finely: parsley, thyme, tarragon, basil or mint. Chives can be used in a larger quantity, say 2 tablespoons.

Vinaigrette with lemon

A very sharp dressing, excellent if the salad is to be eaten with fish. Use the Basic Vinaigrette recipe but instead of wine vinegar use fresh lemon juice.

Vinaigrette with garlic

Use the Basic Vinaigrette recipe but add 1 clove of peeled garlic, crushed in through a garlic press, and 1 teaspoon of sugar.

Vinaigrette with onion

Use the Basic Vinaigrette recipe but add 2 heaped teaspoons of very finely chopped onion, preferably shallot.

Vinaigrette with spring onion

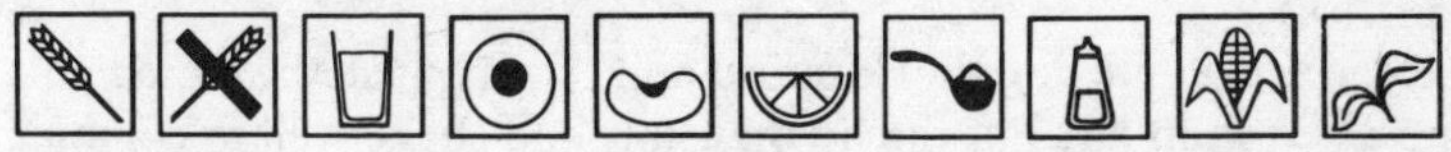

Use the Basic Vinaigrette recipe but add the finely chopped white part of 1 spring onion. This has a more delicate flavour than ordinary onion.

Skimmed Milk Dressing

This is a very low fat dressing. Keep in the fridge for up to 5 days only.

½ cup cold water
1½ tablespoons low fat dried milk granules
2 teaspoons sunflower oil
2 tablespoons cider vinegar
½ teaspoon sugar (fructose, caster or icing sugar)
Sprinkle white pepper

Method

Measure the cold water into a screwtop jar. Sprinkle in the milk granules and stir with a teaspoon to blend. Add all the remaining ingredients and put the lid on firmly. Shake vigorously to combine before using.

Sweet Mustard Dressing

The teaspoon of mustard can be level or heaped, according to taste, as can the type of mustard used: French is milder than English.

  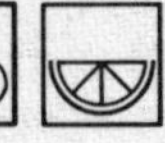   

 Use wheat-free mustard  Use gluten-free mustard

1 tablespoon low fat dried milk granules
½ cup skimmed milk
1 teaspoon made mustard
2 heaped teaspoons sugar (soft brown, fructose or caster)
1 tablespoon wine vinegar
Freshly ground black pepper, to taste

Method

Stir the dried milk into the skimmed milk, then put all the ingredients into a screwtop jar. Put the lid on firmly and shake well to combine before using.

Fruit Dressing (without Oil)

Make this dressing as required. It is good for root salads.

2 tomatoes, washed and chopped
1 teaspoon fresh lemon juice
½ teaspoon caster sugar

Method

Liquidize the tomatoes. Put through a fine mesh wire sieve. The result should be a pale pink purée. Stir in the lemon juice and sugar.

Lime Dressing

Use within a week and store in the fridge.

2 tablespoons sunflower or safflower oil
1 tablespoon fresh lime juice

½ teaspoon caster sugar
Freshly ground black pepper, to taste

Method

Combine all the ingredients in a screwtop jar and shake vigorously before using.

Honey and Lemon Dressing

Serve on salads with nuts and dried fruit.

3 tablespoons sunflower oil
1 generous tablespoon clear honey
2 tablespoons fresh lemon juice
Finely grated rind of ½ lemon
Freshly ground black pepper, to taste

Method

Put all the ingredients into a screwtop jar and put the lid on firmly. Shake well to combine.

Yoghurt Mayonnaise

The traditional thick cream dressing of mayonnaise is exceptionally high in both fat and cholesterol, as it comprises egg yolks and oil. It is possible to make a thick cream dressing using yoghurt as a base, thus reducing the vast amount of fat in the recipe. This yoghurt 'mayonnaise' can be flavoured with herbs etc. as required.

      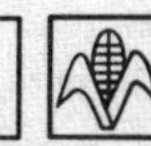 

1 small carton natural (unflavoured) yoghurt
1 tablespoon wine vinegar, preferably white
1 teaspoon caster sugar
1 clove garlic, peeled
Freshly ground black pepper, or white pepper, to taste

Method

Put the yoghurt into a basin. Stir in the wine vinegar and sugar. Crush in the garlic through a garlic press and add the pepper. Stir well to combine.

Yoghurt mayonnaise with curry

Add mild curry powder and ground coriander a pinch at a time to Yoghurt Mayonnaise. Stir in well and keep tasting until you feel you have put in enough. Use on cold, boiled potato, cut into small cubes.

Yoghurt mayonnaise with parsley

To every 2 tablespoons of Yoghurt Mayonnaise stir in 1 heaped teaspoon of freshly chopped parsley. Use on cold boiled potatoes, cut into small cubes, or on cold fish such as tuna or prawns.

Mayonnaise (without Egg) (1)

This mayonnaise will keep in the fridge for up to a week, in a screwtop jar. The tomato purée will colour it a delicate pink. Omit the purée for a white version.

Makes ¼ pint (150 ml)

 Use wheat-free mustard

 Use gluten-free mustard

2 level tablespoons low fat dried milk granules
¼ pint (150 ml) cold water
1 level tablespoon cornflour
1 tablespoon fresh lemon juice
1 tablespoon sunflower or safflower oil
½ level teaspoon made mustard
½ level teaspoon tomato purée
Freshly ground black pepper, to taste
1 level teaspoon sugar (caster or fructose)

Method

Mix the dried milk with the water, then stir in the cornflour. Slowly bring to the boil in a small heavy based saucepan, while you stir. Simmer for 1 minute, still stirring, and then allow to get cold. (A greaseproof 'lid' will stop a skin forming.) Spoon into a liquidizer with the remaining ingredients and blend. Turn into a basin and add a pinch or two more of the sugar or a little more lemon juice to taste. If it has turned out too thick then add a little more skimmed milk.

Salad Dressing with Soya

This makes a good substitute for commercial salad dressing for people who are addicted to it. Store it in the fridge and use as required, shaking well each time before using. This recipe can also be used as the basis for a kind of mayonnaise (see below).

 Use wheat-free mustard  Use gluten-free mustard

1 slightly heaped tablespoon soya flour
3–4 tablespoons wine or cider vinegar
8 tablespoons sunflower or safflower oil
3 heaped teaspoons caster or soft moist sugar
1 level teaspoon made mustard (English)

Method

Put the soya flour into a screwtop jar. Stir and press with the back of a spoon to remove any lumps. Add all the other ingredients and put the lid on firmly. Shake well to combine.

Mayonnaise (without Egg) (2)

  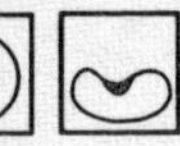    

 Use wheat-free mustard  Use gluten-free mustard

4 tablespoons water mixed with 2 level teaspoons ground rice
4 tablespoons Salad Dressing with Soya (see recipe above)

Method

Cook the ground rice and water in a small saucepan, while you stir for 2 or 3 minutes until smooth and thickened, then leave to cool for 4 or 5 minutes. Stir in the salad dressing until smooth. When cold put into a screwtop jar and store in the fridge. Before using shake well: it keeps for about a week.

Salad Cream

 Use milk-free margarine

2 oz (50 g) soft polyunsaturated margarine
2 slightly heaped teaspoons caster sugar
1 teaspoon wine vinegar
4 teaspoons water
Squeeze fresh lemon juice
1 teaspoon sunflower oil
Pinch allspice
Pinch black or white pepper
½ level teaspoon soya flour

Method

Put the margarine into a bowl with the sugar and beat to a cream. Beat in the vinegar a little at a time until absorbed, then do the same with the water. Add the lemon juice and beat in. Put in the oil and the spice. Beat in. Lastly add the soya flour, through a fine mesh sieve to stop any lumps spoiling the result. Give the mixture a final beating and put into a screwtop jar. Store in the fridge and use as required.

Pink salad dressing

 Use milk-free margarine

Make the above recipe for Salad Cream and add 1 level teaspoon of tomato purée at the same time as the soya flour. A little more sugar may be required, to taste.

SALAD INGREDIENTS

Salads are easy to prepare, requiring no great kitchen skills and only simple equipment – a sharp knife, grater, chopping board and a bowl. A great variety of ingredients can be used, as the following lists will show.

Leaves

Lettuce – Cos, Flat, Webb's Wonder, Iceberg, Little Gem, etc.
Cabbage – red or white, Savoy or any hard cabbage, curly kale, spring greens, sprout tops.
Brussels sprouts.
Spinach – young leaves and wash extra well.
Watercress – dark green sprigs must be washed extra well.
Cress – leave growing in its pack until just before using.
Parsley – use the tenderest leaves of this herb.

Roots

Carrots – use young or old, whatever is in season.
Parsnips – young roots are best.
Turnips – choose small, young roots.
Beetroot – young or old beets can be eaten raw or cooked.
Swede – use young, small roots.
Radish – use small red or white salad radishes, or the equivalent of white kooli can be grated just like carrot.
Onions – can be cut into thin rings or chopped finely, and are cheaper and tastier than spring onions.

Other Vegetables (Raw)

Cucumber – use ridge or prickly cucumbers. No need to peel.
Peppers – green, red, yellow and black peppers are now available. Deseed and chop or cut into strips.
Spring onions – do not eat just the white parts of these, as the tender green parts are also useful in salads.
Cauliflower – crisp and crunchy in its raw state and ideal for salad use.
Mushrooms – small, unopened ones are best for raw eating. Wash extra well but avoid bruising.
Courgettes– choose young, tender ones for eating raw.
Peas – young, freshly shelled raw peas are sweet and delicious.

Cooked Vegetables

Potato – new or old potatoes can be boiled and allowed to get cold before slicing or cubing. Leave the skins on small new potatoes.
Broad beans – boil and allow to get cold before using. Young ones can be eaten whole but older ones will need to be skinned and just the inner green parts eaten.

Peas – cook and allow to get cold. Avoid using dressing which contains lemon juice as this will discolour them.
Mushrooms – small button mushrooms can be cooked and allowed to cool before using.
Leeks – cook in boiling water until tender and then strain extra well. Best cooked in large pieces.
Green beans – cook in boiling water until tender. Allow to grow cold before using.

Sprouting Seeds

Beansprouts – these are mung beans sprouted into long white shoots.
Fenugreek – tiny golden brown seeds with white shoots.
Lentils – sprouts are small.
Aduki beans – yellow beans with a brown covering, short white sprouts.
Alfalfa – tiny brown seeds which produce a tangle of delicate white shoots.
Wheat – golden brown seeds which produce thin, short shoots.

All these beans and seeds are obtainable at good health stores. Mung beansprouts can often be found at good greengrocers and supermarkets. Other seeds, such as barley, mustard, pumpkin, rice, sesame and sunflower seeds, can be sprouted at home. Chickpeas can also be sprouted. Sprouting times vary from 2–7 days. Sprouted beans and seeds are prized for their vitamin and mineral content and are probably used most by vegetarians and vegans.

Nuts

Almonds – a very versatile nut that combines well with other salad ingredients. Do not blanch them, but use with their brown skins left on.
Walnuts – use freshly shelled ones if possible.
Brazil nuts – always serve chopped very finely as they really need a good deal of chewing.
Cashews – sweet tasting, milky flavoured nuts.
Hazelnuts – best served chopped and not whole.

Seeds

Sunflower seeds – sprinkle into salads just as they are.
Sesame seeds – minute seeds for sprinkling.

Fruits

Apple – wash well and leave the skin on.
Pear – peel before using.
Orange – very moist fruit. Other members of the citrus family can also be used, e.g. clementines, tangerines, satsumas, grapefruit, uglifruit, etc.
Banana – use in salads that have a dressing with lemon juice or the banana will discolour.
Grapes – best served both peeled and depipped unless they are the small sultana grapes.
Dried apricots – wash well, dry and chop into small pieces as they are very chewy.
Raisins – wash, dry and leave whole.
Sultanas – wash, dry and leave whole.
Avocado – this is high in fat so should only be used in small amounts. Like banana it discolours without a lemon dressing.

Other Salad Ingredients

Rice – boil, strain in a colander and allow to get cold before using.
Buckwheat – use in the same way as rice; needs long cooking.
Haricot (type) beans – there are many varieties and colours. They need to be soaked overnight and then cooked carefully, i.e. well boiled for the first 10 minutes of cooking and then simmered until tender. Allow to cool before using in salads.
Canned beans – many kinds of beans can be bought already cooked in cans. Flageolets (green haricot beans), red kidney beans and white haricot beans (navy beans) are all suitable for salads. Always strain canned beans in a fine mesh wire sieve before using. If they look sticky, rinse them under the cold tap and drain before use.
Borlotti beans, chickpeas – can be cooked at home or bought already canned.
Pasta – cold, cooked pasta can be used as a salad base. Small shapes or short lengths of noodles are the easiest to eat. See p. 154 for cooking instructions.
Cracked wheat or wholewheat – this can be cooked, strained and allowed to cool before using as a salad base.

High Protein Additions

Egg – hard boil and plunge into cold water. When cool peel and either chop or serve in quarters.
Ham – trim off all fat and discard before using.

Tofu – a bland cheese-like ingredient made from soya beans. It will take up other flavours well. A useful vegetarian and vegan food.
Fish – cold canned fish that has been well drained can be used for salads. Leave sardines whole but flake tuna fish and salmon.
Prawns/shrimps – must be cooked, shelled and allowed to cool before use. Defrost the frozen kinds and wash before use.
Cold meat – chicken or turkey from a cold roast bird can be skinned, trimmed of fat and either cut into slivers, small cubes or pieces.
Bacon – grill lean parts of unsmoked back bacon until crisp and then cut into small pieces. Makes a good garnish for green leafy salads.
See also the list of nuts and seeds for high protein additions.

SALAD PREPARATION

Salad vegetables should be as fresh as possible and prepared just before they are eaten. Dry ingredients with kitchen paper after thorough washing. (A clean tea towel can be used if preferred.) The recipes that follow will tell you how to prepare the ingredients after trimming or peeling.

Use a good sized bowl to help you mix the ingredients for mixed salads. (Avoid using a wooden salad bowl. It is better to use a china or glass one that can be washed properly after use.) A pair of large forks, salad servers or your hands can be used to mix the ingredients, although raw or cooked beetroot should not be mixed by hand as it will stain.

Always dress a salad just before bringing it to the table or it will become soggy. Do not overdress or you will have a puddle at the bottom of the bowl.

GREEN SALADS

Green Salad (1)

For each person you will need:

3 or 4 lettuce leaves
5 or 6 thin slices cucumber
1 teaspoon finely chopped fresh parsley
Freshly ground black pepper, to taste
3 teaspoons basic vinaigrette

Method

Tear the lettuce into small pieces. Add the remaining ingredients and toss in the vinaigrette. Serve immediately.

Green Salad (2)

 Use wheat-free mustard  Use gluten-free mustard

For each person you will need:

2 lettuce leaves each of 3 varieties of lettuce
3 teaspoons vinaigrette with mustard

Method

Tear the lettuce into pieces, toss in the dressing and serve at once.

Green Salad (3)

For each person you will need:

4 or 5 lettuce leaves
¼ packet cress
3 slices cucumber
3 teaspoons vinaigrette or vinaigrette with garlic

Method

Mix all the ingredients and toss in the dressing. Serve at once.

Green Salad (4)

For each person you will need:

3 or 4 lettuce leaves
6 sprigs watercress
3 slices cucumber (optional)
3 teaspoons sweet vinaigrette

Method

Tear the lettuce leaves into pieces and mix with the watercress and cucumber. Toss in the dressing and serve at once.

Green Salad (5)

For each person you will need:

3 lettuce leaves
2 or 3 young spinach leaves
Freshly ground black pepper, to taste
3 teaspoons vinaigrette with lemon

Method

Tear the leaves into small pieces and season. Toss in the dressing and serve immediately.

Green Salad (6) (large)

     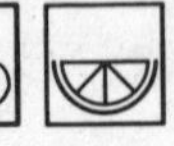   

For each person you will need:

4 or 5 lettuce leaves
¼ green pepper, deseeded and cut into strips
3 slices cucumber
4 or 5 onion rings, thinly sliced
1 teaspoon freshly chopped parsley
Few watercress sprigs or ¼ packet cress, chopped
1 tablespoon sweet vinaigrette (or less)
Freshly ground black pepper, to taste

Method

Tear the lettuce leaves into small pieces. Put into a bowl with all the other ingredients and toss to combine. Serve at once.

MIXED ROOT SALADS

Root Salad (1)

For each person you will need:

1 small raw beetroot, peeled and finely grated
½ medium carrot, finely grated
3 teaspoons vinaigrette

Method
Combine the grated vegetables in a bowl and toss in the dressing. Serve at once.

Root Salad (2)

For each person you will need:

½ medium carrot, finely grated
1 small turnip, finely grated
1 spring onion, finely chopped, or 1 heaped teaspoon raisins
3 teaspoons vinaigrette

Method
Combine the ingredients in a bowl and toss in the dressing. Serve at once.

Root Salad (3)

For each person you will need:

½ medium carrot, finely grated
1 small parsnip, finely grated
1 heaped teaspoon raisins or sultanas
3 teaspoons vinaigrette with lemon

Method
Combine the ingredients in a bowl and toss in the dressing. Serve at once.

Root Salad (4)

        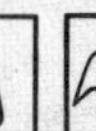  

For each person you will need:

Cube of swede, grated finely
1 small turnip, grated finely
2 stoned dates, chopped finely
3 teaspoons vinaigrette

Method

Combine the ingredients in a bowl and toss to coat with the dressing. Serve at once.

SALADS WITH A CABBAGE BASE

Coleslaw

For each person you will need:

2 crisp cabbage leaves, shredded finely
¼ eating apple, sliced thinly and then chopped
1 heaped teaspoon finely chopped onion
1 heaped tablespoon coarsely grated carrot
Freshly ground black pepper, to taste
3–4 teaspoons vinaigrette with lemon
½ teaspoon sugar

Method

Combine all the ingredients in a salad bowl and toss lightly to coat with dressing. Serve at once.

White Cabbage Salad

For each person you will need:

2 leaves crisp white cabbage, finely shredded
½ stick celery, chopped finely
¼ medium carrot, coarsely grated
1 heaped teaspoon raisins
3 teaspoons vinaigrette or vinaigrette with onion
Freshly ground black pepper, to taste

Method

Combine all the ingredients in a salad bowl and toss to coat with dressing. Serve at once.

Red Cabbage Salad

For each person you will need:

2 leaves red cabbage, finely shredded
1 small shallot (or equivalent), finely chopped
½ eating apple, coarsely grated
¼ packet cress, chopped
3 teaspoons vinaigrette with lemon
¼ red pepper, deseeded and chopped (optional)
Freshly ground black pepper, to taste

Method

Combine all the ingredients in a salad bowl and toss to coat with the dressing. Serve at once.

MIXED SALADS

Red Salad

If the tomato and beetroot are very moist you may require less dressing.

 Use wheat-free mustard for dressing

 Use gluten-free mustard for dressing

For each person you will need:

1 leaf red cabbage, shredded finely
1 tomato, chopped
½ small raw beetroot, finely grated
¼ medium carrot, finely grated
3–4 teaspoons vinaigrette or vinaigrette with mustard
Freshly ground black pepper, to taste

Method

Combine all the ingredients and toss to coat with the dressing. Serve at once.

Cauliflower Salad

A pinch or two of sugar will improve this salad if the carrot is not very sweet.

 Avoid sugar

For each person you will need:

A few crisp cauliflower florets, chopped
3 sprouts, finely shredded, or 3 young leaves curly kale, finely shredded
¼ medium carrot, finely grated
3 teaspoons vinaigrette with lemon
Freshly ground black pepper, to taste

Method

Combine all the ingredients and toss to coat with the dressing.

Courgette and Tomato Salad

     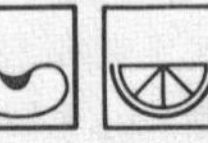    

For each person you will need:

1 small courgette, sliced thinly
1 tomato, cut in half and sliced thinly
1 heaped teaspoon freshly chopped parsley
Vinaigrette with garlic – 3 teaspoons should be sufficient
Freshly ground black pepper, to taste

Method

Combine all the ingredients and toss to coat with the dressing. Leave to marinade for 15 minutes before serving.

Sweet Pepper Salad

Yellow or black peppers may be used instead of the green.

For each person you will need:

¼ red pepper, deseeded and sliced thinly
¼ green pepper, deseeded and sliced thinly
1 spring onion, finely chopped
3 teaspoons vinaigrette with garlic
Freshly ground black pepper, to taste

Method

Combine all the ingredients and toss to coat with the dressing. Serve at once.

Mixed Salad with Avocado

This makes a generous salad for one or will stretch to two with a little more lettuce. It is excellent with Italian food.

 Use wheat-free mustard for dressing

 Use gluten-free mustard for dressing

For each person you will need:

½ clove garlic, unpeeled
3 or 4 lettuce leaves, including heart leaves
2 small tomatoes, quartered
¼ green pepper, deseeded and chopped
4 or 5 thin slices cucumber
¼ stick celery, sliced
3 teaspoons vinaigrette with mustard
¼ avocado, cut into long slices
5 or 6 thin onion rings
Freshly ground black pepper, to taste

Method

Take the garlic and rub round the inside of a bowl. Line with lettuce leaves. Fill with the tomatoes, green pepper, cucumber and celery. Sprinkle the dressing over these and lay the avocado slices on top. Garnish with onion rings, season with the pepper and serve at once.

Pasta Salad with Tomatoes

Use pasta shapes or very short lengths of noodles. Wholewheat pasta will be the tastiest.

 Use egg-free pasta

For each person you will need:

2 heaped tablespoons cooked, drained and cooled wholewheat pasta
2 small tomatoes, chopped
1 spring onion, chopped finely
3 teaspoons vinaigrette with garlic
Freshly ground black pepper, to taste
1 teaspoon freshly chopped parsley

Method

Put the pasta, tomatoes and spring onion into a bowl. Toss with the vinaigrette and a little pepper. Sprinkle with the parsley and serve.

Pasta Salad with Chicken

Use pasta shapes for an attractive dish.

 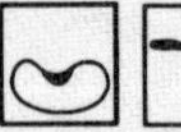   

 Use egg-free pasta

For each person you will need:

2 heaped tablespoons cooked, drained and cooled wholewheat pasta
About 1 oz (25 g) cold chicken, cut into small pieces
4 shelled almonds, cut into slivers
¼ peeled banana, cut into slices
4–5 slices cucumber, chopped
1 heaped teaspoon freshly chopped parsley
1 tablespoon (or less) vinaigrette with lemon
Freshly ground black pepper, to taste

Method

Combine all the ingredients and toss to coat with the dressing. Serve at once.

SALADS WITH FISH

Tuna Salad

A high protein dish.

For each person you will need:

3 or 4 lettuce leaves, torn into pieces
½ small can tuna, drained and flaked
1 tomato, sliced
4 thin slices cucumber
1 tablespoon vinaigrette with lemon
Freshly ground black pepper, to taste
½ hard boiled egg, cut into four

Method

Line a shallow dish with the lettuce. Put the tuna, tomato and cucumber into a basin and pour over the dressing. Toss to combine and pile on the lettuce. Season with the black pepper and lay the slices of egg on the top to decorate.

Tuna Salad with Beans

     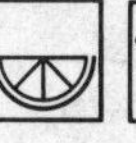 

 Use home-cooked unsalted beans

For each person you will need:

2 heaped tablespoons cooked haricot beans
1 spring onion, chopped finely
1 heaped teaspoon freshly chopped parsley
2 small tomatoes, skinned
½ small can tuna, drained
1 tablespoon vinaigrette with garlic
Freshly ground black pepper, to taste

Method

Combine all the ingredients in a bowl and toss to coat with the dressing. Leave to marinade for 15 minutes before serving.

Sardine Salad

 Use vinaigrette with lemon

 Use vinaigrette with mustard

 Use vinaigrette with lemon

For each person you will need:

6 or 7 heart leaves of lettuce
1 tomato, cut into thin slices
2 or 3 canned sardines, drained on kitchen paper
1 shallot, or equivalent, chopped finely
1 teaspoon chopped parsley
3 teaspoons vinaigrette with mustard or lemon
Freshly ground black pepper, to taste

Method

Line a plate with the lettuce leaves. Cover with the slices of tomato. Lay the sardines on top and sprinkle with the shallot and parsley. Spoon over the dressing, avoiding the sardines. Serve at once, seasoned with black pepper.

Prawn Salad (Prawn Cocktail)

 Serve with wheat-free bread

 Avoid lemon garnish

 Serve with gluten-free bread

For each person you will need:

2 lettuce leaves, torn into pieces
1 heaped tablespoon frozen prawns, defrosted
1 tablespoon pink mayonnaise or pink salad dressing (see recipes), or other thick dressing
½ tomato, cut into 4 wedges
3 sprigs watercress
Lemon twist to decorate

Method

Line a glass dish with the lettuce leaves. Mix the prawns with the mayonnaise and spoon into the centre. Decorate with the tomato, watercress and the lemon twist. Serve within 30 minutes with brown bread and butter.

Egg Salad

For each person you will need:

2 or 3 lettuce leaves
¼ stick celery, sliced
4 slices cucumber
1 hard boiled egg, peeled and halved lengthways
1 tomato, cut into quarters
1 tablespoon yoghurt mayonnaise
1 teaspoon freshly chopped parsley

Method

Line a plate with the lettuce. Sprinkle with the celery and cucumber and place the egg halves on top. Garnish with the tomato quarters. Spoon the dressing over the egg halves and sprinkle with the parsley. Serve at once.

Salads with Onion and Herb Garnish

For each portion of any mixed salad, chop ½ spring onion or 3 chives and mix with 1 teaspoon freshly chopped parsley. Sprinkle over the salad before serving. (If you do not have a spring onion, a small piece of ordinary onion, finely chopped, will make a good substitute.)

Salads with Onion

The method of preparation is the same for the following four salads, which are designed for one person. Sprinkle the vegetable base with the onion and spoon over the dressing.

Bean and onion salad

1 portion cooked green beans, runner or stringless
1 slice onion, chopped finely
3 teaspoons vinaigrette

Tomato and onion salad

    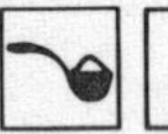   

 Use plain vinaigrette

 Use plain vinaigrette

2 tomatoes, sliced
1 pickling onion (or equivalent), chopped finely
2 teaspoons vinaigrette or vinaigrette with mustard
1 teaspoon freshly chopped parsley to garnish (optional)

Potato salad (1)

     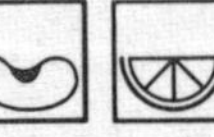    

1 medium cold, boiled potato, or 4 cold, boiled new potatoes in their skins
1 spring onion, chopped finely
1 teaspoon freshly chopped parsley to garnish (optional)

Potato salad (2)

6 small new potatoes, boiled in their skins, cold
1 tablespoon yoghurt mayonnaise
1 teaspoon freshly chopped parsley
2 chives, chopped finely

Spinach Salad

For each person you will need:

About 6 young spinach leaves, well washed and torn into pieces
3 teaspoons vinaigrette with lemon
Freshly ground black pepper, to taste
1 rasher unsmoked back bacon, trimmed of all fat and dry fried in a pan or grilled

Method

Put the spinach into a bowl. Pour over the dressing and season with the pepper. Toss to coat. Sprinkle the bacon over the salad as a garnish. Serve at once.

Carrot Salad

For each person you will need:

½ medium carrot, finely grated
3 teaspoons vinaigrette
1 teaspoon freshly chopped parsley

Method

Toss the carrot in the dressing and serve sprinkled with the parsley.

Mushroom Salad

For each person you will need:

About 6–8 button mushrooms, washed and dried
3 teaspoons vinaigrette with lemon
1 teaspoon chopped chives or parsley
Freshly ground black pepper, to taste

Method

Combine all the ingredients in a small bowl and leave to marinade for 30 minutes before serving.

Green Salad with Egg

Dandelion leaves are rarely sold in Britain, unlike the Mediterranean countries where they are quite a common sight at the greengrocers. If you have a garden, instead of weeding them out and throwing them away, use them for this salad. If dandelion leaves are not available, then use young spinach leaves.

For each person you will need:

A handful young dandelion or spinach leaves
1 cold hard boiled egg, peeled
1 rasher unsmoked back bacon, trimmed of all fat and fried until crisp in 1 teaspoon sunflower oil
1 tablespoon vinaigrette with garlic
Freshly ground black pepper, to taste

Method

Wash and trim the leaves, then cut them into pieces with a pair of kitchen scissors. Chop the hard boiled egg and put it into a bowl with the leaves. Sprinkle with the bacon pieces after tossing in the dressing and pepper.

Egg and Potato Salad

For each person you will need:

1 spring onion, chopped finely
2 cold boiled potatoes, chopped
1 hard boiled egg, chopped
1 small tomato, chopped
2 tablespoons mayonnaise (see recipes)
1 teaspoon freshly chopped parsley

Method

Combine all the ingredients and mix carefully in a bowl, to distribute the dressing. Serve with lettuce or watercress and cucumber.

Salad with Beans

Serves 2

 Use home-cooked, unsalted beans

4 oz (110 g) cooked mixed dried beans (see cooking instructions on p. 265)
4 oz (110 g) stringless beans, cooked
Freshly ground black pepper, to taste
1 tablespoon vinaigrette with garlic
1 spring onion, finely chopped
1 teaspoon freshly chopped parsley

Method

Make sure all the beans are absolutely cold before using them. Put into a bowl, season with black pepper and toss in the dressing to combine. Sprinkle with the onion and parsley and serve with mashed or jacket potatoes, cottage cheese and a green salad for a nourishing vegetarian meal.

Salad with Lettuce and Orange

This salad is excellent with cold poultry, especially cold duck.

For each person you will need:

2 cos lettuce leaves
2 flat lettuce leaves
3 or 4 sprigs watercress
1 tablespoon vinaigrette with lemon
3–4 orange segments, cut away from the membrane and depipped
2 or 3 chopped chives, or 3 or 4 onion rings

Method

Tear the lettuce leaves into pieces and put into a bowl. Add the watercress and dressing. Toss to combine and lay the orange slices on top. Garnish with the chives or onion rings and serve.

Waldorf Salad

This is good with cold pork, jacket potatoes and a green salad.

Serves 2

1 eating apple, cored but not peeled, chopped
1 stick celery, chopped
8 walnut halves, chopped
2 tablespoons mayonnaise (see recipes)
2 teaspoons freshly chopped parsley

Method

Combine all the ingredients, except the parsley, in a bowl and mix lightly to coat the ingredients with the mayonnaise. Sprinkle with the parsley as a garnish and serve.

Cracked Wheat Salad

A nice side salad for grilled meat or fish.

 Serve with eggs or cheese

For each person you will need:

About 2 heaped tablespoons small cracked wheat grains
1 tomato, chopped finely (peel if you have the time)
1 spring onion, chopped finely
1 level tablespoon finely chopped parsley
Freshly ground black pepper, to taste
1 tablespoon vinaigrette with lemon
Watercress sprigs or heart lettuce leaves

Method

Soak the cracked wheat in water for at least an hour. Drain and squeeze dry (see recipe on p. 189). Put into a bowl with the tomato, onion and parsley. Season to taste with the pepper and pour over the dressing. Line a plate with the green leaves of your choice and put the wheat salad in a mound in the centre. Serve immediately.

Mixed Salad

A crunchy salad with delicate colours – pale green, white and yellow. Serve with cold meat or fish and jacket potatoes.

 Use wheat-free mustard for dressing

 Serve with eggs or cheese

 Use gluten-free mustard for dressing

For each person you will need:

4 or 5 lettuce heart leaves, torn into pieces
3 or 4 onion rings, sliced very thinly
Few thin slices green pepper
Few florets cauliflower, chopped
2 sprouts, finely shredded
¼ stick celery, chopped
About 1 tablespoon vinaigrette with mustard
Freshly ground black pepper, to taste

Method

Put all the ingredients into a bowl and toss to combine.

Simple Salad

Not all salads need to be mixed in a bowl. Individual ingredients can be arranged on a serving plate and made to look attractive. Here is a very basic, all-the-year-round salad which always looks good and is easy and quick to prepare. It is also a good salad to serve because it can be made a little in advance of eating. Leave room on the plate for the high protein part of the meal – meat, fish, egg, etc. – and a high starch food such as potatoes. Follow with fresh fruit for an easy, well-balanced meal.

For each person you will need:

2 or 3 lettuce leaves, left whole
About 1 heaped tablespoon of a finely grated vegetable, either carrot, turnip or raw beetroot
1 heaped tablespoon chopped celery

Few thin strips green, red or yellow pepper
1 tomato, sliced
4 or 5 slices cucumber

Method

Arrange the lettuce leaves on a plate. Place the grated vegetable, celery and pepper in small mounds on the lettuce. Lay the tomato and cucumber slices in a fan shape. Serve a dressing of your choice separately (see recipes).

Crudités

     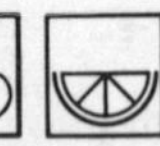    

These are often called 'nibbles'. Use only the freshest vegetables, with one of the mayonnaise recipes from pp. 273–5 or a suitable dressing. Serve attractively on a largish plate with the dressing in a small dish in the centre. Suitable vegetables are small florets of cauliflower, slivers of raw carrot and celery, radishes, spring onions, tiny tomatoes, small heart leaves of lettuce, sprigs of watercress and slivers of green, red or yellow pepper. Simply wash, trim and slice vegetables as required, just before serving.

PUDDINGS

HOT PUDDINGS

Lemon and Fruit Pudding

Avoid too much sweetening. The fruit should be slightly tart and refreshing.

Serves 4

 Use wheat-free bread

 Use artificial sweetener

 Use gluten-free bread

 Avoid margarine, use 1½ tablespoons sunflower oil

 Use milk-free margarine

1 lb (450 g) stewed fruit*
Soft brown sugar or sweetener, to taste
About 2 oz (50 g) butter or margarine
1 lemon
4 oz (110 g) breadcrumbs**

Method

Preheat the oven to Gas Mark 4, 180°C or 350°F. Sweeten the stewed fruit to taste. Grease an ovenproof dish liberally with about half the fat. Grate the lemon finely and mix with the breadcrumbs. Sprinkle a third of this over the base of the dish. Cover with a third of the stewed fruit. Continue in layers using the last of the crumbs for the top. Melt the remaining fat in a small saucepan and pour over the top. Sprinkle with sweetening to taste and bake on the top shelf for about 30 minutes. Serve hot from the oven.

Suitable fruits*

Cooking apples, especially Bramleys; cooking pears; blackberry and apple; plums; apple and plums; apple and black currants; red and black currants; raspberries and apple; apricots; peaches and red currants.

Suitable breads**

Wholewheat, wheat-free and gluten-free bread such as Trufree, or recipes on p. 374.

Steamed Pudding with Fruit

A pudding to replace the fat-heavy, suet type of steamed pudding.

Serves 4–6

Use milk-free margarine and water to mix

4 oz (110 g) plain wholewheat flour
1½ teaspoons baking powder
3 oz (75 g) polyunsaturated margarine
1 small cooking apple, peeled, cored and finely grated
2 oz (50 g) soft brown sugar, or 1½ oz (40 g) fructose
4 oz (110 g) fruit – choose from currants, sultanas, raisins, chopped apricots or chopped, stoned prunes, chopped fresh apricots, peaches, plums, stoned cherries or chopped pineapple
2 slices wholewheat bread made into fine crumbs
Finely grated rind 1 lemon or 1 orange
Milk to mix

Method

Mix the flour and baking powder in a bowl. Add the margarine and blend as well as you can with a fork. Put in the apple, sugar, fruit, crumbs and rind. Mix well, adding enough milk to make a soft dropping consistency. Grease a 1½ pint (900 ml) pudding basin and spoon in the mixture. Cover and steam for about 2 hours. Take off the cover and put a plate over the top. Hold the pudding and plate firmly together and turn upside down. Shake the pudding on to the plate and serve hot with sweet white sauce or custard.

Fruit Cobbler

Serves 4–6

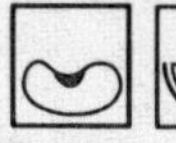   

 Use milk-free margarine, and water to mix

About 1 lb (450 g) stewing fruit*
Brown sugar or fructose, to taste
6 oz (175 g) plain wholewheat flour
1 slightly heaped teaspoon baking powder
3 oz (75 g) polyunsaturated margarine
1 heaped tablespoon brown sugar
1 heaped tablespoon wheat bran
1 egg, beaten
Milk to mix

Method

Prepare the fruit of your choice and stew in a little water until tender. Sweeten to taste with sugar. Remove the fruit with a slotted spoon and put into a pie dish. (Reserve the leftover juice for serving.) Make the scone topping. Put the flour into a mixing bowl and sprinkle in the baking powder. Mix well. Add the margarine and rub in until the mixture resembles breadcrumbs. Stir in the sugar and then the bran. Use a fork to mix in the beaten egg and enough milk to make a soft dough. Knead very lightly and roll out to ½ in. (1 cm) thick on a floured worktop. Cut into rounds. Place around the pie dish, overlapping slightly and on top of the fruit. Bake in a preheated oven, Gas Mark 6, 200°C or 400°F, above the centre for about 20 minutes. After this turn down the heat to Gas Mark 5, 190°C or 375°F for at least another 10 minutes. Serve hot from the oven with a little single cream or just as it is with the leftover juice heated in a small saucepan and poured over each portion.

Suitable fruits*

Apple; blackberry and apple; apple and blackcurrant; apple and plum; plum; greengage; apricots; peaches; peaches and raspberries; red and black currants; stewing pears; cooked prunes; cooked dried apricots.

Batter Pudding with Fresh Fruit

This makes a good breakfast dish as well as a pudding.

Serves 3–4

2 oz (50 g) plain wholewheat flour
1 egg, beaten
¼ pint (150 ml) skimmed milk
1 tablespoon sunflower oil
4 small Conference pears or Bramley cooking apples, peeled, cored and quartered
Brown sugar or fructose, to taste
3 good pinches cinnamon (optional)

Method

Make the batter while you preheat the oven to Gas Mark 7, 220°C or 425°F. Put the flour into a bowl and make a well in the centre. Pour in the egg and mix to a lumpy paste. Add the milk a little at a time. As soon as the mixture can be beaten, beat well. Add the rest of the milk and beat again to a smooth, creamy batter. Heat the oil in a small roasting tin. When it begins to smoke, take off the heat and arrange the fruit over the base. Sprinkle with sugar and the spice, and quickly pour the batter over the fruit. Put straight into the oven on the top shelf and bake for about 30 minutes. (Do not open the door for at least 20 minutes or it will go flat.) Serve right away on hot plates.

Batter Pudding with Dried Fruit

Serves 2, or 1 generously

1 really heaped tablespoon plain wholewheat flour (1 oz/25 g)
1 small egg, beaten
3 tablespoons skimmed milk
3 teaspoons sunflower oil
1 generous tablespoon currants, raisins, sultanas, or chopped dried apricots
Brown sugar, to taste

Method

Put the flour into a basin and add the egg. Mix to a lumpy paste and add the milk a little at a time. As soon as the mixture can be beaten, beat well to get out the lumps. Add the remaining milk and beat to a smooth, thin batter. Put the oil into a small sponge tin or six patty tins and heat until it begins to smoke. Quickly pour in the batter and sprinkle in the dried fruit. Have the oven preheated to Gas Mark 9, 240°C or 475°F. Put the pudding straight into the oven, on the top shelf. Bake for about 5 minutes on this high heat, then turn it down to Gas Mark 6, 200°C or 400°F, and continue baking for about 25–30 minutes. Serve hot from the oven as soon as it is ready, sprinkled with a little sugar.

Apples Baked in Sweet Pastry

Serves 2

 Use milk-free margarine

 Avoid egg glaze

Pastry

2 oz (50 g) polyunsaturated margarine
4 oz (110 g) plain wholewheat flour
1 tablespoon soft brown sugar
Water to bind

Filling

2 cooking apples, peeled and cored but left whole
2 tablespoons blackberry or plum jam
Beaten egg, to glaze (optional)

Method

Preheat the oven to Gas Mark 3, 170°C or 325°F. Make the pastry. Rub the margarine into the flour until the mixture resembles breadcrumbs. Stir in the sugar. Add enough cold water to make a very soft dough, then add a little more flour to make the dough workable. Knead lightly, divide into two and roll out on a floured worktop. Aim for a square shape in each case. Place an apple in the centre of each one and fill the core cavities with the jam. Brush all round the edges of the pastry with water and wrap the pastry up round the apples, like a parcel. Press the edges together where you can, to seal in the apples.

Trim. Cut a slit in the top of each one and use any leftover pastry trimmings to make pastry leaves. Seal on to the tops with water. Bake for about 25 minutes, brushed with egg to glaze. Serve hot from the oven.

Fruit Upside Down Pudding

The fruit for this pudding can be varied according to season, or fruit canned without sugar can be used instead. Fresh fruit in season: apricots, peaches, nectarines, greengages, plums, pineapple rings, pears, blackberries. Canned fruit without sugar: blackberries, peaches, apricots, stoned prunes, pears. To turn out the pudding, put a serving plate upside down over the dish. Hold the dish and plate tightly together and turn upside down. Shake the pudding on to the plate. This will give you a sponge base with a fruit topping.

Serves 4

 Use milk-free margarine and water to mix

4 oz (110 g) soft brown sugar
Approx. 8 oz (225 g) prepared fresh ripe fruit, or fruit canned without sugar
3 oz (75 g) polyunsaturated margarine
4 oz (110 g) plain wholewheat flour mixed with 2 level teaspoons baking powder
1 egg, beaten
Milk to mix

Method

Preheat the oven to Gas Mark 5, 190°C or 375°F, and liberally grease a round ovenproof flan dish, about 7 in. (18 cm) in diameter. Sprinkle a little of the sugar over the base of the dish and arrange the fruit to cover. (If using canned fruit, drain well before using.) Put the remaining ingredients, except the milk, into a bowl and use a wooden spoon to beat to a stiff cream. Add the milk, a little at a time, and beat it until the mixture has a soft dropping consistency. Spoon over the fruit and flatten with a knife. Bake above the centre of the oven for about 25 minutes, until firm to the touch. Leave to cool for 2 minutes, then turn out on to a dish, upside down. Serve warm.

Fruit-filled Pancakes

Serves 4

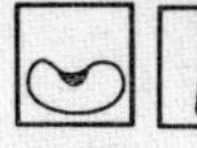   

 Avoid lemon juice

6–8 heaped tablespoons hot stewed fruit for filling*
4 oz (110 g) plain wholewheat flour
1 egg, beaten
½ pint (300 ml) skimmed milk
Oil for the frying pan

Method

Put the flour into a mixing bowl and make a well in the centre. Pour in the egg and a little of the milk. Draw the flour into the liquid and mix. Add the remainder of the milk a little at a time, mixing each amount in. When all the milk has been added, beat well to a smooth batter. Have the filling ready (hot) while you make the pancakes. Oil a heavy based frying pan with sunflower oil by dipping a screw of kitchen paper in the oil and rubbing it over the base of the pan. Put over a high heat and when smoke begins to appear pour in enough batter to cover the base when the pan is tilted to let the batter run all over it. The pancake is ready to turn when bubbles appear. Turn with a spatula and cook on the other side for a minute. Spread each pancake with fruit filling and roll it up. Keep warm in a hot oven while you make the rest and serve immediately.

Suggested fruit fillings for pancakes*

Cooking apples stewed with a little lemon juice and caster sugar or fructose to taste.
Sweet plums, stewed with a little water and brown sugar to taste. Remove stones and chop the plums after stewing. Add cinnamon or allspice to taste.
Stew peeled and stoned peaches with a few raspberries and sweeten to taste with caster sugar or fructose. Chop the peaches after cooking.
Stew fresh apricots with a little lemon juice and caster sugar or fructose to taste. If the fruit is very ripe remove the stones before cooking. If they are a little stubborn, cook first.
Stew raspberries, red currants and black currants in a little water with caster sugar or fructose to taste.

Stew blackberries with cooking apples and sweeten to taste with fructose, caster or brown sugar.
Stew cooking apples with a sprinkle of sultanas and a pinch or two of mixed spice to taste. Sweeten with brown sugar.

Fruit on Bread

For wheat-free or gluten-free diets, use 2 slices of bread made with Trufree Nos 4 or 5 flour. For milk-free diets, use the oil.

Serves 1

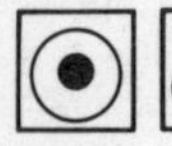    

 Use wheat-free bread

 Avoid butter, use sunflower oil or milk-free margarine.

 Use gluten-free bread

 Use unsalted bread and sunflower oil

Butter, polyunsaturated margarine or sunflower oil
1 slice bread
Brown sugar or fructose, to taste
1 portion ripe fruit – plums, greengages, peaches or apricots – stewed in 1 tablespoon water

Method

Put a little oil in a frying pan and fry the bread on one side until crisp and golden. Turn upside down on to a warm plate and cover with the fruit. Sprinkle with sugar to taste and serve immediately.

Fruit Charlotte

For wheat-free or gluten-free dieters, use bread made with Trufree Nos 1, 3, 4 or 5 flours.

Serves 4 generously

 Use wheat-free bread

 Avoid butter, use milk-free margarine

 Use gluten-free bread

 Avoid lemon rind

2 lb (1 kg) cooking apples, peeled, cored and sliced
4 oz (110 g) soft brown sugar or demerara, or 3 oz (75 g) fructose
Finely grated rind ¼ lemon
About 2 oz (50 g) butter or polyunsaturated margarine
About 10 slices wholewheat bread with crusts removed

Method

Preheat the oven to Gas Mark 4, 180°C or 350°F. Put the apples into a saucepan with about half the sugar, the lemon rind and 2 tablespoons of water. Stir, put the lid on and cook gently until the apples are soft. Use the butter or margarine to spread the bread and cut into halves. Sprinkle with the remaining sugar and line the bottom and sides of a greased soufflé dish, putting aside a few pieces for the 'lid'. (The butter/sugar sides of the bread should be in contact with the sides and bottom of the dish.) Fill the middle with the apple and put on the bread lid, butter/sugar side up. Bake above the centre of the oven for about 35–40 minutes, until the outside is crisp. Serve hot.

Eve's Pudding

Serves 3

 Use milk-free margarine

Base

3 cooking apples, peeled and cored
Sugar, honey or fructose, to taste
¼ teaspoon cinnamon
Water

Topping

2 oz (50 g) polyunsaturated (soft) margarine
3 oz (75 g) plain wholewheat flour
1 teaspoon baking powder
1 large egg, slightly beaten
2 oz (50 g) soft brown sugar

Method

Preheat the oven to Gas Mark 4, 180°C or 350°F. Slice the apples as thinly as you can or grate them coarsely, and put into a greased pie dish. Sprinkle with the sugar to taste, the cinnamon and 1 tablespoon of water. Put the topping ingredients into a bowl and mix/beat to a soft, creamy sponge mixture. Add a little cold water if you think the mixture is too stiff. Spread over the apples and bake on the centre shelf for about 30 minutes. Serve warm from the oven.

Variation

Use ripe stoned plums, greengages or peaches instead of the apple.

Eve's Pudding (wheat free/gluten free)

Serves 2

 Use milk-free margarine

Base

1 cooking apple, peeled, cored and sliced thinly
Sugar to taste

Topping

1 oz (25 g) polyunsaturated soft margarine
1 oz (25 g) sugar
1 oz (25 g) Trufree No. 7 SR flour
2 teaspoons cornflour or maize flour (must be wheat free/gluten free)
1 small egg

Method

Preheat the oven to Gas Mark 5, 190°C or 375°F. Put the topping ingredients into a bowl and beat to a soft consistency. Grease a small ovenproof dish and half fill with the slices of apple. Sprinkle with sugar to taste and spread the topping evenly over the fruit. Bake on the top shelf for about 20–25 minutes. Serve warm from the oven.

Variation

Other fruits can be used such as ripe plums, gooseberries, apricots, peaches, or blackberry and apple. Soaked, dried fruit such as stoned prunes, dried apricots and peaches can be used: soak overnight in cold water and drain and chop before using.

Christmas Pudding

Serves 4

 Use milk-free margarine

1 oz (25 g) of each of the following:
- wholewheat flour
- wholewheat breadcrumbs
- melted polyunsaturated margarine
- chopped almonds
- chopped, stoned prunes
- chopped, dried apricots
- sultanas
- currants
- raisins
- grated carrot
- grated apple
- brown sugar

1 lemon and 1 orange, grated rind and juice
1 egg
1 heaped teaspoon black treacle
2 tablespoons brandy
½ teaspoon each nutmeg, mixed spice and cinnamon

Method

Put all the ingredients into a bowl, mix and leave overnight. Stir well and spoon into a greased basin. Cover and steam for about 5 hours over a gentle heat. Let the pudding grow cold and take off the covers. Put on new ones and store in a cool dry place in the bottom of the fridge until required. On the day of eating, steam again for 1½–2 hours. Remove covers and turn out on to a plate. (Put a plate over the top of the basin, hold basin and plate together and turn upside down. Shake the pudding on to the plate.) Serve with sweet white sauce to which you have added a tablespoon of brandy, stirred in just before serving.

Quick Christmas Pudding

A bantamweight version of the traditional Christmas Pudding, to be made on the day.

Serves 4

 Use milk-free margarine and water to mix

4 oz (110 g) wholewheat flour
1½ teaspoons baking powder
3 oz (75 g) polyunsaturated margarine
2 oz (50 g) each currants, sultanas and raisins
½ cooking apple, peeled and finely grated
3 oz (75 g) wholewheat breadcrumbs (fine)
Finely grated rind of 1 lemon or orange
1 heaped tablespoon chopped almonds or walnuts
2 tablespoons brown sugar
¼ teaspoon each nutmeg, cinnamon and mixed spice
1 tablespoon black treacle
Milk to mix

Method

Mix the flour and baking powder in a bowl. Add the margarine and blend as well as you can with a fork. Put in the dried fruit, apple, breadcrumbs, grated rind, nuts, sugar, spices and black treacle. Mix well, adding a little milk to make a soft dropping consistency. Grease a 1½ pint (900 ml) pudding basin and spoon in the pudding mixture. Cover and steam for about 2 hours. Put a plate over the top, hold pudding and plate firmly together and turn upside down. Shake the pudding on to the plate and serve hot.

Macaroni Pudding

Serves 4

1¾ pints (450 ml) hot water
5 heaped tablespoons low fat dried milk granules

2 oz (50 g) wholewheat macaroni
1 heaped tablespoon brown sugar
1 egg, beaten
4 oz (110 g) dried fruit, soaked overnight*

Method

Put the water into a saucepan with the dried milk and whisk to combine. Add the macaroni and bring to the boil. Simmer on a lower heat, until the macaroni begins to soften. Take off the heat and add in the sugar. Stir until it has dissolved. Let it cool a little, then mix in the beaten egg. Put the soaked fruit into an ovenproof dish and spoon the macaroni over the top. Bake in a preheated oven, Gas Mark 4, 180°C or 350°F, above the centre, for about 30 minutes or until the top is nice and brown.

Suitable fruits

Stoned prunes, dried apricots, dried peaches or nectarines, or mixed dried fruit salad. If you do not have quite enough dried fruit make up the weight with sultanas.

Steamed Plum Pudding

The texture of the pastry will be similar to that of suetcrust. However, the difference is a much, much lower fat content. Other kinds of fruit in season can be used, such as apple and sultana; plain apple; pear and cinnamon; apricot; peach; greengage; blackberry and apple; or a mixture of plum, apple and blackberry.

Serves 4

 Use milk-free margarine

2 oz (50 g) polyunsaturated margarine
4 oz (110 g) ground rice
1 eating apple, finely grated
10–12 ripe plums, stones removed, fruit chopped
Brown sugar or fructose, to taste
1 tablespoon water

Method

Put the margarine, ground rice and grated apple into a bowl and blend with a fork. Knead into a ball using a little more ground rice if the pastry is too wet. Roll two-thirds of the pastry into a ball and flatten it. Grease a 1 pint (600 ml) pudding basin. Put the flattened ball of pastry into the bottom and press out with the fingers, as neatly as you can, until the basin is lined to ½ in. (1 cm) below the rim. Roll out the remaining pastry to make a round 'lid'. Put half the fruit into the pudding and sprinkle with sugar to taste. Add the rest and sprinkle with sugar again. Put on the pastry lid and press to the sides so that it joins all round. Put on a cover and steam for about 45 minutes, topping up the boiling water as required. Take the basin out of the boiling saucepan and put a plate over the top. Hold the plate and basin firmly together and turn upside down. Shake the pudding on to a plate and serve hot.

Bread and 'Butter' Pudding

Serves 2–3

 Use wheat-free bread

 Use artificial sweetener to taste

 Use gluten-free bread

4 or 5 slices wholewheat bread
Polyunsaturated margarine
3 tablespoons sultanas, currants or raisins
Few pinches mixed spice, cinnamon or nutmeg
1 heaped tablespoon brown sugar or fructose
About ½ pint (300 ml) skimmed milk
1 heaped tablespoon low fat dried skimmed milk granules
1 egg

Method

Grease a pie dish. Spread the bread with margarine and cut into quarters. Cover the base of the dish with margarine-side-down bread. Sprinkle with about a third of the raisins, a little of the sugar and two pinches of spice. Make another layer of bread slices and sprinkle with fruit, sugar and spice. Lastly make a layer of the bread slices, margarine-side-up, and sprinkle with fruit, sugar and spice. Whisk the milk and milk granules, add the egg and whisk again. Pour over the bread through a wire sieve and leave to stand for about 20 minutes. Preheat the oven to Gas Mark 5, 190°C or 375°F. Bake on the centre shelf for about 35 minutes, until risen, brown and crisp. Serve still warm from the oven.

Soufflé Omelet with Fruit Filling

Ripe fruit should not need any sugar.

Serves 2

 Use artificial sweetener to taste, avoid icing sugar

2 eggs, separated
2 teaspoons cold water
Few drops vanilla flavouring
2 teaspoons caster sugar, or 1½ teaspoons fructose
2 teaspoons sunflower oil
2 oz (50 g) fresh raspberries, tayberries or loganberries, sliced kiwi fruit, guava or banana, or sliced strawberries
Few pinches icing sugar

Method

Put the egg yolks into a basin with the water, flavouring and caster sugar. Whisk to make a creamy mixture. Whisk the egg whites until they will form peaks. Fold the two mixtures together using a metal spoon. Put a little oil on a screw of kitchen paper and oil an omelet pan. Heat and pour in the egg mixture, flattening it with a spatula. Cook for a couple of minutes over a moderate heat and then put the pan under the grill, again under a moderate heat. Grill for just over 1 minute to set the top. Put the filling of your choice on half the omelet and fold it over with a palette knife. Turn carefully on to a warmed plate and sprinkle with the icing sugar. This must be served immediately, or it will go flat.

Dried Apricot Soufflé

Serves 2

  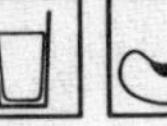   

 Use artificial sweetener to taste

About 6 oz (175 g) dried apricots, soaked overnight
Juice ½ large lemon
1 heaped tablespoon soft brown sugar
2 egg whites

Method

Cook the apricots with the lemon juice and sugar in the soaking water until tender. Cool and spoon into a blender. Pour off most of the liquid and blend. Turn into a bowl. Whisk the egg whites until they will form peaks. Fold into the fruit mixture using a metal spoon. Grease a soufflé dish or two ramekins. Spoon in the mixture. Bake in a preheated oven, Gas Mark 4, 180°C or 350°F, above the centre of the oven for about 20–25 minutes. Meanwhile, heat the cooking juices that were strained off. Serve the soufflés immediately they are ready – they should be well risen and light – with the juice as a sauce if required.

Fruit Brulée

Serves 2

About 8–10 oz (225–275 g) stewed fruit, sweetened to taste
1 small carton natural low fat yoghurt
2 level tablespoons soft brown sugar

Method

Put the fruit into an ovenproof dish and spoon the yoghurt over the top. Spread flat with a knife, taking care not to let any of the fruit show through. Sprinkle with the sugar and put under a hot grill. Watch until the sugar melts, and then serve right away.

Baked Bananas (no added sugar)

The fruit must be ripe and sweet. Other juices to use are unsweetened pineapple juice, a few sweet strawberries liquidized with a little water, or a sweet, ripe peach peeled, stoned and liquidized with a little water. Raspberries or tayberries liquidized with a little water can also be used but the fruit needs to be really sweet or the end result will be too sharp.

Serves 1

 Use pineapple juice

2 small bananas, peeled and cut in half lengthways
Juice 1 sweet (small) orange, clementine or satsuma

Method

Preheat the oven to Gas Mark 3, 170°C or 325°F. Lay the bananas in a shallow ovenproof dish. Squeeze the fruit juice over them and bake above the centre of the oven for about 20 minutes. Serve hot.

HOT OR COLD PUDDINGS

Dried Apricot Crumble

Serves 2

  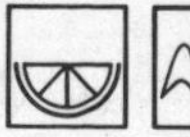 

 Use milk-free margarine

 Avoid margarine, use 1½ tablespoons sunflower oil

Base

About 4–6 oz (110–175 g) dried apricots, soaked for at least 12 hours
Brown sugar or fructose, to taste
¼ teaspoon cinnamon

Topping

2 heaped tablespoons plain wholewheat flour
1 slightly heaped tablespoon polyunsaturated margarine
1 tablespoon brown sugar, or fructose

Method

Stew the apricots in a little water for 15 minutes and sweeten to taste. Preheat the oven to Gas Mark 6, 200°C or 400°F. Put the flour into a bowl with the margarine and rub in with the fingers until the mixture resembles breadcrumbs. Add the sugar and stir. Put the base into an ovenproof dish and sprinkle the topping lightly over the top in a thick layer. Bake on the centre shelf for about 15 minutes. Serve hot or cold.

Prune Crumble with Lemon

Serves 2

 Use Trufree No. 7 SR flour

 Use milk-free margarine

 Use Trufree No. 7 SR flour

 Avoid SR flour and use sunflower oil or unsalted butter instead of margarine

About 10 medium-size dried prunes, soaked overnight
Juice ½ lemon
Brown sugar, honey or fructose to taste
2 heaped tablespoons plain wholewheat flour
1 slightly heaped tablespoon polyunsaturated margarine
Grated rind ½ lemon
1 tablespoon brown sugar, or fructose

Method

Stew the prunes in a little water with the lemon juice. When tender allow to cool a little then remove the stones. Add a little sugar, if necessary, to taste. Put the stoned prunes into an ovenproof dish. Put the flour into a bowl and rub in the margarine until the mixture resembles breadcrumbs. Stir in the lemon rind and sugar. Sprinkle the topping lightly over the prune base. Bake on the centre shelf of a preheated oven, Gas Mark 6, 200°C or 400°F, for about 15 minutes. Serve hot or cold.

Fruit Pie

A deep pie dish may need a pie funnel to hold up the pastry. Put this into the dish before spooning in the fruit. Make a hole in the pastry to correspond with the hole in the pie funnel.

Serves 4

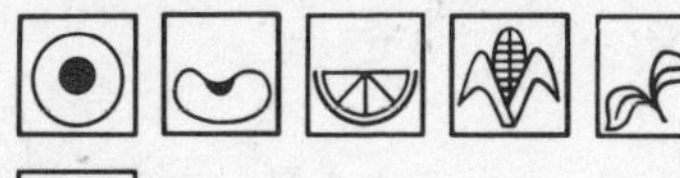

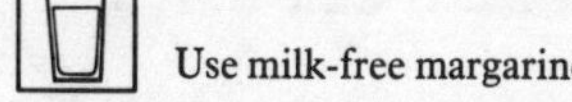

Use milk-free margarine

Filling

About 1½ lb (750 g) fruit for stewing
2 tablespoons water
Few pinches allspice, cinnamon or powdered cloves, to taste (optional)
Brown sugar or fructose, to taste

Pastry

3 oz (75 g) polyunsaturated margarine
6 oz (175 g) plain wholewheat flour
Cold water

Method

Preheat the oven to Gas Mark 7, 220°C or 425°F. Prepare the fruit, stoning, peeling, etc. as required. Cut into pieces or slices. Put into a saucepan with the water, any spice and sugar to taste. Stir and cook for a few minutes, until the fruit begins to soften. To make the pastry, put the margarine and flour into a bowl and rub in with the fingers until the mixture resembles breadcrumbs. Add enough water to make a sticky paste then put in a little more flour to make the dough workable. Roll out on a floured worktop. Put the pie dish upside down on the pastry and cut round (generously) with a knife. Use the trimmings to circle the pie plate, moistening the rim with cold water to make the pastry stick to it. Spoon the partly cooked fruit into the dish. Moisten the pastry border with water, and fit the lid. (Roll back the pastry lid and place the rolling pin on the worktop so the pastry can be rolled back over it. Manoeuvre the pastry on to the pie and remove the rolling pin.) Pinch the edges of the pastry together and cut a hole in the centre. Trim off neatly all round with a knife. Flute the edge with the fingers and thumb. Brush the top with a little water and sprinkle with sugar. Bake on the top shelf for about 20 minutes until the pastry is crisp and just beginning to brown. Serve hot or cold.

Suggested fruit fillings for the pie

Blackberry and apple (no spice); apple and powdered cloves; ripe plums and either cinnamon or allspice; apricots and cinnamon or, if the fruit is really good, just plain apricots; peaches; greengages; a mixture of apples, plums and blackberries (no spice).

Fruit Pie with Gluten-free/Wheat-free Pastry

Serves 2–3

 Use milk-free margarine

Pastry

2 oz (50 g) polyunsaturated margarine
4 oz (110 g) ground rice
3 oz (75 g) finely grated eating apple

Filling

8 oz (225 g) stewing fruit, prepared and chopped or sliced
Brown sugar or fructose, to taste
1 tablespoon water

Method

Preheat the oven to Gas Mark 8, 230°C or 450°F. Blend the pastry ingredients with a fork and knead into a ball of dough. Put the fruit into a saucepan and sweeten to taste. Add the water and cook while you stir until the fruit has softened but not cooked completely. Press out the pastry by hand, or roll out using more ground rice. Put a small pie dish upside down on the pastry and cut round it. Make a border of pastry strips all round the edge of the dish. Brush with water. Use a slotted spoon to remove the partly cooked fruit from the pan and put it into the dish. Cut the pastry for the lid into quarters. Use a spatula to lay them on the fruit so that the edges meet. Press all round the edge and flute between finger and thumb. Sprinkle with a little sugar (optional) and bake on the top shelf for about 25 minutes, until the pastry is crisp and golden. Serve hot or cold, using up any fruit juice as a sauce.

Apple Flan

Serves 4

 Use wheat-free pastry

 Use milk-free margarine for pastry

 Use gluten-free pastry

 Avoid lemon juice

4 oz (110 g) plain wholewheat flour
2 oz (50 g) polyunsaturated margarine
2 or 3 Cox's apples
Brown sugar for sprinkling
2 tablespoons apricot jam
Juice ¼ lemon

Method

Heat the oven to Gas Mark 5, 190°C or 375°F. Make the pastry. Put the flour into a bowl with the margarine. Rub in with the fingers until the mixture resembles breadcrumbs. Add a little water, enough to make a wet paste. Put in enough flour to make a soft but workable dough. Roll out on a floured worktop and line a small flan dish. Halve and core the apples but do not peel them. Cut into thin slices and lay overlapping in circles in the flan case. Sprinkle with a little brown sugar, but only if the apples are not sweet enough. Bake on the top shelf for about 30 minutes. Put the jam into a small saucepan with the lemon juice and heat while you stir. Use a pastry brush to glaze the apples with the mixture. Serve hot or cold.

Rice Pudding

Serves 4

5 heaped tablespoons low fat dried milk granules
1 pint (600 ml) water
1 tablespoon polyunsaturated margarine
1 heaped tablespoon brown sugar, or 1 level tablespoon fructose
Few drops vanilla flavouring
1½ oz (40 g) pudding rice

Method

Preheat the oven to Gas Mark 2, 150°C or 300°F. Dissolve the milk granules in the water. Melt the margarine in a saucepan and add the milk. Heat the mixture but do not let it boil. Stir in the sugar and flavouring. Sprinkle the rice into a greased ovenproof pie dish. Pour over the milk mixture and mix well. Put in the oven on the shelf below the centre. After 20 minutes stir the pudding and put it back into the oven. Stir again after 40 minutes, and on the hour. Leave for the next hour to finish cooking and form a skin. Serve hot or cold.

Variation

Omit the vanilla flavouring. Just before you put the pudding in the oven to bake, grate a little nutmeg over the top.

Milk-free Rice Pudding

Serves 4

1 level tablespoon soya flour
1 pint (600 ml) cold water
1 tablespoon milk-free margarine or sunflower oil
Few drops vanilla flavouring
3 level tablespoons pudding rice
3 heaped teaspoons brown sugar, or 2 heaped teaspoons fructose, or 1 tablespoon liquid honey
1 heaped tablespoon sultanas, raisins, or dried chopped apricots
Freshly grated nutmeg

Method

Put the soya flour and a little of the water into a saucepan. Stir until blended, then gradually add the rest of the water. Bring to the boil and simmer for 5 minutes. Put in the margarine or oil and stir until absorbed, then add the vanilla flavouring. Put the rice, sugar or other sweetening into an ovenproof dish. Pour the soya mixture over and stir well. Sprinkle in the dried fruit. Top with a little grated nutmeg and bake in a preheated oven at Gas Mark 2, 150°C or 300°F for about 2–2½ hours. If the pudding starts to dry out during the cooking, add a little more (hot) water and stir in. Serve hot or cold.

Carob Rice Pudding

Serves 2

1 oz (25 g) pudding rice
2 heaped teaspoons carob powder
2 heaped teaspoons brown sugar
14 fluid oz (400 ml) skimmed milk

Method

Preheat the oven to Gas Mark 2, 150°C or 300°F. Put all the ingredients into a medium sized ovenproof dish and stir well to dissolve the carob. Bake for 2½–3 hours, giving an occasional stir. Serve hot or cold. If the pudding starts to dry out during baking, add a little more skimmed milk, heated in a saucepan.

Baked Apricots

Serves 3

12–15 fresh apricots
Juice ½ lemon
Brown sugar or fructose, to taste

Method

Preheat the oven to Gas Mark 2, 150°C or 300°F. Wash the apricots and, with a sharp knife, make a slit where the natural line occurs on each fruit. (This will ensure that at the end of the cooking time you will be left with whole fruit and not ones that have burst and disintegrated.) Rinse out a shallow ovenproof casserole with cold water. Arrange the fruit to cover the base and spoon over the lemon juice. Sprinkle with sugar and put the lid on. Bake for 45–55 minutes, depending on the size and ripeness of the fruit. Have a look at them after 20 minutes. If they appear to be drying out, add a little water. Serve hot or cold.

Baked Peaches with Red Berries

Serves 1

1 peach
Handful red berries – strawberries, raspberries, tayberries, loganberries or red currants
Caster sugar or fructose, to taste

Method

Do not peel the peach but cut away from the stone in slices. Put in a small ovenproof casserole. Liquidize the berries with a little water and pour over the peach. Sprinkle with sugar to taste and put on the lid. Bake as for baked apricots and serve hot or cold.

Spiced Apples

Serves 2

1 large cooking apple
1 tablespoon sultanas
2 teaspoons lemon juice
¼ teaspoon cinnamon, or mixed spice
Brown sugar or fructose, to taste

Method

Peel and core the apple. Slice thinly and put into a saucepan with the sultanas, lemon juice, spice and sugar to taste. Add a little water and stew for up to 8 minutes, until the apples are soft and the sultanas plump. Serve hot or cold.

Baked Apples

Serves 2

       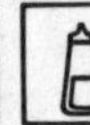  

2 cooking apples
Sugar or honey, to taste
Water

Method

Preheat the oven to Gas Mark 4, 180°C or 350°F. Core the apples and cut a line round the middle of each one with the point of a sharp kitchen knife. (This is to prevent the apples from bursting.) Put the prepared apples into a shallow ovenproof dish and sprinkle with sugar or dribble a little honey over them. Add about a cupful of water to the dish and bake above the centre of the oven for about 30 minutes, or until the apples are soft. Serve hot or cold with the liquid from the dish.

Stuffed Baked Apples

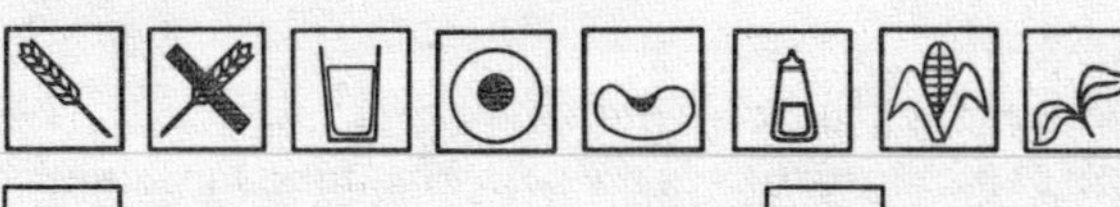

 Avoid mincemeat

 Avoid marzipan or mincemeat

The centre holes left by the cores can be stuffed with dried fruit for variation: fill with sultanas, raisins, chopped dried apricots or dates. Home-made marzipan can also be used. For a really spicy stuffing use home-made mincemeat. Use a teaspoon to put the stuffing into the cavities, and then cook as above.

Fresh Jam Tart

Avoid over-sweetening the fruit, as the filling should be slightly sharp and refreshing. Suitable fruits are raspberries, apricots, peaches, apples, greengages, plums, blackberry and apple, red currants, black currants or any mixture.

Serves 3–4

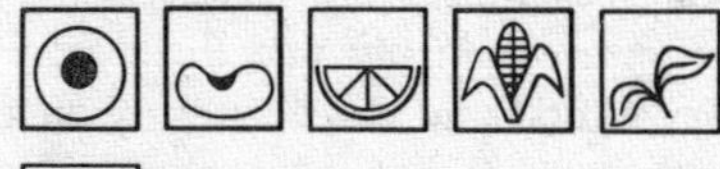

 Use milk-free margarine

About 8 oz (225 g) fresh fruit, e.g. 2 apples, 2 peaches, 10 apricots
Sugar to taste – use either fructose or soft brown sugar
4 oz (110 g) plain wholewheat flour
2 oz (50 g) polyunsaturated margarine
Cold water to mix

Method

Stew the fruit until soft in as little water as possible. Sweeten to taste. Make the pastry. Put the flour into a bowl and rub in the margarine. When the mixture resembles breadcrumbs add enough water to make a sticky paste. Add a little more flour to make the dough workable and knead very lightly. Roll out on a floured worktop and line an 8 in. (20 cm) pie plate. Re-roll the pastry leftovers and cut into strips. Spread the tart base with the stewed fruit. Arrange the pastry strips in a lattice, attaching them to the edges with water and pressing them firmly together. Bake in a preheated oven, Gas Mark 6, 200°C or 400°F, on the top shelf for about 20 minutes. Serve hot or cold.

Custard Tart

This tart has more protein than the kind made with whole milk. The polyunsaturated fat of the margarine in the pastry balances the saturated fat of the egg yolks.

Serves 4–6

2 oz (50 g) polyunsaturated margarine
4 oz (110 g) plain wholewheat flour
Cold water to mix
½ pint (300 ml) lukewarm water
3 heaped tablespoons low fat dried milk granules
2 eggs
2 teaspoons soft brown sugar, or fructose
Freshly grated nutmeg, to taste

Method

Rub the margarine into the flour until it resembles fine breadcrumbs. Add enough water to make a sticky paste, then put in a little more flour to make it workable. Knead very lightly and roll out thinly on a floured worktop. Line a 7 in. (18 cm) flan dish with the pastry. Put the lukewarm water in a basin and add the dried milk. Whisk to combine, making sure there are no lumps. Add the eggs and sugar and whisk again. Pour into the pastry case and grate a little nutmeg over the top. Put carefully into a preheated oven, Gas Mark 5, 190°C or 375°F, above the centre shelf and bake for about 30 minutes or until the pastry is cooked and the custard lightly set. Cool on a wire rack and leave in the dish. Serve slightly warm or cold.

Stewed Fruit

Use artificial sweetener

Many fruits are suitable for stewing, for example, plums, peaches, nectarines, apples (cooking varieties), cooking grade pears, greengages, gooseberries, apricots, raspberries, blackberries, red, black and white currants. (Some fruits such as damsons and rhubarb require a large amount of sweetening and so have not been listed.) Apple combines well with other fruits, e.g. blackberry and apple, plums and apple. Autumn provides the greatest variety of fruit and these can all be stewed together successfully. Use a little brown sugar, fructose or honey for sweetening, to taste. Prepare the fruit, removing stones only if the fruit is very ripe. Put into a saucepan with the sweetening of your choice and a little water. Bring to the boil and simmer until tender and there is plenty of juice. Eat hot or cold.

Stuffed Prunes

Serves 4–5

Avoid sugar

8 oz (225 g) medium prunes
Water
Juice 1 lemon
Brown sugar to taste (this may not be necessary)
As many walnut halves as there are prunes

Method

Wash the prunes in cold water. Put them into a basin and cover with plenty of water, and leave them to plump for at least 2 hours. Transfer them to a saucepan and add the lemon juice and brown sugar. Bring to the boil and simmer with the lid on for about 30–35 minutes. Allow to cool a little, then remove the stones carefully. Replace each stone with a walnut half, and put the prunes back into the liquid. Leave to soak for 1 hour. Serve hot or cold with a little single cream or yoghurt.

COLD PUDDINGS

Fruit and Cheese Mousse

A high protein, low fat pudding. For the fruit use stewed blackberries, black currants, red currants, peaches, apricots, dried apricots or prunes. Raspberries and strawberries can be used fresh, with a little water.

Serves 2

4–5 oz (110–150 g) stewed fruit and juice, or fresh fruit and water
4 oz (110 g) cottage cheese
Brown sugar or fructose, to taste
1 level teaspoon powdered gelatine
1 egg white

Method

Put the fruit and all but 2 tablespoons of the juice or water into a liquidizer with the cottage cheese and sweetening. Blend and turn into a basin. Use a very gentle heat to dissolve the gelatine in the 2 tablespoons of juice or water. Cool and stir into the cheese mixture. Whisk the egg white until it will stand in peaks, then fold into the cheese mixture using a metal spoon. Spoon into two glass dishes and leave to set in the fridge.

Cheese Cake

This is traditionally a high fat dish. However, this version has less than ½ oz (15 g) fat per portion and is a much lighter and more easily digested treat.

Serves 6

4–6 digestive biscuits, depending on size
1 oz (25 g) butter
1 orange
1 tablespoon fresh lemon juice
½ oz (15 g) gelatine crystals

12 oz (350 g) cottage cheese
1 small carton natural low fat yoghurt
1 oz (25 g) fructose, or 1½ oz (40 g) caster sugar
2 egg whites
Fruit for decorating the top – fresh strawberries (halved), raspberries, tayberries, slices of orange, kiwi fruit, peaches, nectarines or depipped grapes are all suitable. Allow enough almost to cover the top.

Method

Grease an 8 in. (20 cm) flan ring and put it on a flat plate. Crush the biscuits in a paper bag, using a rolling pin. Melt the butter in a small pan and sprinkle in the crumbs. Stir with a wooden spoon and use to cover the plate, inside the flan ring. This will form the base. Finely grate the orange rind and put into the blender. Squeeze out the juice and pour into a small pan with the lemon juice. Sprinkle in the gelatine and leave to soak for about 5 minutes, to soften. Put into the blender with the orange rind and add the cheese, yoghurt and sugar. Blend to a smooth, thick cream and turn into a basin. Whisk the egg whites until they will stand up in peaks. Fold them into the cheese mixture until smooth. Carefully smooth the cheese mixture over the biscuit base, flattening it off neatly. Put in the fridge to set. When ready to serve, decorate the top with the fresh fruit.

Fresh Fruit and Nut Dessert Cake

Serves 6

3 oranges
3 eggs, separated
4 oz (110 g) soft moist sugar
2 slices wholewheat bread, made into fine crumbs
4 oz (110 g) ground almonds

Method

Preheat the oven to Gas Mark 4, 180°C or 350°F. Grease and line an 8 in. (20 cm) round cake tin with a removable base. Finely grate the rind from one of the oranges. Squeeze the juice from all three. Put the egg yolks into a mixing bowl with the sugar and beat with a wooden spoon until the mixture is creamy and the yolks become lighter in colour. Put in the breadcrumbs, almonds, orange juice and rind. Stir in, but do not beat, until they are all blended. Put the egg whites into a basin and whisk until they will form peaks. Use a metal spoon to fold into the mixture. Turn into the prepared tin and spread flat with a knife. Bake on the middle shelf until the cake is well risen and feels spongy to the touch – about 40–45 minutes. Make sure the cake will come out of the tin by running a knife between the greaseproof paper and the tin, all round the sides. Leave to get completely cold, then turn out of the tin very carefully. Leave to chill, on a serving plate in the fridge, for at least 30 minutes before serving. Eat on the day of baking.

Apple Cake

This cake can be used for tea, a snack or for a pudding if served with sweet white sauce or single cream.

Serves 6–8

Serve without cream or white sauce, and use milk-free margarine

8 oz (225 g) plain wholewheat flour
2 teaspoons baking powder
1 teaspoon cinnamon
4 pinches ground cloves
4 oz (110 g) polyunsaturated (soft) margarine
4 oz (110 g) soft brown sugar, or 3 oz (75 g) fructose
2 cooking apples, peeled, cored and coarsely grated
1 egg, beaten

Method

Preheat the oven to Gas Mark 5, 190°C or 375°F. Grease and line a 7½ in. (19 cm) square tin. Put the flour and baking powder into a basin with the spices. Mix well. Add the margarine and rub in until the mixture resembles breadcrumbs. Stir in the sugar, apples and egg. Turn into the tin and spread flat with a knife. Bake above the centre of the oven for about 30–35 minutes. Leave to cool in the tin, then cut into squares or rectangles.

Fruit Tartlets

Fruits to use are: raspberries, strawberries, tayberries, peeled kiwi fruit and lychees, peeled ripe apricots, peaches and nectarines cut into slices, seedless or depipped grapes, sweet, destoned cherries. Thin slices of banana can be used but must be glazed immediately or they will discolour.

Makes 12

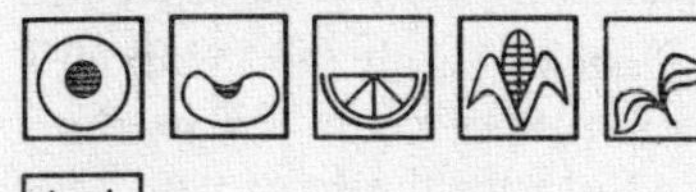

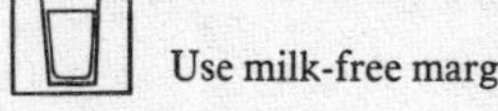

Use milk-free margarine

Pastry

2 oz (50 g) polyunsaturated margarine
5 oz (150 g) wholewheat flour
Water to bind

Glaze

3 generous tablespoons redcurrant jelly
1 tablespoon water
About 8–12 oz (225–350 g) prepared, fresh fruit

Method

Preheat the oven to Gas Mark 7, 220°C or 425°F. Make the pastry. Rub the margarine into the flour until the mixture resembles bread-crumbs. Add enough water to make a sticky dough, then add more flour to make it workable. Roll out thinly on a floured worktop and cut into 12 rounds with a tumbler or a cutter. Use to line 12 patty tins. Bake on the top shelf for about 10 minutes. Take out of the patty tins and cool on a wire rack. Make the glaze. Put the redcurrant jelly into a small saucepan with a tablespoon of water. Stir while you heat until the jelly has melted and blended with the water. Use a pastry brush to brush the bases of the pastry cases. Arrange the prepared fruit on top and brush with the glaze. Allow to set a little and serve.

Pineapple Dessert (milk free)

Serves 1

 Use artificial sweetener

 Avoid orange juice and orange slices

1 slightly heaped tablespoon ground rice
¼ pint (150 ml) pineapple juice
2 teaspoons brown sugar, or 1½ teaspoons fructose
Small knob milk-free margarine
1 slice fresh pineapple, chopped

Method

Put all the ingredients except the fresh fruit into a saucepan. Mix until smooth, heat to boiling point, then simmer while you stir for about 2 minutes until the pudding has thickened. Spoon into a glass dish. Allow to grow cold, then decorate the top with the fresh fruit.

Variation

Use orange juice instead of the pineapple juice, and half an orange, sliced, for the topping.

FRESH FRUIT

Most good quality fresh fruit is excellent just served on its own. In some areas good supplies of imported fruit are available all year round. Fruit in season is the most economical buy. Eat it within two days of purchase. Choose from the following:

eating apples	tangerines	kiwi fruit	apricots
bananas	ugli fruit	guavas	ripe plums
pears	grapefruit	lychees	pineapple
grapes	strawberries	nectarines	cherries
oranges	raspberries	peaches	
satsumas	tayberries	dates	
clementines	loganberries	figs	

FRUIT SALADS

Simple, refreshing desserts can be made from fresh fruit all year round. Some fruits are good just on their own, others are better in combination, while passion fruit and mango are best used for flavouring as they have such a strong taste. Prepare the fruit, peeling and stoning as required. Slice or chop and put into individual dishes or into a bowl. Add 2 tablespoons of fruit juice per portion and sweeten to taste with a little brown sugar or fructose. Really ripe, sweet fruit will not need sugar. Try the following combinations.

All-Year-Round Fruit Salad

   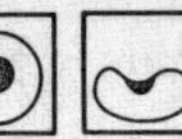   

 Use artificial sweetener

For each person you will need:

½ orange, segmented
½ apple, sliced thinly, peel left on
½ banana, sliced
Orange, pineapple or apple juice to moisten
Sweetening to taste

Exotic Fruit Salad (1)

 Use artificial sweetener

For each person you will need:

1 kiwi fruit, peeled and sliced
1 slice pineapple, cubed
Handful raspberries or strawberries
½ banana, sliced
Pineapple juice to moisten
Sweetening to taste

Exotic Fruit Salad (2)

 Use artificial sweetener to taste

For each person you will need:

3 or 4 lychees, peeled and stoned
1 small slice melon, cubed
Few slices orange, clementine or satsuma
Orange juice to moisten
Sweetening to taste

Mixed Fruit Salad

 Avoid oranges and orange juice, clementines, satsumas, grapefruit

 Use artificial sweetener to taste

Combine 4 or 5 fruits in season, enough to make a portion. Use pineapple or orange juice as a base, and sweeten to taste if necessary. The following combinations are good:

Apple, pear, grape, orange, pineapple.
Peaches, raspberries, strawberries, apple, orange.
Bananas, passion fruit, pineapple, kiwi fruit.
Cherries, peaches, strawberries, oranges, bananas.
Oranges, clementines, satsumas, grapefruit.
Nectarines, peaches, plums, raspberries.
Melon, raspberries, strawberries, oranges.

Red Fruit Salad

 Avoid orange juice

 Use artificial sweetener to taste

Combine any red fruits in season. Sprinkle with brown sugar or fructose to taste and spoon over a little pineapple or orange juice. Suitable red fruits are raspberries, strawberries, tayberries, loganberries, stoned cherries, red plums.

Green Fruit Salad

 Avoid orange juice

 Use artificial sweetener to taste

Combine any green fruits in season. Sprinkle with a little caster sugar or fructose to taste and spoon over a little apple juice. Suitable fruits are green melon, green depipped grapes, green apples, ripe greengages or green plums, and ripe green gooseberries.

Yellow Fruit Salad

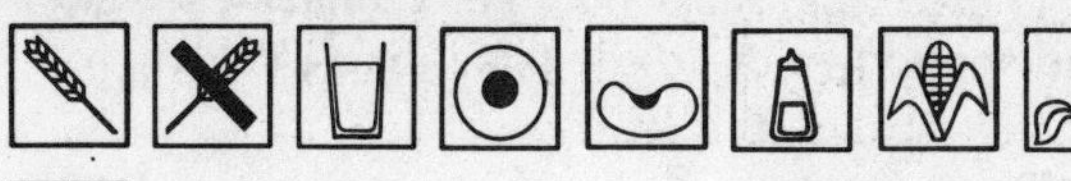

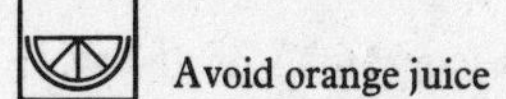 Avoid orange juice

 Use artificial sweetener to taste

Combine any yellow fruits in season. Sprinkle with a little pineapple or orange juice and sugar to taste. Suitable fruits are yellow melon, peaches, yellow plums, yellow apples, bananas, white depipped grapes. Serve in coloured bowls if possible.

Crème Caramel

Serves 4

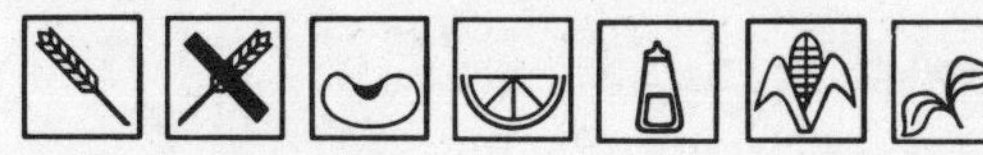

2 heaped tablespoons granulated sugar
3 tablespoons water
1 tablespoon caster sugar, or fructose
2 eggs
4 heaped tablespoons low fat dried milk granules
½ pint (300 ml) water
Few drops vanilla flavouring (optional)

Method

Put the granulated sugar into a saucepan with the 3 tablespoons of water. Over a gentle heat, stir until the sugar has dissolved. Increase the heat slightly and discontinue the stirring. After a few minutes the mixture should have reduced, turned golden brown and be frothy. Take off the heat and add 2 teaspoons of boiling water to disperse the froth. Pour into four ramekins and leave to set and grow cold. When they are ready, put the caster sugar or fructose into a bowl with the eggs. Use a wooden spoon to beat to a pale cream. Mix the milk granules into the water. Put on to heat but do not allow the milk to reach boiling point – catch it just before it boils and remove it from the heat. Add to the egg mixture with the flavouring and stir briskly. Pour through a fine mesh wire sieve into the ramekins. Have ready a roasting tin filled with about 1 in. (2.5 cm) hot water. Place the ramekins carefully in this and bake slowly in a preheated oven, Gas Mark 1, 140°C or 275°F, for about 1 hour. The egg should be set but not too firm. Allow to grow cold. Run a knife round the edge of each one. Invert on serving plates and shake out. The caramel will make a layer on the top and spill down on to the plate. Serve cold.

Summer Pudding

For the fruit choose from red currants, black currants, raspberries, blackberries and strawberries. A mixture of at least three is preferable. This low fat, high fibre pudding is delicious.

Serves 6

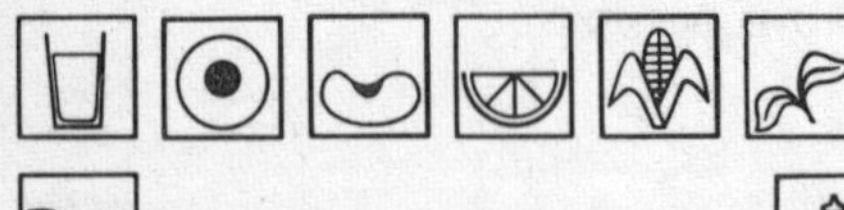

Use artificial sweetener

Use home-made, salt-free bread

2 lb (1 kg) soft fruit in season
Sugar to taste
About 12 slices wholewheat bread, crusts removed

Method

Prepare the fruit and put it into a saucepan with sugar to taste. Put the lid on and cook over a gentle heat, stirring from time to time. Depending on the fruit, 7–10 minutes should be ample to soften it. Rinse out a 1½ pint (900 ml) pudding basin with cold water. Cut the bread into wedges and line the basin, leaving enough over to make a lid. Fill with the fruit and juice. Put on the bread 'lid' and put a plate over the top. Stand several heavy weights on the plate – about 3–4 lb (1.5–1.75 kg) – and leave to stand overnight. The juice from the fruit will be soaked up by the bread and you will be able to turn out the pudding, upside down, on to a plate for serving.

Autumn Pudding

Use artificial sweetener to taste

Use home-made salt-free bread

Make in the same way as for Summer Pudding but use a different selection of fruits in season, e.g. ripe, stoned plums, blackberries, apples, cooking pears.

Vegetarian Fruit Jelly

Avoid using kiwi fruit or pineapple as these do not set well.

Serves 2

½ pint (300 ml) fresh or stewed fruit purée
Sugar or honey, to taste
1 level teaspoon agar-agar

Method

Put the purée into a saucepan and bring to the boil. Stir in the sweetening to taste and stir well to dissolve. Sprinkle in the agar-agar. Stir again until dissolved. Pour into a glass dish and leave to set. Serve chilled from the fridge on the day it is made.

Fruit Jelly

Serves 3–4

1 pint fruit juice (any except pineapple or kiwi fruit)
½ oz (15 g) powdered gelatine

Method

Put about 4 tablespoons of the fruit juice into a cup and sprinkle in the gelatine. Leave to soften for 5 minutes. Heat the rest of the fruit juice almost to boiling point. Take off the heat and add the gelatine mixture after stirring. Stir until you are sure all the gelatine has dissolved. Pour into a glass dish and leave to set. Eat within 12 hours of setting. Serve cold from the fridge.

Dried Fruit Salad

The soaking time can be reduced if boiling water is used. Really good quality dried fruit will be sweet and should not need any added sugar.

Serves 4–5

    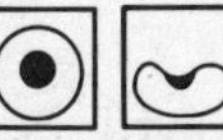     

 Avoid sugar

8 oz (225 g) dried fruit salad
4 or 5 dried figs
Brown sugar or fructose, to taste

Method

Wash the fruit in cold water. Drain in a colander. Put into a basin and cover with plenty of water. Leave to soak overnight. Transfer both fruit and soaking liquid to a saucepan with a little sugar. Bring to the boil. Simmer with the lid on for about 30–40 minutes, or until the fruit is tender. Serve either hot or cold.

Fruit Compote

Serves 2

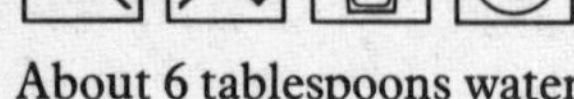

About 6 tablespoons water
Brown sugar or fructose, to taste
8 oz (225 g) prepared fresh fruit – choose from quartered apples, cooking pears, plums, greengages, apricots, peaches, nectarines

Method

Put the water into a saucepan with the sugar and heat while you stir until dissolved. Bring to the boil and carefully put in the fruit. Turn the fruit over so that the syrup coats the pieces all over. Turn the heat right down so that the mixture barely simmers and poach the fruit gently until tender. This will take from 10–20 minutes, depending on the type of fruit. Do not cook for too long and make the fruit fall to pieces. When it is tender remove from the heat and take out of the pan with a slotted spoon. Put into a serving dish. The liquid left in the pan should now be brought to the boil to thicken it. Allow it to cool and then pour over the cooked pieces of fruit. Serve cold.

Berry Water Ice

Serves 4

1 lb (450 g) berries – choose from raspberries, blackberries, tayberries and loganberries
4 oz (110 g) caster sugar, or 3 oz (75 g) fructose
¼ pint (150 ml) water
1 egg white

Method

Boil the sugar and water for a few minutes to make a syrup. Leave to cool. Purée the fruit and syrup in a blender. Whisk the egg white until it will stand up in peaks. Use a metal spoon to fold it into the purée. Put into a freezerproof dish and cover. Freeze for at least 2 hours, until mushy. Take out of the freezer and mix well. Put back into the freezer, covered, and freeze until set for another 2 hours. Spoon into glass dishes and serve cold from the freezer or, if set really hard, allow to defrost a little first in the fridge.

Banana Ice Cream

Serves 6

¼ pint (150 ml) water
2 heaped tablespoons low fat dried milk granules
2 oz (50 g) soft brown sugar
1 large egg, beaten (or 2 small)
Few drops vanilla flavouring
1 small carton single cream
2 bananas, mashed well

Method

Put the water into a saucepan. Stir in the milk granules until dissolved. Add the sugar and egg and stir while you heat gently and the mixture thickens. Strain into a bowl through a wire sieve. Add the vanilla flavouring and stir. Leave to cool, then fold in the cream and lastly the mashed bananas. Turn into a freezerproof container. Cover tightly and freeze for several hours until firm. Allow to soften a little in the fridge before serving.

Brown Bread and Nut Ice Cream

Serves 3–4

 Use salt-free bread

2 slices wholewheat bread, trimmed of crusts and made into fine crumbs
3 oz (75 g) brown sugar
1 oz (25 g) ground hazelnuts, walnuts or almonds (skins left on)
1 large or 2 small egg whites
1 small carton single cream

Method

Mix the crumbs, a third of the sugar and the ground nuts in a bowl. Spread on a baking tray and grill to a light brown colour, giving the mixture an occasional stir. Leave to grow cold. Put the egg white(s) into a basin and whisk until peaks can be formed. Fold in the crumb mixture and then the cream. Spoon into a 1 pint (600 ml) freezerproof basin. Cover tightly and freeze until solid (this takes several hours). Spoon out portions as required, leaving them in the fridge to soften a little before serving.

Lemon Sorbet

Serves 4

½ pint (300 ml) cold water
1 very slightly heaped teaspoon powdered gelatine
3 oz (75 g) fructose, or 4 oz (110 g) caster sugar
Finely grated rind and juice 2 small lemons
1 large egg white

Method

Put a little of the water into a cup and sprinkle in the gelatine. Leave this to soften for about 4 or 5 minutes. Put the rest of the water into a small saucepan with the sugar and rinds. Heat gently while you stir to dissolve the sugar. Take the pan off the heat and stir in the gelatine mixture. Keep stirring until it has completely dissolved. Mix the juice in and leave to grow cold. Pour into a freezerproof container and, without covering, freeze for an hour or so, or until ice crystals have formed around the edge but the middle is still slushy. Whisk the egg white in a basin until it will form peaks. Add the lemon mixture and whisk until light. Put back into the freezerproof container and freeze for several hours, until firm. Spoon into glass dishes and serve.

Peach Sorbet

Serves 4

4 ripe peaches, peeled and stoned
4 oz (110 g) caster sugar, or 3 oz (75 g) fructose
6 tablespoons cold water

Method

Put the prepared fruit into the liquidizer and blend to a smooth purée. Put the sugar into a small saucepan with the water and stir to dissolve. Heat to boiling point, simmer for 1 minute and then allow to cool. Stir into the purée. Spoon into a freezerproof container and freeze for at least 1 hour. By this time small ice crystals should have formed just round the edge of the sorbet. Turn out into a basin and whisk well. Spoon back into the container and freeze for about 6 or 7 hours. Before serving put in the fridge for about 1 hour to defrost slightly. Spoon into glass dishes and serve.

Fruit Yoghurt

Serves 2

 Avoid banana and lemon

1 small carton low fat natural yoghurt
2 heaped tablespoons finely chopped fresh fruit
Sugar or honey to taste

Method

Fold the fruit into the yoghurt with a teaspoon and sweeten to taste.

Suitable fruits

Apple and raspberry; strawberry; kiwi fruit; mango; guava; peach; pear; centre of 1 passion fruit; banana and a squeeze of fresh lemon juice; raspberry; loganberry; tayberries; ripe plums; ripe apricots; ripe nectarines.

Fruit Fool

Serves 2

About 10 oz (275 g) stewed fruit, sweetened to taste
1 small carton low fat natural yoghurt
Sugar to taste

Method

Strain the fruit, reserving the juice. Put the fruit into the blender with the yoghurt. Blend to a purée and turn into a basin. Sweeten to taste. Serve chilled from the fridge. (Use the juice to drink as fruit juice.)

Fruit Snow

Serves 2–3

Many kinds of fruit can be used for this simple sweet. Fresh raspberries or strawberries, loganberries or tayberries, ripe peaches, nectarines, apricots or a mixure of raspberries and ripe peaches. If fresh fruit is not available try stewed apple, stewed apple and blackberries, plums or gooseberries. Cooked fruit should be drained to remove excess liquid. If using fresh fruit keep a little back to decorate the tops. Insead of water use lemon juice for apricot or stewed apple purée.

Approx 8 oz (225 g) prepared, fresh ripe fruit and 2 or 3 teaspoons water, or equivalent drained stewed fruit
Sugar to taste – caster or fructose
2 egg whites

Method

Purée the fruit and liquid in a blender. Turn into a bowl and add sugar to taste. Stir well. Whisk the egg whites until they are stiff enough to form peaks. Sprinkle in a teaspoon of sugar and whisk again. Use a metal spoon to fold the egg whites into the fruit purée. Spoon into glass dishes and serve chilled from the fridge.

Rice Fruit Dessert

This pudding can also be made with semolina instead of the ground rice.

Serves 4

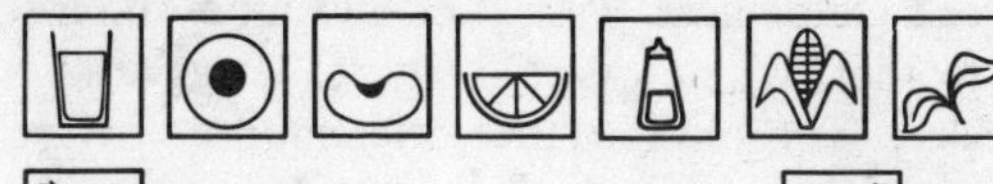

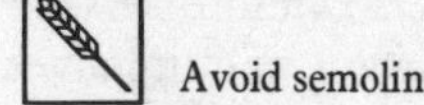 Avoid semolina  Avoid semolina

About 1 lb (450 g) stewing fruit
2 tablespoons ground rice
Brown sugar or fructose, to taste

Method

Put the fruit into a saucepan and heat while you stir. When the juice has accumulated bring to the boil and simmer for a few minutes until the fruit is soft. Cool a little, then purée in a blender. Mix the rice with 4 tablespoons of water in a cup and stir into the fruit. Bring to the boil and cook while you stir until the rice has thickened the mixture. Stir in sugar to taste and spoon into glass dishes. Serve cold.

Coffee Mousse with Walnuts

Serves 4

 Use milk-free margarine

1 oz (25 g) polyunsaturated margarine
2 level tablespoons soft brown sugar
1 scant tablespoon Tia Maria or rum (optional)
2 teaspoons instant coffee powder
3 eggs, separated into whites and yolks in 2 basins
8 walnut halves

Method

Put a bowl over a pan of hot water. Put the margarine, sugar, alcohol and coffee powder into the bowl. Stir until melted and combined. Mix in the egg yolks. Stir occasionally while the mixture cooks very gently for about 5 minutes, over a gentle heat. Take the bowl out of the pan and allow the contents to cool. When it is cold whisk the egg whites until they will form peaks, then fold into the coffee mixture before using a metal spoon. Spoon into individual dishes. Before serving chop the walnuts and sprinkle over the tops, or place 2 walnut halves on each one.

CAKES, BISCUITS, COOKIES AND PASTRIES

From a nutritional point of view, there can be few worse combinations of ingredients that should not be eaten in large quantities than those found in cakes, biscuits, cookies and pastries. High sugar, fat (mainly saturated) from oils, margarine, butter and egg yolks, low fibre white flour and dubious colourings are considered quite normal in most households. It is unfortunate that this kind of food has become such an acceptable part of the weekly diet. Bearing in mind the overnutrition value of such food, this section is very modest. Recipes have been included mainly for psychological reasons, and have been tailored to decrease the sugar and fat and increase the fibre content.

Low-fat Sponge

As there is no margarine or butter in this type of recipe it is often referred to as 'fatless sponge'. However, the egg yolks are a source of both fat and cholesterol, which is a point to remember.

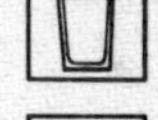    

 Avoid orange, lemon and lime flavourings

3 eggs
4½ oz (125 g) soft brown sugar
3 oz (75 g) wholewheat SR flour
Flavouring*

Method

Grease and line a 9 in. (23 cm) square sponge tin. Preheat the oven to Gas Mark 5, 190°C or 375°F. Put the eggs into a bowl with the sugar and whisk with an electric whisk. When it has reached a mousse-like texture sprinkle in the flour through a fine mesh wire sieve. Tip in the bran which will be left in the sieve and then fold in gently with a metal spoon. Pour into the prepared tin and bake above the centre of the oven for about 35 minutes. (When pressed lightly with the fingers the top should feel springy if it is done.) Remove from the tin and cool on a wire rack. Cut through with a breadknife and sandwich back together with jam, stewed fruit, mashed fresh fruit, or leave just as it is.

Flavourings for Low-fat Sponge*

 Avoid orange, lemon and lime flavourings

Chocolate
Replace 2 heaped teaspoons of the flour with a similar amount of cocoa. Mix into the flour before using.

Ginger
Add 1 teaspoon of ground ginger to the flour and mix well before using.

Spice
Add 1 teaspoon of mixed spice to the flour and mix well before using.

Cinnamon
Add 1 teaspoon of cinnamon to the flour and mix well before using.

Carob
Replace 2 heaped teaspoons of the flour with a similar amount of carob powder.

Orange
Stir in the finely grated rind of 1 orange with the flour.

Lemon
Stir in the finely grated rind of 1 lemon with the flour.

Lime
Stir in the finely grated rind of ½ lime with the flour.

Coffee
Add 1 heaped teaspoon of instant coffee powder to the flour and mix in well before using.

Sponge Mix (wheat/gluten/milk/egg/corn free)

Eat freshly baked. Use stale sponge for jelly or trifle, or to make crumbs. The mixture can also be used for buns, if the baking time is only 15 minutes; spoon into five or six patty tins lined with cake papers. (NB Double the recipe will fill a small sponge tin.)

Avoid lemon, orange and lime flavourings

Use salt-free baking powder

½ oz (15 g) soya flour
1 oz (25 g) sugar
½ level teaspoon dried pectin, or ½ generous teaspoon methylcellulose
¾ oz (20 g) potato flour
2 oz (50 g) ground rice
½ oz (15 g) yellow split pea flour
½ oz (15 g) ground almonds
2 slightly heaped teaspoons special baking powder (see p. 105)
5 tablespoons pineapple juice
2 teaspoons sunflower oil
Flavouring*

Method

Preheat the oven to Gas Mark 6, 200°C or 400°F. Oil a small ovenproof dish with sunflower oil and sprinkle with ground rice. Put all the recipe ingredients into a mixing bowl and mix/beat with a wooden spoon until the mixture is light and creamy. Spoon into the prepared dish and flatten the top with a knife. Bake on the top shelf for about 30 minutes until it is golden. Allow to cool for 2 minutes, then turn out on to a wire rack to cool.

Flavouring*

The basic sponge mix can be flavoured with any of the following: finely grated rind of ½ lemon, orange or lime; 1 heaped teaspoon cocoa or carob powder; ½ teaspoon ground ginger and 1 teaspoon black treacle; few drops vanilla flavouring; ¼ teaspoon mixed spice; ¼ teaspoon cinnamon.

Boiled Fruit Cake

This keeps well, wrapped in greaseproof paper, inside an airtight tin.

2½ oz (65 g) polyunsaturated margarine
3 oz (75 g) black treacle or molasses
14 oz (400 g) dried mixed fruit
3 fluid oz (85 ml) milk

Grated rind 1 orange
1 level teaspoon mixed spice
¼ teaspoon grated nutmeg
4 oz (110 g) plain wholewheat flour
1 egg, beaten
¼ level teaspoon bicarbonate of soda

Method

Preheat the oven to Gas Mark 2, 150°C or 300°F. Line a greased 1 lb loaf tin with greased greaseproof paper. Put the margarine, treacle, fruit, milk and rinds into a large saucepan. Stir while you heat gently to melt the margarine. This should take about 4–5 minutes. Let the mixture cool down to lukewarm. Mix the spices with the flour in a mixing bowl. Add the beaten egg without stirring. Sprinkle the bicarbonate of soda into the mixture in the saucepan. Stir and quickly mix into the flour/egg. Beat well and spoon into the prepared cake tin. Bake in the centre of the oven for about 1½ hours or more. Turn out of the tin to cool on a wire rack.

Rich Fruit Cake (1)

This cake is suitable for weddings, Christmas and birthdays. Make it about five or six weeks before you need it to let the cake mature. It is much less sweet than most traditional versions. To be sure of a really moist cake, every two weeks of storage prick the top with a fork and dribble in a little sherry or brandy.

Use water instead of milk, and use milk-free margarine

Mix the following in a large mixing bowl:

12 oz (350 g) plain wholewheat flour
4 oz (110 g) ground almonds
2 teaspoons each of mixed spice and cinnamon

Whisk the following in a basin:

2 tablespoons skimmed milk
4 tablespoons sherry
4 eggs

Cream the following in a mixing bowl:

4 oz (110 g) brown sugar
1 tablespoon black treacle or molasses
8 oz (225 g) polyunsaturated margarine

Have ready the following:

8 oz (225 g) each seedless raisins and sultanas
4 oz (110 g) each chopped destoned prunes and dried apricots
Grated rind 1 lemon and 1 orange

Method

Preheat the oven to Gas Mark 3, 170°C or 325°F. Grease a 9 in. (23 cm) round cake tin. Line with a double thickness of greased greaseproof paper. (Also tie a double-thickness band of brown paper round the outside of the tin if you wish, so it cooks evenly.) Take the bowl with the margarine mixture and gradually stir in the flour mixture and the egg mixture, alternately. Lastly stir in the rinds and fruit until they are distributed evenly. (You may find this easier with your hands.) Spoon into the prepared tin and flatten the top with a knife. In case it should rise, make a slight dent in the middle. This should make the cake turn out flat. (Alternatively, bake the cake and level it off, if necessary, with a breadknife when it is cold, before icing.) Put it on the centre shelf of the oven and do not open the door for 1½ hours. Turn down the heat to Gas Mark 2, 150°C or 300°F. Leave the cake in for another 1¾ hours at least. If it begins to darken too much put a sheet of greaseproof paper over the top, or move it one shelf down.

When baked, take out of the oven but not the tin. Leave to cool right down overnight. Take out of the tin and store in a large airtight container, still in the greaseproof paper. Peel this off just before cutting. Serve in very small pieces as it is a rich cake just for special occasions.

Rich Fruit Cake (2) (wheat free and gluten free)

Suitable for Christmas, birthday and wedding cake – to be eaten by everybody.

 Use milk-free margarine

 Omit orange and lemon rind

8 oz (225 g) Trufree No. 7 SR flour
1 heaped teaspoon each cinnamon and mixed spice
2 oz (50 g) ground almonds or cashews
6 oz (175 g) polyunsaturated soft margarine
4 oz (110 g) brown sugar
1 tablespoon black treacle
3 eggs
2 tablespoons sherry or brandy
1 lb (450 g) dried mixed fruit
4 oz (110 g) chopped, dried apricots
Grated rind 1 lemon
Grated rind 1 orange

Method

Preheat the oven to Gas Mark 3, 170°C or 325°F. Line a 9 in. (23 cm) diameter cake tin with greased greaseproof paper. Mix the flour, spices and nuts in a basin. In a separate large mixing bowl cream the margarine, sugar and treacle. In a third bowl beat the eggs and sherry or brandy with a fork. Add both the sherry mixture and the flour mixture alternately to the margarine mixture, mixing after each addition. Lastly stir in the fruit and lemon rind. Spoon into the prepared tin and flatten the top with a knife. Bake for 1¼ hours on the centre shelf, then turn the heat down to Gas Mark 2, 150°C or 300°F for another 1–1¼ hours. Let the cake cool in the tin overnight. Remove from the tin but leave the paper on and store for a few weeks until required. Before icing, prick the top of the cake with a fork and dribble in a little sherry or brandy.

Fruit Cake (1)

 Use milk-free margarine, and water to mix

 Omit lemon or orange rind

8 oz (225 g) plain wholewheat flour (fine)
2 level teaspoons baking powder
1 teaspoon each mixed spice and cinnamon
3 oz (75 g) polyunsaturated soft margarine
3 oz (75 g) brown sugar, or 2 oz (50 g) fructose
8 oz (225 g) dried mixed fruit

Finely grated rind 1 lemon or 1 orange
1 egg, beaten
Milk to mix

Method

Preheat the oven to Gas Mark 4, 180°C or 350°F. Grease and flour a 2 lb (1 kg) loaf tin. Mix the flour, baking powder and spices in a mixing bowl. Add the margarine and rub in until the mixture resembles breadcrumbs. Stir in the sugar, dried fruit and rind. Mix in the egg and enough milk to make a soft dropping consistency. Spoon into the prepared tin and bake on the centre shelf for about 1 hour or a few minutes over. Allow to cool and let the sides shrink away a little from the tin, then turn out carefully on to a wire rack to finish cooling. Cut in thick slices for tea, or a snack.

Apricot cake

Instead of the dried fruit, use 8 oz (225 g) chopped dried apricots.

Fruit Cake (2) (eggless)

 Use milk-free margarine and water to mix

1 teaspoon bicarbonate of soda
8 oz (225 g) plain wholewheat flour
4 oz (110 g) polyunsaturated margarine
¼ pint (150 ml) skimmed milk
1 tablespoon black treacle
3 oz (75 g) brown sugar, or 2 oz (50 g) fructose
6 oz (175 g) dried mixed fruit
2 tablespoons wine vinegar

Method

Preheat the oven to Gas Mark 3, 170°C or 325°F. Grease and line a 6 in. (15 cm) diameter cake tin. Put the bicarbonate of soda into a bowl with the wholewheat flour and mix well. Add the margarine and rub in until the mixture resembles breadcrumbs. Pour in the milk and stir. Add the black treacle, sugar and fruit. Use a metal spoon to fold the mixture together, gently. Fold in the vinegar, taking care not to beat the mixture. Put into the oven, above the centre, and bake for

1¼–1½ hours. Leave to cool in the tin for a few minutes and then turn out on to a wire rack to finish cooling. Peel off the paper before the cake gets cold.

Currant cake
Use currants instead of the dried mixed fruit.

Sultana cake
Use sultanas instead of the dried mixed fruit.

Raisin cake
Use raisins instead of the dried mixed fruit.

Fruit and nut cake
Use half dried fruit and half nuts (chopped walnuts) to make up the 6 oz (150 g).

Carob Cake (eggless)

Eat for tea, for a snack, or for pudding with a sweet sauce. Skimmed milk can be used instead of orange juice for citrus-free diets.

Makes 8 slices

Use skimmed milk instead of orange juice

5 oz (150 g) wholewheat flour
1 heaped teaspoon baking powder
2 oz (50 g) polyunsaturated margarine
4 fluid oz (100 ml) orange juice
2 oz (50 g) brown sugar, or 1½ oz (40 g) fructose
1 small cooking apple
2 heaped teaspoons carob powder

Method
Preheat the oven to Gas Mark 5, 190°C or 375°F. Grease a sponge tin or flan dish and line the bottom only with greased, greaseproof paper. Put the flour and baking powder into a mixing bowl. Mix and add the margarine. Rub in until the mixture resembles breadcrumbs. Stir in the orange juice, sugar, cooking apple and carob powder. Stir to a soft, creamy cake mix and turn into the prepared tin or dish. Bake above the centre of the oven for about 30 minutes. Leave to cool on a wire rack and eat within two days.

Variation

Use 1 heaped teaspoon of cocoa instead of the carob, to make Chocolate Cake.

Spiced Apple Cake

Eat freshly baked: good for tea, a snack or a pudding.

Serves 4–5

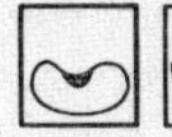   

 Use milk-free margarine and water to mix

2½ oz (70 g) plain wholewheat flour
½ level teaspoon baking powder
2 oz (50 g) sultanas
2 oz (50 g) brown sugar, or 1½ oz (40 g) fructose
4 good pinches cinnamon
1 oz (25 g) polyunsaturated margarine
1 small egg, beaten
About 4 tablespoons skimmed milk
1 small eating apple, grated finely

Method

Preheat the oven to Gas Mark 4, 180°C or 350°F. Grease and line a small cake tin or ovenproof dish with straight sides. Put all the ingredients into a bowl and mix well. Beat to a thick batter and pour into the prepared tin. Spread flat with the back of a spoon and put on the centre shelf to bake for about 55–60 minutes. Turn out on to a wire rack immediately and peel off the greaseproof paper. Allow to cool a little before cutting into slices.

Date and Ginger Cake (eggless)

  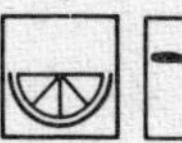   

 Use milk-free margarine and apple or pineapple juice instead of milk

5 oz (150 g) plain wholewheat flour
1 heaped teaspoon baking powder
2 oz (50 g) polyunsaturated margarine
¼ pint (150 ml) skimmed milk
2 oz (50 g) brown sugar
½ cooking apple, grated to give 2 oz (50 g)
1 slightly heaped teaspoon ground ginger
About 10 dates, stoned, chopped and rolled in flour

Method

Preheat the oven to Gas Mark 5, 190°C or 375°F. Grease a sponge tin and line just the base with greaseproof paper. Mix the flour and baking powder in a mixing bowl. Add the margarine and rub in until the mixture resembles breadcrumbs. Add all the remaining ingredients except the dates, and stir well until soft and creamy. Stir in the fruit and turn into the prepared tin. Spread the top flat with a knife and bake above the centre of the oven for about 30 minutes. Cut into squares or wedges and eat within two days.

Digestive Biscuits (1)

Low fat, low sugar, high fibre biscuits.

Makes about 12–14

 Use milk-free margarine and water to mix

4 oz (110 g) plain wholewheat flour
2 oz (50 g) medium oatmeal
Very small pinch powdered cloves or nutmeg (optional)
2 oz (50 g) polyunsaturated margarine
2 oz (50 g) soft brown sugar, or 1½ oz (40 g) fructose
1 small egg
Skimmed milk to mix, if required

Method

Preheat the oven to Gas Mark 6, 200°C or 400°F. Grease baking sheets with sunflower oil. Put the flour, oatmeal and spice into a mixing bowl. Mix and add the margarine. Rub in with the fingers until the mixture resembles fine breadcrumbs. Add the sugar, then the egg and mix to a stiff paste, using a wooden spoon. Add a little milk if needed. Sprinkle the worktop with flour and roll out the dough to about ¼ in. (5 mm) thick. Cut into squares with a knife, or rounds with a cutter and use a spatula to lay the biscuits on the baking sheets. Take a small fork and prick them all over. Bake in the centre of the oven for about 15–18 minutes. (NB These biscuits will still be soft when the baking time is over.) Transfer to a wire rack, where they will gradually grow crisp as they cool down. When quite cold, store in an airtight container.

Digestive Biscuits (2) (eggless)

Makes about 8 or 9

 Use milk-free margarine and water to mix

4 oz (110 g) medium oatmeal
4 oz (110 g) plain wholewheat flour
2 oz (50 g) polyunsaturated soft margarine
1 heaped tablespoon soft brown sugar, or 1 level tablespoon fructose
1 tablespoon black treacle, melted in a small pan and allowed to cool a little
Skimmed milk to mix

Method

Preheat the oven to Gas Mark 4, 180°C or 350°F. Grease a baking sheet with a little sunflower oil. Put the oatmeal and flour into a bowl and mix well. Add the margarine and rub in with the fingers until the mixture resembles breadcrumbs. Stir in the sugar. Pour in the treacle and enough milk to mix to a fairly tough dough. (If you add too much milk, then add more flour.) Sprinkle the surface of the worktop with a little of the oatmeal and roll out the dough to about ¼ in. (5 mm) thick. Cut into squares with a knife, or rounds with a cutter. Use a spatula to transfer the biscuits to the baking sheet, then prick them all over with a fork or a skewer. Bake above the centre of the oven for about 20 minutes. Leave to cool on the tray, then transfer to a wire rack to cool down completely. Store in an airtight tin.

Langues de Chat (1)

Serve with desserts or just as dainty biscuits.

Makes several dozen

 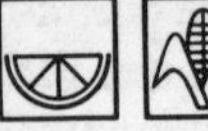  

 Use milk-free margarine

2 oz (50 g) polyunsaturated margarine
2 oz (50 g) soft brown sugar
2 egg whites, lightly whisked with a fork
2½ oz (50 g) fine wholewheat flour
Sunflower oil for greasing

Method

Preheat the oven to Gas Mark 7, 220°C or 425°F and grease two large baking sheets with sunflower oil. Put the fat and sugar into a bowl and beat to a soft cream. Add a little of the egg white and beat in. Put in a little of the flour and beat again. Continue adding the egg and flour alternately until they are used up. Put the mixture into a piping bag fitted with a ¼ in. (5 mm) nozzle. Pipe the mixture on to the baking sheets in 2½ in. (6 cm) lengths, leaving space between each for the biscuits to spread. Bake one baking sheet at a time, for about 4–5 minutes, until they are starting to brown. Use a spatula to loosen them and leave on a wire rack to cool and go crisp. Store in an airtight tin.

Langues de Chat (2) (gluten free and wheat free)

Use instead of ice cream wafers or just as dainty biscuits.

Makes several dozen

2 oz (50 g) butter
2 oz (50 g) caster sugar
2 egg whites
2 oz (50 g) Trufree No. 6 flour
Vanilla flavouring

Method

Preheat the oven to Gas Mark 6, 200°C or 400°F. Put the butter into a bowl with the sugar and beat to a light, fluffy cream. Whisk the egg whites lightly with a fork. Gradually beat the egg whites into the butter/sugar mixture, a little at a time. Fold in the flour and three or four drops of the flavouring. Grease baking sheets and flour with more Trufree No. 6 flour. Put the mixture into a piping bag fitted with a ½ in. (1 cm) nozzle. Pipe 3 in. (7.5 cm) lengths on the prepared baking sheet, leaving space for the biscuits to spread. Bake above the centre of the oven for about 10–12 minutes. The biscuits are ready when they are brown all round the edge but still pale in the middle. Leave to cool on the baking sheet for 2 minutes, then lift off carefully with a spatula and leave to grow cold and crisp on a wire rack. When completely cold store in an airtight tin.

Plain Biscuits (gluten/wheat/egg/milk free)

These biscuits may be flavoured with the finely grated rind of an orange or lemon, or an extra teaspoon of carob powder.

Makes 6–7

 Avoid orange and lemon rind

2 tablespoons sunflower oil
2 oz (50 g) ground rice
1 heaped teaspoon ground almonds
1 level teaspoon carob powder
3 heaped teaspoons brown sugar
½ eating apple, finely grated, including the peel

Method

Preheat the oven to Gas Mark 7, 220°C or 425°F. Put all the ingredients into a mixing bowl and blend together with a fork until you have a stiff paste. Divide into six or seven equal portions and roll each one into a ball. Oil a baking sheet and place them well spaced out. Flatten each one with the back of a spoon into biscuit shapes about ¼ in. (5 mm) thick. Bake on the top shelf until brown – about 20 minutes. Lift off with a spatula and cool on a wire rack. Store in an airtight tin and eat within three days.

Fruit Cookies (gluten free and wheat free)

Makes 4

 Use milk-free margarine

1 oz (25 g) polyunsaturated margarine
2 oz (50 g) ground rice
½ eating apple, finely grated
1 tablespoon brown sugar
1 slightly heaped tablespoon dried fruit
3 pinches mixed spice
Grated rind ¼ orange or lemon

Method

Preheat the oven to Gas Mark 8, 230°C or 450°F. Put the margarine and ground rice into a bowl and blend with a fork. Add the apple, sugar, fruit, spice and rind. Mix with a wooden spoon until the dough forms one ball. Grease a baking sheet with margarine and drop spoons of the mixture on to it. Spread out with the back of a teaspoon or a knife, into cookie shapes. Bake above the centre of the oven for about 20–25 minutes. Allow to cool on the baking sheet for 2 or 3 minutes and then remove to a wire cooling rack, using a spatula. As they grow cold the cookies will crisp. Eat within a day of baking.

Fruit and nut cookies

Make as for Fruit Cookies but add 1 tablespoon of chopped walnuts, almonds or hazelnuts.

Rock Cakes (Cookies)

6 oz (175 g) plain wholewheat flour
1 level teaspoon baking powder
½ level teaspoon mixed spice
2½ oz (65 g) polyunsaturated margarine
3 oz (75 g) soft brown sugar

4–5 oz (110–150 g) dried mixed fruit
Grated rind 1 lemon or 1 orange (optional)
1 egg, beaten
Milk to mix

Method

Preheat the oven to Gas Mark 5, 190°C or 375°F. Grease and flour a large baking sheet. Put the flour, baking powder and spice into a bowl. Mix well and add the margarine. Rub in with the fingers until the mixture resembles breadcrumbs, then add the sugar, dried fruit and rind. Stir and add the egg and enough milk to make a fairly stiff mixture. Put spoonfuls of the mixture on to the prepared baking sheet, leaving room for them to spread. Bake above the centre of the oven for about 15 minutes. (Do not overbake or they will be dry.) Allow to cool on the baking sheet, then remove to a wire cooling rack, using a spatula. Eat soon after baking.

Nut Cookies (gluten free and wheat free)

Makes 12 cookies that keep well

Rice paper
2 egg whites
3 oz (75 g) caster or soft moist sugar, or 2 oz (50 g) fructose
2 oz (50 g) ground rice
5 oz (150 g) ground nuts – almonds, walnuts, cashews, hazelnuts or a mixture
12 pieces of nut for decoration (optional)

Method

Preheat the oven to Gas Mark 4, 180°C or 350°F. Cover baking sheets with rice paper. Put the egg whites into a bowl and whisk until they form peaks. Add the sugar, ground rice and nuts. Mix with a fork to combine. Form by hand into twelve balls and place on the rice paper, well spaced apart. Flatten and press a piece of nut into the centre of each one. Bake on the centre shelf for 20–25 minutes. Leave to cool, then remove with a spatula and cool on a wire rack. Trim off excess rice paper before serving. When cold, store in an airtight container.

Parkin

Makes 12 squares

4 oz (110 g) polyunsaturated margarine
4 oz (110 g) black treacle
4 oz (110 g) soft brown sugar
4 oz (110 g) medium oatmeal or rolled oats
4 oz (110 g) plain wholewheat flour
1 teaspoon each ground ginger and mixed spice
½ teaspoon bicarbonate of soda
1 egg, beaten with 5 tablespoons of milk

Method

Preheat the oven to Gas Mark 3, 170°C or 325°F. Grease a 6 in. (15 cm) square tin and line with greased greaseproof or silicon paper. Use a saucepan with a heavy base to melt the margarine, treacle and sugar, while you stir. When they are reduced to a liquid, leave to cool. Put the oatmeal, flour, spice and bicarbonate of soda into a mixing bowl. Mix well and stir in the egg/milk. Pour in the cooled sugar mixture. Stir with a metal spoon until blended into a batter. Pour into the prepared tin and bake for 1–1½ hours. Leave to cool in the tin for at least 15 minutes to shrink, and then turn out and peel off the paper. Leave to grow completely cold on a wire rack and store in an airtight tin. Wait for at least two days before cutting as this will make the cake nice and moist.

Low-fat Pastry

This pastry has only a sixth of its weight as fat.

 Use milk-free margarine

1 oz (25 g) polyunsaturated margarine
4 oz (110 g) plain wholewheat flour
1 oz (25 g) finely grated apple (mush)
Water

Method

Put the flour into a bowl and add the margarine. Rub in with the fingertips until the mixture resembles crumbs. Stir in the apple mush and enough water to make a soft but firm dough. Knead into a ball, leaving the bowl clean. Flour the worktop and roll out. Use as required, baking at Gas Mark 6, 200°C or 400°F on the top shelf for 15–20 minutes.

Bran Pastry

 Use milk-free margarine

3 oz (75 g) plain wholewheat flour
1 oz (25 g) wheat bran
2 oz (50 g) polyunsaturated margarine
Water to mix

Method

Mix the flour and bran in a bowl. Add the margarine and rub in with the fingers until the mixture resembles crumbs. Add enough water to make a soft dough, then add more flour to make a consistency that can be rolled out. Sprinkle the worktop with more of the flour and roll out the pastry. (It will not be as easy to handle as ordinary pastry.) Use as required, baking at Gas Mark 7, 220°C or 425°F for about 15–20 minutes.

Potato Pastry (1)

Use instead of ordinary pastry, especially for quiches and savoury flans.

 Use milk-free margarine

5 oz (150 g) plain wholewheat flour
1 level teaspoon baking powder
4 oz (110 g) cold mashed potato
3 oz (75 g) polyunsaturated margarine

Method

Put the flour and baking powder into a bowl. Mix well and add the mashed potato. Mix again and add the margarine. Blend with a fork and knead on a floured worktop. Roll out and use to line a flan dish, when making savoury flans or quiches. This kind of pastry can be baked at a lower temperature than the usual kind – Gas Mark 4, 180°C or 350°F – but it needs longer cooking, at 30 minutes.

Potato Pastry (2) (gluten free and wheat free)

 Use milk-free margarine

2 oz (50 g) cold mashed potato
1 oz (25 g) polyunsaturated margarine
4 oz (110 g) ground rice
Water, if necessary

Method

Beat the potato and margarine to a cream. Gradually add the ground rice and combine with a fork. Knead by hand into a large ball, adding a little water if needed. Put the pastry on to a worktop floured with ground rice. Press flat with a spatula. This pastry is difficult to use in large pieces, so is best cut into rounds and used overlapping, or in pieces that can be pressed together. Bake at Gas Mark 7, 220°C or 425°F for 15–20 minutes, until golden.

Almond Pastry (gluten free and wheat free)

      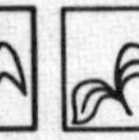

 Use milk-free margarine

2 oz (50 g) polyunsaturated margarine
4 oz (110 g) ground rice
½ large eating apple, grated finely
1 tablespoon brown sugar, or fructose
1 oz (25 g) ground almonds

Method

Put the margarine and ground rice into a bowl and blend with a fork. Add the apple and mix well, then add the sugar and ground almonds. Knead until a ball of dough is formed. Spread out with a knife to make pastry, baking at Gas Mark 7, 220°C or 425°F for 20–25 minutes on the top shelf.

Wheat and Soya Pastry (milk free)

This pastry is higher in protein than ordinary pastry.

3 oz (75 g) plain wholewheat flour
1 oz (25 g) soya flour
1½ tablespoons sunflower oil
Cold water to mix

Method

Put the two flours into a bowl and mix well. Sprinkle in the oil and blend into the flour with a fork. Add enough water to make a workable dough, that is firm but elastic. Roll out, using more wholewheat flour. Bake on the top shelf of a preheated oven at Gas Mark 6, 200°C or 400°F.

Low-fat Pastry with Bread Dough

Use home-made bread dough (see recipes on pp. 366, 375) and roll out as pastry. Leave to rise before baking and bake in a preheated oven at Gas Mark 6, 200°C or 400°F, with a usual baking time of 20 minutes.

Pastry with Oil (1) (milk free)

Suitable for vegans.

8 oz (225 g) plain wholewheat flour
5 tablespoons sunflower oil
3 tablespoons cold water

Method

Put the flour into a mixing bowl. Measure the oil and water into a screwtop jar. Put the lid on firmly and shake well to combine. Pour into the flour and use a fork to bring the pastry together, making a soft paste. Roll out the dough, using more flour and handling it as little as possible for it will not be as strong as ordinary pastry. (If you find it too difficult to handle, put the dough between two sheets of greaseproof paper to roll it out.) Bake at Gas Mark 5, 190°C or 375°F for about 30 minutes on a shelf above the centre of the oven.

Pastry with Oil (2) (milk free)

Most margarines contain a little whey (from milk), but this recipe, which uses oil instead of margarine, will make a useful substitute for those on a milk-free diet. It is also suitable for vegans for the same reason. This amount will line an 8 in. (20 cm) flan dish.

   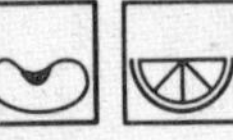   

8 oz (225 g) plain wholewheat flour
1 teaspoon baking powder
Cold water
3 tablespoons sunflower oil

Method

Put the flour and baking powder into a bowl. Mix well. Mix 3 tablespoons of water in a cup with the oil. Stir into the flour and mix well. As quickly as you can, knead lightly and roll out. Bake at Gas Mark 7, 220°C or 425°F.

Sweet Pastry (gluten free and wheat free)

Grease plates, tins, etc. before lining with this pastry.

 Use milk-free margarine

2 oz (50 g) polyunsaturated margarine
4 oz (110 g) ground rice
3 oz (75 g) finely grated eating apple

Method

Use a fork to blend all three ingredients. Knead by hand until it forms a ball of dough. Use the fingers to flatten the dough into a piece that can be cut into wedges, placed in the dish and then pressed together. Alternatively, cut with cutters and use for small items. (Manoeuvre with a spatula.) Bake at Gas Mark 7, 220°C or 425°F for about 20–25 minutes on the top shelf.

Apple Pastry for Steaming

A gluten-free and wheat-free substitute for suet pastry.

 Use milk-free margarine

2 oz (50 g) polyunsaturated margarine
4 oz (110 g) ground rice
1 cooking apple, finely grated to make 3 oz (75 g)

Method

Put the ingredients into a bowl and blend with a fork. Knead by hand into a ball of stiff paste, adding a little more ground rice if required. Press out with the fingers to line a basin. This pastry takes only 45 minutes to steam and provides enough to line a 1 pint (600 ml) basin with enough for the pastry 'lid'.

BREADS, SCONES, CRISPBREADS AND BATTERS

BREADS

Wholewheat Bread and Rolls

Makes 2 small loaves and about 10 rolls

1 oz (25 g) fresh yeast
1 teaspoon brown sugar or runny honey
About 1 pint (600 ml) warm water
2 lb (900 g) plain wholewheat flour
1 tablespoon sunflower, safflower, corn or soya oil

Method

Put the yeast into a cup with the sweetener and mix to a cream. Add a little of the warm water – about 3 tablespoons – stir well and leave to 'work' (grow frothy) for a few minutes. Put the flour into a large, warm mixing bowl. Sprinkle in the oil and rub in with the fingers. When the yeast mixture is frothy, stir in a little more warm water and pour into the flour. Mix with a wooden spoon, pouring in more of the warm water until you have a very wet, sticky dough. Mix and put a sprinkle of flour over the dough. Cover with a clean tea towel and leave to double in size in a warm place. Generously flour the worktop and turn the dough on to this. Add plenty more flour and work it in until you have a much stiffer dough that you can knead. Knead with both hands for about 3 or 4 minutes, or until the dough becomes smooth. Divide into three. Shape two of the pieces into fat sausages and press into two small greased loaf tins. Roll the remaining piece into a long sausage and cut into about ten pieces with a floured knife. Roll each piece into a ball and then flatten it. Place on a greased baking sheet, leaving space for the rolls to expand. Leave both loaves and rolls uncovered to rise in a warm place. Preheat the oven to Gas Mark 7, 220°C or 425°F , and when the rolls have risen put them in on the top shelf for about 12–15 minutes. The loaves will need longer – about 30–35 minutes on the centre shelf. (Do not put the loaves in to bake until the dough has risen to the top of the tins.) Turn out of the tins immediately and cool on a wire rack. Eat the rolls on the day they are baked.

High-protein Bread

Egg, wheatgerm and dried milk give this bread extra protein, making it very nourishing.

12 oz (350 g) plain wholewheat flour
1 oz (25 g) wheat bran
2 oz (50 g) wheat germ
½ pint (300 ml) warm water
½ oz (15 g) fresh yeast
2 teaspoons brown sugar
1 egg, beaten
1 heaped tablespoon low fat dried milk granules, mixed with 3 tablespoons cold water

Method

Put the flour, bran and wheat germ into a warm mixing bowl. Mix well. Cream a little of the water with the yeast, in a basin. Stir in the sugar and a little more of the water. Leave to 'work' (froth) for a few minutes. Beat the egg into the milk. Pour the yeast mixture into the mixing bowl, stir in, and then add the egg/milk and more of the warm water to make a soft, wet dough. Mix with a wooden spoon and sprinkle with a little more flour. Put a clean tea towel over the top and leave to rise in a warm place, for about 45 minutes to 1 hour. Turn out on to a floured worktop and knead, adding more flour. When the dough is smooth, shape into a fat sausage and put into a greased 1½ lb (750 g) bread tin. Leave to rise, uncovered, in a warm place. When nearly doubled in size put on the middle shelf of a preheated oven at Gas Mark 6, 200°C or 400°F for 30 minutes. Turn down the heat to Gas Mark 4, 180°C or 350°F and bake for another 10–15 minutes. Turn out the brown and crusty loaf on to a wire rack to cool.

Barley Bread

Makes 1 loaf

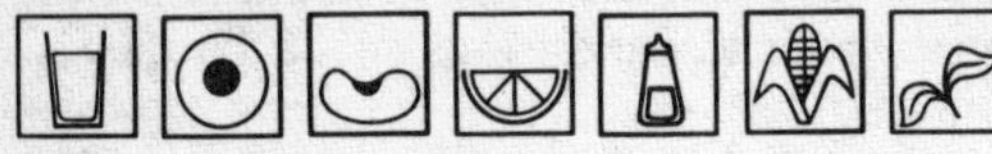

½ oz (15 g) fresh yeast
1 teaspoon brown sugar
About ½ pint (300 ml) warm water
12 oz (350 g) plain wholewheat flour
4 oz (110 g) barley flour

Method

Cream the yeast with the sugar in a cup. Add a little of the warm water and stir well. Leave to become frothy in a warm place. Put the flours into a mixing bowl and mix well to blend. Pour in the yeast mixture and enough of the warm water to make a soft dough. Cover the bowl with a clean tea towel and leave to rise in a warm place. When doubled in size, turn out of the bowl and on to a floured worktop. Knead well until smooth. Grease a 1½ lb (750 g) loaf tin and shape the dough into a fat sausage. Press into the tin and leave to rise in a warm place, uncovered. Bake in a preheated oven at Gas Mark 6, 200°C or 400°F for 40–50 minutes, near the top of the oven. Turn out of the tin and cool on a wire rack.

Rye Bread

Wrap this bread in greaseproof paper, silicon paper or in a polythene bag and do not slice for at least a day. It keeps well and can be sliced thinly.

Makes 2 loaves

½ oz (15 g) fresh yeast
½ teaspoon brown sugar
About ½ pint (300 ml) warm water
8 oz (225 g) light rye flour
8 oz (225 g) plain wholewheat flour
Ground rice for baking sheets

Method

Cream the yeast in a cup with the sugar. Stir in a little of the warm water and leave to grow frothy in a warm place. Put the flours into a mixing bowl and mix well to blend. Add the yeast mixture and enough water to make a medium stiff dough. Use a little more flour to knead the dough for 3 or 4 minutes, then put back into the bowl and cover with a damp, clean tea towel. Leave to rise in a warm place for at least 1 hour. When the dough has risen, knead again and form into two round loaves. Sprinkle a baking sheet with ground rice and place the loaves on it. Leave to rise again, covered with a damp tea cloth. When they have doubled in size cup your hands round them and press the dough up higher. Bake in a preheated oven at Gas Mark 6, 200°C or 400°F, above the centre, for about 1 hour. Leave to cool on a wire rack.

Soya Bread

Makes 1 loaf

½ oz (15 g) fresh yeast
1 teaspoon brown sugar
About ⅔ pint (350 ml) warm skimmed milk
12 oz (350 g) plain wholewheat flour
1 heaped tablespoon soya flour
1 heaped tablespoon ground almonds
Sunflower oil for top and oiling tin

Method

Cream the yeast with the sugar in a cup. Add a little of the warm skimmed milk and stir well. Leave to froth for a few minutes in a warm place. Put the flours and ground almonds into a mixing bowl and mix well. Pour in the frothy yeast and enough of the warm milk to make a wet dough, using a wooden spoon. Cover with a clean tea towel and leave to rise in a warm place. When almost doubled in size turn out on to a floured worktop and use more flour to knead well. When it feels smooth, shape into a fat sausage and put into an oiled 1½ lb (750 g) loaf tin. Brush the top of the loaf with oil. Make shallow cuts in the top with a sharp knife, to form a diamond pattern. Leave to rise, uncovered, in a warm place. When the dough has risen to the top of the tin, bake in a preheated oven at Gas Mark 6, 200°C or 400°F, above the centre of the oven for 35–40 minutes. Turn out of the tin and cool on a wire rack.

Extra Bran Bread

Owing to the extra bran this loaf will tend to dry out quickly and will be stale the next day. Serve in thick slices.

Makes 1 large loaf

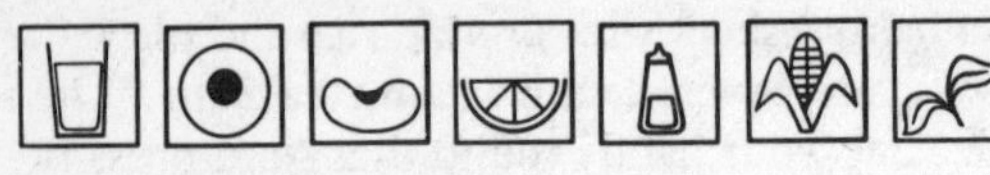

½ oz (15 g) fresh yeast
2 heaped teaspoons brown sugar
About ¾ pint (450 ml) warm water
1 lb (50 g) plain wholewheat flour
1½ oz (45 g) wheat bran
1 tablespoon sunflower oil

Method

Put the yeast into a cup with the sugar and mix to a cream. Add a little of the warm water and leave to grow frothy. Mix the flour and the bran in a warmed mixing bowl. Sprinkle in the oil and rub in with the fingers. Pour in the yeast and enough of the warm water to make a very wet dough. Sprinkle a little flour on the top, cover the bowl with a clean tea towel and leave to rise in a warm place. When almost doubled in size add more flour and turn out on to a floured worktop. Pull into one lump and knead the dough until smooth. Grease a 2 lb (1 kg) loaf tin. Shape the dough into a fat sausage and put into the tin. Press the corners down with your knuckles so the dough takes up the shape of the tin. Leave to rise in a warm place, then bake in a preheated oven at Gas Mark 6, 200°C or 400°F on the centre shelf for about 35–40 minutes. Turn out of the tin and cool on a wire rack.

Corn Bread (gluten free, wheat free and yeast free)

Cornmeal can be bought at most health stores.

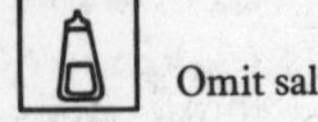 Omit salt

1 tablespoon sugar
3 pinches salt

3 teaspoons baking powder
1 tablespoon plain wholewheat flour
8 oz (225 g) cornmeal
1 egg
Scant ½ pint (300 ml) skimmed milk
1 tablespoon corn or sunflower oil

Method

Put the sugar, salt, baking powder and wholewheat flour into a basin. Mix well and sprinkle in the cornmeal. Stir to combine. Beat the egg and milk together in a small basin, then pour in the oil, add to the flour mixture and mix well. Pour this batter into a 9 in. (23 cm) pie dish which has been well greased. Put immediately into a preheated oven at Gas Mark 7, 220°C or 425°F on the top shelf and bake for about 30–35 minutes, until beginning to brown. Serve straight from the oven: either turn out of the dish and serve in wedges, or use a large spoon and serve by the spoonful.

Soda Bread (1) (gluten free and wheat free)

This kind of loaf is the poor cousin of yeasted bread. It tends to dry out very quickly so avoid overbaking and eat within a couple of hours of baking.

Makes 1 loaf

8 oz (225 g) Trufree No. 4 or 5 flour
1 heaped teaspoon bicarbonate of soda
1 heaped teaspoon cream of tartar
1 teaspoon sugar
1 tablespoon sunflower, soya or corn oil
¼ pint (150 ml) cold skimmed milk

Method

Put the flour, bicarbonate of soda, cream of tartar and sugar into a large bowl. Mix well. Sprinkle in the oil and rub in with the fingertips. Pour in the milk and mix to a stiff dough. Use a little more flour to knead into a ball of dough and shape into a round loaf. Put on to a greased baking sheet and score a cross on top, with a sharp knife. Bake for 20 minutes above the centre of the oven in a preheated oven at Gas Mark 7, 220°C or 425°F. After 30 minutes the loaf should be well risen and crusty. Cool on a wire rack and eat freshly baked.

Soda Bread with Fruit (gluten free and wheat free)

Use the previous soda bread recipe but add 1 oz (25 g) currants, sultanas or raisins to the flour.

Soda Bread (2)

This bread can also be baked in a greased loaf tin, but it will need 5 minutes extra cooking time.

Makes 1 loaf

8 oz (225 g) plain flour – either half-and-half wholewheat and white, or all wholewheat
½ teaspoon bicarbonate of soda
1 slightly heaped teaspoon cream of tartar
3 pinches salt
1 small egg, beaten
Just over ¼ pint (150 ml) skimmed milk

Method

Preheat the oven to Gas Mark 5, 190°C or 375°F. Put the flours, bicarbonate of soda, cream of tartar and salt into a large mixing bowl. Make a well in the centre and pour in the egg and enough milk to make a thick dough that can be stirred with a wooden spoon. Add more of the milk if the mixture seems too stiff. Turn out on to a floured worktop and knead into a ball of dough. Shape into a round and flatten the top slightly. Put on to a greased baking sheet. Use a knife dipped in flour to cut a cross on the top. Bake above the centre of the oven for 45–50 minutes. Immediately you take it out of the oven, wrap it in a clean tea towel to keep it warm. (This will also stop it from drying out.) Eat freshly baked.

Oat Bread

Makes 2 small loaves

 Avoid soya oil  Avoid corn oil

6 oz (175 g) rolled oats
1 pint (600 ml) skimmed milk
½ oz (15 g) fresh yeast
2 heaped teaspoons sugar
3 tablespoons warm water
12 oz (350 g) plain wholewheat flour
2 tablespoons oil – sunflower, safflower, corn or soya

Method

Use a basin to soak the oats in the milk for about 15 minutes. While the oats are soaking, cream the yeast with the sugar and add the 3 tablespoons of warm water. Mix well and leave to become frothy. Put the flour into a large mixing bowl. Sprinkle in the oil and add the soaked oats mixture and the yeast. Stir well with a wooden spoon. Cover the bowl with a clean tea towel and leave to rise in a warm place. When double the size turn the dough out on to a floured worktop. Sprinkle with flour and pull the dough together until it can be kneaded. Knead for about 5 minutes and shape into two equally sized, fat sausages. Press into two greased 1 lb (450 g) loaf tins and leave to rise in a warm place, covered with the clean tea towel. When the dough has risen to the tops of the tins put into a preheated oven at Gas Mark 8, 230°C or 450°F, above the centre of the oven. After about 30 minutes, turn the heat right down to Gas Mark 2, 150°C or 300°F for another 30 minutes. When baked and crusty turn out of the tins and cool on a wire rack. Use as ordinary bread.

Oat Bread (without yeast)

A sweet kind of bread with a good flavour.

2 oz (50 g) rolled oats
½ pint (300 ml) scalded, skimmed milk
6 oz (175 g) plain wholewheat flour
3 pinches salt
2 oz (50 g) sugar
½ oz (15 g) baking powder
1 small egg, beaten

Method

Put the oats into a basin. Pour over the hot milk and leave to soak until cool. Put the flour, salt, sugar and baking powder into a bowl and mix well. Spoon in the oat mixture and add the beaten egg. Mix again. Turn into a greased loaf tin and leave to stand for 15 minutes or so. Bake on the middle shelf of a preheated oven at Gas Mark 4, 180°C or 350°F for about 1¼–1½ hours. Turn out of the tin and leave to cool a little, but serve still warm and eat on the day of baking.

Trufree Brown Bread (gluten free and wheat free)

This bread takes only a couple of minutes to prepare for the oven and does not need to be left to rise. However, amounts ***must*** *be carefully weighed out and not guessed.*

10¼ oz (290 g) Trufree No. 5 flour
1 tablespoon sunflower oil
1 sachet yeast, supplied with the flour, or similar
Exactly 8 fluid oz (225 ml) warm water

Method

Put the flour into a bowl. Add the oil and sprinkle in the yeast. Stir. Pour in the water and mix to a creamy batter with a wooden spoon. (Do not use an electric beater.) Turn into a greased 1 lb (450 g) loaf tin and immediately put into the oven, preheated to Gas Mark 4, 180°C or 350°F, to bake on the top shelf. When well risen and crusty, after 1 hour, turn out of the tin and cool on a wire rack. Handle the loaf gently when it has baked as it must be left to 'set'. Cut when cold.

Trufree White Bread (gluten free and wheat free)

Make in the say way as for Trufree Brown Bread but use Trufree No. 4 flour instead. The blend of special flours used to make the No. 4 are all very pale in colour. The resulting loaf is a cream colour, not really white.

Basic Dough for Gluten-free and Wheat-free Bread

For crusty rolls, breadsticks, French sticks and pizza bases. While most cooking is really an art, this kind of specialized cooking is more scientific, requiring the exact measurement of ingredients. The special Trufree flour can be bought at chemists or by mail order (see p. 106 for details). (This recipe will not work with other types of gluten-free flour.)

Makes about 1 lb (450 g) dough

 Use milk-free margarine

10 oz (275 g) Trufree No. 4 gluten-free and wheat-free flour
1 sachet instant yeast, supplied with the flour, or similar
3 pinches salt
1 heaped teaspoon sugar
1 oz (25 g) margarine
¼ pint (150 ml) warm water

Method

Put the flour, yeast, salt and sugar into a mixing bowl. Mix well to blend and add the margarine. Rub in with the fingers. Pour in all the water and mix with a wooden spoon to a sticky dough. Without adding any more flour, knead into a ball. (If it feels too stiff add another tablespoon of water.) Knead on a cool worktop for 2 minutes until smooth and shiny. Shape as directed in the following recipes *without using more flour*. Leave in a warm place to rise and then bake according to the recipes.

Trufree Crusty Finger Rolls (gluten free and wheat free)

 Use milk-free margarine

Use the Basic Dough recipe above. For each roll use about 1 oz (25 g) of dough. Roll into small sausage shapes without using more flour and place on a greased baking sheet. Leave to rise in a warm place. When doubled in size bake for 15 minutes on the top shelf of a preheated oven at Gas Mark 7, 220°C or 425°F for 15 minutes. Eat freshly baked.

Trufree Baps (gluten free and wheat free)

 Use milk-free margarine  Avoid egg glaze

Use the Basic Dough recipe above. Use 2 oz (50 g) of dough for each bap. Shape in round, flat buns without using more flour and leave to double in size on a greased baking sheet, in a warm place. Bake on the top shelf of a preheated oven at Gas Mark 7, 220°C or 425°F. Take them out of the oven before they brown and cool on a wire rack. Use freshly baked for salad rolls or hamburgers. (For a really professional finish brush the tops with egg before leaving to rise and then sprinkle with sesame seeds before baking.)

Trufree Breadsticks (gluten free and wheat free)

 Use milk-free margarine

Use the Basic Dough recipe above. Use about ½ oz (15 g) of the dough for each breadstick. Roll out on the worktop into long pencil shapes without using more flour and put on greased baking sheets. When on the baking sheets pinch out to about 10 in. (25 cm) long. Leave for just a few minutes to rise in a warm place. Bake on the top shelf of a preheated oven at Gas Mark 7, 220°C or 425°F for 9–10 minutes until golden brown. Eat on the day of baking.

Trufree French Sticks

Makes 2 gluten-free and wheat-free crusty 'French' loaves

 Use milk-free margarine

Use the Basic Dough recipe above. Divide into two and roll each piece into a long sausage without using more flour. Put on to a greased baking sheet, brush the top with beaten egg and then cut slashes with a sharp knife, diagonally. Leave in a warm place to rise for about 15 minutes and then bake on the top shelf of a preheated oven at Gas Mark 7, 220°C or 425°F, for about 15 minutes. Eat the golden, crusty loaves freshly baked and broken into pieces.

Brown Bread (gluten free, wheat free and egg free)

The measurements for this recipe must be exact and carefully made. (The imperial measurements are the most accurate.) The size of tin is also crucial.

     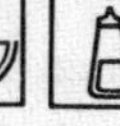  

2 slightly heaped teaspoons dried yeast granules
9 fluid oz (260 ml) warm water
1 oz (25 g) soya flour
4½ oz (125 g) potato flour
4 oz (110 g) brown ground rice
¾ oz (20 g) yellow split pea flour
2 level teaspoons dried pectin, or 1½ level teaspoons methylcellulose powder
1 tablespoon ground almonds
1 slightly heaped teaspoon brown sugar
1 tablespoon sunflower or soya oil
1 heaped teaspoon carob powder

Method

Preheat the oven to Gas Mark 4, 180°C or 350°F. Sprinkle the yeast into the water and leave to soften for a few minutes. Put all the other ingredients into a mixing bowl and stir well, breaking up any lumps. Stir the yeast and water and pour into the flour mixture. Mix, then beat with a wooden spoon (not an electric beater). Grease a medium loaf tin size 7¼ × 3½ × 2¼ in. (18.5 × 9 × 5 cm). Pour the batter into this and put into the oven immediately on the top shelf. Bake for 1 hour until brown and crusty. Turn out on to a wire rack to cool. Do not cut until cold as the loaf needs to set.

White Bread (gluten free, wheat free, egg free and milk free)

Measurements must be exact for this recipe and the size of the tin is also important. (The imperial measurements are the most accurate.)

 Avoid corn oil

2 slightly heaped teaspoons dried yeast granules
9 fluid oz (260 ml) warm water
1 oz (25 g) soya flour
4½ oz (125 g) potato flour
3 oz (75 g) pure maize flour (gluten-free and wheat-free cornflour)
¾ oz (20 g) ground almonds
2 level teaspoons pectin, or 1½ teaspoons methylcellulose powder
1 slightly heaped teaspoon caster sugar
1 tablespoon sunflower, soya or corn oil

Method

Preheat the oven to Gas Mark 4, 180°C or 350°F. Sprinkle the yeast into the warm water and leave to soften for a few minutes. Put all the other ingredients into a mixing bowl and stir well, breaking up any lumps. Stir the yeast and water and pour over the flour mixture. Mix, then beat with a wooden spoon (not an electric beater). Grease a medium loaf tin size 7¼ × 3½ × 2¼ in. (18.5 × 9 × 5 cm). Pour the batter into this and put into the oven immediately on the top shelf. Bake for about 1 hour until well risen, brown and crusty. Turn carefully out of the tin to cool on a wire rack. Leave to set and do not cut until completely cold.

Speckled Bread

Makes 1 small loaf

1½ oz (40 g) polyunsaturated margarine
¼ pint (150 ml) warm milk (or just over)
¼ level teaspoon grated nutmeg
8 oz (225 g) plain wholewheat flour
¼ oz (7 g) fresh yeast
3 oz (75 g) currants
1 small egg, beaten
1 level tablespoon brown sugar

Method

Gently melt the margarine in a small saucepan. Add the milk, stir and leave to cool for a few minutes. Mix the nutmeg and flour in a large mixing bowl. Crumble the yeast very finely and sprinkle into the flour with the currants. Beat the egg in a cup and add to the milk mixture. Add to the flour with the sugar. Mix well, adding more milk if the dough is too stiff. Sprinkle the top with a little flour, cover the bowl with a clean tea towel and leave to rise in a warm place. When doubled in size turn out the dough on to a floured worktop and knead, adding more flour as required. Shape into a fat sausage as soon as the dough feels smooth and put into a greased 1 lb (450 g) loaf tin. Leave to rise, uncovered, in a warm place. Bake on a shelf above the centre of a preheated oven at Gas Mark 4, 180°C or 350°F for about 30 minutes. As soon as it is baked, turn it out of the tin. Serve in thick slices, spread with polyunsaturated margarine. When stale serve as toast.

Banana Bread

Makes 1 small loaf

 Use milk-free margarine

 Avoid lemon rind

2 ripe bananas
8 oz (225 g) plain wholewheat flour
3 level teaspoons baking powder
Grated rind 1 lemon (optional)
2 oz (50 g) polyunsaturated margarine
1 egg, beaten
2 oz (50 g) soft brown sugar

Method

Peel the bananas and mash on a plate. Put the flour, baking powder and lemon rind into a bowl. Mix well and rub in the margarine with the fingertips. Pour in the egg, then add the sugar and mashed banana. Mix well, adding a little water if the mixture is too thick. Turn into a greased and floured 1 lb (450 g) loaf tin and bake on the centre shelf of a preheated oven at Gas Mark 4, 180°C or 350°F for about 45 minutes, or until firm and golden brown. Use as a teabread.

Fruit Teabread (gluten free, wheat free and egg free)

Makes 1 small loaf

 Avoid butter, use milk-free margarine

1 heaped teaspoon dried yeast granules
¼ pint (150 ml) warm water
4½ oz (125 g) ground rice
1 oz (25 g) soya flour
½ oz (15 g) yellow split pea flour
1 heaped teaspoon ground almonds
1½ level teaspoons dried pectin, or methylcellulose
1 oz (25 g) currants, raisins or sultanas
2 heaped teaspoons sugar
1 oz (25 g) polyunsaturated margarine or butter, melted

Method

Preheat the oven to Gas Mark 4, 180°C or 350°F. Sprinkle the yeast into the warm water and leave to soften for a few minutes. Put the remaining ingredients, except for the fat, into a mixing bowl. Mix well and add the margarine or butter. Stir the yeast and water and add to the flour mixture. Mix well, then beat to remove lumps. (Use a wooden spoon and not an electric beater.) Grease a 1 lb (450 g) loaf tin and flour it with ground rice. Turn the mixture into this and flatten off the top with a knife. Bake on the top shelf for 40–45 minutes, until browned. Turn out carefully on to a wire rack to cool. Do not cut until absolutely cold.

Date and Walnut Bread (gluten free, wheat free and egg free)

 Avoid butter, use milk-free margarine

Make as for Fruit Teabread, but instead of the currants put in 1 oz (25 g) chopped walnuts and 2 oz (50 g) chopped, stoned dates.

Fruit and Nut Bread (yeast free)

Makes 1 loaf

12 oz (350 g) plain wholewheat flour
3 level teaspoons baking powder
3 oz (75 g) soft brown sugar
2 oz (50 g) chopped walnuts or almonds
4 oz (110 g) dried fruit – choose from raisins, stoned dates, sultanas or dried apricots
2 eggs, beaten
Scant ½ pint (275 ml) skimmed milk
2 oz (50 g) polyunsaturated margarine, melted

Method

Preheat the oven to Gas Mark 4, 180°C or 350°F. Mix the flour and baking powder in a large mixing bowl. Stir in the sugar, nuts, dried fruit and the beaten eggs. Pour in the milk and mix well. Beat and add the margarine. Make sure it is thoroughly mixed and turn into a large greased and lined loaf tin – 9 × 5 × 3 in. (23 × 13 × 7.5 cm). Use a knife to make the top level and bake on the middle shelf for about an hour. Turn out of the tin carefully and leave to cool on a wire rack. Do not cut until cold. Remove greaseproof paper and cut into thick slices. Spread with polyunsaturated margarine.

MUFFINS AND SCONES

Wholemeal Raisin Muffins

Makes 8–10

8 oz (225 g) (plain) wholewheat flour
½ teaspoon baking powder
Pinch salt
1 oz (25 g) polyunsaturated margarine
2 oz (50 g) brown sugar
2 oz (50 g) raisins
¼ pint (150 ml) skimmed milk, warmed
1 tablespoon runny honey
½ teaspoon bicarbonate of soda

Method

Grease eight patty tins. Preheat the oven to Gas Mark 6, 200°C or 400°F. Put the flour, baking powder and salt into a bowl. Mix well and add the margarine. Rub in until the mixture resembles fine breadcrumbs, then stir in the sugar and raisins. Put the milk and honey into a cup and stir until the honey has all dissolved. Sprinkle the bicarbonate of soda into the flour mixture, add the liquid and beat well. Quickly spoon into the prepared patty tins and bake above the centre of the oven for about 12–15 minutes. Serve warm from the oven spread with polyunsaturated margarine.

Bran Muffins

Makes 8

1 oz (25 g) wheat bran
8 oz (225 g) plain wholewheat flour

Pinch salt
½ teaspoon baking powder
1 oz (25 g) polyunsaturated margarine
2 oz (50 g) brown sugar
¼ pint (150 ml) skimmed milk
1 tablespoon black treacle or molasses
½ teaspoon bicarbonate of soda

Method

Preheat the oven to Gas Mark 6, 200°C or 400°F. Grease eight patty tins. Put the bran, flour, salt and baking powder into a mixing bowl. Mix well and add the margarine. Rub in with the fingers. Stir in the sugar. Gently heat the milk and black treacle while you stir, to melt the treacle. Sprinkle the bicarbonate of soda into the flour mixture and pour in the liquid. Beat well and quickly spoon into the prepared patty tins. Bake above the centre of the oven for 15–20 minutes. Best eaten warm from the oven, spread with polyunsaturated margarine.

Oat Muffins

These are good for breakfast if you have run out of bread.

Makes 10–12

3 tablespoons sunflower oil
1 egg
About 8 fluid oz (225 ml) skimmed milk
4 oz (110 g) plain wholewheat flour
1 level tablespoon baking powder
Just under 4 oz (110 g) rolled oats

Method

Preheat the oven to Gas Mark 7, 220°C or 425°F. Grease patty tins with sunflower oil. Put the oil, egg and milk into a basin and whisk together. Put the flour and baking powder into a mixing bowl and mix. Sprinkle in the oats and mix again. Pour in the milk mixture and stir with a fork to combine the ingredients lightly. (Avoid the temptation to beat the mixture as this is not required.) Divide among the oiled tins and bake for about 20 minutes until firm and well risen. Serve warm, spread with polyunsaturated margarine.

Apple Muffins

Makes 6

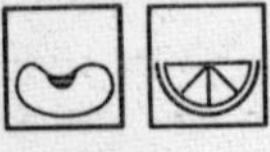

 Use milk-free margarine

4 oz (110 g) plain wholewheat flour
2 teaspoons baking powder
¼ level teaspoon mixed spice (optional)
1½ oz (40 g) polyunsaturated margarine
2 oz (50 g) currants or sultanas
1½ oz (40 g) brown sugar
1 small cooking apple, finely grated including skin
1 egg, beaten

Method

Preheat the oven to Gas Mark 8, 230°C or 450°F. In a bowl, mix the flour, baking powder and spice. Rub in the margarine. Stir in the dried fruit and sugar. Add the grated apple and beaten egg. Mix with a fork to a soft dough. Use more of the flour to shape by hand into six flat cakes, about ½ in. (1 cm) thick. Place on a greased baking sheet and bake above the centre of the oven for about 15 minutes. Serve warm, split and spread with polyunsaturated margarine or butter.

Singin' Hinny

Serves 2

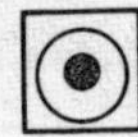

3 oz (75 g) plain wholewheat flour
1 teaspoon baking powder
1 level tablespoon ground rice
¼ teaspoon mixed spice
1 level tablespoon polyunsaturated margarine
1 tablespoon brown sugar
1 slightly heaped tablespoon dried mixed fruit
About 6 tablespoons skimmed milk
Sunflower oil for greasing

Method

Put the griddle or a heavy based frying pan over a medium heat while you make the scones. Put the flour, baking powder, ground rice and spice into a mixing bowl. Mix to blend well. Add the margarine and rub in until the mixture resembles breadcrumbs. Stir in the sugar and dried fruit. Add a little milk – enough to make a soft dough. Flour the worktop and turn the dough on to it. Roll out with a rolling pin to a large round scone, about ¼ in. (5 mm) thick. Screw up a piece of kitchen paper and dip in a little of the oil. Oil the griddle. Cut the scone into wedges (triangles) and use a spatula to place on the hot griddle. Cook for 4–5 minutes and then turn them over and cook on the other side. Serve still warm and spread with butter or polyunsaturated margarine.

Herb and Yoghurt Scones

These scones are good with soups or spread with cottage cheese.

Makes 8 wedges

8 oz (225 g) plain wholewheat flour
1 teaspoon each bicarbonate of soda and cream of tartar
Shake black pepper
2 oz (50 g) polyunsaturated margarine
½ teaspoon dried, mixed herbs
About ¼ pint (150 ml) plain low fat yoghurt
Milk for glaze

Method

Preheat the oven to Gas Mark 7, 220°C or 425°F. Mix the flour, bicarbonate of soda, cream of tartar and pepper in a mixing bowl. Add the margarine and rub in with the fingers until the mixture resembles fine breadcrumbs. Stir in the herbs, using a metal spoon. Pour in most of the yoghurt and work to a soft dough, adding more of the yoghurt if required. Turn on to a floured baking sheet and knead for a minute. Shape into a ½ in. (1 cm)-thick round on a baking sheet. Dip the blade of a knife into some flour and cut the dough half way through to make eight wedges. Brush with milk and bake for 20–25 minutes above the centre of the oven. Serve split and spread with polyunsaturated margarine.

Cheese and Bran Scones

Serve with plain soups such as tomato or watercress, or serve for breakfast, split and spread with polyunsaturated margarine.

Makes 12

8 oz (225 g) plain wholewheat flour
1 heaped tablespoon wheat bran
1 teaspoon dry mustard powder
2 heaped teaspoons baking powder
2 oz (50 g) polyunsaturated margarine
2 oz (50 g) grated Parmesan or Cheddar cheese (as fine as possible)
¼ pint (150 ml) skimmed milk
Paprika

Method

Preheat the oven to Gas Mark 8, 230°C or 450°F, and grease two baking sheets. Put the flour, bran, mustard powder and baking powder into a mixing bowl. Mix well and add the margarine. Rub in with the fingers until the mixture resembles fine breadcrumbs. Sprinkle in the cheese and stir. Add enough of the milk to make a soft dough. Turn out on to a floured worktop and knead for a minute. Roll out on a floured surface and either cut into rounds with a floured cutter or into squares with a floured knife. Place on the baking sheets, brush with milk and sprinkle sparingly with the paprika. Bake above the centre of the oven for about 12–15 minutes.

Plain Scones (gluten free, wheat free and egg free)

Makes 4

 Use milk-free margarine

2 oz (50 g) Trufree flour No. 4
½ level teaspoon each bicarbonate of soda and cream of tartar
Pinch salt

½ oz (15 g) polyunsaturated soft margarine
2 teaspoons sugar
Exactly 1 tablespoon cold water

Method

Put the flour, bicarbonate of soda, cream of tartar and salt into a mixing bowl. Mix well and add the margarine. Rub in with the fingers. Stir in the sugar and add the water. Mix, then knead to a soft dough adding a little more flour. Divide into four, roll into balls and flatten and shape into scones. Put on to a greased baking sheet and bake on the top shelf of a preheated oven at Gas Mark 7, 220°C or 425°F for 15 minutes. Serve freshly baked, split and spread with polyunsaturated margarine, and jam, if liked.

Pikelets

Makes 4–5

1 teaspoon dried yeast granules
3 pinches brown sugar
About 6 tablespoons warm skimmed milk
4 oz (110 g) plain wholewheat flour
1 egg
Oil for greasing

Method

Put the yeast, sugar and warm milk into a cup and leave to soften. After about 15 minutes, or when the mixture looks frothy, whisk lightly with a fork. Put the flour into a bowl and make a well in the centre. Add the egg and half the yeast mixture. Mix to a thick consistency with a wooden spoon. Stir in the rest of the yeast mixture and cover with a clean tea towel. Leave to work in a warm place for about 25–30 minutes. Oil a griddle or heavy based frying pan and heat well. When smoke begins to appear stir the batter and pour on to the griddle to make large scones. Cook until bubbles begin to appear and the edges begin to brown, then turn over with a spatula and cook on the other side. Keep hot in the oven until they are all made, then serve spread with butter or polyunsaturated margarine.

Dropscones

Makes 24

8 oz (225 g) plain wholewheat flour
2 slightly heaped teaspoons baking powder
1 tablespoon soft brown sugar
1 egg
About ½ pint (300 ml) skimmed milk
Oil for greasing

Method

Mix the flour, baking powder and sugar in a mixing bowl. Beat the egg into the milk. Stir in the flour mixture and beat to a smooth batter, adding a little water if it looks too thick. Heat a griddle or heavy based frying pan. Grease lightly with a screw of kitchen paper dipped in a little oil. Pour tablespoons of the batter on to the hot griddle. They will spread and form bubbles as they cook. Allow about 3 minutes cooking, then turn them over with a spatula and cook on the other side. Keep the scones warm and covered with a clean tea towel while you make the remainder. Eat freshly made with a scrape of polyunsaturated margarine or jam.

Dropscones (egg free)

Use instead of yeasted bread with meals, or for a snack.

Makes about 20

4 heaped tablespoons plain wholewheat flour
2 teaspoons sunflower oil
½ pint (300 ml) skimmed milk
Oil for greasing

Method

Put the flour into a bowl and sprinkle in the oil. Stir rapidly while you add the milk. Mix, then beat to a smooth batter. Use kitchen paper to grease the griddle or a heavy based frying pan with oil. Heat and pour tablespoons of the batter on to it. These will spread. When bubbles start to appear, turn them over with a spatula to cook on the other side for about 2 minutes. Serve immediately with a scrape of margarine or butter.

Dropscones (egg free and milk free)

Use the recipe for Dropscones above but make with water instead of milk. Avoid butter and margarine, unless they are milk free. Serve with jam, or just plain.

Dropscones (gluten free and wheat free)

Makes 5

4 oz (110 g) Trufree No. 7 flour
2 pinches salt
1 heaped teaspoon sugar
½ beaten egg
Just over 2½ fluid oz (60 ml) cold, skimmed milk
Oil for greasing

Method

Put the flour, salt and sugar into a basin. Mix well and stir in the egg and enough milk to make a creamy batter. Beat well, making sure there are no lumps. Grease the griddle or a heavy based frying pan with a little oil on a screw of kitchen paper. Heat and pour tablespoons of the batter on to it, allowing them to spread. Cook for about 2 minutes, or until bubbles appear on the surface, then turn over with a spatula and cook on the other side for 2 more minutes. Keep warm in a clean tea towel or napkin. Serve still warm with polyunsaturated margarine or butter.

Buckwheat Scones (gluten free and wheat free)

These scones can be made with water instead of milk.

Makes 7 or 8

 Use water

 Avoid sugar

2 heaped tablespoons buckwheat flour
Pinch salt
½ teaspoon sugar (optional)
8 tablespoons skimmed milk
Oil for griddle

Method

Mix the flour, salt and sugar in a basin. Stir in the milk to make a smooth batter. Beat well. Grease the griddle or a heavy based frying pan with a little oil on a screw of kitchen paper. Heat and pour tablespoons of the batter on to it, allowing them to spread. Cook over a medium heat for about 2 minutes, then turn them over with a spatula and cook for another 2 minutes on the other side. Eat while still warm instead of bread.

Oat Bannocks

Use the barley flour for wheat-free diets. These are good for breakfast.

Makes 12

 Avoid wholewheat flour, use wheat-free baking powder

 Use milk-free margarine

7 oz (200 g) medium oatmeal
2 slightly heaped tablespoons wholewheat or barley flour
½ teaspoon baking powder
2 oz (50 g) polyunsaturated margarine
Hot water from the kettle

Method

Put the griddle or a heavy based frying pan (ungreased) on to heat gently while you make the dough. Put the oatmeal, flour and baking powder into a mixing bowl. Mix and add the margarine. Rub in with the fingers and make a well in the centre. Pour in a little hot water – about 4 tablespoons – and mix to a soft dough. (Add a little more of the hot water if you think it necessary.) Sprinkle the worktop with oatmeal and roll out the dough to ¼ in. (5 mm) thick. Cut into shapes with a floured knife or cutter. Cook over a gentle heat on the griddle for 5 minutes each side, turning once. Eat with a meal, warm from the griddle, instead of bread.

CRISPBREADS AND FLATBREADS

Rye Biscuits

Makes about 12 oz (350 g) biscuits

 Use milk-free margarine

4 oz (110 g) plain wholewheat flour
2½ oz (65 g) rye flour
½ teaspoon baking powder
2 oz (50 g) polyunsaturated margarine
Beaten egg to bind
1 tablespoon soft brown sugar

Method

Put the flours into a basin with the baking powder. Mix well. Rub in the margarine with the fingertips. Stir in the sugar and add enough beaten egg to make a stiff dough. Flour the worktop and roll out pieces of the dough thinly. Cut into shapes with a sharp knife or cut into rounds with a pastry cutter. Use a spatula to place on greased baking sheets. Bake at the top of a preheated oven at Gas Mark 3, 170°C or 325°F for about 15 minutes or until firm. Put on to a wire rack to grow cold. Store in an airtight tin.

Oatmeal Biscuits

Makes about 12 oz (350 g) biscuits

 Use milk-free margarine

5 oz (150 g) medium oatmeal
3 oz (75 g) plain wholewheat flour
1 tablespoon soft brown sugar
½ teaspoon baking powder
3 oz (75 g) polyunsaturated margarine
Beaten egg to bind

Method

Mix the oatmeal, flour, sugar and baking powder in a bowl. Melt the margarine in a small saucepan and allow to cool a little. Pour into the flour mixture. Stir and add enough beaten egg to make a stiff paste. Knead lightly and roll out the dough thinly on a floured worktop. Cut into rounds with a floured cutter or into squares with a floured knife. Use a spatula to put the biscuits on a greased and floured baking sheet. Bake near the top of the oven, preheated to Gas Mark 3, 170°C or 325°F for about 15 minutes. Cool on a wire rack and store in an airtight container when cold.

Crackers (gluten free and wheat free)

Dried pectin can be bought in some health stores or by mail order. Try chemists for methylcellulose, which is much cheaper than pectin. Yellow split pea flour can be bought at Asian stores or health shops. Carob powder can be bought at health stores, also soya flour and potato flour.

Makes about 4 oz (110 g) biscuits

1 oz (25 g) yellow split pea flour
1½ oz (40 g) ground rice
½ oz (15 g) soya flour
½ oz (15 g) potato flour
½ level teaspoon dried apple pectin or methylcellulose
1 level teaspoon carob powder
1 heaped teaspoon sugar
3 pinches salt
2 teaspoons sunflower oil
2 tablespoons cold water

Method

Put all the ingredients except the water into a bowl and rub in the oil with the fingertips. Measure in the cold water and mix by hand to a stiff paste until the mixture makes a ball of dough. Use ground rice to roll out thinly. Cut into square or rectangular biscuits and use a spatula to place on lightly greased baking sheets. Prick all over with a fork and bake until lightly browned, in an oven preheated to Gas Mark 6, 200°C or 400°F, on the top shelf. The crackers should still be slightly soft when they are baked, but will gradually grow crisp as they cool down. Cool on a wire rack. Store in an airtight tin.

Rye Crispbreads

Makes about 8 oz (225 g) biscuits

 Avoid salt

1 lb (450 g) boiled, floury potatoes
4 pinches salt (optional)
6 oz (175 g) rye flour
Sunflower oil for greasing

Method

When the potatoes have cooled, mash them and put through a wire mesh sieve. Sprinkle in the salt and gradually add the rye flour to make a stiff, sticky dough. Use more rye flour to flour the worktop. Roll out portions of the dough until paper thin. Use a sharp knife to cut into shapes and prick all over with a fork. Heat a griddle or heavy based frying pan. Use a piece of kitchen paper to grease lightly. Cook the crispbreads on both sides until browned, and cool on a wire rack. Store in an airtight tin but eat within two or three days of baking.

Oat Crispbreads (wheat free)

These are not easy to make but are well worth the trouble. Use water to mix for milk-free diets.

Makes 12

 Use water

8 oz (225 g) medium oatmeal
2 pinches salt
6 tablespoons skimmed milk or water
More oatmeal for rolling out

Method

Mix the oatmeal and salt in a bowl. Add the liquid and mix by hand to a soft dough. Knead into a ball. Liberally sprinkle the worktop with oatmeal and roll out the dough thinly. (As it breaks very easily it is better to do this in small amounts.) Trim with a sharp knife into neat shapes and lift on to a hot, ungreased griddle or heavy based frying pan. Cook for about 2 minutes on each side, turning once. Cool on a wire rack. Eat freshly baked.

Crispbreads (gluten free and wheat free)

Makes 16

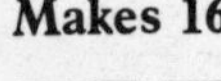

 Use milk-free margarine

1 oz (25 g) rice bran
2 pinches salt
7 oz (200 g) Trufree No. 6 flour
2 oz (50 g) polyunsaturated margarine
Exactly 6 tablespoons cold water

Method

Put the rice bran, salt and flour into a bowl. Mix well. Rub in the margarine with the fingertips until the mixture resembles breadcrumbs. Add the water and mix by hand into a ball of stiff dough. Use more of the Trufree No. 6 flour to roll out thinly. Cut into rectangles with a sharp knife. Use a spatula to place the crispbreads on ungreased baking sheets and prick them all over with a fork. Bake in a preheated oven at Gas Mark 8, 230°C or 450°F on the top shelf of the oven for about 12–15 minutes. Remove from the baking sheets with a spatula and leave to cool on a wire rack. As they cool down they will go crisp. When cold they can be stored in an airtight container.

Rye Flatbreads (wheat free and milk free)

Makes 8–10

2 heaped tablespoons rye flour
3 pinches salt
2 teaspoons sunflower oil
5 tablespoons water
More oil for greasing

Method

Mix the flour and salt in a basin. Sprinkle in the oil and stir in the water. Mix to a light batter. Grease the griddle or a heavy based frying pan with a little oil on a screw of kitchen paper. Heat and pour spoonfuls of the batter on to it. Spread them out as thin as you can with the back of a spoon and cook for about 3 minutes. Turn them over with a spatula and cook on the other side for another 2 minutes. Serve still warm instead of bread.

Barley Flatbreads (wheat free)

Makes 8–10

3 heaped tablespoons barley flour
1 teaspoon sunflower oil
4 tablespoons cold water
More oil for greasing
More barley flour for rolling out

Method

Put the flour into a basin and sprinkle in the oil. Add the water and mix by hand to a soft dough. Roll out very thinly, using more barley flour. Cut into crispbreads with a sharp knife. Heat the griddle or a heavy based frying pan and use a screw of kitchen paper to grease with oil. Place the crispbreads on the surface and press down with a spatula. Cook over a high heat for about 4 minutes, then turn them over and cook on the other side. (If you prefer them really crisp, grease the griddle again before you cook them on the other side.) Cool on a wire rack. Use as crispbreads.

Wheat Flatbreads (yeast free)

Makes 6

4 oz (110 g) plain wholewheat flour
About 3 tablespoons cold water
Oil for greasing pan (optional)
More flour for rolling out

Method

Put the flour into a basin and gradually stir in the water to make a soft dough. Knead into a ball, flatten and put back into the bowl. Cover with a clean cloth and leave to rest for about 20 minutes in a cool place. (If you do not have the time, omit this stage.) Knead again and break off pieces of the dough to roll out as thinly as you can, on a floured worktop. Dip a screw of kitchen paper in oil and grease a heavy based frying pan or a griddle. Heat and lay the flatbreads on the hot surface, pressing them flat with a spatula. After about 1 minute, turn them over to cook on the other side. (If preferred, they can be lightly greased and put under a very hot grill. They will need about 30 seconds each side.) They should be crisp and blistered whichever way you cook them. Serve with meals instead of bread.

Chappatis (gluten free and wheat free)

Makes 4

    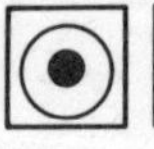   

2 heaped tablespoons Trufree No. 7 flour
Pinch salt
3 teaspoons sunflower oil
Exactly 2 tablespoons cold water
Sunflower oil for frying

Method

Put all the ingredients into a bowl and mix to a paste. Use more of the flour to knead. Divide into four and roll out thinly, using more flour. Heat, but do not grease, a griddle or heavy based frying pan. Cook the chappatis on both sides for about 1 minute or until crisp. When ready to use, heat a little oil in a frying pan. Fry quickly on both sides for a few seconds, just to recrisp them. Stack on a plate after draining on kitchen paper. Serve with curry and rice.

Tortillas (gluten free and wheat free)

Makes about 6

4 oz (110 g) cornmeal
Cold water to mix

Method

Put the cornmeal into a bowl and gradually add water to make a firm dough, while you mix. Break off pieces of the dough and roll them out as thin as you can, between sheets of greaseproof or silicon paper. Heat a griddle or heavy based frying pan and cook the tortillas for 1 minute on each side, without greasing. Use instead of bread, with meals.

Tacos

        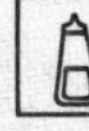 

Make as for Tortillas and, while still warm from cooking, fold lightly in half. Leave to cool on a wire rack. Use to stuff with salad vegetables or any sandwich fillings.

BATTERS

Yorkshire Pudding (with wholewheat flour)

Do not open the oven door for at least 25 minutes or the pudding will collapse. Try to bake the pudding to be ready at the same time the beef is to be served, as it will not stand too much waiting, tending to go flat and leathery.

Serves 4

4 oz (110 g) plain wholewheat flour
1 egg
2 slightly heaped tablespoons low fat dried milk granules
Water
Sunflower oil for greasing tin

Method

Preheat the oven to Gas Mark 6, 220°C or 425°F. Put the flour into a basin and add the egg. Stir. Put the milk granules into a measuring jug and add water up to the ½ pint (300 ml) mark. Stir well to combine and gradually add to the flour mixture, stirring after each addition. Beat to a smooth batter. Oil a sponge tin with a screw of kitchen paper dipped in a little sunflower oil. Put the tin into the oven on the top shelf for 5 minutes to heat. Pour in the batter and put back in the oven, again on the top shelf, for about 40 minutes. The pudding should be well risen, brown and crisp on the outside with a soft layer inside and a large hole. Serve hot with roast beef.

Yorkshire Pudding (wheat free and gluten free)

Do not open the oven door for at least 15–20 minutes.

Makes 12 small puddings and can be eaten by all the family

4 oz (110 g) Trufree No. 7 SR flour
1 tablespoon sunflower oil
1 egg
½ pint (300 ml) skimmed milk
More oil for the baking tins

Method

Preheat the oven to Gas Mark 9, 240°C or 475°F. Put the flour and oil into a bowl. Mix and add the egg. Stir and gradually add the milk, still stirring. Beat well to make a batter. Grease twelve patty tins with oil and put them to heat in the oven. Spoon in the batter and return to the oven on the top shelf. Bake for 5 minutes, then turn down the heat to Gas Mark 7, 220°C or 425°F for 30 minutes. Serve hot with roast beef.

Pancake Batter

Makes about 12

1 tablespoon low fat dried milk granules
Cold water
1 egg
2 teaspoons sunflower oil
4 oz (110 g) wholewheat flour

Method

Put the milk granules into a measuring jug and add water up to the ½ pint (300 ml) mark. Stir well to combine. Add the egg and oil and whisk with an egg whisk until smooth. Put the flour into a basin and pour in a little of the egg mixture. Mix, then beat, gradually adding the remaining egg mixture, a little at a time. Beat to a creamy batter. Use to make pancakes for sweet or savoury dishes.

Pancake Batter (gluten free and wheat free)

  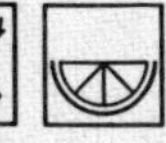 

2 oz (50 g) Trufree No. 7 SR flour
1 egg
¼ pint (150 ml) skimmed milk
1 teaspoon sugar

Method

Put the flour into a basin with the egg and mix to a stiff paste. Add the milk, a little at a time, beating it in after each addition. Beat well and add the sugar. Beat again, and the batter is ready to use.

Pancakes

 Avoid lemon and orange

 Avoid meat and fish fillings

 Avoid sugar

Pancake batter – see recipes above
Sunflower oil for greasing pan

Method

Heat the pancake pan or a heavy based frying pan. Screw up a piece of kitchen paper and dip in a little oil. Use to grease the pan. Get the pan really hot, then pour in about 2–3 tablespoons of the thin batter. Tip the pan to let the batter coat the base. Cook for about 1 minute, then loosen with a spatula and turn over to cook on the other side. Use for both sweet and savoury dishes.

Sweet Pancakes

Lemon pancakes

Make pancakes. Sprinkle with fresh lemon juice and a little sugar to taste – soft brown, caster or fructose. Roll up and serve on a hot plate.

Orange pancakes

Make pancakes. Sprinkle with a little fresh orange juice mixed with a few drops of lemon juice and soft brown sugar, caster or fructose to taste. Roll up and serve on a hot plate.

Savoury Pancakes

Make the pancakes and spread with filling. Roll up and serve on a hot plate. Allow two per person for a main course, or one for a starter.

The amounts of filling listed below are for two pancakes.

Ham filling

1 slice of lean ham, with the fat trimmed off, cut into small squares and mixed into 3 tablespoons of Basic White Sauce (see recipe on p. 403).

Prawn filling

Put 2 heaped tablespoons of defrosted prawns into boiling water and heat through for a minute. Drain and add to 3 tablespoons of Basic White Sauce (see recipe on p. 403). Season with black pepper to taste and add a few drops of lemon juice and a teaspoon of freshly chopped parsley.

Chicken and mushroom filling

Put 3 tablespoons of Basic White Sauce (see recipe on p. 403) into a small saucepan and add 1 heaped tablespoon of chopped, cooked chicken and the same of mushrooms. Heat through and sprinkle in 1 teaspoon of freshly chopped parsley.

Dumplings

Makes 8 small dumplings for casseroles and stews or 16 mini dumplings for soups: serves 4

 Use milk-free margarine

2 oz (50 g) plain wholewheat flour
½ teaspoon baking powder
1 oz (25 g) polyunsaturated margarine
Cold water

Method

Put the flour and baking powder into a bowl and mix well. Add the margarine and rub in with the fingers until the mixture resembles breadcrumbs. Add 2–3 tablespoons of water and mix to a soft dough. Dip your hands into flour and divide the dough into equal-sized pieces. Roll into balls. The dumplings are ready to cook. In casseroles and stews they will require about 25–30 minutes. In soups, mini dumplings will need only 15–20 minutes. Place them on top of the casserole, stew or soup, where they should float. (See individual recipes for the base dishes in which to cook them.)

Variations

Add ¼ level teaspoon dry mustard powder to the flour.
Add 1 heaped teaspoon dry wheat bran to the flour.
Add 2 pinches dry mixed herbs to the flour.

SAUCES, GRAVIES, CHUTNEYS, JAMS AND DRINKS

SAUCES

See also sauces for Pasta Dishes, pp. 156–68.

Bread Sauce

To eat with roast chicken. For wheat-free/gluten-free diets, use any of the appropriate breads in this book, or Trufree Nos 1, 4 or 5 breads. If just making for one person, use half the quantities in this recipe but still use 1 slice of the special bread.

Serves 2

 Use wheat-free bread

 Avoid Trufree Nos 4 and 5 flours

 Use gluten-free bread

 Avoid Trufree Nos 4 and 5 flours

1 slice bread
½ pint (300 ml) skimmed milk + 1 tablespoon low fat dried milk granules
1 small onion
1 teaspoon sunflower oil
Pinch powdered cloves
Freshly ground black pepper, to taste

Method

Make the bread into fine crumbs. Stir the granules into the milk. Peel the onion and put into a saucepan with the other ingredients. Bring to the boil, gently, then transfer to a warm ovenproof dish. Put in the bottom of the oven while the chicken is roasting, which should just keep it warm. When ready to serve, remove the onion and discard, and beat the sauce with a wooden spoon.

Sage and Onion Stuffing

For roast chicken or pork. Stuffing used inside a joint or bird will absorb a good deal of unwanted fat. This method of cooking stuffing keeps the fat to a minimum yet the stuffing still has a good flavour. (NB Use special bread for gluten-free/wheat-free diets.)

Serves 2–3

Use wheat-free bread

Avoid lemon rind

Use gluten-free bread

2 slices bread, made into crumbs
½ medium onion, chopped finely
½ teaspoon dried sage, or 1 teaspoon chopped fresh
2 teaspoons sunflower oil
A little water
Freshly ground black pepper, to taste

Method

Oil a small ovenproof dish with sunflower oil. Mix all the ingredients, adding enough water to make a rather wet mixture. Spoon into the dish and bake at the top of the oven until crisp (about 30 minutes should be enough). Move to the bottom of the oven to keep warm after it has finished cooking.

Variations

Add ½ cooking apple, finely grated, for use with pork.
Add the finely grated rind of ½ lemon for use with chicken.

Basic White Sauce (with cornflour) (gluten free and wheat free)

This recipe can form the basis for both savoury and sweet sauces: it makes about ½ pint (300 ml) or 2 servings of low fat sauce. A list of flavourings follows. (NB If using this recipe for gluten-free/wheat-free diets, make sure the brand of cornflour (or maize flour) is suitable, as some brands have wheat flour added.)

2 heaped tablespoons low fat dried milk granules
½ pint (300 ml) cold water
1 level tablespoon cornflour

Method

Mix the dried granules into the water to make the milk. Put the cornflour into a jug and add about 3 tablespoons of the milk. Stir until smooth, then gradually add the rest of the milk. Pour into a heavy based saucepan and heat gently while you stir. When the mixture is almost at boiling point, reduce the heat and stir for another 2 minutes until it has thickened.

Savoury Flavourings for Basic White Sauce

Onion sauce

Peel and boil 2 medium onions for about 30 minutes, until soft. Drain, chop and add to the Basic White Sauce. Serve with fish or lamb.

Egg sauce

Hard boil an egg. Peel and chop finely. Stir into the Basic White Sauce with a little freshly ground black pepper, to taste. Excellent with white fish such as cod, haddock or plaice.

Parsley sauce

Chop a few sprigs of parsley to make 1 heaped tablespoon. Stir into the Basic White Sauce and serve with boiled root vegetables or fish.

Cheese sauce

Make the Basic White Sauce but add an extra 2 teaspoons of milk granules, when you make up the milk. Stir in 1 tablespoon of finely grated Parmesan cheese until it melts. (Also stir in 1 teaspoon of French mustard for a tastier sauce.) Cheese sauce is usually a high fat food but this recipe keeps the fat content very low.

Tomato sauce

Make the Basic White Sauce and stir in 1 heaped tablespoon of tomato purée. Taste. If it seems too sour, add a pinch or two of sugar until it is correct.

Cheese and onion sauce

    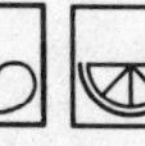   

Make the Basic White Sauce. Have ready 1 medium onion, chopped and fried for 5 minutes in 2 teaspoons of sunflower oil. Add to the sauce with 1 tablespoon of finely grated Parmesan cheese. Serve with white fish or on cauliflower to make Cauliflower Cheese (see recipe on p. 249).

Mushroom sauce

Chop 2 oz (50 g) mushrooms and fry in 2 teaspoons of sunflower oil for about 3 or 4 minutes. Make the Basic White Sauce and stir in the cooked mushrooms. Serve with fish or nutburgers.

Cucumber and lemon sauce

Cut 10 thin slices of cucumber and chop them. Finely grate the rind of just ¼ lemon. Make the Basic White Sauce and add both the cucumber and the rind. Stir in while you heat gently. Serve with white fish. (NB Leave the skin on the cucumber, otherwise it will have no colour in the sauce.)

Sweet Flavourings for Basic White Sauce

Vanilla custard

Make the Basic White Sauce and stir in 1 tablespoon of sugar or less of fructose (to taste). Add a few drops of vanilla flavouring and stir well.

Carob sauce

Make the Basic White Sauce and add a little sugar to taste. Stir in 2 heaped teaspoons of carob. Serve on plain or orange low-fat sponge for a pudding (see recipe on p. 345).

Chocolate sauce

 Use wheat-free cocoa

 Use gluten-free cocoa

Make the Basic White Sauce, adding 2 heaped teaspoons of cocoa to the cornflour before you start. Stir in sugar to taste. Serve on low-fat chocolate sponge (see recipe on p. 345).

Orange sauce

Make the Basic White Sauce and add sugar to taste. Stir in the grated rind of ½ orange. Serve with low-fat sponge for a pudding.

Lemon sauce

Make the Basic White Sauce and stir in sugar to taste. Add the finely grated rind of ½ lemon and stir in well. Use on low-fat plain or lemon sponge as a pudding (see recipe on p. 345).

Passion fruit sauce

Halve a passion fruit and squeeze out the centres. Put through a fine sieve to remove the pips and catch all the resulting juice. Make the Basic White Sauce and sweeten to taste with sugar. Stir in the passion fruit juice. Serve on plain low-fat sponge for a pudding.

Non-dairy 'Cream'

Use instead of cream. It can be flavoured to taste with vanilla flavouring, cocoa, carob, grated lemon or orange rind, mashed banana, etc.

1 level tablespoon maize starch
5 tablespoons cold water
1½ oz (40 g) milk-free margarine
2 heaped teaspoons caster sugar or icing sugar
Few drops fresh lemon juice

Method

Put the maize starch into a small saucepan with the water. Heat gently while you stir, until the mixture begins to form blobs. Turn the heat down and continue to stir until the mixture has thickened. Use a wooden spoon to beat to a smooth consistency. Allow to grow completely cold. Cream the margarine and sugar in a basin. Beat in the lemon juice and the cold maize mixture, adding a little at a time. Beat until fluffy.

GRAVIES

  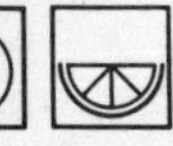  

 Avoid wholewheat flour, and use wheat-free soy sauce

 Use unsalted home-made stock and avoid tomato purée

 Avoid wholewheat flour, and use gluten-free soy sauce

 Avoid cornflour

 Avoid soy sauce

Unless gravy is made with care it can contain a good deal of unwanted saturated fat. Three ingredients are required to make good gravy – liquid of some kind, a thickener and some sort of stock.

Suitable Liquids

Water – use only if nothing else is available. Vegetable strainings – when straining cooked vegetables in a colander, put over a saucepan to catch the strainings. Those from greens and root vegetables are always useful and can be topped up with water if there is not enough.

Suitable Thickeners

As even a thin gravy needs a little thickening it is advisable to keep one or two suitable starches in the store cupboard.

Cornflour

A smooth thickener, but one which may form a skin if allowed to grow cold. Useful for gluten-free/wheat-free diets, providing the cornflour is not the kind that is a mixture of starches including wheat flour.

Wholewheat flour

Fine plain wholewheat flour is best for gravy. It will make a robust gravy without upsetting the flavour.

Potato flour

This tastes slightly of potato but has the advantage over cornflour and wheat flour that it does not form lumps, so is easy to use.

Rice flour

A fine white flour with only a slight taste of rice; coarser versions are the ground rices – brown and white – which can also be used if rice flour is not available.

Arrowroot

This is very finely ground starch, but it is very expensive; useful for allergics, as it is grain-free.

Suitable Stock

Soy sauce

The thin varieties are best, but make sure you choose one which does not contain MSG, a favourite ingredient for stock manufacturers. Some brands are gluten free and wheat free for special diets. Unless the bottle says 'low salt', soy sauce will contain salt as one of its main ingredients.

Yeast extracts

These are blends of yeast and spices plus a good deal of salt. Some brands are low salt, such as Natex low salt yeast extract.

Meat stock for gravy

Avoid wholewheat flour, and use wheat-free soy sauce

Use unsalted home-made stock, and avoid tomato purée

Avoid wholewheat flour, and use gluten-free soy sauce

Avoid cornflour

Avoid soy sauce

If you are roasting a joint or poultry there will be some juices that leak out from the meat into the pan. These usually congeal to form a brown deposit under and around the meat. There will always be some fat in the roasting tin and this should be carefully drained off before using the juices. The gravy can then be made in the roasting tin, by adding a mixture of liquid and thickener. After pouring these into the tin, rub with the back of a spoon to release the stock juices. Bring to the boil, then simmer while you stir for 2 minutes.

Tomato purée

This can be added to gravies to increase flavour.

Home-made vegetable or meat stock

This can also be used, but at least 1 tablespoon per person is required (see recipes).

Gravy

For each portion you will need 1 teaspoon of the thickener of your choice.

 Avoid wholewheat flour, and use wheat-free soy sauce

 Use unsalted home-made stock, and avoid tomato purée

 Avoid wholewheat flour, and use gluten-free soy sauce

 Avoid cornflour

 Avoid soy sauce

About 5 or 6 tablespoons liquid
½ teaspoon soy sauce, ¼ teaspoon yeast extract, or 1 tablespoon home-made stock

Method

Put the thickener into a cup with 1 tablespoon of cold water and stir well. Pour in the liquid and add the stock. Heat in a saucepan while you stir until the mixture comes to the boil. Simmer, still stirring, until the gravy thickens – about 1½–2 minutes. Serve immediately.

Onion Gravy

 Avoid wholewheat flour, and use wheat-free soy sauce

 Use unsalted home-made stock, and avoid tomato purée

 Avoid wholewheat flour, and use gluten-free soy sauce

 Avoid cornflour

 Avoid soy sauce

Fry ½ medium onion, chopped finely, in a little sunflower oil. Stir while you cook for about 6 minutes and let the onions brown. (The browner the onions, the tastier the gravy.) Add a mixture of thickening and liquid and stir well. Season to taste with black pepper and add the stock of your choice. Bring to the boil and simmer for 2 minutes. Strain and serve.

Vegetable Stock

3 onions, peeled and sliced
1 tablespoon vegetable oil such as sunflower, corn or soya oil
1 turnip, peeled and chopped
2 carrots, trimmed and cut lengthways
4 or 5 celery stalks (outer ones)
2 small leeks, sliced and thoroughly cleaned
Water to cover

Method

Stir/fry the onions in the oil for 4 minutes. Add the remaining ingredients and enough water to cover, and bring to the boil. Turn down the heat and simmer with the lid on for about 3 hours. This should produce a good stock when strained and the vegetables discarded. Cool and store in the fridge for not more than two days before using in soups and casseroles.

Meat Stock

Use for home-made soups and casseroles.

2 lb (1 kg) veal and beef bones, plus scraps of meat from the butcher (ask him to chop the bones)
Water to cover
1 each onion, carrot and turnip
Few sprigs parsley

Method

Trim off and discard any visible fat from the meat and bones, then put them into a large saucepan and cover with water. Bring to the boil slowly. Any scum that rises to the top must be skimmed off and discarded. Add the vegetables cut into long pieces (not slices) and the parsley. Put the lid firmly on the saucepan and simmer for at least 4 hours. Strain into a basin and discard the vegetables, bones, etc. Allow to cool, then cover and put into the fridge overnight. Fat will rise to the surface and harden. This can be removed before the stock is used. Keep in the fridge and use within two days.

QUICK CHUTNEYS

Like jam, this can be made in very small amounts for immediate use. Use for sandwiches, with cold meats and curries.

Apricot Chutney

4 oz (110g) dried apricots
2 teaspoons sunflower oil
1 medium onion, chopped finely
2 heaped tablespoons sultanas
4 tablespoons wine vinegar
Finely grated rind 1 small orange, with its juice
4 good pinches cinnamon
¼ teaspoon French mustard
Brown sugar or fructose, to taste

Method

Soak the apricots overnight in cold water. Heat the oil in a small saucepan and stir/fry the onion for 4 minutes, until transparent. Add all the other ingredients and bring to the boil. Turn down the heat and simmer for 10 minutes, or until the apricots are soft. (If the chutney begins to dry out while cooking, add a little hot water.) Allow to cool and store covered in the fridge. Eat within two days.

Date and Apple Chutney

½ medium onion, chopped finely
2 teaspoons sunflower oil
2 cooking apples, peeled, cored and coarsely grated
3 tablespoons wine vinegar
5 dates, stoned and chopped finely
¼ level teaspoon ground ginger
3 grinds black pepper
Brown sugar or fructose, to taste

Method

Fry the onion in the oil for 4 minutes, while you stir. Add all the other ingredients and a little water. Bring to the boil while you stir. Simmer with the lid on for about 10–15 minutes, or until the chutney has reduced. Put into the fridge when cold and eat within two days.

Tomato Chutney

2 spring onions, chopped finely
2 teaspoons sunflower or olive oil
1 lb (450 g) ripe tomatoes
2 tablespoons wine vinegar
Small pinch cayenne pepper
Small pinch mixed spice
4 good pinches paprika
Brown sugar or fructose, to taste

Method

Use a small saucepan to fry the onion in the oil for 30 seconds while you stir. Peel the tomatoes and chop. Add all the other ingredients and stir well. Bring to the boil. Simmer while you stir for another 5 minutes, then allow to cool and store in the fridge. Eat within two days.

Spiced Plum Chutney

2 or 3 teaspoons sunflower oil
1 small onion, chopped finely
Small piece root ginger, peeled, chopped finely
About 10 plums
1 cooking apple, peeled, cored and coarsely chopped
4 tablespoons wine vinegar
4 good pinches allspice
4 good pinches cinnamon
2 grinds black pepper
1 pinch powdered cloves
Brown sugar or fructose, to taste

Method

Heat the oil in a small saucepan and fry the onion while you stir for 4 minutes. Put in all the other ingredients and bring to the boil, adding a little water. Simmer for about 10–15 minutes, stirring occasionally. Allow to cool and store in the fridge. Eat within two days.

QUICK JAMS

This is a most economical way to make jam – just make enough for one or two days. There is no need to add lots of sugar to set it. Regard these jams as fruit spreads and not preserves.

Dried Apricot Jam

Soak a dozen or so dried apricots for 24 hours. Put into the liquidizer with the soaking liquid and a little honey or brown sugar to taste. Blend and use as a spread instead of jam.

Quick Kiwi Jam

Mash a peeled kiwi fruit and use immediately, instead of jam. Ripe fruit will not need the addition of a sweetener.

Quick Berry Jam

Mash a few raspberries, strawberries, tayberries or loganberries and sweeten to taste (if necessary) with a little fructose or caster sugar. Use immediately instead of jam.

Stewed Fruit Spread

 Use artificial sweetener

Stew any suitable fruit in a little water. Add sweetening to taste and cook while you stir to thicken it. Use within two days instead of jam. The following fruits are all suitable: apple (cooking varieties); blackberry and apple; plum; greengage; peach; nectarine; black, red and white currants.

Sweet Mincemeat

Commercially made mincemeat usually contains suet that has been rolled in wheat flour. This recipe is vegetarian, vegan and suitable for wheat-free/gluten-free diets.

      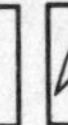 

2 oz (50 g) each seedless raisins, chopped walnuts and brown sugar
3 oz (75 g) each of currants and sultanas
1 tablespoon sunflower oil
½ teaspoon each allspice, cinnamon and nutmeg
1 eating apple, finely grated
Juice 1 orange

Method

Blend all the ingredients in a basin and put into jars. Store in the fridge, covered, and use as required.

FRUIT JUICES AND MILKSHAKES

These should be regarded as liquid foods, not just drinks. Freshly squeezed or blended fruit juices have a higher nutritional value than canned and frozen brands, whose vitamins can be lost as the juice ages or is left open. Although citrus juices can be squeezed by hand, this is rather a wasteful way of preparing them. A rotary electric citrus squeezer is probably the most efficient. Peeled fruit that is liquidized will have a higher fibre content than squeezed juice, as the membranes and some of the pith will also be used. Discolouring of some fruits due to oxidization can be prevented by the addition of lemon juice.

The following juices can be freshly made and offer a vitamin boost to any diet. Ripe fruits will not need any added sugar; however, the addition of a little fructose can sometimes make a juice palatable that would otherwise seem too sour.

Fruit Drinks

Use water

Use artificial sweetener or very sweet fruit

Avoid lemon juice, orange, clementine, satsuma, grapefruit

Amounts are for 1 drink in each case:

½ grapefruit and 1 orange or 1 satsuma or 2 clementines, squeezed
1 orange, 2 clementines, squeezed.
1 banana, few drops of fresh lemon juice, juice of ½ passion fruit, strained; blend with a little water or skimmed milk in the liquidizer.
1 orange, peeled and segmented, 4 or 5 strawberries or a handful of raspberries; liquidize with a little water.
1 slice of fresh pineapple and a little water, liquidized (cut the pineapple into chunks before using).
3 fresh stoned apricots, 5 or 6 orange segments, liquidized with a little water.
1 ripe peeled and stoned peach and a few raspberries, liquidized with a little water.
1 peeled and cored apple, a few drops of fresh lemon juice and a little water with a pinch of cinnamon, liquidized.
1 cupful of dried apricots, soaked for 12 hours and liquidized with a few drops of lemon juice.
Juice of 1 orange and 4 or 5 stoned, soaked prunes, liquidized with a little water.
A handful of raisins (seedless), soaked overnight in water and liquidized with 1 peeled and cored sweet eating apple and a little water.
Juice of ½ lemon and 1 orange, a little water and fructose to taste.

Milk-based Drinks

Avoid wheat germ

Avoid honey and sugars, use artificial sweetener

Avoid egg

1 heaped tablespoon low fat dried milk granules, 1 cup water, 2 heaped teaspoons wheat germ, 1 teaspoon liquid honey, ½ banana; liquidize and serve immediately.

1 heaped tablespoon low fat dried milk granules, 1 cup water, a handful of raspberries or strawberries or 1 ripe, peeled and stoned peach or nectarine; add sugar to taste, liquidize and serve immediately.

1 heaped tablespoon low fat dried milk granules, 1 small raw egg, 1 cup water, 1 teaspoon wheat germ, 1–2 teaspoons liquid honey; liquidize and drink immediately; a good breakfast substitute.

1 heaped tablespoon low fat dried milk granules, 1 level tablespoon ground almonds, sweetening to taste, 6 dried apricot halves soaked overnight; liquidize with 1 cup of water and drink immediately.

Home-made Lemonade

Use instead of squash, diluted a little with water.

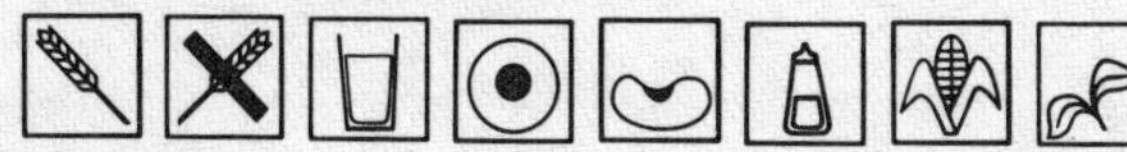

2 lemons
2 tablespoons brown sugar, or 1½ tablespoons fructose
About 1½ pints (900 ml) boiling water

Method

Wash the fruit and cut into thin slices. Put into a jug and sprinkle with the sugar. Pour the boiling water over the fruit and leave to steep for about 12 hours. Strain and discard the fruit slices.

Mixed Fruit Squash

1 lime
2 lemons
2 oranges
3 tablespoons brown sugar, or 2 tablespoons fructose
2 pints (1 litre) boiling water

Method

Make as for Home-made Lemonade and use instead of fruit squash, diluted with a little water.

Limemade

2 limes
1 lemon
Sugar to taste
1 pint (600 ml) boiling water

Method

Make and use as for Home-made Lemonade.

FURTHER READING

For more details and an updated look at the Hay Diet, see *Food Combining for Health* by Doris Grant and Jean Joice, published by Thorsons.

Index

A

appetite 13
apricot crumble 315
apricot chutney 412
apricots, baked 321
apple baked in sweet pastry 303
apple cake 328
apple flan 319
apples, spiced 322
apples, stuffed 323
autumn pudding 334

B

baking powder 105
banana ice cream 339
bananas, baked 315
batter pudding with dried fruit 302
batter pudding with fresh fruit 302
beans, dried 265
beefburgers 212
beef casserole with prunes 214
beef in stout 220
beef stew with vegetables 215
beef with ginger 219
berry water ice 338

biscuits
- crackers 392
- digestive (1) 354
- digestive (2) eggless 355
- fruit cookies (gluten/wheat free) 358
- langues de chat (1) 356
- langues de chat (2) gluten wheat free 356
- nut cookies (gluten/wheat free) 359
- oatmeal 391
- plain (gluten/wheat/egg/milk free) 357
- rye 391

blancmange 335
Boston baked beans 247
bran pastry 361
bread and 'butter' pudding 312
breadsauce 402

breads
- banana 379
- barley 368
- basic dough for gluten/wheat free 375
- brown, gluten/wheat free 377
- corn, gluten/wheat free 370
- date and walnut 381
- extra bean bread 370
- extra protein 367

flatbreads
- fruit and nut, yeast free 381
- fruit teabread, gluten/wheat free 380
- oat 372
- oat without yeast 372
- rye 368
- soda, wheat/gluten free 370
- soya 369
- speckled 379
- Trufree baps, wheat/gluten free 376
  - brown 374
  - white 374
  - breadsticks 376
  - crusty finger rolls 375
  - French sticks 377
- white, gluten/wheat free 378
- wholewheat bread and rolls 366

broccoli 259
brown bread and nut ice cream 339
burgers, high protein 246

C

calabrese 259
cakes 345–54
canneloni 165
  fillings for 169–70
carbohydrate 19–20
carob cake, eggless 352
carob rice pudding 321
carrots 260
cauliflower 259
  cheese 249
chappatis, wheat/gluten free 396
cheese and vegetable pie 250
chicken
  and mushroom casserole 224
  baked in fruit juice 229
  casserole 226
    with leeks 228
  cold 225
  dinner for one 236
  in red wine 235
  roast 228
  roast with herb gravy 227
  with tarragon 223
  with yoghurt and ginger 230
cod
  baked 202
  creole 203
  marinaded 202
coffee mousse 243
cooked vegetables 258–67
cracked wheat 189
creme caramel 333
crispbreads
  gluten/wheat free 394
  oat 393
  rye 393
  see also flatbreads
curried TVP with vegetables 254
custard tart 324

D

date and apple chutney 412
date and ginger cake 353
diets
  ancient and modern 1–8
  citrus free 58–68
  corn free 60–72
  egg free 50–4
  gluten free 40–4
  high calcium 86–7
  high iron 89–91
  high potassium 78–9
  low cholesterol 80–3
  low purine/weight reducing 84–5
  low salt 65–8
  milk free 45–9
  no added sugar 61–4
  slimming 76–7
  soya free 55–7
  tapwater free 73–5
  The Hay Diet 92
  vegetarian 98–9
  wheat free 35–9
dressings for salads 268–76
  fruit, without oil 272
  honey and lemon 272
  lime 272
  sweet mustard 272
  soya 275
  vinaigrette 269–71
  basic 269
  sweet 269
  with garlic 271
  with herbs 270
  with lemon 270
  with mustard 270
  with onion 271
  with spring onion 271
  see also mayonnaise and salad cream
dropscones 388
  egg free 388
  egg/milk free 389
dried apricot crumble 315
  soufflé 314
  fruit salad 337
dumplings 401

E

eggs
baked 116
filled omelet 117
hardboiled 115
herb omelet 118
poached 117
scrambled 116
soft boiled 115
Eve's pudding 307
wheat/gluten free 308

F

fats 9, 12
animal 23
content of meat 24
deficiency 25
problems 25
saturated 22
unsaturated 22
fibre 9, 17, 18
fish
cakes 191–92
casserole with leeks 205
cod 202, 203
grilled 195
hotpot 206
in breadcrumbs 196
in white sauce 205
kebabs 201
mackerel 198
pie 204
poaching liquid, for 191
prawns 200
salmon 198
sole 199
stew 207
trout with almonds 193
whiting 200
with parsley sauce 208
food
high carbohydrate 11
lack of 10
high fat 11
high mineral 11
high vitamin 11
high protein 11
French beans 260
dressing 269
fresh fruit and nut dessert cake 327
fruit – see puddings
fruit dressing 269
fresh jam tart 323
fruit cake (1) 350
fruit cake (2) eggless 351
fruit cakes
boiled 347
rich 348
wheat/gluten free 349
fruit juice/drinks 415–18
fruit squash 417

G

goulash with TVP 253
granola 110
grapefruit 147
gravies 407–10
greens 258

H

ham in cider 223
ham and egg casserole 235
herb butter for pasta 156
herrings in oatmeal or millet 197
hunger 13
hummus 149

I

Irish stew 234

J

jams, quick 414
dried apricot 414
quick kiwi 414
quick berry 414
stewed fruit spread 414

K

kebabs, fish 201

L

lamb with apples 231
lamb, roast leg of 210
with garlic and rosemary 233
Lancashire hotpot 232
leeks 259
in cheese sauce 249
lemonade 417
limeade 418
liver and orange 210
casserole 211

M

macaroni cheese 171
mackerel stuffed with fruit 198
margarines 27
marrow stuffed with nuts 241
mayonnaise 273–75
with curry 274
with parsley 274
with yoghurt 273
without egg (1) 274
without egg (2) 275
melon 147
meat
beef
casseroles 217–19
in stout 220
stew 215
chilli con carne 213
ham 223
liver 210, 211
pasties 234
pork casserole 222
roasting tables 209
stock 411
veal 221
meatballs 213
milk based drinks 416
milkshakes 415
mincemeat, sweet 415
minerals 11
mouth 13
mouth problems 13
muesli 111–13
muffins
apple 384
bran 382
oat 383
wholemeal raisin 382
mushrooms, creamed 114
stuffed 148

N

nutrients 10
nutrition 9
tables 17
nutburgers, grilled 246
nut
roast 242
pâté 242
rissoles with egg 244
rissoles without egg 243
spicy rissoles 245

O

oat bannocks 391
oatmeal biscuits 391
oils 22
content of fish 25
vegetable 22
omelet 117
soufflé with fruit filling 373
onion gravy 410
onions 260
onions with cheese stuffing 251
orange and grapefruit 148

P

packed foods 118
paella 187
pancakes 390–400
batter for 399
batter for wheat/gluten free 399
potato 114

parkin 360
parsnips 262
  roast 264

pasta 153
  cold for salads 178
  easy dishes 175
  green 155
  homemade 154
  wheat/gluten free 154

pasta with
  bacon and mushrooms 117
  broccoli and potato 176
  chicken and mushroom 177
  (chow mien) with beef 178
  (chow mien) with chicken 179
  ham and beansprouts 180
  prawn and tomato 176

pastry
  apple for steaming 365
  bran 361
  low fat 360
  potato (1) 361
  potato (2) gluten/wheat free 362
  sweet pastry, gluten/wheat free 364
  wheat and soya, milk free 363
  with oil (1) milk free 363
  with oil (2) milk free 364
peaches and red berries 322
peas 260
pikelets 387
pizza 122
pork dinner for one 237
pork sausages 113
pork, spiced casserole 222

porridges
  millet 109
  oat 108
  oatmeal 108
  roasted buckwheat 110
  rice 109
potato pancakes 114

potatoes
  baked 263
  provençale 265
  roast, dry 263
see also vegetables 258
potatoes Lyonnaise 266
potatoes with cheese and bacon 260
poultry
  chicken 223–30
  turkey 230
proteins 10
prawns with lettuce and ginger 200
prunes, stuffed 325
puddings 299–344

Q

quiches 120
quick Boston baked beans 247
quick jams 414

R

rice
  Chinese style 189
  fried 188
  savoury 183

rice with
  chicken and mushroom 185
  eggs and lemon 186
  ham and peas 183
  nuts 185
  vegetables 184
risotto with prawns 187
risotto with vegetables and ham 182
runner beans 259

S

salads
  bean and onion 292
  carrot 293
  cauliflower 286
  coleslaw 284

courgette and tomato 286
crudités 298
egg 291
egg and bean 295
egg and potato 294
green 280–82
green with egg 294

salad ingredients
cooked 271
fruits 279
leaves 277
other ingredients 279–80
raw vegetables 271
roots 277
seeds 278
sprouting seeds 278
lettuce and orange 296
mixed root 282–84
mushroom 293
pasta and chicken 288
pasta and tomatoes 288
pasta, pink 172

salads, pasta with
cheese and tomato 174
chicken and pineapple 175
ham and peas 174
pepper and celery 172
prawns 173
potato (1) 292
potato (2) 292
prawn cocktail 290
preparation of 280
red cabbage 285
sardine 290
spinach 298
sweet pepper 286
tomato and onion 292
tuna 289
tuna and bean 289
with avocado 287
with onion and herbs 291
white cabbage 291
salads and dressings 268–98
salad cream 276
salmon, poached 198
sandwiches 119–20
sauce, basic white 403
sauce, basic white, gluten/wheat free 410

sauces for pasta
almond 166
bacon and egg 165
bolognese 162
cheese with vegetables 167
courgette 159
mushroom 159
onion 158
parsley and nut 164
pea and ham 161
pepper 157
prawn and tomato 163
tomato and herb 163
tomato and tuna 156
vegetable 165
wine and rosemary 162

sauces, savoury
cheese 404
cheese and onion 405
cucumber and lemon 405
egg 404
mushroom 405
onion 405
parsley 404
tomato 404

sauces, sweet
carob 406
chocolate 406
lemon 406
orange 406
passion fruit 407
vanilla (custard) 406
sausages 113

scones
buckwheat, gluten/wheat free 389
cheese and bran 386
herb and yoghurt 385

plain scones, gluten/wheat free 386
small intestine 15

soups
avocado 152
beetroot 123
celery 130
chicken broth 139
clear vegetable broth 143
cold cucumber 143
courgette 141
cream of mushroom 132
leek and potato 138
lentil 125
lettuce 145
minestrone 136
mushroom 131
French country 136
fresh pea 126
onion (1) 127
onion (2) 128
onion and potato 126
parsley 144
quick beef broth 146
spinach 133
split pea 124
thin leek 134
tomato 142
turnip 135
starters 146–52
steak dinner for one 239
stewed lentils 255
stick beans 259
stomach 14
problems 14
stuffing, sage and onion 403
summer pudding 334
wheat/gluten free 335
swedes 261
symbols for recipes 103–104

T

tacos 397
tomato appetizer 247
tomato chutney 413
tortillas, gluten/wheat free 397
trout, grilled 195
with almonds 193
herbs 194
tarragon 194
turnips 261
turkey and chestnuts 230
TVP dishes 251–54
TVP and bean loaf 251

V

veal and mushrooms 221
vegetarian main meals 240–57

vegetables
baked 263
casserole with TVP 252
cooked 258–67
mashed 262
mixed 262
nut curry 242
pâté 248
roast 263
steamed 262
stew with barley 256
stir/cook 264
stock 411
vinaigrette 269
vinaigrettes, flavoured 270–71

W

walnut pâté 150
walnuts, roast 240
water 9
white sauces 403
whiting with mushrooms 200
wheat/gluten free
baking powder 105
ingredients 104–5
special ingredients 106–7

Y

Yorkshire pudding, wheat/gluten free 398
wholewheat 397

Wheat-free and Gluten-free Summer Pudding

 Make salt-free bread

 Avoid Trufree flours Nos 4 and 5

Make as for ordinary Summer Pudding but use home-baked Trufree bread (see the recipes on pp. 374, 375). If making it for one person, reduce the amounts in the recipe right down and use a small basin, but go on in exactly the same way.

Blancmange

Serves 2

 Use wheat-free flavourings

 Use artificial sweetener

 Use gluten-free flavourings

1 heaped tablespoon low fat dried milk granules
½ pint (300 ml) skimmed milk
3 tablespoons cornflour (maize flour)
1 heaped tablespoon caster sugar, or 1 level tablespoon fructose
Flavouring*

Method

Stir the milk granules into the milk and mix well to combine. Put 4–5 tablespoons of the milk into a basin and add the cornflour, sugar and flavouring. Mix well. Meanwhile heat the remaining milk to just below boiling point. Pour over the cornflour mixture and stir briskly. Put back into the saucepan and cook while you stir for about 3 minutes. The mixture will thicken. Rinse out a ½ pint (300 ml) decorative mould or a basin with cold water. Pour the hot mixture into this and leave to cool and set. When completely cold and ready to serve, very gently, with the fingertips, pull the blancmange away from the sides of the mould. Put a plate on top, hold the mould and plate firmly together and turn upside down, shaking the blancmange gently on to the plate. Serve on its own or with stewed or fresh fruit.

Suggested flavourings*

3 heaped teaspoons carob powder.
2 heaped teaspoons cocoa powder.
2 heaped teaspoons drinking chocolate.
Few drops vanilla flavouring.
1 heaped teaspoon instant coffee mixed with 2 teaspoons boiling water.

Milk Jelly

Serves 3–4

 Use wheat-free flavouring  Use gluten-free flavouring

3 heaped tablespoons low fat dried milk granules
Water
½ oz (15 g) powdered gelatine
2 tablespoons sugar, or 1½ tablespoons fructose
Flavouring*

Method

Put the milk granules into a measuring jug and top up with water to just below the 1 pint (600 ml) mark. Put about 4 tablespoons of the milk into a cup and sprinkle in the gelatine. Leave to soften for 5 minutes, then stir well. Put the rest of the milk into a saucepan with the sugar and the flavouring of your choice. Stir well and bring to the boil, stirring all the time so as not to let it catch. Take off the heat and stir in the gelatine mixture. Keep stirring until it has completely dissolved. Pour into a bowl or individual dishes and leave to set. Serve cold from the fridge.

Suggested flavourings*

Few drops vanilla flavouring.
3 teaspoons instant coffee added to the hot milk and stirred well.
3 heaped teaspoons cocoa powder or carob powder, added to the hot milk and stirred in well.